Wolfgang Bibel

Automated Theorem Proving

W0263518

Wolfgang Bibel

Automated Theorem Proving

Friedr. Vieweg & Sohn   Braunschweig / Wiesbaden

CIP-Kurztitelaufnahme der Deutschen Bibliothek

Bibel, Wolfgang:
Automated theorem proving / Wolfgang Bibel. —
Braunschweig; Wiesbaden: Vieweg, 1982.

1982
All rights reserved
© Friedr. Vieweg & Sohn Verlagsgesellschaft mbH, Braunschweig 1982

No part of this publication may be reproduced, stored in a retrieval system or transmitted in
any form or by any means, electronic, mechanical, photocopying, recording or otherwise, without prior permission of the copyright holder.

ISBN-13: 978-3-528-08520-9   e-ISBN-13: 978-3-322-90100-2
DOI: 10.1007/978-3-322-90100-2

Preface

Among the dreams of mankind is the one dealing with the mechanization of human thought. As the world today has become so complex that humans apparently fail to manage it properly with their intellectual gifts, the realization of this dream might be regarded even as something like a necessity. On the other hand, the incredible advances in computer technology let it appear as a real possibility.

Of course, it is not easy to say what sort of thing human thinking actually is, a theme which over the centuries occupied many thinkers, mainly philosophers. From a critical point of view most of their theories were of a speculative nature since their only way of testing was by Gedanken-experiments. It is the computer which has opened here a wide range of new possibilities since with this tool we now can model real experiments and thus test such theories like physicists do in their field.

About a quarter of a century ago, scientific activities of that sort were started under the label of **artificial intelligence** . Today these activities establish a wide and prosperous field which the author, in lack of any better name, prefers to call **intellectics** . Without any doubt, the computer programs developed in this field have tought us much about the nature of human thinking.

One of its prominent features is the ability for logical reasoning which had been studied extensively by the logicians of many centuries. In particular, their contributions within the last hundred years have prepared the grounds for the mechanization of this special feature. Although reasoning certainly is part of most intellectual activities, it naturally plays a particularly important role in mathematics. Not surprisingly then, the first attempts towards automatic reasoning were made in mathematical applications focusing on generating proofs of mathematical theorems. For this historical reason, this subarea within intellectics is still identified as **automated theorem proving** although proving mathematical theorems is just one in a wide variety of applications.

The purpose of this book is to provide a comprehensive development of the most advanced basic deductive tools presently available in this area and to give an idea of their usefulness for many important applications. Because of the rapid expansion of this field, which in a wider sense also is termed **automated deduction** , it is certainly not possible any more to cover all its aspects in a single book. Hence our attention will focus on the classical tool of proof procedures for first-order logic which in our opinion are to be regarded as basic for the whole field, at least for the time being.

In the 1970's much research in this area has concentrated on how to eliminate the enormous redundancy experienced in running computer systems which realized such proof procedures. Much of it was based on **resolution** , but some was carried out also with a rather different background. With our uniform treatment based on what we call the **connection method** we hope to have re-combined these various attempts into one single stream of research, which culminates in the description of what, according to current technology, appear to be the features of a most advanced proof procedure for first-order logic.

Unfortunately, these features have become so complex that any author dealing with this topic faces a real problem of presentation. On the one hand, because of this complexity a rigorous treatment is of essential importance in order to avoid serious errors or misjudgements. On the other hand, many readers will be frightened by the resultant formalism, thus creating the need for plenty of illustrations and informal descriptions. We have made an attempt to serve both these needs by pairing the rigorous definitions, thorems and proofs with informal descriptions and discussions, illustrated with many examples.

If this attempt has been successful then the book might actually serve for a wide spectrum of readers. On the one extreme, there would be those who just want to understand the ideas behind all the formalism and thus study the examples guided by the informal discussions without going much into the details of formal definitions, theorems and proofs. On the other extreme, well-trained logicians might easily skip much of the informal text. And in the middle there are those readers who are grateful for informal explanations but also acknowledge the necessity of preciseness for such a complex topic, and thus read both these approaches **in parallel** .

The ability to read mathematical definitions, theorems and proofs together with some basic knowledge about elementary set theory and about algorithms are actually all the pre-requisites needed for a full understanding of most parts of the book. However, some familiarity with mathematical logic and/or some previous training in abstract mathematical think-ing will certainly be helpful for coping with the intrinsic complexity of some of the results.

Although this book has not been explicitly designed as a textbook it may well be used in instructor-student settings. For such purposes a number of exercises of varied difficulties may be found at the end of each chapter listed in the sequence of the presented topics. The selection of material for such a course should be easy with the following hints.

Chapter I provides a short introduction into logic as the formal structure of natural reasoning. The basic connec-tion method is then developed, first, in chapter II, on the level of propositional logic and second, in a strictly par-allel treatment in chapter III, on the level of first-order logic. This, together with the first two sections in chapter IV, which introduce resolution and embed it into the connec-tion method, is regarded as the basis for the field of auto-mated theorem proving.

The rest of chapter IV contains more specialized material on the connection method towards a most advanced proof system for first-order logic, which will be of partic-ular interest for researchers specializing in this field. Readers with a more general interest might rather consider the material in chapter V, perhaps even at an earlier stage of their reading. It briefly introduces some of the possible applications and extensions of first-order theorem proving.

Each chapter is preceded by a more detailed overview of its contents for further orientation. Moreover, the many references to previous or later parts of the book within the text should ease to begin reading at any of its parts. For this purpose we use a familiar numbering scheme. For instance, (III.3.5) refers to the item labeled 3.5 in chapter III. By convention, the number of the chapter is deleted for any reference within the actual chapter, that is, within chapter III the previous reference is simply (3.5) rather than (III.3.5). The same applies to figures and tables which, however, are numbered independently.

The abbreviations used are generally familiar and are listed in table 1 below. Also with our denotations we have tried to follow common practice as listed in table 2 and 3.

Both, the historical remarks at the end of each chapter and the bibliography as a whole are by no means comprehensive. Rather, they reflect both, the author's limited knowledge of an exploding literature and their direct relevance to the topics we consider in this book. Finally, we hope that the reader acknowledges the author's difficulty in expressing the material in a non-native language.

München, Dezember 1981

W. Bibel

ACKNOWLEDGEMENTS

Man ist geneigt, die Vollendung eines solchen Buches als ein persönlich wichtiges Teilziel zu interpretieren, das stellvertretend für vieles andere im eigenen Leben steht. Deshalb sieht man sich bei solcher Gelegenheit auch zum Rückblick auf die Einflüsse veranlaßt, die den Weg bis hierher mitbestimmt haben. Ich muß gestehen, daß mir jede Auswahl unter solchen Einflüssen und die damit verbundene Gewichtung zumindest anfechtbar, wenn nicht sogar willkürlich erscheint. Deshalb möchte ich nur feststellen, daß ich dankbar an viele Menschen denke, die mich in Liebe, Freundschaft, manche auch in Haß oder Gegnerschaft auf meinem Weg gefördert haben.

Die vorbildliche Gestaltung des Textes selbst verdanken wir alle dem außerordentlichen Geschick von Frl. H. Höhn, die mit unermüdlichem Einsatz alle Schwierigkeiten zu meistern verstand. Bei den Zeichnungen und Sonderzeichen war zudem Frau A. Bussmann behilflich. Dr. K.-M. Hörnig sowie Herrn A. Müller bin ich für viele Korrekturen und Verbesserungsvorschläge dankbar. Ihnen verdanke ich auch manche Anregung aus der gemeinsamen Projektarbeit. Dem Fachbereich Informatik der Hochschule der Bundeswehr München, insbesondere Herrn Prof. W. Hahn, bin ich für die Erlaubnis zur Benutzung eines Textautomaten verpflichtet. Herrn Prof. K. Mehlhorn sei für die an den Verlag gegebene Anregung eines solchen Buches gedankt.

Meine Musikfreunde, jedoch besonders meine Frau und meine Kinder haben mir die mit der Niederschrift verbundenen Mühen erträglicher gemacht, wodurch sie einen nicht unbeträchtlichen Anteil an der Fertigstellung haben.

Abbreviation	Intended meaning
ATP	Automated Theorem Proving
fol	first-order logic
w.r.t.	with respect to
iff	if and only if
A iff B iff C	A iff B and B iff C
D.	Definition
T.	Theorem
L.	Lemma
C.	Corollary
F.	Formula
q.e.d.	quod erat demonstrandum (what had to be proved)
□	end of proof or definition

Table 1. List of abbreviations

Kind of objects	Standard Symbols
propositional variables	P, Q, R
constant symbols	a, b, c
function symbols	f, g, h
terms	s, t
predicate symbols	P, Q, R
signum or arity	n
literals	K, L, M
object variables	x, y, z
formulas, matrices	D, E, F
clauses	c, d, e
paths	p, q
connections	u, v, w
sets of connections	U, V, W
connection graphs	G, H
natural numbers	m, n, l
indices	i, j, k
sets of indices	I, J
occurrences, positions	r
substitutions	ρ, σ
truth values	τ

Comment. All symbols may be decorated with indices etc.

Table 2. Standardized denotations

Notation	Meaning
$\sum\limits_{i=1}^{n} m_i$, $\prod\limits_{i=1}^{n} m_i$	sum, product
$\mathbb{N}$	set of natural numbers with $0 \in \mathbb{N}$
$\emptyset$	empty set
$\cup$, $\cap$	union, intersection
$\setminus$	set difference
$X \cup Y$	union in the special case $X \cap Y = \emptyset$
$\bigcup\limits_{i=1}^{n} X_i$, $\bigcap\limits_{i=1}^{n} X_i$	union, intersection with $\bigcup\limits_{i=1}^{0} X_i = \emptyset$, $\bigcap\limits_{i=1}^{0} X_i = \emptyset$
$|X|$	number of elements in set X, i.e. cardinality of X
$X \times Y$	cartesian product of X and Y
X^n, X^*, X^+	n-fold product, $\bigcup\limits_{i=0}^{\infty} X_i$, $\bigcup\limits_{i=1}^{\infty} X_i$
2^X	set of subsets in X
$n \bmod m$	n modulo m

Table 3. Standard notations

Contents

Chapter I

Natural and formal logic

In this first chapter the close connection between a natural text and a corresponding formalized statement in first-order logic will be demonstrated with a simple example. It comprises an informal description of well-known rules of inference (modus ponens, contraposition, and instantiation). As a first illustration the corresponding proof with the connection method is presented. Because of its introductory nature this chapter might well be skipped by alert readers. On the other hand, readers who have no background in mathematical logic at all, might feel a need for a broader introduction. They should consult [Ro3], or any elementary introduction to mathematical logic, such as [He1]. In [Ko3] they would find many more examples of practical interest.

1.   LOGIC ABSTRACTED FROM NATURAL REASONING

1.1.E.   DEATH IN THE SWIMMINGPOOL. Frank is suspected of having murdered Jane at her home. But he has a seemingly perfect alibi: at the critical time he had a telephone conversation with Bill. Frank claims, he called Bill from his office far away from Jane's place. This call by chance was tape-recorded. Detective Shane, however, is able to convict Frank of lying on the basis of the following chain of reasoning.

The existing tape proves that there was such a conversation. The background noises - a radio report of a football-game - allow even the exact determination of the time of this call which is 2.55 - 3.05 p.m.. But the tape also proves that Frank was not in his office at that time as he claims since the chime of his office clock at the full hour (3 p.m.) is missing on the tape; thus he may well have called Bill from Jane's villa.   □

We all would agree with the detective's way of reasoning in this little story (if we take for granted that the guy
has checked some further details). This experience can be made
not only in detective stories but in everyday's life - and it
has been made for at least 2000 years - that our intelligent
thinking follows certain logical rules which apparently are
the same for everyone.

What are the rules which have been applied in this
story, and how could we destillate them out of this text with
all its irrelevancies and redundancies? For this purpose we
list the core of Shane's argument in the form of several statements.

(i)   Any (sufficiently loud) noise reaches the telephone in
the same room.
(ii)   Any noise, which reached the telephone used by Frank at
the time in question must be on the tape.
(iii)   The 3 o'clock chime of Frank's office clock is a noise
but
(iv)   it is not on the tape.
(v)   Hence the telephone mentioned in (ii) was not the one
in Frank's office.

Note that none of the statements (i) - (iii) was in fact mentioned within the story although they are crucial for this
chain of reasoning. This is typical for natural communication,
where people share a lot of common **world knowledge** which is
understood without explicit mentioning. In order to study and
apply logical rules, however, it is necessary to make such
facts or hypotheses explicit as they belong to the complete
chain of reasoning.

The logic within our example is not expressed in any
or all of these statements per se, rather it consists of implying (v) from (i) through (iv). However, even in this form it is
still hard to see what kind of general logical rules are
applied in this implication. This explains why it is desirable
to further formalize or standardize the way of presentation.

Consider fact (i) through (v) once more for this purpose. There is only a single telefone in question described in

some detail in (ii). Let us briefly call it tel. Now, the main part of the content of fact (i) is expressed by the phrase "noise reaches tel". Apparently, this phrase relates two objects, noise and tel, and this relation is established with the verb reach. Any such structure will be written in the form REACHnoise,tel where the relating **predicate** (written in capital letters) is followed by the list of related objects (written in small letters). Of course, the important issue here is the use of some standard form, which captures the essence of the phrase as described above; in special applications a different (but equivalent) form than the one introduced here might well be more comfortable (e.g. semantic nets in natural language applications).

Fact (i) is not completely represented by REACHnoise,tel , however, since it involves two conditions under which noise reaches tel. First, it is important to notice that the object noise is to be regarded as a noise in the same way as chime in (iii) where this property is explicitly stated. This distinction between noise as an object and noise as a property applying to objects is not made explicit in the natural language phrase, but it is crucial to implement it within our standard form. Hence, the one condition appropriately reads NOISEnoise expressing that object noise in fact has the property of being a (sufficiently loud) noise. The second condition in (i) can be found in the phrase "in the same room" relating again the objects noise and tel; it is thus formalized by SAME-ROOMnoise,tel .

Thus we have formalized all parts in statement (i) except for the single word "any" which generalizes the statement to apply for all objects which satisfy the given conditions. This generalization or **quantification** may be expressed in natural language in various ways such as "noises reach the .." or "all noises reach the .." or "whenever something is a noise then it reaches the ..", etc. In our formalization we prefer a single standard form for all these variants, namely " **for-all** noise ...". Therefore statement (i) in a formalized version now reads

(i')   **for-all** noise

     NOISEnoise **and** SAME-ROOMnoise,tel

          imply REACHnoise,tel

This is no more perfect English, but it reveals the logical structure of the original statement in a much clearer way than before.

Since the connectives **for-all, and, imply** , etc. occur again and again in such statements, logicians prefer to use the short symbols $\forall, \wedge, \rightarrow$, etc. instead of the respective words. Also they find it boring to write whole words denoting objects or predicates and rather use a single letter. If we apply this abbreviation using the first (capital or small) letter of the respective word, we then obtain the following version of (i).

(i") $\forall n\ (Nn \wedge Sn,t \rightarrow Rn,t)$

Many readers might be frightened by such abstract formulas. Often such a psychological reaction is extended to the whole topic leading to awful misunderstandings. In order to avoid such misunderstandings we have spent so much time to develop (i") out of (i). The version (i") is all we need to study its logical structure. But we urge the reader to clearly realize that (i') and (i") are exactly the same statements except for the abbreviations, and that (i') is the same statement as (i) only structured in a logically clearer way. For this reason we may even identify all three versions in the discussion.

The details of the analog transformation of (ii) through (v) is left to the reader. We only give here the result of it.

(ii')   **for-all** noise

          NOISEnoise **and** REACHnoise,tel   **imply** ON-TAPEnoise

(ii") $\forall n\ (Nn \wedge Rn,t \rightarrow On)$

(iii')   NOISEchime

(iii") Nc

(iv')   **not** ON-TAPEchime

(iv") $\neg Oc$

(v')   **not** SAME-ROOMchime,tel

(v") $\neg Sc,t$

We have mentioned before that the logic within our example consists of implying (v) from (i) through (iv). In other words, we
apply the inference (i) **and** (ii) **and** (iii) **and** (iv) **imply** (v).
In the double-prime version this inference is represented by
the following formula.

1.2.F.
$$\forall n(Nn \wedge Sn,t \to Rn,t) \wedge \forall n(Nn \wedge Rn,t \to On) \wedge Nc \wedge \neg Oc \to \neg Sc,t$$

The main concern in this book is a mechanism which guarantees
the correctness or validity of such inferences or formulas.
Such mechanisms are called **proof procedures** and their activity
is called **theorem proving** since there is no qualitative
distinction between our detective's way of reasoning and a
mathematican's way of proving a mathematical theorem.

In the former case the situation has been described by
the four statements (i) through (iv) used as **hypotheses** or
axioms in (1.2). In mathematics any work is performed in some
theory which is specified by a number of axioms playing exactly the same role as the present statements (i) through (iv).
Statement (v) is then what a mathematician regards as the
theorem which is implied by the axioms. Once, the validity of
the theorem has been established it may itself be added to the
list of axioms for proving further theorems. This addition
certainly does not change the situation as described by the
original axioms which again is illustrated by our story where
fact (v) of course was part of the szenario independently of
the detective's discovering it. In that sense logical reasoning only uncovers knowledge which implicitly is contained
already in previous knowledge or assumptions. The term **axioms**
henceforth is used to denote all statements which are currently used to derive a new theorem, unless explicitly stated
otherwise.

Above we have stressed the point of transforming a description like in the story (1.1) into a precise statement like
the formula (1.2). There is some work going on in artificial
intelligence (or **intellectics** , to use a better name for this
field), in particular in natural language understanding, with
the research goal of performing such a transformation automat-

ically. This certainly is not the topic of the present book ([Gro], [SPe], and [Win] are sources for more information in this respect). But it should be mentioned at this point that such research is supplementary to the field of Automated Theorem Proving (ATP) in the sense that the ultimate goal would be the use of the computer as a reasoning assistant with which we communicate in natural language rather than in any formal language.

On the other hand, automated natural language understanding is not imaginable without ATP. How else could a computer understand the last sentence in the story in (1.1)? In fact, a further sophisticated automation in many areas will require the use of ATP. Some of these applications will be discussed in chapter V . This does not exclude the ultimate possibility that the techniques originally developed in ATP eventually become so integrated in the particular application that their origins are hardly recognizable any more. For instance, we extracted the implicit condition NOISEnoise from the text in (1.1). A future smart system might well avoid this explicit extraction, after we will have mastered all the problems which are present already without this extra complication.

2.   LOGICAL RULES

In the previous section the core of the chain of reasoning in the story (1.1) has been abstracted to yield formula (1.2). But still we have not isolated any logical rules of some generality which have been applied by the detective in establishing his conclusion.

Consider the first two axioms (i) and (ii). They are statements applying to **any** noise. Hence, in particular, they apply to chime. Thus we obtain from (i) and (ii)

(vi) $Nc \wedge Sc,t \rightarrow Rc,t$ and
(vii) $Nc \wedge Rc,t \rightarrow Oc$

by **instantiation** . This is a familiar logical principle; whenever we assume the truth of a statement of the form

" **for-all** objects   ... objects ..."

then this implies the truth of any statement obtained by canceling the **prefix "for-all** objects" and substituting "objects"
all-over by a particular object-1, illustrated by

"... object-1 ..."

Since (iii) guarantees Nc , the condition Nc in both (vi) and
(vii) may be dropped thus obtaining

(viii)   Sc,t → Rc,t   and
(ix)   Rc,t → Oc.

These two immediately imply

(x)   Sc,t → Oc

according to our natural logical intuition, always assuming
that the reader still has present the whole natural statements
which are abbreviated by these formulas.

   The last steps are variants of the familiar logical
rule called **modus ponens** : whenever we have statement1, and
also know that statement1 implies statement2 then we may infer
statement2. In particular, we may infer Oc from Rc,t and
Rc,t → Oc . This is exactly what happened in the last step
except that there was the additional condition Sc,t to be carried over from the premisse to the conclusion. Similarly in the
previous steps, again with additional conditions (Sc,t and
Rc,t, resp.).

   Again natural intuition allows to restate (x) in the
form of

(xi)   ¬Oc → ¬Sc,t.

Also this step follows a familiar general principle called
contraposition : whenever statement1 implies statement2 then
not statement2 implies **not** statement1. Since (iv) asserts
¬Oc, modus ponens may now be applied once more to yield ¬Sc,t,
quod erat demonstrandum.

   Altogether we thus needed instantiation, contraposition and modus ponens for this proof, three completely general
logical principles or rules. In fact, these rules apparently

are of a purely syntactical nature; they completely ignore the
intended meaning behind the symbols. In the last step, for
instance, ¬Oc was chosen as statement1 in order to apply modus
ponens. This requires to locate a second formula which begins
precisely, i.e. symbol by symbol, with   "¬Oc → ". Formula (xi)
is exactly of that structure. Statement2, mentioned in the
definition of modus ponens, in this particular case must then
be the formula to the right of the symbol → , namely ¬Sc,t.

In this **matching** process, which just compares symbols
(or bits in the machine) the isolated meaning of Oc to be
ON-TAPEchime is not relevant anymore since it is encoded in
the description (1.2) as a whole, as far as it is logically
relevant. Therefore it may well happen that a completely different story by abstraction may lead to exactly the same formula (1.2). This is expressed in logic by saying that such a
formula may have several **interpretations** or **models** . The
situation described in the story (1.1) is just one such model
for formula (1.2).

Having thus isolated three logical rules which may be
processed in a completely mechanical way, we are faced with
several questions. One might be whether these rules are **natural** to the extent that our brain processes exactly these
rules while following the reasoning in the detective's story.
Although one would doubt it based on self-observation, science
at present does not give any definite answer for this. All we
can say is that experience (over hundreds of years) makes it
evident that these rules are compatible with what is realized
in our brains in the sense that they never produced a conclusion which we felt not to be acceptable.

Another question is how many more rules we might dis-
cover by examining many more such chains of reasoning. Of
course, also in this respect we have to rely on all the experience compiled and analysed over the centuries beginning with
Aristoteles in the 4th century b.c., if not earlier. According
to the present state of the art this book will concentrate on
that part of logic which covers most but not all of our natural
reasoning, called **first-order logic (fol)**. In chapter V we
will briefly discuss several extensions covering further such
rules.

Incidentally, the issue in fact is not the quantity of rules; rather it is their quality such as their generality or computational effectiveness. Actually, it is the purpose of this book to isolate essentially a single first-order rule which is as general as to cover any other first-order rule and at the same time computationally most effective. In order to give the reader a first taste of this rule, we apply it to formula (1.2) in a way which simulates the previous proof.

The given formula thus is

$$\forall n(Nn \wedge Sn,t \rightarrow Rn,t) \wedge \forall n(Nn \wedge Rn,t \rightarrow On) \wedge Nc \wedge \neg Oc \rightarrow \neg Sc,t \ .$$

In the first 2 steps just 2 connections are added,

$$\forall n(Nn \wedge Sn,t \rightarrow Rn,t) \wedge \forall n(Nn \wedge Rn,t \rightarrow On) \wedge Nc \wedge \neg Oc \rightarrow \neg Sc,t \ .$$

This simulates the instantiation and the dropping of condition Nc above where we derived (viii) and (ix). Note that dropping (together with instantiating) corresponds to connecting. The newly derived formulas above apparently correspond here to those parts in the formula which have not yet been connected. This correspondence applies once more in the next step where we simulate the elimination of Rc,t above which yielded (x):

$$\forall n(Nn \wedge Sn,t \rightarrow Rn,t) \wedge \forall n(Nn \wedge Rn,t \rightarrow On) \wedge Nc \wedge \neg Oc \rightarrow \neg Sc,t \ .$$

In this **connection** rule there is no action corresponding to contraposition. Therefore the last two steps simulate the application of modus ponens in the last step above:

$$\forall n(Nn \wedge Sn,t \rightarrow Rn,t) \wedge \forall n(Nn \wedge Rn,t \rightarrow On) \wedge Nc \wedge \neg Oc \rightarrow \neg Sc,t \ .$$

This completes the 5-step proof with the connection rule, which simply consists in adding one connection in each step, otherwise leaving the given formula unchanged. Hence only a single copy of the formula is required, of which the 4 copies within this paragraph are to be considered as snapshots during the proof.

The correspondence just mentioned might have given the reader a rough idea of this connection rule, not more of course. The precise definition of this rule and the termination criterion signaling the completion of a proof, together with their justification will require the treatment of many technical details. Because of their complexity this treatment will be split into 2 parts, one exclusively concerned with the features already present in a restricted part of fol called **propositional logic** (chapter II), the other concerned with extending this to the complete fol (chapter III). This distinction may be illustrated once more with formula (1.2).

Recall the instantiation which has been applied before to yield (vi) and (vii). Substituting these 2 formulas for the respective parts in (1.2) gives

2.1.F. $(Nc \land Sc,t \to Rc,t) \land (Nc \land Rc,t \to Oc) \land Nc \land \neg Oc \to \neg Sc,t$

If we completely ignore the internal structure of the connected units Nc, Sc,t, Rc,t, and Nc then this is a **formula in propositional logic** , and the same connections, now with a simplified meaning, establish its validity.

Chapter II

The connection method in propositional logic

This chapter provides an introduction into propositional logic, mainly under the aspect of ATP. In particular, its formulas are mostly considered as **matrices** which are sets of sets of ... of literals thus providing a strictly set-theoretical approach to propositional logic.

The fundamental syntactic concept characterizing the validity of a formula is that of a **complementary** matrix which is discussed in section 3. At many occasions in this book we will see that questions concerning the consistency and completeness of a number of proof methods may be elegantly answered by recurrence to this basic notion. For the first time this happens in the sections 4 through 6 where we introduce a first version of our basic proof method, called the **connection method** . This version is applicable to formulas in normal form only. The casual reader might get a feeling for its nature from a look to the figures 1 and 2 in section 4 and to the surrounding informal discussion.

1.   THE LANGUAGE OF PROPOSITIONAL LOGIC

At the end of the last chapter we have seen an example of a formula (I.2.1) in **propositional** (or **sentential**) **logic** which studies the logical combination of whole propositions. For instance, the intended meaning of Sc,t was the proposition "the chime is in the same room as the telephone". We have mentioned that in propositional logic the internal structure of such a sentence is completely disregarded. Therefore we may even abbreviate such a whole proposition by a single letter, say L for Sc,t such that formula (vi) from (I.2) might now

read K ∧ L → M . This suggests to define such formulas in propositional logic as syntactic structures built from a basic
alphabet with the familiar logical connectives.

On the way to presenting this definition we prefer to
first meet the concept of a matrix which from technical points
of view will turn out to be the more appropriate one for our
purposes.

1.1.D. An **alphabet** is any non-empty, finite or denumerably
infinite set.

Let $\mathbf{P}^o$ be an alphabet. Its elements are called **propositional symbols** or **variables** (or **nullary predicates**). By
convention, they are denoted by P, Q, or R.

A (**ground**) **literal** is a pair (n,P) such that $n \in \{0,1\}$
and $P \in \mathbf{P}^o$. Literals are denoted by K, L, or M.

For any literal L=(n,P) and for $m \in \{0,1\}$, ^mL denotes the literal (n+m mod 2; P). By convention, (n,P) may be
abbreviated by P in the case n=0, and by ¬P in the case n=1.

Let **R** be an alphabet. Its elements are called **occurrences** or **positions** and are denoted by r.

(**Propositional**) **matrices** (over $\mathbf{P}^o$ and **R**), denoted by
D, E, or F, the **size** $\sigma(F)$, the set $\Omega(F) \subset \mathbf{R}$ of positions in
a matrix F , and the **depth** $\delta(r)$ of r in F for any $r \in \Omega(F)$
are defined inductively by (m1) and (m2).

(m1)   For any literal L and for any $r \in \mathbf{R}$ the pair (L,r), or
shortly L^r , is a matrix with $\sigma(L^r)=0$, $\Omega(L^r)=\{r\}$, and
$\delta(r)=0$.

(m2)   If $F_1,\ldots,F_n$ with n>0   are matrices such that
$\Omega(F_i) \cap \Omega(F_j)=\emptyset$ for   i≠j   and $1 \leq i,j \leq n$ then   the   set
$\{F_1,\ldots,F_n\}$ is   a   matrix   with $\sigma(\emptyset)=0$ for   n=0   and
$\sigma(F)=1+\sum_{i=1}^{n}\sigma(F_i)$ for n>0 ,
$\Omega(\{F_1,\ldots,F_n\}) = \Omega(F_1) \cup \ldots \cup \Omega(F_n)$,   and $\delta(r)=m+1$ for any
$r \in \Omega(F_i)$, $1 \leq i \leq n$, where m is the depth of r in F_i.   □

As a general convention throughout this book, the introduction
of any new alphabet implicitly infers that it does not contain
any elements from previously introduced alphabets. This conven
tion here assures $\mathbf{P}^o \cap \{0,1\} \cap \mathbf{R} = \emptyset$.

Another such convention applies to any standard denotations agreed upon within this book. They may be decorated with

indices, primes, bars and the like; moreover, we may even take
the freedom to substitute them by any appropriate **mnemonic**
denotations whenever this might improve readability. In that
that sense, K_1, M', L_i, $\tilde{K}$, M1, PROPOSITION, PROPi, all are
correct denotations for literals, but F, E_i, $\tilde{D}$ are not since
these are reserved for matrices (and the formulas below).

The atomic parts of matrices (or formulas) obviously
are the literals which by convention either are of the form P
or ¬P where $P \in P^o$. As mentioned at the beginning of this section they are intended to abbreviate whole sentences. In view
of fol (first-order logic) they may be regarded as nullary
predicates, hence the index o attached to P . Our preference
for regarding literals as pairs (n,P) stems from the resultant
notational comfort which will be felt in more complicated
situations. In particular note that the pairs have not to be
displayed themselves, rather the form of literals will be L and
^1L (or ¬L) only, since obviously $^0L = L$ for any L.

Matrices, which are not literals, are nested sets of
occurrences of literals. The occurrences are needed in the
formalism to be able to distinguish different occurrences of
the same literal within a matrix. For the display of matrices,
however, the occurrences need not to be named explicitly since
they may be identified with the places where they are written
down. Hence, $\{\{L\},\{^1L\}\}$ and $\{\{\},K,\{\{K\},M\}\}$ are two examples of
matrices.

Such a nested structure becomes more illustrative if
it is unfolded in form of a **tree** . The two trees naturally
associated with the two matrices just given are

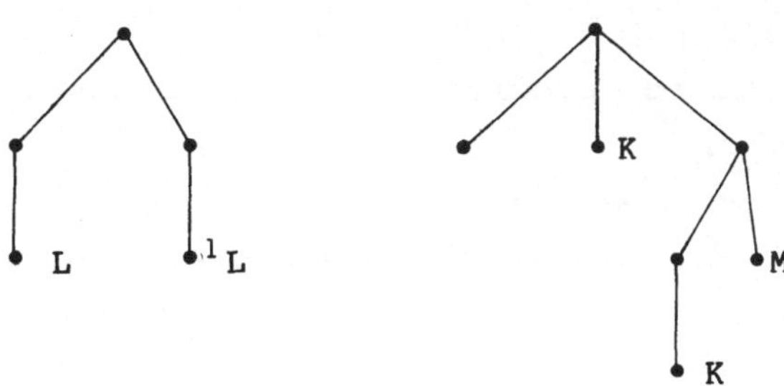

To be sure that each reader is familiar with this important concept we insert its definition.

1.2.D. A (**directed**) tree t over an alphabet R is a pair $(\Omega(t), A(t))$, with a set of **nodes** or **positions** $\Omega(t) \subseteq R$, and a set of **arcs** $A(t) \subseteq R \times R$, defined inductively by (t1) and (t2), together with its **root** , its **leaves** , and its **subtrees** $t_{:r}$ with root r for any $r \in \Omega(t)$.

(t1)   For any $r \in R$, $(\{r\}, \emptyset)$ is a tree, say t ; r is called its root and in this degenerate case it is also a leave; its only subtree $t_{:r} = t$.

(t2)   If $(\Omega(t_1), A(t_1)), \ldots, (\Omega(t_n), A(t_n))$, $n > 1$,   are trees with roots $r_i \in \Omega(t_i)$, $i=1, \ldots, n$, and $\Omega(t_i) \cap \Omega(t_j) = \emptyset$ for $i \neq j$, $1 \leq i, j \leq n$, then for any

$$r \in R \setminus \bigcup_{i=1}^{n} \Omega(t_i) \;, \quad (\; \{r\} \cup \bigcup_{i=1}^{n} \Omega(t_i), \quad \bigcup_{i=1}^{n}(r, r_i) \cup \bigcup_{i=1}^{n} A(t_i)\;)$$

is a tree, say t with root r . Its leaves are all the leaves of t_i for $i=1, \ldots, n$. Its subtrees are $t_{:r} = t$, and $t_{:r_i} = (t_i)_{:r_i}$, for any $r_i \in \Omega(t_i)$, $1 \leq i \leq n$.

The number of the nodes in a tree t is also called its **length** $\lambda(t)$, and the number of nodes that are not leaves is called its **size** $\sigma(t)$.

A **branch** in a tree is a sequence $(r_1, \ldots, r_m)$ of nodes such that r_1 is the root, r_m is a leave and (r_i, r_{i+1}) is an arc, $i=1, \ldots, m-1$; r_{i+1} is called a **successor** of r_i and r_i a **predecessor** (or **parent**) of r_{i+1}, $i=1, \ldots, m-1$; r_j is called a   **descendant** of r_i and r_i an **ancestor** of r_j , $1 \leq i < j \leq m$; further we say r_{i+1} has **depth** $\delta(r_{i+1}) = i$ in the tree.

A tree is called **ordered** if the successors of any of its nodes are ordered.

For a **binary** tree n=2 in (t2).

A **labeled** tree has labels associated with nodes and/ or arcs.   □

Returning to our two examples of matrices, we observe that in their representation as trees some leaves are labeled with literals. The depth of these leaves in the tree is the same as the depth of the occurrence of the labeling literal in the matrix as defined in (1.1). Thus it is 1 for K, 2 for L, ^{1}L, and M, and 3 for the second occurrence of K. Each of the remaining nodes corresponds to a certain pair of braces.

The size of a matrix is the number of its pairs of braces except the empty ones; its length is the number of its pairs of braces and its (occurrences of) literals. Thus the first matrix has size 3 and length 5, the second one has size 3 and length 7.

The representation of matrices in form of trees is appropriate for the discussion of its nesting structure. However, it ignores their intended meaning which may be displayed in a more suitable form introduced at the end of this section.

As might have been expected by the reader, the matrices are meant to be used as representatives for formulas. It will provide us technical convenience to work with matrices rather than formulas. This does not mean that we ignore the more traditional and thus more natural concept of formulas, in particular for the human dialogue. Therefore the following definition not only introduces the class of formulas, but also describes their relation with the class of matrices.

1.3.D. For any matrix F and for $l,m \in \{0,1\}$, the set of **formulas** $\tilde{F}$ **represented by** F w.r.t. (l,m) is defined inductively by (r1) through (r4).

(r1)   If F is a literal, $F = L^r$, and if $l = 0$ then $\tilde{F} = L$.

(r2)   If F is a literal, $F = L^r$, and if $l = 1$ then $\tilde{F} = {}^1L$.

(r3)   If $F = \{F_1,..,F_n\}$, $n > 0$, and if $m = 1$ then $\tilde{F} = \wedge(\tilde{F}_1,...,\tilde{F}_n)$, where $\tilde{F}_i$ are any formulas represented by F_i w.r.t. $(l,0)$, $i=1,...,n$.

(r4)   If $F = \{F_1,..,F_n\}$, $n > 0$, and if $m = 0$ then $\tilde{F} = \vee(\tilde{F}_1,...,\tilde{F}_n)$, where $\tilde{F}_i$ are any formulas represented by F_i w.r.t. $(l,1)$, $i=1,...,n$.

A formula $\tilde{F}$ is called (**positively**) **represented by** a matrix F if it is represented by F w.r.t. $l=m=0$; $\tilde{F}$ is called **negatively represented by** F if it is represented by F w.r.t. $l=m=1$. A (**propositional**) **formula** is any formula which is represented by some matrix. Formulas are also denoted by D, E, or F.

The following seven abbreviations or conventions may be used for representing such formulas.

(c1)   In the case n=0, $\wedge(F_1,\ldots,F_n)=\wedge(\ )$ is abbreviated by **T** , and $\vee(\ )$ is abbreviated by **F** .

(c2)   In the case n=1, $\wedge(F_1,\ldots,F_n)=\wedge(F_1)$ and $\vee(F_1)$ both are abbreviated by F_1.

(c3)   In the case n≥2, $\wedge(F_1,\ldots,F_n)$ is called a **conjunction** and its elements F_i are called **conjuncts** . It may be written as $(F_1\wedge\ldots\wedge F_n)$. Similary for $\vee(F_1,..,F_n)$ which is called a **disjunction** of the **disjuncts** F_i, and which may be written as $(F_1\vee\ldots\vee F_n)$. In both cases, any two or more subsequent such **juncts** may be grouped together with additional parentheses.

(c4)   For any formula F, the formula $\neg F$, called the **negation** of F, is defined inductively by (c4-1), (c4-2), and (c4-3).

(c4-1)   If F is a literal then $\neg F = {}^{\perp}F$.

(c4-2)   If $F = \wedge(F_1,\ldots,F_n)$, n≥0, then $\neg F=\vee(\neg F_1,\ldots,\neg F_n)$.

(c4-3)   If $F = \vee(F_1,\ldots,F_n)$, n≥0, then $\neg F=\wedge(\neg F_1,\ldots,\neg F_n)$.

(c5)   Any formula of the form $(\neg D\vee E)$ may be written as $(D\rightarrow E)$, pronounced "D implies E" and called an **implication** . It may also be written as $(E\leftarrow D)$ and pronounced "E is implied by D".

(c6)   Any formula of the form $((D\rightarrow E)\wedge(E\rightarrow D))$ may be written as $(D\leftrightarrow E)$, pronounced "D if and only if E" and called an **equivalence** .

(c7)   We take the convention that the order of precedence decreases in the sequence $\neg,\wedge,\vee,\rightarrow,\leftrightarrow$. Any parentheses, which are redundant on the basis of this convention, may be deleted.

□

This relatively complicated definition for the simple concept of a formula needs justification and explanation. As we said before, it has been meant to also specify the relation between matrices and formulas. This correspondence relation has been established in two parts.

In the first part, matrices are related with formulas containing literals, disjunctions and conjunctions only, since these are their closest counterparts. Obviously, the most natural way of considering a formula is to take the formula itself without any change. Unfortunately, for certain historical

reasons it has become customary in the field of ATP to handle
the negation of a given formula rather than the formula itself
(see section IV.1). We have decided not to follow this unnat-
ural and unnecessary custom, and the concept of matrices enables us to do so without causing any confusion, if the reader
is conscious of the following fact.

1.4.L. If a formula $\overset{\smile}{F}$ is (positively) represented by a matrix
F then $\neg\tilde{F}$ is negatively represented by F.
        The proof consists of a trivial induction (see E2 in
section III.8).

As a consequence of this lemma, both $\tilde{F}$ and $\neg\tilde{F}$ may be represented by the same matrix F, only the interpretation of the
relation "represented by" differs. In this book, however, we
will always have in mind the positive representation unless
stated otherwise.
        As an example, consider the matrix F = {{K,L},M} . For
determining a formula $\tilde{F}$, which is represented by F , we let
l = m = 0 . Hence, according to (r4), $\tilde{F}$ must be of the form
$v(\tilde{F}_1,\tilde{F}_2)$. In order to determine $\tilde{F}_i$, i=1,2 , we have to set
m=1 (l=0 remains) and to determine a correspondence between
$\tilde{F}_1$ and $\tilde{F}_2$ on the one side and the elements {K,L} and M on
the other side. Say, $\tilde{F}_1$ corresponds to M; hence $\tilde{F}_1$ = M by
(r1). Consequently $\tilde{F}_2$ is of the form $\wedge(\tilde{F}_3,\tilde{F}_4)$ by (r3). For
instance, we may now choose $\tilde{F}_3$ = K and $\tilde{F}_4$ = L . Altogether we
thus have $\tilde{F}$ = v(M,$\wedge$(K,L)) . A similar exercise with l = m = 1
yields $\wedge(^1M,v(^1K,^1L))$ as the formula which is negatively represented by F. Obviously, this is the negation of F according to (c4), as it has to be by (1.4).
        We now turn our attention to the second part of defini-
tion (1.3), in which arbitrary formulas are introduced in terms
of those from the first part via the abbreviations (c1) through
(c7). They are built from the literals using the usual **boolean
connectives** or **operators** which are listed once more in table
1 together with their arity, their natural pronounciation, and
with other symbols in use for them.

logical operator	arity	other symbols in use	natural pronounciation
T	0	$t, \curlyvee$	true, verum
F	0	$f, \curlywedge \perp$	false, falsum
¬	1	$\sim, ^-$	not
∧	$n > 0$	&	and
∨	$n > 0$		or, vel
→	2	⊃	if-then-, implies
↔	2	≡	if and only if, equivalent

Table 1. The boolean connectives in use

Let us trace this whole chain of definitions backwards with the formula $K \wedge L \to M$. According to (c7), ∧ has a higher order of precedence than → ; thus its fully parenthesized form is $((K \wedge L) \to M)$. According to (c5), this is an abbreviation of $(\neg(K \wedge L) \vee M)$. By (c4-2) this is to be regarded as $((\neg K \vee \neg L) \vee M)$, which actually is a variant of $\vee(\neg K, \neg L, M)$ according to (c3), and of $\vee(^1K, ^1L, M)$ according to (1.1). By our preference for the positive representation we have $l = m = 0$. There is a unique rule, namely (r4), resulting in such a formula; hence the corresponding matrix F must be of the form $\{F_1, F_2, F_3\}$ which immediately gives $F = \{^1K^{r1}, ^1L^{r2}, M^{r3}\}$ by (r1) for any positions $r_i \in R$, $i = 1, 2, 3$.

This process apparently may be applied to any "well-formed" formula resulting in a uniquely determined matrix which is stated in the following lemma.

1.5.L. Any formula $\tilde{F}$ uniquely determines a matrix F , such that $\tilde{F}$ is represented by F .

The proof is obvious by definition (1.3). Note that (c2) has to be applied if $\tilde{F}$ is of the form $\wedge(\tilde{F}_1, \ldots, \tilde{F}_n)$ to yield $\vee(\wedge(\tilde{F}_1, \ldots, \tilde{F}_n))$. $\square$

Conversely, any matrix may represent more than one formula. For instance, $K \wedge L \to M$, $K \to \neg L \vee M$, $L \wedge K \to M$, $\neg M \to \neg(L \wedge K)$ all are represented by $\{^1K^{r1}, ^1L^{r2}, M^{r3}\}$, the matrix derived

before from the first formula of this list. Incidentally, the
last one is its contraposition which indicates the reason why
in the connection rule to be introduced in section 4 there is
no action corresponding to contraposition as mentioned already
in section (I.2). What is it, then, which characterizes a set
formulas being represented by a single matrix such as these
four ones? The answer is that they differ only w.r.t. associativity and commutativity of the logical operators $\wedge$ and $\vee$, which
will be expressed in precise mathematical terms as follows.

1.6.D. Two formulas D and E are called **m-equivalent** if they
are represented by the same matrix which symbolically is expressed by $D \stackrel{m}{\sim} E$.

On the other hand, **ac-equivalence** (i.e. equivalence
w.r.t. associativity and commutativity) of two formulas D and
E, expressed symbolically by $D \stackrel{ac}{\sim} E$, is defined inductively
by (1), (2), and (3).

(1)   If $D = E$ then $D \stackrel{ac}{\sim} E$.

(2)   If $D = \wedge(F_1,\ldots,F_n)$, $E = \wedge(F_1',\ldots,F_n')$ for $n \geqslant 2$, and if
$F_{\pi i} \stackrel{ac}{\sim} F_i'$, $i=1,\ldots,n$, for some permutation π then $D \stackrel{ac}{\sim} E$.

(3)   If $D = \vee(F_1,\ldots,F_n)$, $E = \vee(F_1',\ldots,F_n')$ for $n \geqslant 2$, and if
$F_{\pi i} \stackrel{ac}{\sim} F_i'$, $i=1,\ldots,n$, for some permutation π then $D \stackrel{ac}{\sim} E$. $\square$

1.7.L. For any two formulas D and E, $D \stackrel{m}{\sim} E$ iff (if and only
if) $D \stackrel{ac}{\sim} E$.

The proof is trivial by (1.3), specifically (r3) and
(r4). $\square$

Apparently, associativity has not played any explicit rule in
this statement, since it has been implemented within the concept of formulas as a convention, specifically (c3).

As we will see in the next section, associativity and
commutativity have no influence on the validity of formulas.
Thus the restriction of our treatment to matrices rather than
formulas in their conventional representation, which provides
many technical advantages, is without any loss of information
for the general proof process. It might be regarded as a loss
of information from a strategical point of view for an actual

implementation. Since the transition from formulas to matrices is precisely defined, however, there is no reason why an actual implementation could not take care of this information, even if it is based on the matrix concept (see section IV.7). Thus when talking of matrices, implicitly we also have in mind the corresponding formulas, and vice versa.

Matrices (and formulas) have been introduced in (1.1) and (1.3) in the most general form. Often we will restrict the discussion to special matrices (and their corresponding formulas), in particular to those which are determined by the following concepts.

1.8.D.   A matrix F is called **in normal form** if $\max_{r \in \Omega(F)} \delta(r) \leq 2$.

The elements of a matrix in normal form are also called **clauses** , denoted by c, d, e.

A clause is called a **Horn clause** if it contains at most one literal of the form $(1, P)$ for $P \in \mathbf{P}^0$.

A matrix is called a **Horn matrix** if it is in normal form, and all its clauses are Horn clauses.

$\square$

With the relation established between matrices and formulas, these definitions also apply to the represented formulas. But as we said before, this goes without explicit mentioning. We should note, however, that a formula represented positively or negatively by a matrix in normal form is also called in **disjunctive** or **conjunctive** normal form, respectively, where "disjunctive" is the standard case throughout this book.

The matrices in normal form are the ones which justify the use of the name "matrix" known from linear algebra. This becomes clear if their clauses, which are sets of literals, are represented as columns in a two-dimensional display. This will turn out to be very illustrative for our purposes. As an example, the formula (I.2.1) at the end of section (I.2) arranged in this way reads

1.9.F.	Nc	Nc	*	*	*
	Sc,t	Rc,t	¬Nc	Oc	¬Sc,t
	¬Rc,t	¬Oc	*	*	*

It contains five clauses, two containing three literals and the remaining three containing one literal. Thus this may be regarded as a (5x3)-matrix in the sense of algebra in which six items have no value (or the value **T** , if you like). The ordering of the clauses within the matrix and of the literals within each clause suggested by such a display should be regarded as accidental, since no such orderings are involved in our concept of matrices. (The generalization of this form of representation to arbitrary matrices is deferred until section 3.)

In this particular example, the formula is even a Horn matrix since all clauses contain only a single or no negated literal.

There are two very special matrices. One is $\{\} = \emptyset$ which corresponds to $v() = F$ (in the positive representation); therefore **F** will also be used to denote this empty matrix. The other is $\{\{\}\} = \{\emptyset\}$ which will be denoted also by **T** since it corresponds to $v(\wedge()) = \wedge() = T$. These two will play an important role in the following section.

2.   THE SEMANTICS OF PROPOSITIONAL LOGIC

In the previous section we have introduced the language of propositional logic in two forms. In the view taken in this book it consists of the set of matrices while in its traditional form it consists of the set of formulas. Both forms are so closely related, however, that in most cases we may even ignore the difference and identify the two concepts.

Any such matrix corresponds to a compound statement in natural language as has been illustrated in the first chapter. Such statements are of a special nature because for any of them it makes sense to ask whether they are true or false. Statements of this nature are sometimes called **aristotelian statements** .

The question whether such a statement E is true or false in fact lies at the heart of ATP. Typically, it is posed together with information about the truth of other statements $E_1,...,E_n$, $n \geqslant 0$. For example, remember once more the formula (I.2.1) where E is $\neg Sc,t$ and $E_1,...,E_4$, respectively, are

the four conjuncts in its if-part, which are assumed to be
true. In terms of definition (1.1), their four atomic statements Nc , Sc,t , Rc,t , Oc are to be regarded as elements
in $\mathbf{P}^0$. If we would know explicitly for these whether they
are true or false then the question on E could be solved easily, not only in this particular example but also in general as
we will see in a moment. This simplest case therefore appears
to be a good candidate to start with.

Note that such knowledge may be regarded as the description of the whole situation given in atomic pieces of the
form "Nc is true", "Sc,t is false", etc. Had we chosen to say
"Nc is false", etc., then this obviously would describe a different situation, another **possible world** or **model** . For determining such a model it is sufficient to just say which
pieces are true. Thus we have the following definition.

2.1.D. A **model for** $\mathbf{P}^0$ is a finite subset of $\mathbf{P}^0$.   □

In the next step, we have to express statements like "F is
true", within our formalism. For that purpose recall that
"true" and "false" may be regarded as elements in our language,
previously denoted by **T** and **F** , respectively. This identification is a natural one. Just be aware of the fact that any statement, which is a conjunction of other statements, naturally
is regarded to be true iff all conjuncts are true. In $\mathbf{T} = \wedge()$
this condition is trivially satisfied since there is no conjunct. Therefore the truth of statements may be expressed by a
function $\tau_{\mathfrak{M}}$ which for a given model $\mathfrak{M}$ reduces any matrix to
the **truth values T** and F .

2.2.D. Inductive definition of $\tau_{\mathfrak{M}}(i,F) \in \{ \mathbf{T},\mathbf{F} \}$ for any
model $\mathfrak{M} \subseteq \mathbf{P}^0$, $i \in \{0,1\}$, and any matrix F.
(t1)   For a literal $F = (j,P)$, if j=0 and $P \in \mathfrak{M}$ or if j=1
and $P \notin \mathfrak{M}$ then $\tau_{\mathfrak{M}}(i,F) = \mathbf{T}$ otherwise $\tau_{\mathfrak{M}}(i,F) = \mathbf{F}$.
(t2)   For a matrix $F = \{F_1,\ldots,F_n\}$, $n>0$, if i=0   then
$\tau_{\mathfrak{M}}(0,F) = \bigvee_{k=1}^{n} \tau_{\mathfrak{M}}(1,F_k)$ otherwise $\tau_{\mathfrak{M}}(1,F) = \bigwedge_{k=1}^{n} \tau_{\mathfrak{M}}(0,F_k)$.
We say, a matrix F **is true** , or **has the truth value**
T or **holds in** $\mathfrak{M}$, or $\mathfrak{M}$ **is a model of** F, in symbols $\mathfrak{M} \vDash F$,

if $\tau_{\mathfrak{M}}(0,F) = T$; otherwise F **is false** or **has the value** F in $\mathfrak{M}$.

A formula $\tilde{F}$ is called **true in** $\mathfrak{M}$, in symbols $\mathfrak{M} \models \tilde{F}$, if $\mathfrak{M} \models F$ for the matrix F which represents $\tilde{F}$; otherwise it is **false in** $\mathfrak{M}$.   □

For instance, let $\mathfrak{M} = \{Nc\}$ in our previous example and consider $E_1 = (Nc \wedge Sc,t \rightarrow Rc,t)$.
$\tau_{\mathfrak{M}}(0,E_1) = \tau_{\mathfrak{M}}(0,\{\neg Nc,\neg Sc,t,Rc,t\}) =$
$\tau_{\mathfrak{M}}(1,\neg Nc) \cup \tau_{\mathfrak{M}}(1,\neg Sc,t) \cup \tau_{\mathfrak{M}}(1,Rc,t) = \{\}\cup\{\{\}\}\cup\{\} = \{\{\}\} = T$.
Similarly, E_i for $i = 2,3,4$, E , and the whole formula (I.2.1) are true in this model which may be easily checked by the reader. Further there is no other model with this property differing on the four propositional variables in question only. Hence, it is this model which adequately describes the situation given in (I.1.1). It is unique if we disregard any other facts or propositional variables which have not been mentioned in this description.

If a natural statement consists of substatements combined by any of our boolean connectives then the knowledge of the truth values for the substatements naturally determine a truth value for the whole statement. This functional connection is displayed for all our connectives in table 2 which is called a **truth table** . On the other hand, such a truth table is also determined by our definition (2.2). It goes without saying that our definition is a natural one in the sense that both tables coincide which is stated in the following lemma.

2.3.L. The truth table for the boolean connectives $\neg$, $\wedge$, $\vee$, $\rightarrow$, and $\leftrightarrow$ determined by definition (2.2) is the one displayed in table 2.

The proof follows immediately from the definitions (2.2) and (1.3).   □

As we have just seen, for a given model the truth value for any formula may be calculated in a straightforward way determined by (2.2). Unfortunately, in practice it is a rare case that a model is known. Rather, the information about an appropriate model is encoded in the form of information about the

D	E	¬D	D∧E	D∨E	D→E	D↔E
T	T	F	T	T	T	T
T	F	F	F	T	F	F
F	T	T	F	T	T	F
F	F	T	F	F	T	T

Table 2. Truth table for the boolean connectives

truth values for compound statements such as E_1 and E_2 above. Such a truth value for a matrix in general does not determine a unique truth value for each of its occurring propositional variables. For instance, the knowledge that E_1 is true in $\mathcal{M}$, allows any model for $\mathcal{M}$ which contains Rc,t or does not contain Nc or Sc,t. Therefore we must consider the following more general truth relation.

2.4.D. For any finite set $\mathcal{E}$ of formulas or matrices, and any formula or matrix F, we say that F is a (**semantical**) **consequence of** or (**logically follows from**) $\mathcal{E}$, in symbols $\mathcal{E} \vDash F$ if $\mathcal{M} \vDash E$ for any $E \in \mathcal{E}$, implies $\mathcal{M} \vDash F$, for any model $\mathcal{M}$. □

2.5.T. (Deduction theorem) For any finite set $\mathcal{E}$ of formulas, and any two formulas E, F, $\mathcal{E} \cup \{E\} \vDash F$ iff $\mathcal{E} \vDash E \to F$.
        The easy proof is left to the reader. □

This (finite version of the usual) deduction theorem may be applied repeatedly until the set of formulas on the left side is empty. The right side is then of the form $(E_1 \to \ldots (E_n \to F) \ldots)$ for some $n \geqslant 0$, which is true iff $E_1 \wedge \ldots \wedge E_n \to F$ is true. In other words, $\{E_1, \ldots, E_n\} \vDash F$ may be tested by verifying $\vDash E_1 \wedge \ldots \wedge E_n \to F$ which in turn means $\mathcal{M} \vDash E_1 \wedge \ldots \wedge E_n \to F$ for any model $\mathcal{M}$. This special case is worth a special concept.

2.6.D. A matrix or formula F is called a **valid** formula or a **tautology** if $\vDash F$, i.e. $\mathcal{M} \vDash F$ for any model $\mathcal{M}$. □

As we said before the typical question in ATP is whether we may infer the truth of E from that of $E_1,\ldots,E_n$ which, as we have just seen, equivalently may be answered by testing the validity of $E_1 \wedge \ldots \wedge E_n \rightarrow E$. Formula (I.2.1) is of this form, and in fact it is a valid formula which is true in any model. The simplest method for deciding whether any formula F is valid or not is the following so-called **truth table method** .

Obviously, only a finite subset of the propositional variables may occur in F, say, $\{P_1,\ldots,P_n\} \subseteq \mathbf{P}^0$. In order to determine the truth value of F in any model $\mathcal{M}$ according to (2.2) , only $\mathcal{M}\,|\,F = \mathcal{M} \cap \{P_1,\ldots,P_n\}$ must be known. There are only finitely many different possibilities for $\mathcal{M}\,|\,F$, consisting of the set of subsets of $\{P_1,\ldots,P_n\}$ which has the cardinality 2^n. By calculating for each of these 2^n possibilities the truth value of F, we may decide whether F is valid (truth value **T** in each case) or not.

In the case of formula (I.2.1) where n = 4 this truth table method requires 16 such calculations, as opposed to the only 5 connections which, as we claim, are required to yield the same result. Therefore let us head for a better method.

3.   A BASIC SYNTACTIC CHARACTERIZATION OF VALIDITY

In the first two sections of this chapter we have presented standard material from mathematical logic. In the present section a syntactic charaterization of the set of valid formulas will now follow, based on the set-theoretic approach which has been chosen for our presentation. The following definition introduces the most important notion in this connection.

3.1.D. A **path through** a matrix F is a set of (occurrences of) literals which is defined inductively by (p1), (p2), and (p3).

(p1)   If $F=\emptyset$ then the only path through F is the empty set $\emptyset$.

(p2)   If $F=L^r$ for a literal L at position r then the only path through F is the set $\{L^r\}$.

(p3)   If $F = \{F_1,\ldots,F_m,F_{m+1},\ldots,F_{m+n}\}$, $0 \leqslant m,n$, $1 \leqslant m+n$, for m literals $F_1,\ldots,F_m$ and n matrices $F_{m+1},\ldots,F_{m+n}$

which are not literals then for any matrix E_i such that $E_i \in F_{m+i}$ and any path p_i through E_i, $i=1,\ldots,n$, the set $\bigcup_{j=1}^{m} \{F_j\} \cup \bigcup_{i=1}^{n} p_i$ is path through F. $\qquad\square$

Let us first consider a matrix E in normal form, viz. $\{\{K_1,K_2\},L_1,\{M_1,M_2,M_3\}\}$, representing the formula $(K_1 \wedge K_2) \vee L_1 \vee (M_1 \wedge M_2 \wedge M_3)$ in (disjunctive) normal form. In the two-dimensional display introduced in section 1 it looks as follows.

$$
\begin{array}{ccc}
 & & M_1 \\
K_1 & & \\
 & L_1 & M_2 \\
K_2 & & \\
 & & M_3
\end{array}
$$

In order to determine the paths through E it might be a helpful exercise in reading such an inductive definition to apply (3.1) in a meticulous way.

E is of the form addressed in (p3) there, with $m=1$, $F_1=L_1$, $n=2$, $F_2=\{K_1,K_2\}$, and $F_3=\{M_1,M_2,M_3\}$. From F_2 and F_3 we have to select a matrix E_1 and E_2 , respectively. There are two possibilities for E_1, viz. K_1,K_2 , and three for E_2 . Since this selection may be done independently for E_1 and E_2 , altogether we thus have six different selections resulting in six different paths. Whatever this selection K_k for E_1 and M_1 for E_2, $k \in \{1,2\}$, $l \in \{1,2,3\}$, is, for the determination of a path p_i through E_i, $i=1,2$, (p2) now applies. Thus the formula in (p3) in this case gives

$$
p_{kl} = \bigcup_{j=1}^{1} \{F_j\} \cup \bigcup_{i=1}^{2} p_i = \{L_1\} \cup \{K_k\} \cup \{M_l\} = \{L_1,K_k,M_l\} \ .
$$

In the two-dimensional display these paths may be nicely illustrated as paths crossing the matrix from left to right, constrained to pass the clauses (to be interpreted as barriers) through any of its literals (to be interpreted as gates), shown in the following picture for the path $p_{21} = \{L_1,K_2,M_1\}$.

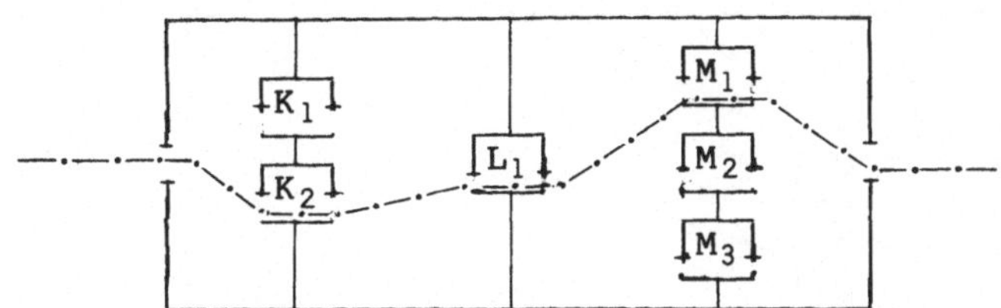

The reader is encouraged always to imagine or even to draw such a picture whenever paths are the topic of discussion. Usually, we will not draw the barriers and their gates explicitly, rather we will use the following simpler way of illustration.

$$\begin{array}{cccc}
K_1 & & M_1 & \\
-\cdot-K_2-\cdot- & -\cdot-L_1-\cdot- & M_2 & \\
& & M_3 &
\end{array}$$

It should now be clear how this generalizes to arbitrary matrices in normal form, where there may be more clauses, each with an arbitrary number of literals. Perhaps we should mention the special case in (p3) where $F_{m+i} = \emptyset$. Since there is no matrix E_i, hence no path p_i, a path through the whole matrix cannot be given. This nicely fits into our interpretation since a clause without a literal is a barrier without a gate which cannot be crossed.

The way of calculation of the number of paths for E above is applicable in general, as the following lemma shows.

3.2.L.   For a matrix $F = \{F_1, \ldots, F_m, F_{m+1}, \ldots, F_{m+n}\}$ as in (p3) of (3.1) but in normal form, the number of paths through F is $\prod_{i=1}^{n} |F_{m+i}|$.

The proof by induction on n is trivial. $\square$

The next step now is to extend this illustration to general matrices not necessarily in normal form. Consider the matrix $E' = \{\{K_1', \{\{K_1, K_2\}, L_1, \{M_1, M_2, M_3\}\}\}, L_1', \{M_1', M_2', M_3'\}\}$, which represents the formula $(K_1' \wedge [(K_1 \wedge K_2) \vee L_1 \vee (M_1 \wedge M_2 \wedge M_3)]) \vee L_1' \vee (M_1' \wedge M_2' \wedge M_3')$ Note that it may be regarded as a copy of the matrix E before with primes attached to its literals, but with K_2' substituted by the whole matrix E. This immediately suggests to use the same two-dimensional way of representation as for normal form matrices but now in a nested form.

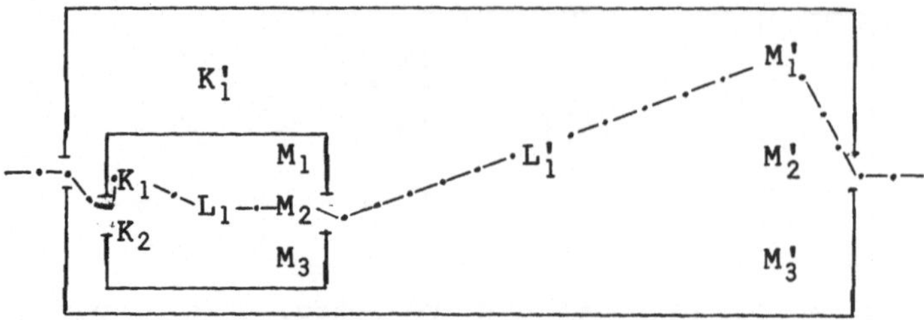

The **submatrix** E within E' has been fenced with straight
lines in order to expose the nesting structure in this picture.
It also shows a path p through E'. If the matrix would contain
K_2' rather than E, then this path would be identical with the
path p_{21} shown further above. But now instead of K_2' we have to
consider a more complicated matrix in normal form, viz. E .
According to (p3) in (3.1) there is nothing peculiar with this
situation. (p3) simply asks for a path through this submatrix
E. This time we have selected $p_{12} = \{K_1, L_1, M_2\}$. Hence,
$p = \{L_1'\} \cup \{K_1, L_1, M_2\} \cup \{M_1'\} = \{K_1, L_1, M_2, L_1', M_1'\}$.

In our illustrative "gate" interpretation we might say
that any gate in the sense before within matrices in normal
form may be split into an entrance and an exit gate with a
whole matrix in between. In that sense even the whole matrix
itself may be regarded as such a generalized gate which has
already been realized in the previous picture. This now also
nicely illustrates why the empty matrix does in fact have a
path, namely the empty one: ——— . It should now also be
clear that this nesting structure may be arbitrarily complicated without causing any principal problems, both w.r.t. the
depth of the nesting and w.r.t. the number of items in each
fenced area.

Considerable space has been spent for the digestion of
definition (3.1) because paths in matrices are fundamental for
the approach to ATP taken in this book. With the following
definition we are now approaching the main result of this section.

3.3.D. A (**partial**) **path in** a matrix F is any subset of a
path through F.

A **connection** in a matrix F is a path in F of the form $\{L^{r0}, {}^1L^{r1}\}$.

A set W of connections in a matrix F is called **spanning for** F if for each path p through F there is an $w \in W$ such that p **contains** w which is to say $w \subseteq p$.

A matrix F is called **complementary** if there exists a spanning set of connections for F.

For any matrix F and any set W of connections in F, the pair (F,W) is called a **connection graph** or **connection matrix** .   □

In our two-dimensional display connections are exposed by connecting its two literals with an arc as in the matrix

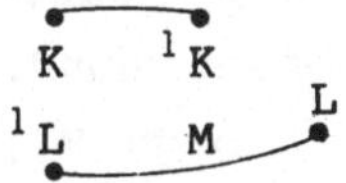

The two connections in this matrix are not spanning since none of them is contained in the path {K,M,L}, i.e. this matrix is not complementary. The word "spanning" has its origin in the imagination of the paths being the basic constructing parts, fixed in themselves. But in order to span out the whole matrix, each needs the support of at least one connection (like of a pillar). In

which was obtained from the previous example by adding the further clause ${}^1M$, the three connections in fact are spanning; hence this matrix is complementary. Another complementary matrix is (1.9). If the reader inserts the five connecting arcs, he/she may notice that these arcs connect exactly those pairs of literals which correspond to the connected pairs of literals in the original formula (I.2.1).

Since any path containing a connection itself is a complementary matrix, we may talk of **complementary paths** in this case. For the same reason in the particular case of a connection its two literals are also called **complementary literals** . Incidentally, this is not the simplest complementary matrix since the matrix {{}} has no paths at all; therefore the empty set of connections is spanning for it which makes it complementary.

The complementarity of a matrix obviously is a purely syntactical property, as opposed to the validity of a matrix which refers to models, a semantical concept. But we are now in the position to bring the two together.

3.4.T. A matrix is complementary iff it is valid.

Proof. We prove this statement by induction on the size $\sigma(F)$ of the matrix, denoted by F .

(i)   If $\sigma(F) = 0$ then by definition (1.1) this means that F is a literal or the empty matrix. If F is a literal then according to definition (2.2.t1) there is a model in which F is false. Hence F is not valid. On the other hand, by definition (3.1.p1) there is exactly one path through F , viz. $\{F\}$, which obviously is not complementary. Since for $F=\emptyset$ the theorem trivially holds, we are done in this case.

(ii)   If $\sigma(F) = 1$ then by definition (1.1) this means that $F=\{(k_1,P_1),\ldots,(k_n,P_n)\}$ for n literals (k_i,P_i), $n \geqslant 1$, or $F=\{\{\}, L_1,\ldots,L_m\}$, $m \geqslant 0$.

If $\emptyset \in F$ then for any model $\mathcal{M}$,

$$\tau_{\mathcal{M}}(0,F) = \tau_{\mathcal{M}}(1,\emptyset) \cup \bigcup_{i=1}^{m} \tau_{\mathcal{M}}(1,L_i) = T \cup \bigcup_{i=1}^{m} \tau_{\mathcal{M}}(1,L_i) = T$$

by definition (2.2.t2), thus F is valid in this case. It is also complementary by default since by definition (3.1.p3) there are no paths through such a matrix, thus settling this case. Now assume $\emptyset \notin F$.

If F is complementary containing a connection $\{L,{}^1L\}$ then for any model either L or ${}^1L$ is true, in both cases yielding the truth-value T for F by definition (2.2), i.e. F is valid.

Otherwise if F is not complementary then by (2.2) F is false in the model $\{P_i \mid k_i=1, i \leqslant n\}$.

(iii)   If $\sigma(F) > 1$ then by definition (1.1) this means that $F = \{\{E_{11},\ldots,E_{1m}\}, E_2,\ldots,E_n\}$ for $m \geqslant 1$, $n \geqslant 0$.

Consider the m matrices $F_i = E_{1i} \cup \{E_2,\ldots,E_n\}$, $i=1,\ldots,m$ (regarding any literal E_{1i} as singleton set). Their size is $\sigma(F)-1$ since in comparison with F at least one pair of braces has gone, hence they are candidates for apply-

ing the induction hypothesis. This will be achieved by proving
the following two statements (I) and (II).

(I)   F is valid iff F_i is valid for any $i \in \{1,\ldots,m\}$.

(II)   F is complementary iff F_i is complementary for any
$i \in \{1,\ldots,m\}$. Obviously, with the induction hypothesis for
F_i, $i=1,\ldots,m$, saying that F_i is complementary iff F_i is
valid, these two statements immediately imply the statement of
the theorem for F.

Proof of (I). Let $\mathfrak{M}$ be any model. We introduce the
following abbreviations.

$E_1 = \{E_{11},\ldots,E_{1m}\}$; $\tau_1 = \tau_{\mathfrak{M}}(0,\{E_1\}) = \tau_{\mathfrak{M}}(1,E_1)$;

$\tau_2 = \tau_{\mathfrak{M}}(0,\{E_2,\ldots,E_n\})$; $\tau_{1i} = \tau_{\mathfrak{M}}(0,E_{1i})$, $i=1,\ldots,m$.

Definition (2.2.t2) provides the following equations.

(e1) $\tau_{\mathfrak{M}}(0,F) = \tau_1 \cup \tau_2$

(e2) $\tau_{\mathfrak{M}}(0,F_i) = \tau_{1i} \cup \tau_2$, $i = 1,\ldots,m$

(e3) $\tau_1 = \bigwedge_{i=1}^{m} \tau_{1i}$

Now, in order prove the "only-if"-case, assume
$\tau_{\mathfrak{M}}(0,F) = T$. If $\tau_2 = T$ this implies $\tau_{\mathfrak{M}}(0,F_i) = T$ by
(e2) for all $i=1,\ldots,m$. Otherwise, $\tau_1 = T$ by (e1). This yields
$\tau_{1i} = T$ by (e3), hence $\tau_{\mathfrak{M}}(0,F_i) = T$ by (e2), for all
$i=1,\ldots,m$.

Conversely, assume $\tau_{\mathfrak{M}}(0,F_i) = T$, $i=1,\ldots,m$, for
proving the "if"-case. If $\tau_2 = T$ then $\tau_{\mathfrak{M}}(0,F) = T$ by (e1).
Otherwise, $\tau_{1i} = T$ for all $i=1,\ldots,m$, by (e2). This yields
$\tau_1 = T$ by (e3), hence $\tau_{\mathfrak{M}}(0,F) = T$ by (e1).

Since in both directions the chain of reasoning holds
for any model, this establishes (I).

The proof of (II) is an immediate consequence of the
following equation.
$\{p \mid p$ is a path through $F\} = \bigvee_{i=1}^{m} \{p \mid p$ is a path through $F_i\}$
In order to etablish it, we simply have to notice that by defi-
nition (3.1.p3) any path through F is of the form $p = p_{1i} \cup p_2$
for some $i \in \{1,\ldots,m\}$, some path p_{1i} through E_{1i} , and
some p_2 , hence is also a path through F_i , and vice versa. $\square$

With this theorem, any formula may be tested for validity without considering any models or truth-values and in a purely syntactical way, simply by checking all its paths for complement-

arity. It remains to be seen how this may be done in an efficient algorithmic way.

4.   THE CONNECTION CALCULUS

Theorem (3.4) provides the basis for a powerful proof method
which naturally may be called the **connection method** . Roughly
speaking it consists in selecting connections in the given
matrix F, one after the other, until the set of selected connections becomes spanning for F. This sounds like a method
easy to be understood, which it is, as far as its main features
are concerned. In its most general and presently most efficient
form, however, so many details have to be accounted for that it
will be helpful for the reader to explain the main features
first by means of a less general and less efficient version
which is the purpose of the remaining sections of this
chapter. More advanced versions will then be discussed in
chapter IV.

In particular, we restrict our attention in these sections to the important special case of matrices in normal form
(see exercise E5 in section 7 or section III.4. w.r.t. the
generality of this restriction). For example,

$$K \quad {}^1K \qquad \qquad {}^1M$$
$$L \qquad {}^1L \qquad \qquad M$$

is of that sort, called E for the following discussion. E
differs from the general case (within the present restriction)
only w.r.t. the number of clauses and the number of literals
in each clause.

There are four paths through E in accordance with
(3.2). On the other hand, there are only three connections in
E which are spanning for E. Hence, at least one connection
must be contained in more than one path. For instance, this is
true for $\{L, {}^1L\}$ which is contained in $\{L, {}^1L, {}^1K, {}^1M\}$ and in
$\{L, {}^1L, M, {}^1M\}$. For the general case this means that one connection may establish the complementarity for more than one, in
fact for arbitrarily many paths as the matrix $\{L, {}^1L\} \cup F$ with
an arbitrarily big matrix F demonstrates. Our envisioned method
should take this into consideration.

Assume that the method first considers the connection $\{K,{}^1K\}$ in E. Then the set B of all paths through E naturally is divided into the set B_0 of those paths containing $\{K,{}^1K\}$ and the set $B \smallsetminus B_0$ of the remaining ones. One way of encoding these two sets is shown in the second copy of the matrix of figure 1. There the horizontal arrow encodes the set B_1 of all paths containing ${}^1L$. Obviously, $B_1 \subseteq B \smallsetminus B_0$. The vertical arrow pointing to the second clause together with the dot after ${}^1K$ and the dashed line through K encodes the set B_2 of paths containing the literal in the second clause which has no dot, i.e. M, and containing the literal with the dashed line through it, i.e. K . Obviously, B_1 and B_2 partition the set $B \smallsetminus B_0$ into two disjoint subsets. Hence altogether we have $B = B_0 \cup B_1 \cup B_2$ which is encoded the way just described. Note that the arc illustrating the connection is not actually needed for this encoding but certainly is a helpful additional illustration.

There may be several other encodings serving for the same purpose, but this one has the advantage that it may be continued in a sequential way. Assume that it is B_2 which should be handled next by the method. The easiest way to process B_2 in the same way as B before (without loosing the information encoded before) is by selecting the next connection such that it contains a literal without a dot in the clause indicated by the vertical arrow which is $\{M,{}^1M\}$.

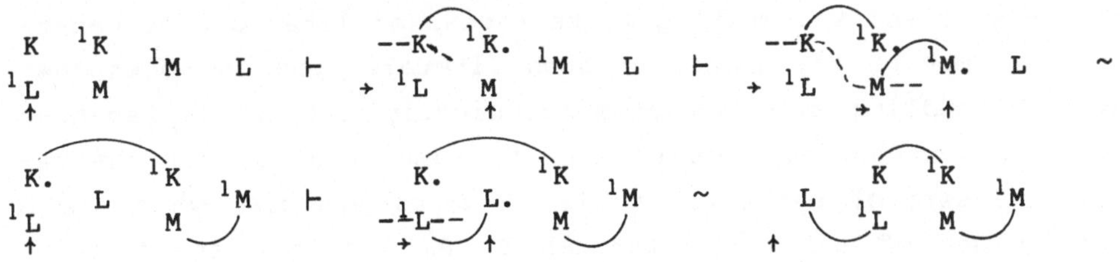

Figure 1. A connection deduction for the matrix E

As before B_2 is divided into the set B_{20} of all paths containing $\{M,{}^1M\}$ and the set $B_2 \smallsetminus B_{20}$ of the remaining ones. Obviously, $B_2 \smallsetminus B_{20} = \emptyset$ in this special case, which is encoded in the third copy of the matrix by the horizontal arrow below its second clause and by the vertical arrow pointing to the third clause containing no literals without a dot. For this reason the method may now turn to any set which still has to be processed in this way. In the present example only B_1 is left over which is settled in the same way as B_2 just before.

At this point all paths in E have been shown to be complementary. For achieving this exactly three steps of selecting a further connection were needed. Purposely, the description of these three steps was given in rather general terms in order to give the reader a first feeling for the performance of this method in general. In fact, the essence of this method already should have become visible even with this trivial example. In particular, it should have been noted that the matrix itself never changes. What will follow in this and the subsequent chapters are the descriptions of many more details, both in an informal and a precise form; in particular this includes the generalization to first-order logic and to formulas not necessarily in normal form.

In order to get experience with further details of this method's behavior for the restricted case of discourse, we are now testing it with a more complicated example, say D, which is shown in figure 2 together with all required steps for establishing complementarity.

The first step is as in the previous example with the only difference that there are now two (instead of one) literals, viz. L and M , waiting to be processed later on. In general there may be any number of such literals, and the postponement of handling such **subgoals** technically may be implemented by a stack-mechanism. Let us use the same notation for the respective sets of paths as in the previous example, which is B for the set of all paths through D, B_0 for the set of paths through the first selected connection $\{K, {}^1K\}$, B_1 the set of paths containing those two subgoals L and M , and B_2 the set of the remaining paths in B.

The second step demonstrates an additional feature. There is not only a connection $\{L, {}^1L\}$ selected as usual but also a second connection $\{K, {}^1K\}$ installed to leave N as the only subgoal in the third clause. The justification for this may be understood by noticing that any path from B_2 , the set of paths of discourse at this stage, contains the literal K.

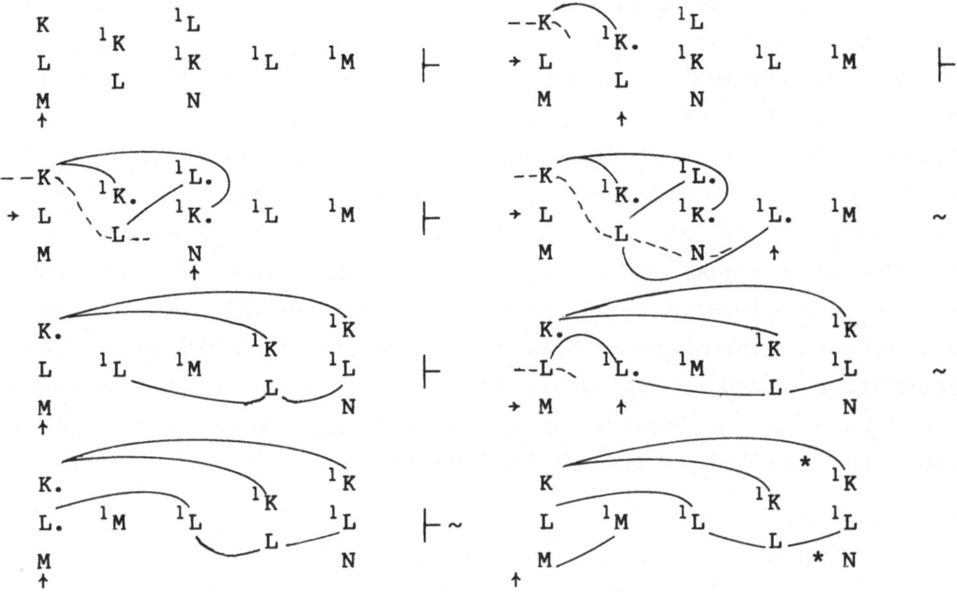

Figure 2. A connection deduction for the matrix D

Hence not only all paths in B_2 which contain $\{L, {}^1L\}$ turn out to be complementary at this step but also all those which contain the literal ${}^1K$ from the third clause; let us denote both these sets of paths by B_{20}. B_{21} is empty since there are no sub-goals in the second clause (from now on we delete a horizontal arrow pointing to nothing as in figure 1). Therefore, we have to consider now the set $B_{22} = B_2 \setminus B_{20}$.

Doing this in the third step, there seems to arise a problem since in the remaining clauses, which are to be encountered for B_{22}, there is no complementary literal for N. Remember, however, what has been done with ${}^1K$ in the previous step. The same, of course, may be applied to ${}^1L$ also in the absence of a complementary literal for N, namely establishing a connection with one out of the set of literals hit by the dashed line; this set is also called the **active path** . This completes this chain of reasoning **solving** the subgoal K in the first clause. It required three steps of a kind which will be called **extension** in definition (4.3) below.

Let us briefly interrupt to explain what would have happened if this matrix D would be changed to contain the clause {M} instead of clause {^{1}L} . Then none of the remaining clauses would contain a literal complementary to any of the literals in the currently active path. Apparently, in this case the whole matrix, say D', is complementary only if this is true for the partial matrix consisting of the remaining clauses only since each path in the latter together with this active path gives a path through D', and the literals in this active path cannot contribute to a connection in it under this assumption. Consequently, in this case the remaining clauses would have to be considered only and all previous subgoals could be regarded as solved leading to

$$\text{4.1.F.} \qquad
\begin{array}{ccccc}
K. & & ^1L. & & \\
 & ^1K. & & & \\
L. & & ^1K. & M & {}^1M \\
 & L. & & & \\
M. & & N. & &
\end{array}$$

after the third step for this variant which below will be called a **separation** step.

Returning to our original matrix D, we see in figure 2 that the matrix turns out to be complementary after two further steps solving the two subgoals in the first clause. Thus altogether we needed 5 steps although, as the reader might have noticed, with a more clever selection of connections or of the start clause only 4 steps would have been required. For the same reason the two connections labeled with an asterix in the last copy of the matrix are in fact redundant for ensuring the spanning property. We will learn in the section 6 how the method may be improved to behave optimal for this particular example. There is no efficient way to find such an optimal solution in general, however, which will be discussed in section (IV.3).

Any two subsequent matrices related by the equivalence sign ~ have not been counted as a step since only the structure imposed to the matrix is rearranged without encountering further connections. Below we will call this a **truncation** . Recall in this connection that clauses and matrices are sets, not lists as the illustrations might suggest. It is hoped that these illustrations have prepared the understanding of this method to a point where the following precise formalism may support this understanding rather than confusing it.

4.2.D. A matrix **structured in view of the linear normal-form connection method for propositional logic** is a matrix F in normal form paired with a structure S defined below; if the kind of deduction is clear from the context, the pair (F,S) will be simply called a **structured matrix** .

The structure S is a triple (α,β,γ) of functions wich satisfy the properties (i), (ii) and (iii).

(i) α is an integer function defined on a subset of the set of clauses in F, i.e. $\alpha(c)=n>1$ where $c\in F$ and $n\in N$. Let F_1^S denote the domain of α, shortly written F_1 if S is clear.

(ii) β is a boolean function on the set of occurrences of literals in F_1, i.e. $\beta(L^r)\in\{0,1\}$ for any literal $L^r\in c$ for some clause $c\in F_1$. Let $c_i = \{L^r\,|\,L^r\in c\in F_1$ and $\beta(L^r)=i\}$.

(iii) γ is defined on some subset $F_1'\subseteq F_1\setminus\{d\}$ for $d\in F_1$ with $\alpha(d)>\alpha(e)$ for any other $e\in F_1$, such that $\gamma(c)$ is an occurrence of a literal $L^r\in c_0\subseteq c$, i.e. $\gamma(c)=L^r\in c'$ for any $c\in F_1'$, such that $\beta(L^r)=0$.   The set $\{L^r\,|\,\gamma(c)=L^r,\ c\in F_1'\}$ is called the **active path** p_a^S, or shortly p_a, in F structured by S. $\square$

The matrices in figures 1 and 2 in fact illustrate such structured matrices. For example, let us consider the first, the fourth, and the last matrix in the deduction of figure 2, denoted by (D,S_1), (D,S_4), and (D,S_8), respectively.

α is illustrated by the vertical arrow pointing to a clause c_n with the convention that α is undefined for any clause to the right of c_n and $\alpha(c_j)+1=\alpha(c_{j+1})$ for the remaining clauses $c_1,\ldots,c_n$ in the displayed order. Let $S_i = (\alpha_i,\beta_i,\gamma_i)$, $i=1,4,8$. Then in particular, $\alpha_1(\{K,L,M\})=1$ and $\alpha_1(c)$ is undefined for $c\neq\{K,L,M\}$, $\alpha_4(\{^1M\})$ is undefined, and $\alpha_4(\{K,L,M\})=1$, $\alpha_4(\{^1K,L\})=2$, $\alpha_4(\{^1L,^1K,N\})=3$, $\alpha_4(\{^1L\})=4$, finally $\alpha_8(c)$ is undefined for any $c\in D$.

All literals in F_1 with a dot to the right and all those hit by the dashed line have the value 0 under β. All others in F_1 have the value 1; in each clause the horizontal arrow points to the first one of them from top to down. For instance, $\beta_1(K) = \beta_1(L) = \beta_1(M) = 1$, while $\beta_4(K) = 0$ and $\beta_4(L) = \beta_4(M) = 1$ for the literals from the first clause; further, $\beta_4(^1L) = \beta_4(^1K) = \beta_4(N) = 0$ for the literals from the third clause; β_4 is not defined for any literal in (D,S_8).

γ is defined for all clauses which are crossed by the dashed line and its value is the literal threaded by it. Hence the active path is empty for (D,S_1) and (D,S_8) while it is $\{K,L,N\}$ for (D,S_4) .

4.3.D. All the following concepts are introduced **in view of the linear normal-form connection method** ; by convention, this extra specification will never be mentioned if it is clear by the context.

For any two structured matrices (F,S) and $(\tilde{F},\tilde{S})$, we say that $(\tilde{F},\tilde{S})$ **is obtained from** (F,S) **by extension** if $F = \tilde{F}$ and $S = (\alpha,\beta,\gamma)$ is related to $\tilde{S} = (\tilde{\alpha},\tilde{\beta},\tilde{\gamma})$ in the way described in (i), (ii), (iii), and (iv).

(i) There is a unique clause d such that $\alpha(d) \geq \alpha(e)$ for any $e \in F_1$ (the domain of α).

(ii) The domain $\tilde{F}_1'$ of $\tilde{\gamma}$ is $F_1' \cup \{d\}$ (F_1' is the domain of γ) and $\tilde{\gamma}(d) = L$ for some $L \in d$ with $\beta(L) = 1$.

(iii) $\tilde{F}_1 = F_1 \cup \{e\}$ for some clause $e \in F \smallsetminus F_1$ which is required to contain at least one literal L such that ^1L is in the active path $\tilde{p}_a$ of $(\tilde{F},\tilde{S})$.

(iv) For any $L \in e$, $\tilde{\beta}(L) = 0$ iff $^1L \in \tilde{p}_a$; for d from (i) , $\tilde{\beta}(\tilde{\gamma}(d)) = 0$; for any $L \in d$ with $L \neq \tilde{\gamma}(d)$ and for any $L \in c$ with $c \in F_1 \smallsetminus \{d\}$, $\tilde{\beta}(L) = \beta(L)$.

If $\tilde{\beta}(L) = 0$ for all $L \in e$, the clause from (iii) , then we say $(\tilde{\tilde{F}},\tilde{\tilde{S}})$ **is obtained from** (F,S) **by extension followed by truncation** if in addition $\tilde{\tilde{F}} = \tilde{F}$ and $\tilde{S}$ is related to $\tilde{\tilde{S}} = (\tilde{\tilde{\alpha}},\tilde{\tilde{\beta}},\tilde{\tilde{\gamma}})$ the way described in (v), (vi), and (vii).

(v) The domain $\tilde{\tilde{F}}_1$ of $\tilde{\tilde{\alpha}}$ is empty if $c_0 = c$ (recall 4.2.ii for c_0) for any $c \in \tilde{F}_1$; otherwise, $\tilde{\tilde{F}}_1 = \{c \in \tilde{F}_1 \mid \tilde{\alpha}(c) < \tilde{\alpha}(e')\}$ where e' is determined by $e' \neq e'_0$ and $c = c_0$ for any c with $\tilde{\alpha}(c) > \tilde{\alpha}(e')$; $\tilde{\tilde{\alpha}}(c) = \tilde{\alpha}(c)$ for any $c \in \tilde{\tilde{F}}_1$.

(vi) $\tilde{\tilde{\beta}}(L) = \tilde{\beta}(L)$ for any $L \in c$ with $c \in \tilde{\tilde{F}}_1$.

(vii) The domain $\tilde{\tilde{F}}_1'$ of $\tilde{\tilde{\gamma}}$ is $\tilde{F}_1' \smallsetminus ((\tilde{F}_1 \smallsetminus \tilde{\tilde{F}}_1) \cup \{e'\})$, where e' is as in (v) ; $\tilde{\tilde{\gamma}}(c) = \tilde{\gamma}(c)$ for any $c \in \tilde{\tilde{F}}_1'$.

We say that $(\tilde{F},\tilde{S})$ **is obtained from** (F,S) **by separation** if $F = \tilde{F}$ and S is related to $\tilde{S}$ in the way described in (i) above, and in (viii), (ix), and (x) below.

(viii) For no literal L in $F \setminus F_1$ is ^1L contained in $p_a \cup \{K\}$ where p_a is the active path in (F,S) and $K \in d$.

(ix) $\tilde{F}_1 = F_1 \cup \{e\}$ for an arbitrary clause $e \in F \setminus F_1$; $\tilde{\alpha}(e) = \alpha(d) + 1$ and $\tilde{\alpha}(c) = \alpha(c)$ for any $c \in F_1$.

(x) For any $L \in e$, $\tilde{\beta}(L) = 1$; for any $L \in c$ with $c \in F_1$, $\tilde{\beta}(L) = 0$. The domain $\tilde{F}_1'$ of $\tilde{\gamma}$ is empty.

The unique structure S_0 with $F_1 = \emptyset$ is called **terminal** , for any matrix F . Likewise, a structure S_1 is called **initial** if F_1 contains a single clause c with $\alpha(c) = 1$ and with $\beta(L) = 1$ for all its literals L . For these two special kinds of structures we say that (F,S_1) is **obtained from** (F,S_0) **by an initial step** .

The transition from (F,S) to $(F,\tilde{S})$ by an initial step, by extension, by extension followed by truncation, or by separation is called a **connection inference** , in symbols $(F,S) \vdash_c (F,\tilde{S})$. If no confusion may arise we simply write $\vdash$ instead of $\vdash_c$. A sequence of connection inferences $(F,S_1) \vdash (F,S_2) \vdash \ldots \vdash (F,S_n)$, $n \geqslant 1$, is called a **connection deduction of** (F,S_n) **from** (F,S_1) , and also written $(F,S_1) \vdash^+ (F,S_n)$. A connection deduction of the form $(F,S_0) \vdash (F,S_1) \vdash^+ (F,S_0)$ or of the form $(\{\{\}\},S_0)$ is called a **connection proof of** F , if S_0 is the terminal and S_1 any initial structure. F is called **deducible** or **derivable** , in symbols $\vdash F$, if there is a connection proof of F. $\qquad\Box$

The figures 1 and 2 show connection proofs of E and D, respectively, and the reader is encouraged to match the precise definition (4.3) with these instances. There, all transitions represented by the symbol $\vdash$ are in fact extensions. The unique clause d referred to in (i) is the clause pointed to by the vertical arrow on the left side of any step. As a clause on the right side of the previous step, at the same time it plays the role of e referred to in (iii). Separation was illustrated in the third step applied to D' , the variant of D above, resulting in the structured matrix (4.1). Truncation is represented in these figures by the symbol $\sim$. Note that extension followed by truncation actually is a single step according to definition (4.3), as in the last step in figure 2 ; but often we will take the liberty of explicitly illustrating the two parts of such a step the way which has been used in these two figures. Note that the trivial initial step which simply sets the vertical arrow in the first matrix has not been shown explicitly.

Incidentally, the names "extension" and "truncation" have been borrowed from linear resolution, the justification for which will be given in section (IV.2). The discussion of the two deductions in figures 1 and 2 now supports the expectation that any matrix may be tested for complementarity by providing such a deduction. The next section will in fact establish this result. The section thereafter will provide details about the algorithmic realization of the connection method.

5.   CONSISTENCY, COMPLETENESS, AND CONFLUENCE

Definition (4.3) has introduced the notion of a deducible matrix, $\vdash F$, which in the present context spelled out in full length means deducible in view of the linear normal-form connection method. This indicates that there are other, in fact many, kinds of deducibilities, even for propositional logic. It is therefore helpful to introduce some general terminology which views these different kinds under common aspects.

5.1.D. For any set $\mathcal{E}$ and any binary relation $\vdash \subseteq \mathcal{E} \times \mathcal{E}$ on $\mathcal{E}$ the following notations are used.

$\iota = \{(X,X) \mid X \in \mathcal{E}\}$ is the **identity relation** on $\mathcal{E}$.

For any binary relation $\Rightarrow$ on $\mathcal{E}$,

$\vdash \Rightarrow = \{(X,Y) \mid X \vdash Z$ and $Z \Rightarrow Y$ for some $Z\}$ denotes the **relation composition** of $\vdash$ and $\Rightarrow$.

$\vdash^0 = \iota$, and for any $i > 0$, $\vdash^i = \vdash \vdash^{i-1}$, which is called the **i - fold composition of** $\vdash$.

$\vdash^+ = \bigcup_{i=1}^{\infty} \vdash^i$ is called the **transitive closure** of $\vdash$.

$\vdash^* = \vdash^+ \cup \iota$ is called the **transitive-reflexive closure** of $\vdash$.

□

5.2.D. A **logic calculus** of the **recognition** or of the **generative** type consists of

a set $\mathcal{F}$, the elements of which are called **formulas** , or **matrices** ,

a set $\Sigma(F)$ associated to $F \in \mathcal{F}$ via function Σ, the elements of which are called **structures** ,

a binary **inference relation** $\vdash$ on $\mathcal{E}$, the set of sets of pairs $(F, \Sigma(F))$ with $F \in \mathcal{F}$, i.e. $\mathcal{E} = 2^{\mathcal{F} \times \Sigma(\mathcal{F})}$,

a subset $\mathcal{E}_0 \subseteq \mathcal{E}$, the elements of which are called **axioms** , and an element $S_0 \in \Sigma(F)$ called the **terminal structure** .

　　　　If $(E_1, E_2) \in \vdash$ holds for any $E_1, E_2 \in \mathcal{E}$ then this usually is expressed in infix notation by $E_1 \vdash E_2$, and called an **inference** or a **deduction** or **derivation step** .

　　　　A sequence $(E_1, \ldots, E_n)$, $n \geqslant 1$, such that $E_i \in \mathcal{E}$, $i=1, \ldots, n$, and $E_i \vdash E_{i+1}$, $i=1, \ldots, n-1$, is called a **deduction** or **derivation of** E_n **from** E_1 , and is written $E_1 \vdash \ldots \vdash E_n$ or simply $E_1 \vdash^n E_n$. n is called the **length** of the deduction.

　　　　If all elements in E are axioms, i.e. $E \in \mathcal{E}_0$, then
(i)   in the case of a recognition type calculus any deduction of the form $\{(F, S_0)\} \vdash^* E$ and
(ii)   in the case of a generative type calculus any deduction of the form $E \vdash^* \{(F, S_0)\}$, is called a **proof** of F ,
where $F \in \mathcal{F}$.

　　　　If there exists a proof of F , for $F \in \mathcal{F}$ then F is called **deducible** or **derivable** , in symbols $\vdash F$.   ☐

This is a generalization of the usual concept of a logic calculus generalized by associating structures with formulas. Any traditional calculus is a special case hereof, in which $\Sigma(F)$ consists of the single element S_0 ; then the associated structure becomes redundant and thus is deleted. For instance, the resolution calculus to be discussed in section (IV.1), is of that sort.

　　　　The **connection calculus** introduced in (4.3) crucially depends on structures, however, which have been specified in (4.2). Its set $\mathcal{E}$ consists of singleton sets each containing a structured matrix, hence it may in fact be identified with the set of structured matrices by deleting the set braces for these singletons. This justifies why we have simply written

$(F,S) \vdash (F,S')$ in the previous section. According to (4.3) its axioms are the pairs (F,S_0) with the terminal structure S_0 .

5.3.D. A logic calculus as defined in (5.2) is called **consistent** (or **sound** or **correct**) (**w.r.t. a unary relation** $\models$ on the set F of formulas) if $\vdash F$ implies $\models F$ for any $F \in \mathcal{F}$. It is called **complete** (**w.r.t.** $\models$) if $\models F$ implies $\vdash F$ for any $F \in \mathcal{F}$.

Its inference relation $\vdash$ is called **confluent** if for any $E, F \in \mathcal{F}$, $D_0 \vdash^* E$ and $D_0 \vdash^* F$ for some $D_0 \in \mathcal{F}$ implies $E \vdash^* D_1$ and $F \vdash^* D_1$ for some $D_1 \in \mathcal{E}$. Further it is called **bounded** if for any $E \in \mathcal{E}$, $\max\{n|\ E \vdash^n F$ for some $F \in \mathcal{E}\} < \infty$. $\square$

Since $\models$ will be always clear from the context we will simply speak of a consistent and complete calculus. The third property of confluency is illustrated with the diagram

$$D_0 \subset {\vdash^* \atop \vdash^*} {- E - \atop - F -} {\vdash^* \atop \vdash^*} \supset D_1$$

These four are properties of fundamental interest for any logic calculus. As a first application we are now going to show that they are satisfied for the connection calculus which has been introduced in the previous section. Therefore, after this excursion to some general notions we now resume the discussion of this particular calculus which means that all notions have the special meaning introduced in the previous sections, in particular in (4.2) and (4.3).

5.4.T. For any matrix F in normal form, $\vdash F$ iff F is complementary.

Proof. Let D denote the set of all paths through F. For any structure S associated with F, D is partitioned into two disjoint subsets D_0^S and D_1^S . If S is terminal then $D_0^S = D$; otherwise, for any path $q \in D_0^S$ and any clause $c \in F_1$, we have $\beta(L) = 0$ for the single literal in $q \cap c$; $D_1^S = D \setminus D_0^S$. In the illustration of the figures 1 and 2 , D_1^S consists of those paths through F which contain subgoals, i.e. literals with no dots and no crossing dashed line, from clauses in F_1 .

If $F = \emptyset$ then F is not complementary and there is no proof for F, since according to the definition (4.3) the required initial step may not be applied. If $F = \{\emptyset\}$ then F is complementary and by (4.3) $(\{\emptyset\}, S_0)$ is a proof for F . Thus the theorem holds in these two special cases. Therefore we may now assume that F contains literals.

Only-if-case. Consider the following statement.

(S)   If $(F, S_n) \;\vdash^n\; (F, S_0)$ with no initial step and if each path in $D_0^{S_n}$ is complementary then F is complementary, $n > 0$.

The only-if-case is an immediate consequence of (S) since $\vdash F$ means that there is a deduction of the form $(F, S_0) \vdash (F, S_n) \;\vdash^n\; (F, S_0)$, for which $D_0^{S_n} = \emptyset$. Thus we are left to prove (S) which will be done by induction on n.

The case $n=0$ is trivial since $D_0^S = D$. Hence, assume $n > 0$ in which case we have $(F, S_n) \vdash (F, S_{n-1}) \vdash^* (F, S_0)$. Let $S_i = (\alpha_i, \beta_i, \gamma_i)$, $i = 0, \ldots, n$.

If $(F, S_n) \vdash (F, S_{n-1})$ is an extension then by (4.3) $D_0^{S_n} \subset D_0^{S_{n-1}}$ and for any path $q \in D_0^{S_{n-1}} \setminus D_0^{S_n}$, we have $p_a^{S_{n-1}} \subset q$, and $L \in q$ for some literal $L \in e$ with $\beta_{n-1}(L) = 0$ where e is the clause described in (iii) of (4.3). The complementarity of such a path q is ensured by (iv) in (4.3); together with the assumption on $D_0^{S_n}$ in (S) this means all paths in $D_0^{S_{n-1}}$ are complementary. Hence, the induction hypothesis may be applied to $(F, S_{n-1}) \vdash^* (F, S_0)$ which establishes the complementarity of F .

If $(F, S_n) \vdash (F, S_{n-1})$ is an extension followed by a truncation then we may write $(F, S_n) \vdash (F, S'_{n-1}) \sim (F, S_{n-1})$ for it. Obviously, we have $D_0^{S'_{n-1}} \subseteq D_0^{S_{n-1}}$ by (v) and (vi) in (4.3). But the converse $D_0^{S_{n-1}} \subseteq D_0^{S'_{n-1}}$ holds as well. Namely consider any path $q \in D_0^{S_{n-1}}$. By (v) in (4.3), $\beta'_{n-1}(L) = 0$ for any literal L from a clause $c \in F_1^{S'_{n-1}} \setminus F_1^{S_{n-1}}$; in particular, this holds for the literal in $c \cap q$ which implies $q \in D_0^{S'_{n-1}}$. Thus we have $D_0^{S'_{n-1}} = D_0^{S_{n-1}}$ for which we have seen before that it only contains complementary paths. Therefore the induction hypothesis may be applied as before.

If $(F, S_n) \vdash (F, S_{n-1})$ is a separation then let $\tilde{F} = F \setminus F_1^{S_n}$ and let $\tilde{S}_i$ be the structure obtained from S_i by restricting its functions to $\tilde{F}$, $i = 0, \ldots, n-1$.   Since $F_1^{S_n} \subseteq F_1^{S_i} \setminus \tilde{F}_1^{S_i}$ for all $i = 1, \ldots, n-1$,   no step in $(F, S_{n-1}) \vdash^{n-2} (F, S_1)$ causes any change in any clause of $F_1^{S_n}$.

Only in the last step $(F,S_1) \vdash (F,S_0)$ these clauses from F_1^{Sn} become involved by truncation. Therefore $(\tilde{F},\tilde{S}_{n-1}) \vdash^{n-1} (\tilde{F},S_0)$ is a connection deduction. Formally, this argument is again an induction (on n-1) which is left to the reader as an easy exercise. For this deduction the induction hypothesis (of the main induction) may be applied since n-1<n and $D_0^{\tilde{S}n} = \emptyset$. Thus we know that $\tilde{F}$ is complementary which in turn implies that $F = F_1^{Sn} \cup \tilde{F}$ is complementary by definition of this notion.

If-case. We now assume that F is complementary. For any structure S such that $S = S_0$, or (i) from (4.3) holds for S, and for k^S such that $k^S = |F| \cdot |D_1^S| + |F \setminus F_1^S|$ if $S \neq S_0$ and $k^S = 0$ if $S = S_0$, we prove by induction on k^S that there is a deduction of (F,S_0) from (F,S) . By applying this to any selected initial structure S_1 for F, we obtain $(F,S_0) \vdash (F,S_1) \vdash^+ (F,S_0)$, i.e. $\vdash F$, as an immediate consequence.

If $k^S = 0$ then $S = S_0$ and (F,S) is the desired deduction. Hence assume $k^S > 0$ which, by the assumption (4.3.i) for S, implies $|D_1^S| > 0$. Now, either we have the case, say (s), where (viii) from (4.3) holds, or the one, say (e), where this does not hold.

In the case (s), the properties (ix) and (x) from (4.3) required for separation may be satisfied by an appropriate selection for e and L as described there. This results in a separation step $(F,S) \vdash (F,\tilde{S})$. For this we have, $|D_1^{\tilde{S}}| < |D_1^S|$ and $|F \setminus F_1^{\tilde{S}}| = |F \setminus F_1^S| - 1$; thus $k^{\tilde{S}} < k^S$, and we are done by application of the induction hypothesis on $(F,\tilde{S})$.

In the case (e), the properties (ii),(iii), and (vi) from (4.3) required for extension may be satisfied by an appropriate selection for $\tilde{\gamma}(d)$ and e as described there . This results in an extension step $(F,S) \vdash (F,\tilde{\tilde{S}})$. Now, either $\tilde{\tilde{\beta}}(L)=1$ for some $L \in e$, in which case we let $\tilde{S}=\tilde{\tilde{S}}$, or otherwise $\tilde{S}$ is uniquely determined by application of truncation to $(F,\tilde{\tilde{S}})$. By definition of extension, we have $|D_1^{\tilde{\tilde{S}}}| < |D_1^S|$. As we have seen in the only-if-case, $|D_1^{\tilde{\tilde{S}}}| = |D_1^{\tilde{S}}|$ holds. Obviously, in both subcases $|F \setminus F_1^{\tilde{S}}| < |F \setminus F_1^S| + |F| - 1$. Thus altogether we obtain
$$k^{\tilde{S}} = |F| \cdot |D_1^{\tilde{S}}| + |F \setminus F_1^{\tilde{S}}| < |F| \cdot (|D_1^S| - 1) + |F \setminus F_1^S| + |F| - 1 < |F| \cdot |D_1^S| + |F| = k^S$$
which allows the application of the induction hypothesis on $(F,\tilde{S})$. $\square$

5.5.C. The connection calculus is consistent.

This is an immediate consequence of the only-if-case in (5.4) together with the only-if case in (3.4).   □

5.6.C. The connection calculus is complete.

This is an immediate consequence of the if-case in (5.4) together with the if-case in (3.4).   □

5.7.C. The inference relation $\vdash$ in the connection calculus restricted to complementary matrices is confluent.

The proof of the if-case of (5.4) showed that for a complementary matrix F a deduction of (F,S_0) may be obtained, no matter which selections are being made in any step. Thus, $(F,S) \vdash^* (F,\tilde{S})$ and $(F,S) \vdash^* (F,\overset{\approx}{S})$ implies $(F,\tilde{S}) \vdash^* (F,S_0)$ and $(F,\overset{\approx}{S}) \vdash^* (F,S_0)$.   □

The result in (5.7) is not true for non-complementary matrices as the example $F=\{L,K\}$ with $L\neq^1 K$ demonstrates. $\underset{L}{K}$ and $\underset{K}{L}$ represent two different initial structures S_1 and S_1' for F . $(F,S_0) \vdash (F,S_1)$ and $(F,S_0) \vdash (F,S_1')$ are the only deductions from (F,S_0) , and both may not be continued, i.e. S_1 and S_1' are **final** structures in that sense but not terminal.

5.8.C. The inference relation $\vdash$ in the connection calculus is bounded.

According to the proof of the if-case in (5.4) by induction on k^S it is clear that $|F|.(|D|+1)$ is an upper bound for k^S , and thus also for the number of possible deduction steps, even for a non-complementary matrix.   □

6.   ALGORITHMIC ASPECTS

With the results (5.5), (5.6), and (5.7) it is now easy to formulate the connection method, which already has been illustrated in section 4, in an algorithmic way, that is to spell out a precise procedure which for a given matrix (or formula) determines whether it is valid or not. Later on in this book (see section IV.3) we will discuss the fact that such a procedure requires an awful lot of steps for complicated matrices. Therefore every possible tool, which reduces the given matrix and with it the costs of the procedure, should be implemented into it. Such tools do exist and will now be introduced before we integrate them into the envisaged procedure later in this section. The reader is reminded of our current restriction to normal form matrices.

Specifically, we will now define a number of reduction operations on matrices and prove for each that their application does not affect the property of validity of the matrix. By the first such operation, multiple occurrences of a literal in a clause may be substituted by a single one, which in formal terms reads as follows.

6.1.D. For two matrices $F, \tilde{F}$ in normal form we say that $\tilde{F}$ **is obtained from** F **by MULT- reduction** , in symbols $F \vdash_{MULT} \tilde{F}$, if they are of the form $F = \{\{L^{r1},\ldots,L^{rn}\} \cup c\} \cup F'$ and $\tilde{F} = \{\{L^{r1}\} \cup c\} \cup F'$, for any L, c, F', ri, $i = 1,\ldots,n$, and $n \geqslant 2$.   □

6.2.L. For any two matrices $F, \tilde{F}$ in normal form, if $F \vdash_{MULT} \tilde{F}$ then $\models F$ iff $\models \tilde{F}$.

Proof. With the notation from (6.1), any path through F of the form $\{L^{ri}\} \cup p'$ is complementary, $1 \leqslant i \leqslant n$ iff $\{L^{r1}\} \cup p'$ is complementary. This implies that F is complementary iff $\tilde{F}$ is complementary, from which the lemma follows by (3.4).   □

This kind of proof will become a routine tool for all lemmata in this section and for several results later on. Therefore the reader should acquire a good acquaintance with it. The next reduction says, that clauses containing a literal L such that ^{1}L does not occur elsewhere in the matrix, may be deleted.

6.3.D. A literal L is called **pure in** a matrix F, if ^{1}L does not occur in F.

For two matrices $F, \tilde{F}$ in normal form we say that $\tilde{F}$ is **obtained from** F **by pure literal elimination** or PURE- **reduction,** in symbols $F \vdash_{PURE} \tilde{F}$, if F is of the form $\tilde{F} \cup \{c\}$ for some clause c which contains a pure literal L in F.

   □

6.4.L.   For any two matrices F, $\tilde{F}$ in normal form, if
$F \vdash_{PURE} \tilde{F}$ then $\models F$ iff $\models \tilde{F}$.

Proof. With the notation from (6.3), any path through
F of the form $\tilde{p} \cup \{L\}$ is complementary iff $\tilde{p}$ is complementary
since $^1L \notin \tilde{p}$. This implies that F is complementary iff $\tilde{F}$ is
complementary (since $\tilde{p}$ is a path through $\tilde{F}$) from which the lemma follows by (3.4).   □

The next reduction says, that any clause which, considered as
a matrix itself, is a tautology, may also be deleted.

6.5.D.   A clause c in any matrix in normal form is called **tautological** , if $\{L,^1L\} \subseteq c$ for some literal L .

For two matrices F, $\tilde{F}$ in normal form we say that $\tilde{F}$ **is
obtained from** F **by tautology elimination** or TAUT- **reduction** ,
in symbols $F \vdash_{TAUT} \tilde{F}$, if $F = \tilde{F} \cup \{c\}$ for a tautological
clause c.   □

6.6.L.   For any two matrices F , $\tilde{F}$ in normal form, if
$F \vdash_{TAUT} \tilde{F}$ then $\models F$ iff $\models \tilde{F}$.

Proof. With the notation from (6.5), let K^c denote
any literal K in clause c. Since any path p through F is of the
form $\tilde{p} \cup \{K^c\}$ for some K^c and some path $\tilde{p}$ through $\tilde{F}$, it is obvious that F is complementary if $\tilde{F}$ is complementary. In order to
show the converse, assume that F is complementary. In particu-
lar, this says that $\tilde{p} \cup \{L^c\}$ and $\tilde{p} \cup \{^1L^c\}$ is complementary each
containing a connection $\{M,^1M\}$ and $\{N,^1N\}$, respectively. We
want to show that $\tilde{p}$ is complementary, which is trivial if one
of these two connections is contained in $\tilde{p}$. However, if this
is not the case then $\{M,^1M\} = \{L^c,^1L^r\}$ and $\{N,^1N\} = \{L^r,^1L^c\}$,
thus $\{L^r,^1L^r\} \subseteq \tilde{p}$ and $\tilde{p}$ is complementary also in this case .
Since this argument applies for any path p through F , we
are now done by (3.4).   □

We will often use this convention of writing simply K_i^c rather than $K_i^{r_i}$, $1 \leq i \leq n$, for any literal from a clause
$c = \{K_1^{r_1},\ldots,K_n^{r_n}\}$, $n \geq 1$.

The next reduction is a generalization of the obvious
observation that a statement $L \wedge K \vee K$ is true iff K is true

(think of any statements in natural language for L and K).
In this case one says that K **subsumes** L∧K . Note that L∧K
implies K , i.e. L∧K→K is a valid formula.

6.7.D. For any two clauses c, d , we say c **subsumes** d if
c ⊆ d after dele tion of positions, i.e. $c = \{K_1^{r_i},\ldots,K_m^{r_m}\}$ and
$d = \{K_1^{q_i},\ldots,K_m^{q_m},K_{m+1}^{q_{m+1}},\ldots,K_n^{q_n}\}$, for some $K_i^{r_i},K_j^{q_j}$, $1 < i < m$,
$1 < j < n$, $1 < m < n$.

   For two matrices F , $\tilde{F}$ in normal form we say that $\tilde{F}$
is **obtained from** F by **subsumption** or SUBS- **reduction** , in
symbols $F \vdash_{SUBS} \tilde{F}$, if they are of the form $F=\tilde{F}'\cup\{c,d\}$ and
$\tilde{F}=\tilde{F}'\cup\{c\}$ for some $\tilde{F}'$, c, and d such that c subsumes d. □

6.8.L. For any two matrices F , $\tilde{F}$ in normal form, if
$F \vdash_{SUBS} \tilde{F}$ then $\models F$ iff $\models \tilde{F}$.

   Proof. With the notation from (6.7), any path p through
F is of the form $\tilde{p} \cup \{K^c\} \cup \{L^d\}$ where $\tilde{p} \cup \{K^c\}$ is a path
through $\tilde{F}$. Hence F is complementary if $\tilde{F}$ is complementary.
Conversely, if   F   is complementary then in particular
$\tilde{p} \cup \{K^c\} \cup \{K^d\}$, thus also $\tilde{p} \cup \{K^c\}$ is complementary which
implies that $\tilde{F}$ is complementary. The lemma, then, follows by
(3.4).   □

The final reduction will be **unit resolution** a special case of
resolution which is the most widely used deduction rule and
will be discussed in detail in section (IV.1). If there is a
unit clause containing a single literal L then all literals L
and ^1L may be canceled in the matrix in one or more steps.

6.9.D. For any two matrices F , $\tilde{F}$ in normal form, we say that
$\tilde{F}$ **is obtained from** F **by unit resolution** or UNIT- **reduction** ,
in symbols $F \vdash_{UNIT} \tilde{F}$, if F and $\tilde{F}$ are of the form
$F = \tilde{F}' \cup \{c \cup \{^1L\}\} \cup \{L\}$ and $\tilde{F} = \tilde{F}' \cup \{c\} \cup \{L\}$, for some $\tilde{F}'$,c,
and L , including the special case $c \cup \{^1L\} = {}^1L$, i.e. $c=\emptyset$. □

6.10.L. For any two matrices F , $\tilde{F}$ in normal form, if
$F \vdash_{UNIT} \tilde{F}$ then $\models F$ iff $\models \tilde{F}$.

   Proof. The set D of paths through $\tilde{F}$ obviously is a
subset of the set D of paths through F , and for any $p \in D \setminus \tilde{D}$

we have $\{L,{}^1L\} \subseteq p$ in the notation of (6.9). Hence F is complementary iff $\widetilde{F}$ is complementary, and the lemma follows by
(3.4).   □

6.11.D. For two matrices F , $\widetilde{F}$ in normal form we say $\widetilde{F}$ is
obtained from F **by reduction** , in symbols $F \vdash_{RED} \widetilde{F}$, if
$(F,\widetilde{F}) \in \ \vdash_{MULT} \cup \vdash_{PURE} \cup \vdash_{TAUT} \cup \vdash_{SUBS} \cup \vdash_{UNIT}$.   □

In other words, reduction means any of the previous five kinds
of reductions. Note that the number of occurring literals
strictly decreases in a reduction step. Therefore if a matrix F with m occurring literals may be reduced to **T** by
reduction only, i.e. $F \vdash_{RED}^{n} \textbf{T}$, then F turns out to be
valid with n≤m . This is a very small number of steps compared
to the general case (see section IV.3). For this reason
reduction obtains the highest priority in the algorithm below.

In particular, this algorithm first exhausts the application of reductions to a matrix F to be tested for validity.
Then the terminal structure S_0 is associated with the resulting matrix $\widetilde{F}$ and connection steps are applied with arbitrary
selections. Whenever this leads to $(\widetilde{F},S_0)$ the original matrix
F is valid otherwise it is not valid.

6.12.A. The first (hence lower index 1) **connection procedure**
CP_1^0 for propositional logic (hence upper index 0) applicable to
any formula or matrix F in normal form.
STEP1. If $F \vdash_{RED} \widetilde{F}$ holds for any $\widetilde{F}$ then $F \leftarrow \widetilde{F}$ and
goto STEP1;
STEP2. If $\emptyset \in F$ then return "valid"; if $F=\emptyset$ then return
"not valid";
$F \leftarrow (F,S)$ for any initial structure S ;
STEP3. If S is terminal then return "valid"; if $F \vdash \widetilde{F}$ for
some $\widetilde{F}$ then $F \leftarrow \widetilde{F}$ and goto STEP3; return "not valid".   □

6.13.C. For any matrix F in normal form the connection procedure CP_1^0 terminates, and it returns "valid" iff $\models F$.
Proof. Any application of STEP1 preserves validity according to (6.2), (6.4), (6.6), (6.8), and (6.10) . After

entrance into STEP3 the result is covered by (5.5), (5.6), and
(5.7). The guarantee for termination (after a finite number of
steps) is provided by (5.8).   □

The reader who has followed the exposition from the very beginning might now be interested how well this procedure CP_1^0 from
(6.12) does for the formula (I.2.1) from chapter I which has
been presented as a matrix in (1.9). This can be seen from figure 3 which shows a deduction for this formula simulating the
steps of CP_1^0 . In this case the deduction consists of 9 reduction steps, as many steps as there are literals; STEP3 in
CP_1^0 has not even been entered. Hence for this trivial example
we obtain a fast proof as it should be which favorably compares
with the truth table method of section 2 requiring 16 times the
evaluation of the truth value for the whole formula.

        For any appropriate appreciation of this performance
of CP_1^0 it should be noted that in an actual implementation
a run of CP_1^0 would operate on a single copy of the matrix
only. In that sense the representation of such a deduction as
in figure 3 is misleading unless we are aware that after each
step the same physical object is displayed as before this step
except for canceling one of its literals (to be realized in
practice e.g. by changing the value of an associated boolean
function). This is true not only for the **reduction phase** of
STEP1 but also for the **connection phase** of STEP3 which already
has been illustrated in figures 1 and 2 (see section 4). The
matrix remains always the same except for changes in the values
of the functions of its structure.

        The algorithmic language used in (6.12) certainly is
of a very high-level nature ; in particular, the test $F \vdash \tilde{F}$
cannot be realized but by a number of actions in a more conventional language. Therefore we are now going to present a dif
ferent version of the main part of CP_1^0 in such a more conventional form which might be easily translated into a programming
language in actual use.

        As in (6.12), by $X \leftarrow Y$ it is meant that the value of
Y is assigned to X . If the value of Y is a list of n items
$Y_1,\ldots,Y_n$ then $(X_1,\ldots,X_n) \leftarrow Y$ is an abbreviation for
$X_1 \leftarrow Y_1,\ldots,X_n \leftarrow Y_n$. Further our language uses the well-known

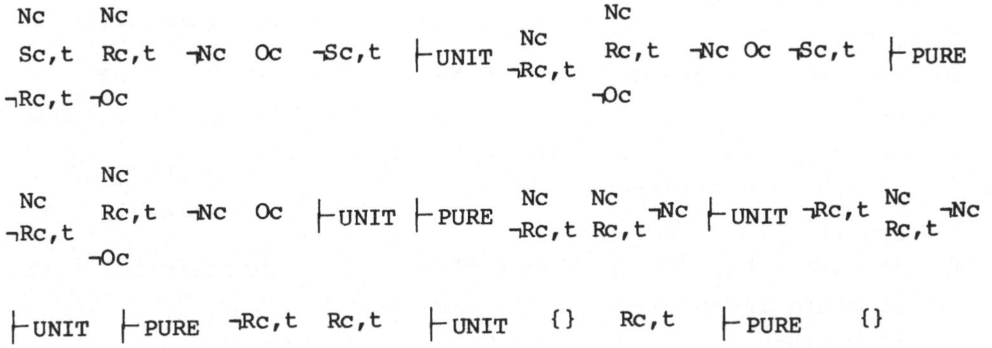

$$Sc,t^{Nc}\ Rc,t^{Nc}\ \neg Nc\ Oc\ \neg Sc,t\ \vdash\text{UNIT}\ {}^{Nc}_{\neg Rc,t}\ Rc,t^{Nc}\ \neg Nc\ Oc\ \neg Sc,t\ \vdash\text{PURE}$$
$$\neg Rc,t\ \neg Oc \qquad\qquad\qquad\qquad\qquad \neg Oc$$

$$\neg Rc,t^{Nc}\ {}^{Nc}Rc,t\ \neg Nc\ Oc\ \vdash\text{UNIT}\ \vdash\text{PURE}\ {}_{\neg Rc,t}^{Nc}\ {}_{Rc,t}^{Nc}\ \neg Nc\ \vdash\text{UNIT}\ \neg Rc,t\ {}_{Rc,t}^{Nc}\ \neg Nc$$
$$\neg Oc$$

$$\vdash\text{UNIT}\ \vdash\text{PURE}\ \neg Rc,t\ Rc,t\ \vdash\text{UNIT}\ \{\}\ Rc,t\ \vdash\text{PURE}\ \{\}$$

Figure 3. Reduction of (1.9) to T

notion of a **stack** , i.e. a list of items which may be accessed
at a distinguished end only for addition or deletion of items.
We will denote these two basic operations by the function
push(STACK,item), the value of which is STACK extended by item
at the distinguished end, and by the function pop(STACK), the
value of which is (STACK,item) where item denotes the entry a
the distinguished end, and STACK denotes the previous value of
STACK but with this item having been deleted. The empty list
will always be denoted by NIL. All other notions have their
natural meaning.

6.14.A. The connection procedure CP_1^o from (6.12), but without
reductions, in a more conventional algorithmic form, applicable
to any matrix $F \neq \emptyset$ in normal form. Using the terminology from
(4.2), the occurring variables are of the following type.

D   at any state denotes $F \setminus F_1$.

c   at any state denotes that part of the (currently consid-
          ered) clause with maximal α-value , such that $\beta(L) = 1$
          for any of its literals.

p   at any state denotes the set of literals from the active
          path.

WAIT   at any state denotes a stack of entries, storing the in-
          formation for processing the subgoal literals L^c from
          $F_1 \setminus \{c\}$ with $\beta(L^c) = 1$; the format for these entries
          is (c,p,D) .

```
 0:  D←F; WAIT←NIL;                              ⎫ initialization
 1:  p←∅;                                        ⎭
 2:  select a clause  c  from the matrix D;      ⎫ selection of
     D←D\c;                                      ⎭ initial structure
 3:  select a literal  L  from  c ; c←c L;       ⎫
     if c≠∅ then WAIT←push(WAIT,(c,p,D));        ⎬ preparation of
     p←p∪{L} ;                                   ⎭ inference
 4:  if  D=∅  then return 'invalid' ;            } unsuccessful exit
 5:  if there is no clause d ∈D  such that
      ¹L ∈ D then                                ⎫
 6:  ⌈if there is no clause d ∈ D such that      ⎬ separation
       ¹K ∈ d  for some  K ∈ p  then
     ⌈WAIT←NIL ; goto 1;⌉                        ⎭
 7:  else select  c  from  D  such that
      ¹K ∈ c for some  K ∈ p ;⌉
 8:  else select  c  from  D  such that
      ¹L ∈ c ;                                   ⎫
 9:  D←D\c ;                                      ⎬ execution of
10:  c←c\¹L ;                                        extension
     for all literals K such that
      ¹K ∈ c  and  K ∈ p  do  c←c\¹K ;
11:  if  c≠∅  then goto 3 ;                       ⎭
12:  if WAIT = NIL then return 'valid';          } successful exit
13:  (WAIT,(c,p,D))← pop(WAIT); goto 3;          } truncation   □
```

It is obvious that this algorithm is but a more detailed version of (6.12). Its structure already takes into account that later in this book this algorithm will be extended in various ways. A good familiarity with it will therefore be quite helpful later on. Hence the reader is strongly encouraged to hand-simulate a run with the examples of the figures 1 and 2 in section 4 (exercise E10 in section 7).

It should be noted that the presentation of (6.14) stresses structural clearness rather than optimal code. Hence, for an efficient implementation one has to note that for instance the entries in WAIT may share a lot of information. Also, an appropriate data structure has to be chosen for storing the matrices such that locating connections may be perform-med in a fast way. One possibility for this is to order the literals in the clauses, so that they can be accessed in a more directed way. Another one would be to store for each literal L the list of references to the positions where it occurs. Thus for any such L a connection may be determined simply by selecting any reference in this list for ^1L . This possibility justifies that we always regard the selection of a connection as a single step in performance considerations.

The memory space for this extra feature equals the space for storing one further copy of the matrix. The remaining storage requirements can be easily seen to be less than that for storing the matrix. Thus altogether the required space amounts to less than three times the size of the matrix.

The number of steps required for a given matrix is not as easy to predict. Therefore the discussion of this point will be approached in a more general context (see section IV.3). It should only be mentioned here that different selections of literals in each step may drastically change this number. Therefore these selections will have to be subject to strategical consideration (see section IV.11).

With these few remarks concerning implementation and analysis we have reached the end of this chapter which has provided the theoretical material for ATP on the ground level, i.e. in propositional logic, and has introduced a first basic proof procedure CP_1^o . This will be **lifted** to the first-order level in the following chapter and improved to more sophisticated versions in the chapter thereafter, in particular to ones which are not restricted to normal forms.

7.   EXERCISES

(E1)   Write down a number of propositional formulas and determine their representing matrices. Conversely, for such matrices F determine the set of all formulas $\tilde{F}$ represented by F and built with the connectives $\neg, \wedge, \vee, \rightarrow, \leftrightarrow$.

(E2)   Same as (E1) but with the negative representation.

(E3)   Calculate the truth-table for the formula (I.2.1).

(E4)   Carry out the details of the induction proof for (3.2).

(E5)   Spezify a binary relation $\vdash_{DSTR}$ on matrices such that the following two properties hold.

(i)   For any matrix F, $F \vdash^n_{DSTR} \tilde{F}$ for some matrix $\tilde{F}$ in normal form and some $n > 0$.

(ii)   For any matrices $F, \tilde{F}$, if $F \vdash^*_{DSTR} \tilde{F}$ then $\vDash F$ iff $\vDash \tilde{F}$.

Prove these two properties for $\vdash_{DSTR}$.

(Hints: Recall the distributivity law $F_1 \wedge (F_2 \vee F_3) \rightarrow (F_1 \wedge F_2) \vee (F_1 \wedge F_3)$ and use 3.4 in the proof)

(E6)   Carry out the details of the induction proof in the only-if-case of (5.4) establishing that $(F', S'_{n-1}) \vdash^{n-1} (F', S_0)$ is a connection deduction.

(E7)   The **full** matrix F^n in normal form in n variables $P_1, \ldots, P_n$ for $n > 0$ is the matrix consisting of the 2^n clauses $\{(i_1, P_1), \ldots, (i_n, P_n)\}$, where $i_j \in \{0, 1\}$ for $j = 1, \ldots, n$.
Define the binary relation $\vdash_{CNCL}$ such that $F^n \vdash_{CNCL} F$ holds if F is obtained from F^n by canceling in each clause c in F i_c literals with $0 \leq i_c \leq n-1$.

Prove that the set of matrices F in n variables such that $F^n \vdash_{CNCL} F$ essentially is the same as the set of valid matrices in normal form. More precisely, define an equivalence relation $\sim$ on matrices such that for any matrix F in normal form we have $\vDash F$ iff $F^n \vdash_{CNCL} \tilde{F}$ and $\tilde{F} \sim F$.

(Hint: $\sim$ takes care of multiple occurrences of literals or clauses. Cf. theorem 2.5 in [Bi7])

(E8)   Use $\vdash_{CNCL}$ from (E7) to generate valid matrices and apply CP^o_1 to them . Further use $\vdash'_{CNCL}$, which is defined as $\vdash_{CNCL}$ but allows $i_c = n$, to generate valid and invalid matrices and apply CP^o_1 to them.

(E9)   Write a program which automatically transforms any propositional formula into a matrix.

(E10)   Simulate by hand a run of (6.14) with the matrices
from figure 1 and 2 in section 4 and other matrices as input,
and note the values of all occurring variables at each entry
of line 3. Generally verify that (6.14) simulates correct connection deductions.

(E11)   Write a program that realizes CP_1^o .

8.   BIBLIOGRAPHICAL AND HISTORICAL REMARKS

This is certainly not the place to give any bibliographical or
historical details on propositional logic itself. In that
respect the reader is referred to standard textbooks of mathematical logic (such as [He1]). We only note that our approach
seems to be the first one which is of a purely set-theoretic
nature w.r.t. both, syntax and semantics. It has been used
first in [Bi7], and seems to provide more technical comfort in
view of ATP than the standard approach although it is less
natural of course. There was always a tendency towards set
theory within ATP where everyone talks of a **set** of clauses;
yet, a clause itself mostly is defined as a **disjunction** not a
set of literals (see [ChL], [Lo4], etc.).
    The notion of a **path** first appears in [Pr2]. That of a
connection has emerged in the early seventies in [YHR] and
[Ko3]. **Spanning** sets of connections have been introduced in
[B10]. Theorem (3.4) first has been stated in this form in
[Bi7]. All these references in a sense are not original, however, since these notions and insights implicitly are contained
in earlier work on ATP and logic. For instance, the earlier
researchers would consider (3.4) as a simple variant of the
analogue statement on the **conjunctive normal form** of the formula which may be defined as the conjunction of all paths each
regarded as a disjunction of its literals. The notion of a
connection has been anticipated by that of **mate** in [Da2].
    Similarly, with the procedure CP_1^o , which has been in-
troduced in [B11] in the form of (6.14), but may actually be
regarded as a variant of linear resolution (see [Lo4] for references and section (IV.2) for further details). Its reduction
steps even are well-known for decades (e.g. see [Da2] and

[DuN]). Nevertheless, the point of view that these notions and the procedure are defined in terms of (a single copy of) the very given formula, in a direct way and without technical tricks such as structure sharing, this view in fact was not taken before [B11] which derives from [BiS]. It has changed the perspective and with it the notions even that of a logical calculus, which thus has been introduced here in a more general form then usual. For the notions of **confluency** and **boundedness** in such a calculus the reader is refered to [Hu2]. Of course, this kind of a calculus immediately reminds of the concept of an automaton (e.g. see [Sal]) with our structures as its states. The set of states of an automaton usually is not input dependent as are our structures; therefore our notion is more general also under this point of view.

Chapter III

The connection method in first-order logic

The expressive power of propositional logic is too restricted for practical use. Therefore we have to encounter the considerably richer language of first-order logic which will be introduced in the first section of the present chapter. We did not waste our time, however, by the previous development of the connection method for sentential logic. Rather we shall see that the method may be **lifted** from the **ground** level to the level of first-order logic by **adding** some features **without** any change of the features developed thus far.

In order to clearly work out this very important **lifting** technique, the material in the present chapter is developed in exact parallelity with the previous one. Again we point out the set-theoretical aspects of formulas, captured in the notions of **matrices, paths, connections** , etc. The fundamental characterization of the **valid** formulas introduced in section 2 is then provided by the completeness and consistency of the so-called **standard procedure** in section 3 which applies to **any** formula. This characterization is more general than the usual ones in ATP or in logic, since the formulas are not restricted in any way and their sentential structure is not changed at all. Furthermore, given the corresponding characterization (II.3.4) from the ground level, this extra-generality is obtained without any additional efforts. Herbrand's theorem for formulas in **Skolem normal form** is just a special case of this characterization, which in turn comprises Herbrand's theorem for **normal form formulas** usually considered in resolution theory.

In order not to confuse the reader with too many technical details the development of the connection method in the rest of the chapter is restricted to normal form formulas (as usual in resolution theory), deferring the generalization to the next chapter. In detail, the transformation to this normal

form is developed in   section 4, then unification is first
encountered in section 5, and finally the connection calculus
is presented in section 6 with several algorithmic aspects in
section 7.

The casual reader might be served well by the discussion related to the figures 1 and 2 in the first part of section 6 only. For all those, however, who have in mind to contribute to the field of ATP in any substantial way, all the
material in this chapter is considered mandatory **including**
the proofs.

1.   THE LANGUAGE OF FIRST-ORDER LOGIC

In the first chapter we have discussed sentences like "any
noise that reaches the telephone", abbreviated by $\forall n\ Rn,t$. Propositional logic, which has been explored in the previous chapter, is not expressive enough to model the internal structure
of such a sentence, rather it has to regard it as an atomic
unit, viz. a literal, without any (relevant) internal structure.

In any non-trivial application, however, the need for
modelling such an internal structure will certainly arise and
may be satisfied by the language of **first-order logic** . In
this language, a literal is no more regarded as an atomic unit,
rather it offers a rich internal structure of considerable
expressive power.

In detail, there is always a predicate talking about a
number of objects like the predicate R (for REACHES) above
which talks about the objects n (for noise) and t (for
telephone). But this is the simplest way of specifying objects
only since, rather than naming them directly, they may be determined in terms of other objects as well. For instance, any
clock, say cl , causes individual noises, say its tic-tac, say
tic(cl), or its chime, say ch(cl), accordingly, Rtic(cl),t
would express the sentence saying that the tic-tac noise
caused by the clock, denoted by cl , reaches the telephone,
denoted by t , and similarly for Rch(cl),t . Obviously, tic
plays the role of a function defined on clocks with the respec-

tive noise as its value.

This kind of functional denotation of objects may be applied in a nested way. Think of the tic-tac noise of the clock owned by a person with name John and of the telephone also owned by John which may be expressed in the previous context as Rtic(clock-owned-by(john)),tel-owned-by(john). This is still a literal relating two objects, viz. a noise and a telephone; but these objects are determined by more complicated **terms** than simple names. By allowing an arbitrary number of terms related by the predicate, an arbitrary number of arguments for the functions in these terms, and an arbitrary nesting-depth of these functions, we arrive at the general notion of a literal as defined in (1.1) below.

The generalization of the concept of a literal is only the one aspect of first-order logic as an extension of propositional logic. The other aspect is the introduction of further logical connectives, viz. **quantification** , specifically **universal** quantification and **existential** quantification. These two distinguish whether we talk about all elements in some **universe** of objects like in ∀n Rn,t above, or only about some of them expressed by ∃n Rn,t . Here "some" is meant in the sense of "at least one", therefore the latter formula should be regarded as an abbreviation of the natural statement "there is an – at least one – object n such that n (the noise) reaches t (the telephone)". In general, these two unary connectives apply not only to literals such as Rn,t but to arbitrary **first-order formulas** which are now going to be defined in precise terms.

As in chapter II, we will actually be interested in **first-order matrices** which represent first-order formulas in a technically more comfortable way. Thus we proceed as in section (II.1), first introducing the matrices and only then the formulas, both in normal form to begin with.

1.1.D.   The language of **first-order logic** is built upon the following alphabets.

V – the set of **object variables** or simply **variables** , denoted by x,y,z.

F – the set of **function symbols** , denoted by f,g,h.

P - the set of **predicate symbols** , denoted by P,Q,R.

R - the set of **occurrences** or **positions** , denoted by r.

F and **P** are graded by an **arity** function $\alpha: \mathbf{F} \cup \mathbf{P} \rightarrow \mathbf{N}$.

$\mathbf{F}^n = \{f \in \mathbf{F} \mid \alpha(f) = n\}$ and $\mathbf{P}^n = \{P \in \mathbf{P} \mid \alpha(P) = n\}$, $n \geqslant 0$. The elements of $\mathbf{P}^0$ are also called constants and are denoted by $a,b,$ c. The set **T** of **terms** (over $V \cup F$), denoted by s,t, is a set of labeled trees defined inductively by (t1) and (t2), together with the set $\Omega(t)$ of positions in any term $t \in T$.

(t1)   For any variable $x \in V$ and any position $r \in R$, the pair (x,r) , or shortly x^r , is a term with $\Omega(x^r)=\{r\}$.

(t2)   For any function symbol $f \in F^n$, $n \geqslant 0$, for any n terms $t_1,\ldots,t_n$, such that $\Omega(t_i) \cap \Omega(t_j) = \emptyset$ for $i \neq j$ and $1 \leqslant i,j \leqslant n$, and for any $r \in R \smallsetminus \bigcup_{i=1}^{n} \Omega(t_i)$ the pair $(ft_1 \ldots t_n, r)$, or shortly $f^r t_1 \ldots t_n$, is a term with $\Omega(f^r t_1 \ldots t_n)=\{r\} \cup \bigcup_{i=1}^{n} \Omega(t_i)$.

A (**first-order**) **literal** is of the form $^m P t_1 \ldots t_n$ where $m \in \{0,1\}$, $P \in P^n$, $n \geqslant 0$, $t_i \in \mathbf{T}$, and $i=1,\ldots,n$. Literals are denoted by $K,L,$ or M.

For any literal $L = {}^m P t_1 \ldots t_n$, $\Omega(L) = \bigcup_{i=1}^{n} \Omega(t_i)$, and for $k \in \{0,1\}$, $^k L$ denotes the literal $^j P t_1 \ldots t_n$ where $j=m+k \bmod 2$. By convention, $^m P t_1 \ldots t_n$ may be abbreviated by $P t_1 \ldots t_n$ in the case $m=0$ and by $\neg\, P t_1 \ldots t_n$ in the case $m=1$. Therefore $^0 P t_1 \ldots t_n$ is called **unnegated** and $^1 P t_1 \ldots t_n$ **negated** .

A (**first-order**) **quantified matrix in normal form** is (a triple) of the form $\{c_1,\ldots,c_m\}$ $\{x_1,\ldots,x_n\}$ F_0 , where F_0 is a propositional matrix in normal form but with first-order (rather than propositional) literals, $\{c_1,\ldots,c_m\}$ is the set of constants occurring in F_0 , and $\{x_1,\ldots,x_n\}$ is the set of variables occurring in F_0 . $\{c_1,\ldots,c_m\}$ $\{x_1,\ldots,x_n\}$ is called a **prefix** and F_0 a (**quantifier-free**) **matrix** whose elements are called **clauses** . $\square$

As in the case of propositional logic we ignore the positions wherever this does not cause any confusion. Also we use the names of clauses for the identificaton of the occurrences of their literals; thus L^d denotes the occurrence of literal L

in clause d . As another convention we use parentheses and commas whenever they are helpful for the eye to catch the structure of a term, as in the literal MARRIED(mother(john),father(john)) which in accordance with (1.1) actually would read MARRIEDmotherjohnfatherjohn. With respect to quantified matrices in normal form we often use the convention to delete the prefix since it is uniquely determined in this special case. Hence the literal just mentioned may in fact be regarded as an example of a quantified matrix in normal form with its prefix {john} {} deleted by this convention (or of a quantifier-free matrix). This example should remind the reader of the close connection with natural language (which was discussed in the first chapter) even when we prefer the more prosaic form Pfc,gc for such a literal.

As a second example consider the quantified matrix {c} {x,y} {{Pc,Pfx},^{1}Py} . As in propositional logic this syntactic structure may be regarded and actually has been defined as a labeled tree as shown in figure 1. Sometimes we are only interested in that part of the tree in which the subtrees representing the literals are regarded as single nodes, viz. leaves (the boxes in figure 1). In that case we will speak of the **logical part** of the tree of the quantified matrix. Note that this logical part is unordered while the remaining subtrees (in the boxes) are ordered trees.

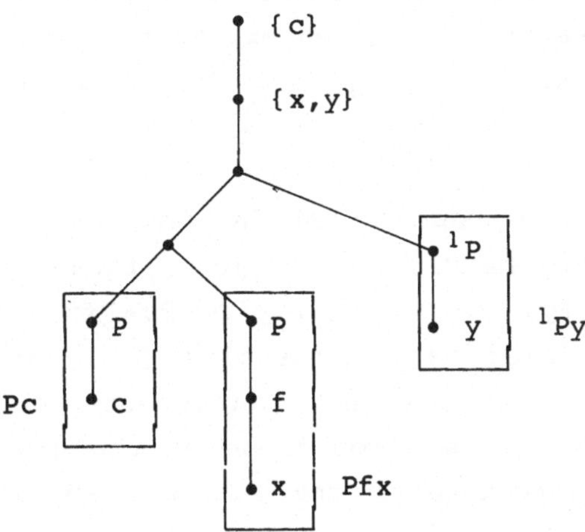

Figure 1 The matrix {c} {x,y} {{Pc,Pfx},^{1}Py} as a tree

More revealing for our purposes, however, is the representation in matrix form which for the present example is

$$1.2.F. \qquad \begin{matrix} Pc \\ Pfx \end{matrix} \qquad {}^{1}Py$$

where again the prefix   {c} {x,y}   has been suppressed. As another example remember the matrix $\overset{\pi}{(1.9)}$ the prefix of which is   {c,t} {} . In fact, any of the examples in chapter II, which are in normal form, are instances of the present definition (1.1) as well since nullary predicates are included in (1.1). Hence in this special case of normal form matrices the step from the ground to the first-order level conceptually is a rather simple one. This fact is reflected also in the following definition of the formulas in normal form.

1.3.D. For any quantified matrix F in normal form, $F = \{c1,\ldots,c_m\}\ \{x_1,\ldots,x_n\}\ \ F_0$, a formula $\tilde{F}$ is called (**positively**) **represented** by F, if $\tilde{F} = \forall c_1 \ldots c_m \exists x_1 \ldots x_n\ \tilde{F}_0$ where $\tilde{F}_0$ is positively represented by F_0 according to (II.1.3.); $\tilde{F}$ is called **negatively represented** by F , if $\tilde{F} = \exists c_1 \ldots c_m$ $\forall x_1 \ldots x_n\ \tilde{F}_0$ where $\tilde{F}_0$ is negatively represented by F_0 according to (II.1.3). A (**first-order**) **formula in normal form** is any formula which is represented by some quantified matrix in normal form. Formulas are denoted as before by D, E, or F. $\forall$ is called a **universal** , $\exists$ an **existential quantifier** , and $\forall c_1 \ldots c_m\ \ \exists x_1 \ldots x_n$ or $\exists c_1 \ldots c_m\ \ \forall x_1 \ldots x_n$ is called the **prefix.** $\square$

Formulas, which are represented by the two matrices shown above, are $\forall$john MARRIED(mother(john),father(john)) , and $\forall c\ \exists x,y(Pc \wedge Pfx \vee {}^{1}Py)$ or $\forall c\ \exists x,y(Py \rightarrow Pc \wedge Pfx)$. Note that the existential quantifier as a convention does not occur in the first formula since it does not contain any variables. As we see these formulas differ from those on the ground level only by the internal structure of the literals and by the prefix; everything else is as it has been before.

Research in ATP in the past was mainly concerned with formulas in normal form, and we will see in section 4 that this does not imply a restriction of generality. It does affect the issue of efficiency, however, therefore it will be necessary to discuss general formulas as well. Unfortunately, it becomes very difficult to display more complicated general formulas in the matrix representation on two-dimensional paper although - as on the ground level - this is the very appropriate form of representation. For this reason, we will now introduce the general first-order formulas directly in the more conventional form without recourse to their (positively) representing matrices, not without the hope that the reader has acquired enough familiarity with the close connection of matrices and formulas to be able to imagine the matrices within the formulas (see also E1 in section 8).

In order to keep the amount of details in the following definition small anough, full use will be taken of all our conventions in it. In this respect, the reader is reminded of the definition (II.1.2) of trees and related concepts, in particular the fact that all their nodes are always assumed to be different, and last not least of table 2 after the Preface. In contrast to previous definitions we will introduce the short-hand notation only, assuming the reader to be aware now that for instance a quantifier indexed by a position formally means a pair, etcetera.

1.4.D. The set of (**first-order**) **formulas** , denoted by D, E,F , over the alphabets **V, F, P,** and R from (1.1) is a set of labeled trees, defined inductively by (f1) through (f4) , together with their **free** and **bounded** occurrences of variables and constants, and the **scopes** of their quantifiers.

(f1)   For any literal L as defined in (1.1), L^r is a formula. Any position $\tilde{r} \in \Omega(L^r)$ associated with a variable or constant cx , i.e. $L^r_{:\tilde{r}} = cx^{\tilde{r}}$, is a free occurrence of cx.

(f2)   If $F_1,\ldots,F_n$ with $n>0$ are formulas then $v^r(F_1,\ldots,F_n)$ and $\wedge^r(F_1,\ldots,F_n)$ are formulas, say F whenever the following condition is satisfied: If $r_i \in \Omega(F_i)$

and $r_j \in \Omega(F_j)$, $1 < i, j < n$, $i \neq j$, are both associated with a variable or constant cx_i and cx_j , and at least one of them occurs bounded then $cx_i \neq cx_j$. Any free or bounded occurrences of variables or constants in F_i, $1 < i < n$, are also free or bounded, respectively, in F .

(f3)   If F_0 is a formula then $\exists^r x_1 \ldots x_n F_0$, say F , is a formula, provided $n > 1$ and x_i, $i = 1, \ldots, n$, occurs free in F_0 . All occurrences of x_i, $i = 1, \ldots, n$, in F are bounded occurrences; any other free or bounded occurrences of variables or constants in F_0 are also free or bounded, respectively, in F . F_0 is the scope of $\exists^r$.

(f4)   If F_0 is a formula then $\forall^r c_1 \ldots c_n F_0$, say F , is a formula, provided $n > 1$ and c_i, $i = 1, \ldots, n$, occurs free in F_0 . All occurrences of c_i, $i = 1, \ldots, n$, in F are bounded occurrences; any other free or bounded occurrences of variables or constants in F_0 are also free or bounded, respectively, in F . F_0 is the scope of $\forall^r$.

The **subformulas** of a formula are naturally determined by its subtrees. A formula is called **closed** if it does not contain any free variables or constants.

All conventions listed in (II.1.3) also apply to first-order formulas, completed by the following ones.

(c4-4) If F is a formula of the form $\forall c_1 \ldots c_n F_0$ then $\neg F$ means $\exists c_1 \ldots c_n \neg F_0$ where c_i , $i = 1, \ldots, n$, in $\neg F$ stands for a variable (thus violating our notational convention).

(c4-5) If F is a formula of the form $\exists x_1 \ldots x_n F_0$ then $\neg F$ means $\forall x_1 \ldots x_n F_0$ where x_i , $i = 1, \ldots, n$, in $\neg F$ stands for a constant (thus violating our notational convention).

(c7)   The order of precedence of $\forall c_1 \ldots c_n$ and of $\exists x_1 \ldots x_n$ is the same as that of $\neg$. $\Box$

As always, the positions in a formula are taken into account only if necessary. Thus $\forall y Py \rightarrow \forall c Pc \wedge \exists x Pfx$ is a formula as defined just before. In contrast to the one after (1.3) above it is not in normal form. Note that we have used a universal quantifier for the variable y since by the conventions (c4) and (c5) in (II.1.3) and (III.1.3) it abbreviates $\exists y^1 Py \vee \forall c Pc \wedge \exists x Pfx$.

Once more we stress the point that the matrix representation should be kept in mind even for such general formulas. For the present example it is displayed by

(F1) $\forall c$
$$\exists x \quad \boxed{\begin{array}{c} \boxed{Pc} \\ \boxed{Pfx} \end{array}} \quad \exists y \quad \boxed{^{1}Py}$$

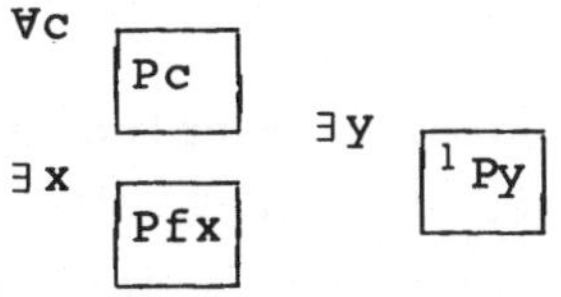

The very (and only) function of quantifiers is the display of their scope. Here the scopes have been shown with labeled boxes which demonstrates the difficulty of an appropriate and illustrative display for more complicated examples. Thinking in three dimensions certainly might support the reader's imagination.

In terms of matrices rather than formulas $(F_1,\ldots,F_n)$ in (1.4.f2) actually is to be regarded as a set rather than a list; the same applies to $x_1\ldots x_n$ in (1.4.f3) and to $c_1\ldots c_n$ in (1.4.f4). We will often take the freedom of making use of this set-theoretic interpretation without an explicit warning (see E1 in section 8).

Note that in the present examples the occurrences of c, x, and y all are bounded. The condition in (1.4.f2) above does not allow $\exists x^{1}Px \vee \forall cPc \wedge \exists xPfx$ or $^{1}Px \vee \forall cPc \wedge \exists xPfx$ as formulas thus ensuring that variables or constants in different context are also denoted different.

In parallel to the treatment of propositional logic in section (II.1) we now mention the generalization of lemma (II.1.4) to first-order logic referring the reader to what has been said before and after (II.1.4) about its meaning.

1.5.L. If a formula $\tilde{F}$ in normal form, is (positively) represented by a matrix F in normal form then $\neg\tilde{F}$ is negatively represented by F .

Proof by structural induction (see E2 in section 8). □

Before concluding this section we will introduce the extremely important syntactic notion of a substition. Often this will be used to substitute in a formula some term for some free variable, such as fc for x in P(x,y) to obtain P(fc,y) .

1.6.D.   A **substitution** is a function mapping a set **S** into another set **T** , and is denoted by σ . If a substitution is finite then it may be represented as a set of pairs of the arguments, say x, y,... ∈ **S** and their values xσ,yσ,... ∈ **T** under σ in the form {x\xσ,y\yσ,...} . Note that in this case of substitutions the function symbol σ is written behind its argument.

If **S** and **T** are sets of (labeled) trees then a substitution σ mapping **S** in **T** is also called a **tree substitution** and for any (labeled) tree t, tσ is defined inductively by (s1) and (s2).

(s1)   If t\t' ∈ σ for some t' then tσ=t' .

(s2)   If t\t' ∉ σ for any t' then tσ consists of the (labeled) root r of t and of the subtrees $t_1\sigma,...,t_n\sigma$ (with nodes different from r) where $t_1,...,t_n$ are the subtrees of r in t .

By convention, if the nodes in t are specified by their labels only then this means that the definition is to be applied with any nodes.   □

The example mentioned before, is a substitution {x\fc} ; thus its application is expressed by P(x,y){x\fc} = P(fc,y) . Note that it is a tree substitution which disregards the nodes by the convention in (1.6). Similarly, P(x,x){x\fc} = P(fc,fc), but $P(x^{r_1},x^{r_2})\{x^{r_1}\backslash fc\}$ = $P(fc,x^{r_2})$ in which case, of course, the nodes in the tree fc are required to be different from the remaining nodes in $P(fc,x^{r_2})$. More examples are discussed in section 3 (after 3.3).

2.   THE SEMANTICS OF FIRST-ORDER LOGIC

In this section we continue the treatment of first-order logic in the way parallel to that of propositional logic in chapter II. Hence we have now the task to define models in first-order logic (which have been introduced as sets of literals on the ground level). Here a literal, such as $P(fc,gc)$, has a richer structure than on the ground level. It might be interpreted in this particular example by MARRIED(mother(john),father(john)) as in section 1, and under this interpretation this literal might get the value **T** , i.e. it would be a member of the model.

This suggests that on the first-order level models are defined via an interpretation of the syntactic elements building up the literals rather than via the literals as a whole. Such an interpretation obviously must specify the objects such as "john" for "c", the functions such as "mother" for "f" and "father" for "g", and the relations such as "MARRIED" for "P", which is carried out formally in the following definition.

2.1.D. An **interpretation**   **I**   (of **V** , **F** , and **P** from 1.1) is a pair (**A** ,ι) where A is an alphabet, called the **universe,** and ι is a function, the **interpreting function** , which assigns
- to each element from $\mathbf{VUF^0}$ an object from **A** ,
- to each n-ary function symbol $f \in \mathbf{F_n}$, $n \geqslant 1$, an n-ary function from $\mathbf{A^n}$ to **A** ,
- to each nullary predicate symbol $P \in \mathbf{P^0}$ a truth value from $\{\mathbf{T,F}\}$, and
- to each n-ary predicate symbol $P \in \mathbf{P^n}$, $n \geqslant 1$, an n-ary relation over **A** .

For any interpretation (**A** ,ι) a **partially interpreted term** $\tilde{t}$ or **formula** $\tilde{F}$ is obtained from a term t or formula F , respectively, in the following way:
For any node r in t or F which is labeled by a constant or variable cx which in the formula case is free in F , cx is or is not substituted by an element $a \in \mathbf{A}$. $\square$

In our previous example **A** might be the set
{john,mrs.miller,mr.miller} , and ι might be defined by
ιc = john, ιf = mother = {(john,mrs.miller)},
ιg = father = {(john, mr.miller)} , and
ιP = MARRIED = {(mrs.miller,mr.miller),(mr.miller,mrs.miller)}.
With the partially interpreted formulas it is now straightforward to define the truth-value $\tau_I(F)$ of a formula F , analogue to (II.2.2).

2.2.D. Inductive definition of $\iota t \in \mathbf{A}$ and $\tau_I(F) \in \{ \mathbf{T},\mathbf{F} \}$ for
any interpretation $\mathbf{I} = (\mathbf{A} ,\iota)$, any term t , and any partial-
ly interpreted formula F .
(t1)   For any $a \in \mathbf{A}$ let $\iota a = a$.
(t2)   For any $f \in \mathbf{P^n}$ and any $ax_i \in A \cup V$, i=1,...,n ,
n>0 , let $\iota(f(ax_1,...,ax_n)) = (\iota f)(\iota(ax_1),...,\iota(ax_n))$.
(t3)   If $F = {}^m Pax_1...ax_n$ with $m \in \{o,1\}$, $P \in \mathbf{P^n}$, n>0,
$ax_i \in \mathbf{A} \cup \mathbf{V}$, i=1,...,n , then let $\tau_I(F) = \mathbf{T}$ if
$(\iota(ax_1),...,\iota(ax_n)) \in \iota P$ and m=0 or
if $(\iota(ax_1),...,\iota(ax_n)) \notin \iota P$ and   m=1 , otherwise let
$\tau_I(F) = \mathbf{F}$.
(t4)   If $F = v(F_1,...,F_n)$ then $\tau_I(F) = \mathbf{T}$ if
$\tau_I(F_i) = \mathbf{T}$ for some $i \in \{1,...,n\}$, otherwise $\tau_I(F) = \mathbf{F}$.
(t5)   If $F = \wedge(F_1,...,F_n)$ then $\tau_I(F) = \mathbf{F}$ if
$\tau_I(F_i) = \mathbf{F}$ for some $i \in \{1,...,n\}$, otherwise $\tau_I(F) = \mathbf{T}$.
(t6)   If $F = \exists x_1...x_n F_0$ then $\tau_I(F) = \mathbf{T}$ if
$\tau_I(F_0\{x_1 \setminus a_1,...,x_n \setminus a_n\}) = \mathbf{T}$ for   some $a_1,...,a_n \in \mathbf{A}$,
otherwise $\tau_I(F) = \mathbf{F}$.
(t7)   If $F = \forall c_1...c_n F_0$ then $\tau_I(F) = \mathbf{F}$ if
$\tau_I(F_0\{c_1 \setminus a_1,...,c_n \setminus a_n\}) = \mathbf{F}$ for   some $a_1,...,a_n \in \mathbf{A}$,
otherwise $\tau_I(F) = \mathbf{T}$.

We say, a formula F **is true** or **has the value** **T**
or **holds in I** , or I **satisfies** F or I **is a model of**
F , in symbols $\mathbf{I} \models F$, if $\tau_I(F) = \mathbf{T}$; otherwise F is
false or **has the value F in I** .

The **model** **M** determined by an interpretation **I** is
the set of exactly those literals L , for which $\tau_I(L) = \mathbf{T}$.

$\mathcal{C} \models F$ and $\models F$ are defined exactly as in (II.2.4) and
(II.2.6).   □

Recalling once more the example above, we notice that $\tau(Pfc,gc) = T$ under the interpretation given before (2.2): $(\iota(fc),\iota(gc)) = ((\iota f)(\iota c),(\iota g)(\iota c)) =$ (mother(john),father(john)) = (mrs.miller,mr.miller) $\in$ MARRIED = ιP , in accordance with (t3). The model determined by this interpretation is $\{Pfc,gc,Pgc,fc\}$ since any other literal such as $Pfgc,c$ is false. Note in this context that our models are sets of literals exactly as in propositional logic since in the literature this term often is used for what we call an interpretation because of the close relationship between these two.

(t4) and (t5) above are equivalent with (t2) in (II.2.2) which once more shows that the set theoretic approach in fact is the technically elegant (though less familiar) one. (t6) and (t7) reveal the reason why (2.2) has been formulated for the more general partially interpreted terms and formulas among which the usual terms and formulas are a special case. Namely, consider $\exists x\ Px,c$ for which by (t6) and (1.6) $\tau(\exists x Px,c) = \tau(Pa_1,c)$ for some $a_1 \in \mathbf{A}$. In a strict sense Pa_1,c is not a formula since a_1 is neither a variable nor a constant, but it is a partially interpreted formula. This example also explains why in (2.1) a constant or variable cx could or could not be substituted as in $P(a_1,c)$ where the x has been substituted by a_1 but c is still an uninterpreted constant.

In view of the matrix interpretation of formulas it should be noted that the substitutions in (t6) and (t7) might as well be performed one by one in any sequence. Thus we have the following trivial observation.

2.3.L.   For any interpretation, any formula $\exists x_1 x_2 \ldots x_n\ F$ has the same truth-value as $\exists x_{\pi 1} \exists x_{\pi 2} \ldots \exists x_{\pi n}\ F$ for any permutation π , and the same for $\forall c_1 \ldots c_n\ F$. $\Box$

This lemma allows the flexible usage of the sequence following any quantifier in a formula. It may be splitted, or the splitting may be reversed. Or the sequence may be reordered. Or it may be restricted to the length 1. In other words, it may simply be regarded as a set, and we will make extensive use of this comfort, similar as with the propositional connectives.

Since the notions of (semantical) consequence, $\mathscr{C} = F$, and of validity, $\models F$, are exactly as in chapter II, the deduction theorem (II.2.5) obviously holds also on the first-order level (see E5 section 8). This seems to be like a good place to point out once more the advantage of our approach splitted into the ground and the first-order level. Since first-order logic is such a complex structure (as the reader will experience) it is so helpful to treat those concepts separately which may be interpreted on the much easier ground level, such as the matrix structure of a formula, to mention one more of these concepts. The reader should have noted that all these concepts of a propositional nature have been (and further will be) carried over to the first-order level without changing this propositional aspect of their nature, only by extending it with more, viz. first-order, aspects.

3.   A BASIC SYNTACTIC CHARACTERIZATION OF VALIDITY

A reader, who has attentively followed the parallel way of presentation in this and the previous chapter, might have missed at the end of the last section an analogue to the truth table method of section (II.2). Such an analogue method has not been presented simply because there is none. W.r.t. a propositional formula we could restrict our attention to a finite part of any model. For first-order formulas, however, generally we have to take into account models with infinite universes. For instance, think of any statement over the natural numbers, such as $(n+1) \cdot m = n \cdot m + m$ formalized by
$\forall n,m(\text{EQUAL}(\text{TIMES}(\text{PLUS}(n,1),m),\text{PLUS}(\text{TIMES}(n,m),m)))$. According to (2.2.t7), any kind of truth table method would have to evaluate this formula for all pairs n,m of natural numbers, which obviously is impossible.

We, therefore, turn our attention right away to **lifting** the syntactic characterization of validity given in (II.3.4) form the ground level to the first-order level. This, first, requires the lifting of the respective concepts as follows.

3.1.D. A (**propositional**) **path through** a formula F is a set of (occurrences of) literals or subformulas with a quantifier at their root which is defined inductively by (p1),(p2), and (p3).

(p1)   If $F = L^r$ for a literal L , or $F = \exists^r x F_0$ or $F = \forall^r c F_0$ for some F_0 , then the only propositional path through F is the set {F} .

(p2)   If $F = \vee(F_1,\ldots,F_n)$, n>0 , then for any path p_i through F_i , i=1,…,n, $\bigcup_{i=1}^{n} p_i$ is a propositional path through F .

(p3)   If $F = \wedge(F_1,\ldots,F_n)$, n>0 , then any path p_i through F_i , $i \in \{1,\ldots,n\}$, is a propositional path through F .

For any formula F , any element A from any path p through F , i.e. $A \in p$, is called a (**propositionally**) **minimal subformula** of F .   ◻

For instance, $\{^1 Pc, Pc\}$ and $\{^1 Pc, \exists x Px\}$ are all the propositional paths through $Pc \rightarrow Pc \wedge \exists x Px$ which is more obvious if this formula is represented in matrix form

$$\neg Pc \quad \begin{array}{c} Pc \\ \exists x Px \end{array}$$

If in this formula Px would be replaced by any other formula F_0 , the only resulting change for these paths would be the same replacement in the second path to obtain $\{^1 Pc, \exists x F_0\}$. Thus these propositional paths may never "look beyond" a quantifier, regarding the corresponding subformula as an atom.

Except for this point, (3.1) is exactly the same definition as (II.3.1), here presented in logical rather than set-theoretical terms so that the reader may get used to both of these representational variants. Therefore, w.r.t. any further illustration of this notion section (II.3) might be consulted once more as a repetition if necessary.

The definition of the concepts from (II.3.3) is even literally the same on the first-order level, and thus has not to be repeated. These concepts are [**partial**](**propositional**) **paths** , (**propositional**) **connections** , **spanning** sets of propositional connections, (**propositionally**) **complementary**

formulas, and (**propositional**) **connection graphs** . The adjective "propositional" is necessary for distinction of these
notions from their generalized versions to be introduced in
section 6; but whenever it is clear by the context what is
meant, this adjective will be dropped for all these notions.
For instance, in the present context a connection in a (first-
order) formula F actually means a propositional connection,
i.e. a set of two complementary literals like $\{^1Pc,Pc\}$ in the
previous example, incidentally its only connection.
With these notions our basic theorem   (II.3.4)   from propositional logic may now be restated on the first-order level
in the following way.

3.2.C.   A propositionally complementary formula is valid.

     Conversely, if F is a valid formula such that all of
its propositionally minimal subformulas are literals then F
is propositionally complementary.

     Proof. The formula F in question is interpreted as a
propositional formula over an alphabet $\mathbf{P}^0$ of propositional
variables which contains $Pt_1...t_n$ for any literal
$^mPt_1...t_n$ which occurs as a minimal subformula in F , and
any other minimal subformula in F which is not a literal
(thus some of the "symbols" in $\mathbf{P}^0$ might be of a form like
$\exists x_1...x_n \; F_0$ - cf. II.1.1). By (2.2) any interpretation I
uniquely determines a model $\mathbf{M}$ for $\mathbf{P}^0$ with $\tau_I(F) = \tau_\mathbf{M}(F)$
where τ_I is given by (III.2.2) and $\tau_\mathbf{M}$ by (II.2.2).
With this propositional interpretation of F , the corollary is
an immediate consequence of (II.3.4). $\Box$

Remember the formula (I.2.1) as an example of such a complementary formula of a first-order nature. $Pc \to Pc \lor \exists xQx$ is
another but trivial example.

     Of course, (3.2) gives a satisfactory syntactic charac-
terization for a small subset of all valid formulas only. We
now prepare its generalization to all valid formulas with the
following three lemmas.

3.3.L.   For any formula F and any interpretation I ,
$\tau_I(F) = \mathbf{F}$ iff $\tau_I(C) = \mathbf{F}$ for all minimal subformulas   C

in some path p through F .

Proof by induction on the length of F .

(i)   If F is its own minimal subformula then the lemma is trivial.

(ii)   If $F = \vee(F_1,\ldots,F_n)$ then $\tau_I(F) = F$ iff $\tau_I(F_i) = F$, $i=1,\ldots,n$, by (2.2), and $\tau_I(F_i) = F$ iff $\tau_I(C_i) = F$ for any $C_i \in p_i$ for some p_i through F_i , by induction hypothesis. This implies the lemma for $p = \bigvee_{i=1}^{n} p_i$ by (3.1).

(iii)   If $F = \wedge(F_1,\ldots,F_n)$ then $\tau_I(F) = F$ iff $\tau_I(F_i) = F$, $i \in \{1,\ldots,n\}$, by (2.2), and $\tau_I(F_i) = F$ iff $\tau_I(C_i) = F$ for any $C_i \in p_i$ for some p_i through F_i , by induction hypothesis. This implies the lemma for $p = p_i$ by (3.1). $\square$

This is a typically **trivial** induction proof in the sense that all cases are settled immediately by the definitions and the induction hypothesis, which will often be left to the reader.

In the following lemmas we will make use of the notion substitution in its full generality as defined in (1.6). So far in our examples, the substituted subtrees have been leaves only. Now, for instance, consider a formula F of the form $\forall cE$. By definition (1.6) $F\{F\backslash E\}$ means that the subtree F in F is replaced by the tree E , hence $F\{F\backslash E\} = E$. As another example let $F = D \vee \exists xE$ for which in the same way we have $F\{\exists xE\backslash E\} = D \vee E$. Even more complicated, we have $F\{\exists xE\backslash(E\{x\backslash t\} \vee \exists xE)\} = D \vee (E\{x\backslash t\} \vee \exists xE)$ for the same F and for some term t , where the subtree $\exists xE$ in F has been replaced by the subtree $(E\{x\backslash t\} \vee \exists xE)$ which in turn is the result of a previous substitution $\{x\backslash t\}$ in E . Apparently, this nesting of substitutions might be continued as the need arises.

There is a subtle syntactical point with this last example when we wish the result of the substitution to be a formula as we always do. For this point we have to remind the reader of the condition in (1.4.f2), the definition of formulas. Under this condition, for t=x and E=Px the previous result $D \vee (Px \vee \exists xPx)$ would not be a formula since x occurs

both, free and bounded in it. Thus t actually is subject to
the restriction that t must not contain x (or any bounded
variables in D , as well) which may be easily satisfied by
substituting the bounded x by some other appropriate variable
y to yield ∃yPy . As a convention, we will not mention such
necessary renamings explicitly, rather take them for granted
wherever they are required.

        But this is only the one side of this subtle point. For
the other let E = ∀cPx,c in the previous example, thus yielding D ∨ (∀cPt,c ∨ ∃x∀cPx,c) as a result of the previous substitution. Even if t satisfies the restriction described before,
this result still does not meet the same condition in (1.4.f2)
since there are two distinct subformulas each containing a
quantifier which binds the same constant c . In order to meet
this condition, c must be changed to some other constant, say
d , in one of them. This will be expressed by (∃x∀cPx,c){c\d} =
∃x∀dPx,d . Strictly speaking, this is not a tree substitution
as defined in (1.6), since ∀c and ∀d are no subtrees. But it
abbreviates one as defined now.

3.4.D. For any formula F with a subformula ∀cE , we let
F{c\d} = F{∀cE\∀d(E{c\d})} , and analogously for a subformula
∃xE . This kind of substitution is called **renaming** of bounded
variables or constants.   □

In most cases it is really not worth to distinguish ∃x∀cPx,c
from ∃x∀dPx,d , say, and thus bother with those substitutions.
In such cases we simply adopt the convention that an intended
formula in fact is a formula according to (1.4) where possibly
some renamings have not been written down explicitly. This **renaming convention** is justified by the following lemma.

3.5.L. Renaming of bounded variables or constants in formulas
does not change their truth-value under any interpretation.
        The proof is obvious by definition (2.2).   □

We first apply implicit renaming in the following important
lemma.

3.6.L. For any formula F with a non-literal minimal subformula C, F is valid iff (i) or (ii) holds.

(i)   If $C = \exists x C_0$ then $F\{C\backslash(C_0\{x\backslash t\} \vee C)\}$ is valid for any term t .

(ii)   If $C = \forall c C_0$ then $F\{C\backslash(C_0\{c\backslash\tilde{c}\})\}$ is valid where $\tilde{c}$ is any constant which does not occur free in F .

Proof. (i) $C = \exists x C_0$. For any term t , let $C' = C_0\{x\backslash t\} \vee C$ and $F' = F\{C\backslash C'\}$. For any interpretation $I = (\mathbf{A}, \iota)$ we have to prove that $\tau_I(F) = \mathbf{T}$ if $\tau_I(F') = \mathbf{T}$.

Assume $\tau_I(F) = \mathbf{T}$. If $\tau_I(C) = \mathbf{F}$ then by (3.3) $\tau_I(F\{C\backslash C'\}) = \mathbf{T}$ even for an arbitrary C' under the present assumption, hence in particular $\tau_I(F') = \mathbf{T}$. Otherwise, $\tau_I(C) = \mathbf{T}$ by (2.2.t4) which in turn yields $\tau_I(F') = \mathbf{T}$ by (3.3).

Conversely, assume $\tau_I(F') = \mathbf{T}$. If $\tau_I(C') = \mathbf{F}$ then as before by (3.3) $\tau_I(F'\{C'\backslash C\}) = \tau_I(F) = \mathbf{T}$. Otherwise, $\tau_I(C') = \mathbf{T}$ implies $\tau_I(C) = \mathbf{T}$ or $\tau_I(C_0\{x\backslash t\}) = \mathbf{T}$. Since by (2.2) $\tau_I(C_0\{x\backslash t\}) = \tau_I(C_0\{x\backslash \iota t\})$, we see by (2.2.t6) that in either case $\tau_I(C) = \mathbf{T}$. Thus $\tau_I(F) = \mathbf{T}$ by (3.3).

(ii) $C = \forall c C_0$. Since $\tilde{c}$ is assumed not to occur free in F , we may assume $\tilde{c} = c$, without restricting generality. Let $F_0 = F\{C\backslash C_0\}$.

We first show that for any $I = (\mathbf{A}, \iota)$, $\tau_I(F) = \mathbf{T}$ implies $\tau_I(F_0) = \mathbf{T}$. Since the case $\tau_I(C) = \mathbf{F}$ is exactly as in (i), we may assume $\tau_I(C) = \mathbf{T}$. By (2.2.t7), this implies $\tau_I(C_0\{c\backslash a\}) = \mathbf{T}$ for any $a \in \mathbf{A}$. In particular, $\tau_I(C_0\{c\backslash\iota c\}) = \mathbf{T}$ which by (2.2) is the same as saying $\tau_I(C_0) = \mathbf{T}$. This yields the desired $\tau_I(F_0) = \mathbf{T}$ by (3.3).

Conversely, assume that F_0 is valid. We have to show that F is valid. Assume to the contrary, that there exists an $I = (\mathbf{A}, \iota)$ such that $\tau_I(F) = \mathbf{F}$. By (3.3), there is some path p through F such that $\tau_I(D) = \mathbf{F}$ for any $D \in p$. If $C \notin p$ then the substitution $\{C\backslash C_0\}$ leaves p unchanged, thus by (3.3) we would have $\tau_I(F_0) = \mathbf{F}$, contradicting the validity of F_0 . Otherwise, if $C \in p$ then $\tau_I(C) = \mathbf{F}$. By (2.2.t7), this implies $\tau_I(C_0\{c\backslash a\}) = \mathbf{F}$ for some $a \in \mathbf{A}$. We define an interpreting function ι' by $\iota'c = a$ and $\iota'e = \iota e$

for any $e \in \mathbf{V} \cup \mathbf{F}$ such that $e \neq c$; i.e. ι' is the same as ι except for c. Let $\mathbf{I'} = (\mathbf{A} , \iota')$. Now by this construction, $\tau_I(C_0) = \mathbf{F}$ which, by (3.3), implies the existence of a path p_0 through C_0 such that $\tau_{I'}(D) = \mathbf{F}$ for any $D \in p_0$. Because of the condition on bounded constants in (1.4.f2), c does not occur in any subformulas of F different from C ; thus their truth values under $\mathbf{I'}$ are the same as under $\mathbf{I}$. Hence we have, $\tau_{I'}(D) = \mathbf{F}$ for all $D \in (p \setminus C) \cup p_0$, which, by (3.3), implies $\tau_{I'}(F_0) = \mathbf{F}$ again a contradiction. $\square$

This lemma is the key to proving completeness and consistency of any syntactic first-order proof method. Note that its proof in fact is straightforward relying, besides the simple observation (3.3), on our definitions only.

The condition on $\tilde{c}$ in (3.6.ii) is recommended for careful consideration by the reader. It cannot be dropped as the formula $\exists x \forall c P(c,x)$ demonstrates if $P(c,x)$ is interpreted as $c=x$. Of course, this formula will not be true in any useful universe, e.g. the natural numbers, while $c=c$ would be valid (w.r.t. to this interpretation). Without this condition, however, two applications of (3.6) imply that $\exists x \forall c(c=x)$ is valid iff $c=c$ is valid, a contradiction. A liberalization of this condition will be discussed in section (IV.10).

As an application of (3.6) let us consider now the formula $\forall c P c \ \mathbf{V} \ \exists x \neg P x$ w.r.t. validity. With (3.6.ii) we arrive at $P c \ \mathbf{V} \exists x \neg P x$ which, by (3.6.i), is transformed to $P c \lor \neg P t \lor \exists x \neg P x$ for any term t ; e.g. for $t=c$, which is $P c \lor \neg P c \lor \exists x \neg P x$. This is a complementary formula, hence, by (3.2), a valid formula, which proves the validity of the original one. Note that this comes out in a purely syntactical way, without reference to any interpretations or other semantical concepts. Namely, we have dropped $\forall c$, then **instantiated** $\exists x \neg P x$ with c , and finally checked for complementarity, say with the connection procedure CP_1^0 from (II.6.12) . Thus the contours of a first-order proof method become visible.

In particular, for formulas in normal form, $\forall c_1 \ldots c_n \ \exists x_1 \ldots x_m \ F$ say, it appears to spring to the mind immediately. Namely, drop the $\forall c_1 \ldots c_n$ yielding $\exists x_1 \ldots x_m \ F$. Instantiate a first time, $F\{x_1 \setminus t_{11}, \ldots, x_m \setminus t_{1m}\} \lor \exists x_1 \ldots x_m \ F$, a

second time
$$F\{x_1\backslash t_{11},\ldots,x_m\backslash t_{1m}\} \vee F\{x_1\backslash t_{21},\ldots,x_m\backslash t_{2m}\} \vee \exists x_1\ldots x_m\, F \ ,$$
and so forth, at each time testing for complementarity. In fact, the behavior of any known proof method is of this general type. They do vary only in the details, which are important, however, in view of the method's efficiency. The simplest but least efficient method is the following one.

It requires a **fixed enumeration** of all terms from T over $V \cup F$ (recall 1.1). Such an enumeration, i.e. an indexing, trivially may be assumed for V and F^n , $n>0$. From that, one for T may be easily constructed, e.g. by defining finite subsets T^i , $i=1,2,\ldots,$ each with a fixed alphabetic order on its elements, such that in T^i the index of any symbol, the arity of any function symbol, and the nesting of the function symbols, each is not greater than i , and $T^i \cap T^{i-1} = \varnothing$. Thus
$$T^1 = (x_1,c_1,f_1^1 x_1,f_1^1 c_1),$$
$$T^2 = (x_2,c_2,f_1^1 x_2,f_1^1 c_2,f_2^1 x_1,\ldots,f_1^2(x_1,x_1),\ldots,f_1^1 f_1^1 x_1,\ldots),\ \text{etc.}$$
would be appropiate (see E6 in section 8).

3.7.A. The **standard procedure** SP for first-order logic applicable to any formula F , based on a standard enumeration $t_1,t_2\ldots$ of the set T of terms.

STEP0. In F , substitute any subformula $\exists x_1\ldots x_n E$ by $\exists^1 x_1\ldots \exists^1 x_n E$, and $\forall c_1\ldots c_n E$ by $\forall c_1\ldots \forall c_n E$; let $i\leftarrow 1$;

STEP1. If F is (propositionally) complementary then return "valid";

STEP2. If there is no minimal part of the form $\exists^k x E_0$ for $k \leq i$ or $\forall c E_0$ in F then $i \leftarrow i+1$, and if there are still no minimal parts of the form $\exists^i x E_0$ in F then return "invalid";

STEP3. Select a minimal part E in F of the form $\forall c E_0$ or $\exists^k x E_0$ for $k \leq i$; in the case $E = \forall c E_0$ substitute E by $E_0\{c\backslash c_j\}$ in F and go to STEP1, where j is the smallest index such that c_j does not occur free in F ; in the case $E = \exists^k x E_0$ subsitute E by $E_0\{x\backslash t_j\} \vee \exists^{k+1} x E_0$ in F and go to STEP1, where j is the smallest index such that t_j has not been used before in a substitution of $\exists^{\tilde{k}} x E_0$ with $\tilde{k} < k$, and no variable or constant in t_j is bounded by some quantifier in E_0 .   ☐

For example, let F be $\exists x \, \forall c \, \exists y \, P(x,y,c)$. Upon arrival at STEP3 F has the form

$\exists^1 x \forall c \exists^1 y P(x,y,c)$, $\forall c \exists^1 y P(t_1,y,c) \vee \exists^2 x \forall c \exists^1 y P(x,y,c)$,

$\exists^1 y P(t_1,y,c_1) \vee \exists^2 x \forall c \exists^1 y P(x,y,c)$,

$P(t_1,t_1,c_1) \vee \exists^2 y P(t_1,y,c_1) \vee \exists^2 x \forall c \exists^1 y P(x,y,c)$,

$P(t_1,t_1,c_1) \vee P(t_1,t_2,c_1) \vee \exists^3 y P(t_1,y,c_1) \vee \exists^2 x \forall c \exists^1 y P(x,y,c)$,

$P(t_1,t_1,c_1) \vee P(t_1,t_2,c_1) \vee \exists^3 y P(t_1,y,c_1) \vee \forall c \exists^1 y P(t_2,y,c)$, etc.,

in the first, second, etc., resp., round. It is obvious that for this example SP would run forever.

As we see the length of these formulas grows (linearly in the number of rounds), an obvious disadvantage for storage. As a further defect note that we have not specified in detail the test for complementarity in STEP1 of SP . In the case of normal form formulas only we could use C_1^O from (II.6.12) for that purpose. But the worst drawback of this procedure is one demonstrated by the previous example, $F = \forall c P c \vee \exists x \neg P x$. SP as before produces the sequence $\forall c P c \vee \exists^1 x \neg P x$, $P c_1 \vee \exists^1 x \neg P x$, $P c_1 \vee \neg P t_1 \vee \exists^2 x \neg P x$, $P c_1 \vee \neg P t_1 \vee \neg P t_2 \vee \exists^3 x \neg P x$, etc. If the first term t_1 in the fixed enumeration of **T** is c_1 , then SP is lucky and terminated successfully in the third round; however, if c_1 happens to be the term t_{1000} then SP needs 999 more rounds for this trivial example! It is easy to see that such disasters will occasionally occur with any fixed enumeration. Because of this very feature SP got the nickname **British Museum method** (never behave like that in the British Museum!). It is of no use at all in practice. But with the subsequent theorems it provides the theoretical grounds from which we may quickly develop more efficient methods. For their proof we need the following rather obvious result from graph theory.

3.8.T. (König's lemma) A tree with a finite number of successors per node such that each of its branches has finite length, has only a finite number of nodes, i.e. it has finite length.

Proof. If there is a uniform upper bound to the length of all branches, then clearly the tree has finite length. We only must convince ourselves that under the condition in the theorem such a uniform upper bound does exist.

Assume to the contrary, that for each positive integer i there exists a branch of length exceeding i . Then we may

select for each   i   such a branch of length exceeding   i ,
which amounts to an infinite number of such selected branches.
Now the following procedure enumerates the nodes r_j of one
of these branches.
STEP1.   j←1 ; let r_1 be the root of the tree;
STEP2.   Select a successor r_{j+1} of r_j such that an
infinite number of selected branches contain r_{j+1} ; let
j←j+1 ; goto STEP2.

     Obviously, this procedure never terminates successful-
ly selecting a node at each round, thus enumerating the nodes
of a branch of infinite length – a contradiction.   □

Of course,   SP   may be viewed as a logic calculus as defined
in (II.5.2). Its axioms are the complementary formulas (STEP1
in 3.7), and the inference relation   F $\vdash$ F'   is defined by the
substitution in STEP3. Thus the notions of consistency and completeness as defined in (II.5.3) make sense for it.

3.9.T.   The standard connection procedure   SP   is consistent.
     Proof. We have to prove that a formula   F   in fact is
valid if   SP   applied to   F   returns "valid" after   n rounds.
At this point, SP has generated a derivation $F_1 \vdash F_2 \vdash \ldots \vdash F_n$
with F_1 = F . If   n=1   then   F   is valid by (3.2). If   n>1
then F_2 is valid by the hypothesis of this induction, which
implies the validity of   F   by (3.6).   □

3.10.T. The standard connection procedure   SP   is complete.
     Proof. Here we have to prove that for a valid formula
F, SP   does return "valid" after a finite number   n   of rounds.
     The formula F_i , derived in the i-th round of   SP
applied to   F , is valid because of (3.6). Hence, if F_i
does not contain any non-literal minimal parts, then it must be
complementary by (3.2), and thus guarantees the termination in
STEP1 rather than in STEP2 in this case.
     But we also have to worry about the possibility that
SP   might not terminate at all. In this case, we may assume an
infinite sequence of derived formulas, $(F=)F_1, F_2, \ldots$ which
are not complementary. Under this assumption, we shall now
define an interpretation $\mathbf{I} = (\mathbf{A} , \iota)$ for which $\tau_I(F) = F$,

thus contradicting the validity of F which shows that this case actually is not possible.

      For that purpose we define a tree such that the root r_0 is labeled with $\emptyset$ and the nodes r_i of depth $i \geqslant 1$ are labeled with the non-complementary paths through F_i , each with exactly one of them, satisfying the following successor relation. Let E denote the minimal part in F_i selected, and E' the formula in F_{i+1} substituted for E in F_i , in STEP3 of SP , for any $i \geqslant 1$. Then r_{i+1} labeled with p_{i+1} is a successor of r_i labeled with p_i , if $p_{i+1} = p_i$ in the case $E \notin p_i$, and if $p_{i+1} = (p_i \setminus E) \cup p'$ for some p' through E' in the case $E \in p_i$. Obviously, this tree has only a finite number of successors per node, and it must be infinite by the present assumptions. Hence, König's lemma implies that we may select an infinite branch, $((r_0,\emptyset),(r_1,p_1),\ldots,(r_i,p_i),\ldots)$ say. Define $p = \bigcup_{i=1}^{\infty} p_i$.

      Now, let $\mathbf{A} = \mathbf{T}$ and $\iota t = t$ for any term $t \in \mathbf{T}$. Further let $(t_{i1},\ldots,t_{in}) \in \iota P$ iff $^1Pt_{i1}\ldots t_{in} \in p$. With this interpretation we claim:

(*) $\tau_I(C) = \mathbf{F}$ for any $C \in p$.

Since $p_1 \subseteq p$ is a path through F , (*) together with (3.3) implies $\tau_I(F) = \mathbf{F}$. Hence, we are done with the following proof of (*) by induction on the length of C .

(i)   If C is a literal then $\tau_I(C) = \mathbf{F}$ by definition of **I** since by assumption p is not complementary and thus does not contain both L and ^1L for any literal L .

(ii)   If $C = \exists xD$ then by the construction there are infinitely many nodes $(r_{i1},p_{i1}),(r_{i2},p_{i2}),\ldots$ in the selected branch such that $C \in p_{ij}$ and $p_{ij+1} = (p_{ij} \setminus C) \cup p'_{j+1}$ where p'_{j+1} is a path through $D\{x \setminus t_j\}$ and t_j is the j-th term in the fixed enumeration of **T** in SP . By the induction hypothesis any minimal part in p'_{j+1} is false , hence $D\{x \setminus t_j\}$ is false by (3.3), for any $j \geqslant 1$. According to (2.2.t6), this means that $\tau_I(C) = \mathbf{F}$.

(iii)   If $C = \forall cD$ then by construction there is a node (r_i,p_i) in the selected branch such that $C \in p_i$ and $p_{i+1} = (p_i \setminus C) \cup p'$ where p' is a path through $D\{c \setminus c_j\}$ for some c_j . $\tau_I(C) = \mathbf{F}$ now follows by the induction hypothesis, by (3.3), and by (2.2.t7) exactly as in (ii).   □

With this theorem we have completed the desired syntactic characterization of the valid formulas which is restated in the following corollary.

3.11.C. A formula F is valid iff SP , with input F , terminates after a finite number of steps returning "valid". $\square$

This characterization is particularly illustrative for a restricted class of formulas which, among other concepts, will be introduced in the following definition.

3.12.D. For any formula F , let $\mathbf{F}^n$ (F) denote the set of n-ary function symbols occurring in F , $n > 0$, and $\mathbf{F}$ $(F) = \bigcup_{i=0}^{\infty} \mathbf{F}^n$ (F). Then the **Herbrand universe** $H(F)$ of F is the set of terms over $\mathbf{F}$ (F) or over $\mathbf{F}$ $(F) \cup \{c\}$ for some constant c , depending whether $\mathbf{F}^0$ $(F) \neq \emptyset$ or not, respectively, and its members are called **Herbrand terms** or **ground terms of** F .

A formula F is called in **Skolem normal form** if it is a closed formula of the form $\forall c_1 \ldots c_m \, \exists x_1 \ldots x_n \, F_0$ in which the matrix F_0 does not contain any quantifier.

For any such formula F in Skolem normal form $F_1 \vee \ldots \vee F_k$ is called a **compound instance of** F if $F_i = F_0 \{x_1 \backslash t_{i1}, \ldots, x_n \backslash t_{in}\}$ for any Herbrand terms $t_{i1}, \ldots, t_{in}$ of F , $1 \leq i \leq k, k \geq 1$. In the case $k=1$ we also speak of a (**ground**) **instance** of F . Also, these substitutions of variables by Herbrand terms are called **instantiations.**
                                                                   $\square$

For instance, for $E_1 = \forall c \exists x (Pc \vee \neg Px)$ the Herbrand universe $H(E_1)$ is $\{c\}$, and $Pc \vee \neg Pc$ is a compound instance of F. Incidentally, $\exists xy(Py \vee \neg Px)$ has the same Herbrand universe and compound instance as E_1 just before. As another example, the Herbrand universe of $E_2 = \forall c \exists x (Pfc \vee \neg Px)$ is $\{c, fc, ffc, \ldots\}$ and $(Pfc \vee \neg Pfc) \vee (Pfc \vee \neg Pfffc)$ is a compound instance of E_2. Again the same is true for $\exists xy(Pfy \vee \neg Px)$.

Apparently, all these formulas are in Skolem normal form. Even they are in normal form as defined in (1.1) which differs from the former by the additional requirement of the quantifier free matrix being in (propositional) normal form.

Thus E_3 = $\forall c \exists xy((Pc \lor Qx) \land Pfx \lor \neg Py \lor \neg Qc)$ still is in Skolem normal form but not in normal form. As for normal form formulas (see section 1) we adopt the convention that the prefix may be deleted since it is uniquely determined by the matrix. The remaining matrix may then be displayed in matrix form as in propositional logic.

For this restricted class of formulas in Skolem normal form our general characterization may be rephrased in the following form which actually is a version of the famous **Skolem-Gödel-Herbrand theorem** , which in ATP often is briefly called **Herbrand theorem** .

3.13.C. A formula in Skolem normal form is valid iff it has a complementary compound instance.

Proof. Let   F   denote the formula in Skolem normal form. If it is valid, SP terminates after a finite number of steps. Deletion of any disjuncts of the form $\exists xE$ and (uniform) substitution of any ground terms for variables in the resultant complementary formula provides the complementary compound instance of   F   in this special case.

Conversely, if $F_1 \lor ... \lor F_k$ is a complementary compound instance of the form defined in (3.12) then we assume that the substituted terms t_{jl} , $1 \leq j \leq k$, $1 \leq l \leq n$, are among the first   h   terms in the standard enumeration of   **T** . This obviously guarantees that SP terminates before the   i   in (3.7) adopts the value $l+1$, returning "valid" , since the F_j must have been instantiated before in this special case. $\square$

For instance, all the formulas E_1, E_2, and E_3 and their variants mentioned above are valid by this theorem since the compound instances presented for them are complementary as is the one

$$\begin{array}{cc} \begin{array}{cc} Pc & Qc \\ Pfc & \end{array} & \quad \neg Pfc \quad \neg Qc \end{array}$$

for E_3 .

Usually in the field of ATP, Herbrand's theorem is presented and proved for normal form formulas only. Our version (3.13) is more general since it applies to Skolem normal form formulas. But this in turn is only a restricted form of (3.11) which characterizes all valid formulas without any restriction. Its transformation into a form which justifies to call it a version of Herbrand's theorem, will require very little efforts. Hence our proof yielded a much stronger result than usual although the extra complication is marginal.

Reviewing this proof it apparently consists in a straightforward application of the definitions which provided the results stated in (II.3.4) or (3.2), in (3.3), and in (3.6), the first two by a straightforward induction. With these results (3.11) was obtained again in a straightforward way, with one more induction necessary for (3.10). The only tool left out in this list and worth to be mentioned from a proof-theoretical point of view is König's lemma which, though intuitive and easy to prove, is really a strong statement since its proof is non-constructive (cf. [Sc4]). The reader's attention should not miss the interesting fact coming along with this proof that the set of terms may serve as a **canonical** universe, easily mapped into any universe of any interpretation, a fact which has been established in (3.6) and used in (3.10). It is obvious that in view of a formula this set of terms may even be restricted to its Herbrand universe.

The first-order procedure SP differs from the propositional procedure CP_1^O in an essential feature. Namely, CP_1^O always terminates while SP may run forever as we have seen with the example immediately after (3.7). This is not a specific defect of SP. Rather it is known that first-order logic is an **undecidable** theory while propositional logic is a **decidable** theory. This means that for the latter there are **decision procedures** which for any formula decide whether it is valid or not - and CP_1^O in fact is such a decision procedure - while for the former such decision procedures do not exist in principle. Thus SP, according to these results for which the reader is referred to any logic texts such as [End], [DrG] or [Lew], is of the kind which we may expect, it is a **semi-decision procedure** which confirms if a formula is valid but may run forever for invalid formulas. Therefore, termination by running out of time or space after any finite number of steps will leave the question for the validity of a formula unsettled.

Only for certain subclasses of formulas, SP may be extended to a decision procedure, a point which will be discussed in section (IV.1).

4.   TRANSFORMATION INTO NORMAL FORM

It was already mentioned in the last section that the standard connection procedure SP is of no use in practice because of efficiency reasons. Therefore we will now turn our attention to the development of a more efficient proof method. As in chapter II with CP^O , this development will first be carried out for the restricted class of formulas in normal form, starting in the next section. As a prelude it will be shown in the present section that this restriction is without any loss of generality. But we hasten to note that there is a distinction to be made between "loss of generality" and "loss of efficiency". From an efficiency point of view this restriction is in fact a serious one although it is without loss of generality; therefore it will be removed in the next chapter.

In the subsequent definition we specify a transformation process which converts any formula F into a formula F' in normal form. In a first reading the example given afterwards might be consulted first or in parallel. Later we will then justify this process by showing that F is equivalent with F'.

4.1.A. Transformation of any formula F   into a formula   F' in normal form.
STEP0. [**Close the formula and check the formula properties**] For any variable x occurring free in it, substitute x by a new constant c in F , i.e. $F \leftarrow F\{x\backslash c\}$; for any constant c occurring free in F let $F \leftarrow \forall cF$; assure that no two quantifiers share the same variable or constant (by possible renaming) and remove any conventional connectives such as $\neg$, $\rightarrow$, $\leftrightarrow$ according to the conventions c4, c5, and c6 in (II.1.3) and in (III.1.4). Optionally perform **antiprenexing** as described in (IV.11).
STEP1. [**Introduce Skolem functions**] For each subformula of F of the form $\forall cD$ and in the scope of at least one existen-

tial quantifier, replace $\forall cD$ in F by $D\{c \backslash fx_1...x_k\}$; here $x_1,...,x_k$, $k \geqslant 1$, denote all those bounded variables in F for which the subformula $\forall cD$ in question occurs in the scope of $\exists x_i$, $i=1,...,k$, in F ; further f denotes any k-ary function symbol not occurring in F .

STEP2.   [**Transform into Skolem normal form**] If $c_1,...,c_m$ denote all bounded constants, and $x_1,...,x_n$ all bounded variables in F , and if F_0 denotes the result of deleting all quantifiers in F then $F \leftarrow \forall c_1...c_m \exists x_1...x_n F_0$.

STEP3. [**Transform into normal form**] Replace each subformula of the form $A \wedge (B \vee C)$ in F_0 by $(A \wedge B) \vee (A \wedge C)$, until F_0 is in (disjunctive) normal form; $F' \leftarrow \forall c_1...c_m \exists x_1...x_n F_0$.   □

STEP0 has been included only as a reminder of the special form of our formulas which has to be achieved before the actual transformation may be started.

In order to illustrate the remaining steps consider the formula $\exists x \forall c \ P(x,c)$ which is converted to $\exists x P(x,fx)$ in STEP1 with no further change in STEP2 and 3. As another example, $\forall a \exists x \ (\forall b^1 P(a,x,b) \wedge \exists y(\forall c P(y,x,c) \vee P(a,y,x)))$ becomes $\forall a \exists x(^1 P(a,x,fx) \wedge \exists y(P(y,x,gxy) \vee P(a,y,x)))$ by STEP1. In STEP2, this formula is converted to $\forall a \exists x,y(^1 P(a,x,fx) \wedge (P(y,x,gxy) \vee P(a,y,x)))$. STEP3, finally produces $\forall a \exists x,y (^1 P(a,x,fx) \wedge P(y,x,gxy) \vee ^1 P(a,x,fx) \wedge P(a,y,x))$ thereof.

The justification for these transformations is provided by the following well-known results from mathematical logic which are treated in more details in elementary logic texts (such as [He1], ch. VII). The first lemma covers the closing of the formula in STEP0.

4.2.L. A formula F with a variable or constant ax occurring free in it is valid iff the formula $\forall b \ F\{ax \backslash b\}$ is valid for any constant b such that b does not occur free in F or b=ax .

See exercise (E9) in section 8.   □

The introduction of Skolem functions in STEP1 of (4.1) is covered by the following lemma.

4.3.L.   Let   F   be a closed formula with an occurrence of a subformula $\forall cC$ which is in the scope of exactly   n   existential quantifiers $\exists x_1,\ldots,\exists x_n$, $n \geqslant 1$; further let   f   be any function symbol not occurring in   F , let $C' = C\{c\backslash fx_1\ldots x_n\}$ and $F' = F\{\forall cC\backslash C'\}$. Then   F   is valid iff   F'   is valid.

Proof. **If-case** . Here we assume that   F'   is valid and claim the validity of   F . Assume to the contrary that $\tau_I(F) = F$ for some interpretation   I . Under this assumption we will define an interpretation   I'   such that $\tau_{I'}(F') = F$, thus contradicting the validity of   F' .

Let $I = (A ,\iota)$. Then $I' = (A ,\iota')$ where for any symbol different from   f, ι' has the same value as ι ; hence we are left to specify $\iota'f$ appropriately. For any $(a_1,\ldots,a_n) \in A^n$ this will be performed by induction on the number   k   of those quantifiers in   F   which have $\forall cC$ within their scope, in such a way that $\tau_I(F) = \tau_{I'}(F') = F$. For this induction we allow   F   to be a partially interpreted formula. Let a denote any fixed element from   A . Under the present assumption there is a path   p   through   F   such that $\tau_I(D) = F$ for any minimal subformula $D \in p$, by (3.3).

Case   k=0 . If $\forall cC \in p$ then $\tau_I(C\{c\backslash b\}) = F$ for some $b \in A$ by (2.2.t7); in this case we let $(\iota'f)(a_1,\ldots,a_n) = b$ which implies $\tau_{I'}(C') = F$ and $\tau_{I'}(F') = F$ by (2.2) and (3.3). Otherwise, $\tau_I(F') = F$ by (3.3) independently of the interpretation for f ; thus we may define $(\iota'f)(a_1,\ldots,a_n) = a$.

Case   k>0 . If $\forall cC$ does not occur in any $D \in p$ then $\tau_I(F') = F$ for $(\iota'f)(a_1,\ldots,a_n) = a$ exactly as in the last case. For the remaining two subcases we thus may assume that $\forall cC$ occurs in some $D \in p$.

If $D = \exists xE$ and $\forall cC$ is in the scope of   n-i   existential quantifiers, $0 \leqslant i \leqslant n-1$, then the application of the induction hypothesis to $E\{x\backslash a_{i+1}\}$ yields
$\tau_I(E\{x\backslash a_{i+1}\}) = \tau_{I'}(E\{x\backslash a_{i+1}\}\{\forall cC\backslash C'\}) = F$.   Since a_{i+1} is arbitrary this implies $\tau(F') = F$ by (2.2.t6) and (3.3).

If $D = \tilde{\forall cE}$ then for some $\tilde{a} \in A$, $\tau_I(E\{\tilde{c}\backslash\tilde{a}\}) = F$. As just before, application of the induction hypothesis, of (2.2.t7) and of (3.3) implies $\tau(F') = F$, which completes the if-case.

Only-if-case . Given the assumption that F is valid, we have to show that $\tau_I(F') = T$ for any interpretation $I = (\ A\ ,\iota)$.

If $\tau_I(\forall cC) = T$ then $\tau_I(C') = T$ by (2.2). With this observation we may infer $\tau_I(F') = T$ from $\tau_I(F) = T$ with the same induction on k as in the if-case in a straight-forward way which is left to the reader as an exercise (see E10 in section 8).   □

The remaining part of the transformation (4.1) will be covered by the following lemma.

4.4.L. If for any formula F some subformula D is replaced by D' to yield F' , where D and D' are related as shown in table 1, then F is valid iff F' is valid.

#	D	D'	comments
(i)	$A \wedge (B \vee C)$	$(A \wedge B) \vee (A \wedge C)$	note that each of
(ii)	$A \vee (B \wedge C)$	$(A \vee B) \wedge (A \vee C)$	these rules repre-
(iii)	$\exists xA \vee B$	$\exists x(A \vee B)$	sents in fact two
(iv)	$\forall cA \wedge B$	$\forall c(A \wedge B)$	rules, and that x
(v)	$\exists xA \wedge B$	$\exists x(A \wedge B)$	in (iii), (v) and
(vi)	$\forall cA \vee B$	$\forall c(A \vee B)$	c in (iv), (vi) must
(vii)	$\exists xA \vee \exists yB$	$\exists x(A \vee B\{y\backslash x\})$	not occur in B, by
(viii)	$\forall aA \wedge \forall bB$	$\forall a(A \wedge B\{b\backslash a\})$	our conventions

Table 1. Equivalence transformations

Proof. As for (4.3) the proof consists of a straightforward in-duction on the number of quantifiers in F which have D within their scope. Alternatively, it may be carried out by induction on the number of rounds in a run of the standard connection procedure SP . For both versions of the proof the details are left to the reader as an exercise (see E11 in section 8).   □

Altogether, these results provide the justification for (4.1) as follows.

4.5.C. For any formula F which is transformed by (4.1) into
a formula F' in normal form, F is valid iff F' is valid.

  Proof. If F_0 denotes the result of an application of
STEP0 of (4.1) to F then F is valid iff F_0 is valid, by
(3.5) and (4.2). If F_1 denotes the result of an application
of STEP1 of (4.1) to F_0 then F_0 is valid iff F_1 is valid,
by (4.3). If F_2 denotes the result of an application of STEP2
of (4.1) to F_1 then F_1 is valid iff F_2 is valid, by (iii)
through (vi) in (4.4). Finally, after application of STEP3 of
(4.1) to F_2, F_2 is valid iff the resultant F' is valid, by
(i) in (4.4). Of course, any of these for arguments actually
includes a trivial induction.   □

Concluding this section we note that the sequence of the steps
in (4.1) might be changed without affecting the result in
(4.5). Such a change may have an influence to the running time
required by a theorem prover applied afterwards. This is discussed in more details in section (IV.11), where we will see
that (4.1) offers the most efficient sequence of steps in this
sense, unless the extra-feature of **antiprenexing** is added
which provides a further improvement.

5.   UNIFICATION

In order to prove a theorem in normal form, according to (3.13)
it is sufficient to determine a compound instance which is complementary. For example, for the theorem
KINDfather(john) $\to$ $\exists x$ KINDx   its instance
KINDfather(john) $\to$ KINDfather(john) obviously is complementary.
Now, SP would provide a proof for this theorem by substituting x by all terms t_i , i=1,...,n ,in the fixed enumeration
of T with t_n=father(john), testing for complementarity
after each of these substitutions, an infeasible task as
already noted since n may happen to be very large.
  The cause of this drawback is obvious, however. SP does
things in the wrong order. It **first** substitutes in a blind
way, and **then** checks for complementarity. In the other way
around, we would **first** neglect all the terms and check for

complementarity, and only then consider the required substitutions. For instance, in the previous example KIND→KIND obviously is complementary. This rudimentary instance might be
extended to a full instance, if we were able to determine, as a
second step, a substitution which **unifies** the terms
father(john) and x by instantiation without destroying the
complementarity. In the present case the substitution
{x\father(john)} serves for this purpose, since its application
to both terms leads to identical terms, viz. father(john),which
completes the proof for this example.

The idea of interchanging the sequence in which to
solve the two main subproblems, this fundamental idea really
lies at the heart of modern theorem provers. It may, however,
be realized in a favorable way only if the newly emerged problem of unifying two terms like father(john) and x , in general
even sets of such pairs of terms (since the arity of the predicate like KIND may be any positive number), may be solved in an
efficient way even for arbitrary terms. This problem is known
as the **unification problem** which will be discussed in the
present section in a way which has been adapted from section 11
in [Ro3].

We begin this discussion by making precise this notion
of unification.

5.1.D. A substitution which substitutes variables by terms is
called a **variable substitution** . Since all substitutions in
connection with unification will be variable substitutions we
may simply call them **substitutions** in the present context.

If for any set $S = \{E_1,\ldots,E_n\}$, $n \geqslant 1$, of formulas
without quantifiers or terms E_i , i=1,...,n , referred to as
expressions in the present context and for any substitution
α, $S\alpha$ is a singleton set, i.e. $E_1\sigma=\ldots=E_n\sigma$, then σ is
called a **unifier** of $E_1,\ldots,E_m$; in this case the **unifi-
cand** S will be referred to as a **unifiable** set, and the application of σ will be called **unification** .   ☐

The substitution {x\ father(john)} **unifies** the set
{KINDfather(john), KINDx} in the sense of this definition, as
we have seen before. As a more abstract example, the set

$$S = \{f(g(x)), \; y, \; f(z)\}$$

is unified by the substition
$$\sigma = \{x\backslash t, \; y\backslash f(g(t)), \; z\backslash g(t)\}$$
for any term t, since
$\{f(g(x)), \; y, \; f(z)\}\sigma =$
$\{f(g(x)))\sigma, \; y\sigma, \; (f(z))\sigma\} =$
$\{f(g(t)), \; f(g(t)), \; f(g(t))\} = \{f(g(t))\}$.

As this example demonstrates, a set may have even infinitely many unifiers, since t denotes an arbitrary term. Let τ denote the substitution $\{y\backslash f(gx), \; z\backslash gx\}$. Then $S\sigma = (S\tau)\rho$ for $\rho = \{x\backslash t\}$. τ may be regarded as a more general substitution in comparison with σ , in the sense that σ is kind of an instance of τ , viz. $\sigma = \{x\backslash x\rho \; , \; y\backslash(f(gx))\rho \; , \; z\backslash(gx)\rho\}$. This observation naturally leads to the following definition.

5.2.D. For any two substitutions τ and ρ , their **composition** $\sigma = \tau\rho$ is defined by $\sigma = \{x\backslash(x\tau)\rho \mid (x\backslash t) \in \tau$ or $(x\backslash t) \in \rho$ for some term $t\}$. The empty set $\emptyset$ regarded as a substitution is denoted by ε .

A unifier τ of a set S of formulas of terms is called a **most general unifier** , if for any unifier σ of S, $\sigma = \tau\sigma$. $\qquad\qquad\qquad\qquad\qquad\qquad\qquad\qquad\qquad$ $\Box$

For instance let $\tau = \{y\backslash f(gx), \; z\backslash gx\}$ and
$\sigma = \{x\backslash t, \; y\backslash f(g(t)), z\backslash g(t)\}$ as before, then
$\tau\sigma = \{x\backslash(x\tau)\sigma, \; y\backslash(y\tau)\sigma, \; z\backslash(z\tau)\sigma\} =$
$\quad = \{x\backslash x\sigma, \; y\backslash(f(gx))\sigma, \; z\backslash(gx)\sigma\} =$
$\quad = \{x\backslash t, \; y\backslash f(g(t)), \; z\backslash g(t)\} = \sigma$.

Since any unifier of the set S above obviously must be of the form of σ , we see that τ is a most general unifier of S.

This also explains the reason for this name since the effect on any S by any unifier σ is **first** that of the most general one τ , **followed** by further modifications of the singleton set $S\tau$. Thus every particular way of shrinking S to a singleton in this sense must include the way that τ does it.

It is certainly not obvious, and indeed rather subtle, that for any unifiable set S there exists at least one such most general unifier. We will establish this result in a **constructive** way (similar as with our version of Herbrand's theorem 3.13), by specifying a process here called **unification algorithm** which for any set S of expressions determines whether it is unifiable, and in the affirmative case produces a most general unifier of S .

As we shall see, it will suffice to give the unification algorithm for the case when S has **two** expressions in it; the cases when S has more than two expressions in it will be easy to handle once we work out the case of two expressions. For any such two expressions say X, Y, we must analyse them to find how they differ. The following definition is to serve exactly for this purpose.

5.3.D. For any two expressions X and Y (i.e. formulas without quantifiers or terms regarded as labeled and ordered trees), the **difference** DIFF(X,Y) of X and Y denotes a set of unordered pairs of subexpressions, one from X the other from Y , defined inductively as follows.
(d1) If X and Y are the same expression then DIFF(X,Y) = $\emptyset$,the empty set.
(d2) If X and Y are not the same expression, but their roots have the same labels and the same number n of ordered successor nodes determining corresponding subexpressions $X_1,\ldots,X_n$ and $Y_1,\ldots,Y_n$ then
DIFF(X,Y) = DIFF(X_1,Y_1) $\cup\ldots\cup$ DIFF(X_n,Y_n) .
(d3) In all other cases, DIFF(X,Y) = {{X,Y}} . $\square$

For example, if X is f(hx,g(x,ky)) and Y is f(kx,z) then
DIFF(X,Y) = DIFF(hx,kx) $\cup$ DIFF(g(x,ky),z)   [by d2]
         = {{hx,kx}} $\cup$ {{g(x,ky),z}}   [by d3]
         = {{hx,kx},{g(x,ky),z}} .

5.4.D. For any two expressions X and Y , we say DIFF(X,Y) is **negotiable** if it is non-empty and for any of its elements {x,t} , x is a variable which does not occur in t .

If this holds then the substitution $\{x\backslash t\}$ is called
a **reduction** of DIFF(X,Y) . $\square$

In the previous example, DIFF(X,Y) is not negotiable since
none of the terms in $\{hx,kx\}$ is a variable. If we replace
hx by x in X then DIFF(X$\{hx\backslash x\}$,Y) still is not negotiable since x occurs in kx in $\{x,kx\}$. Replacing hx by y
in X , however, results in a negotiable set
DIFF(X$\{hx\backslash y\}$,Y) = $\{\{y,kx\},\{g(x,ky),z\}\}$.
Note that because of the set notation the variable may be written at the first or the second place in each pair. Thus both,
$\{y\backslash kx\}$ and $\{z\backslash g(x,ky)\}$ are reductions in the last
example.In the case of two variables in such a pair as in
$\{x,y\}$, both $\{x\backslash y\}$ and $\{y\backslash x\}$ are reductions. With these
notions the algorithm reads as follows.

5.5.A. The **unification algorithm** $UNIF_1$ applicable to any
formulas without quantifiers or terms X and Y .
STEP0.   Put $\sigma = \varepsilon$.
STEP1.   While DIFF(Xσ,Yσ) is negotiable
         do   replace σ by $\sigma\rho$
         where ρ is any reduction of DIFF(Xσ,Yσ) .
STEP2.   If   DIFF(Xσ,Yσ) is empty
         then $\{X,Y\}$ is unifiable and σ is a most general
                 unifier
         else $\{X,Y\}$ is not unifiable. $\square$

Let us work an example to get the feel of a computation
carried out by $UNIF_1$, taking the input expressions to be
X = P(x, f(gy), fx) and Y = P(h(y,z), fz, f(h(u,v))) . The
whole computation may be summarized in table 2, which shows how
the successive states of σ bring about, successively, pairs
$\{A\sigma,B\sigma\}$ whose difference is "smaller" each time until it van-
ishes.

    In detail, after initializing σ to the empty substi-
tution, $UNIF_1$ enters the loop in STEP1. First it computes
the difference of Xσ and Yσ , that is, of X and Y . This
situation, referred to as state 0, is shown in the first line
of table 2, with the current value of σ and of DIFF(Xσ,Yσ).

State	σ	DIFF(Xσ,Yσ)
0	{}	{{x,h(y,z)},{z,gy},{x,h(u,v)}}
1	{z\gy}	{{x,h(y,gy)},{x,h(u,v)}}
2	{z\gy,x\h(u,v)}	{{u,y},{v,gy}}
3	{z\gu,x\h(u,v),y\u}	{{v,gu}}
4	{z\gu,x\h(u,gu),y\u,v\gu}	{}

Table 2. Unification of $P(x,f(gy),fx)$ and
$P(h(y,z),fz,f(h(u,v)))$

The latter apparently is negotiable, therefore a reduction
will be made up from one of its pairs; say the choice is
{z\gy} . Thus in state 1 the value of σ will be
ε{z\gy} = {z\ gy} .   With this substitution we obtain
Xσ = P(x, f(gy), fx) and Yσ = P(h(y,gy), f(gy), f(h(u,v))) .
The difference of these two literals is shown in the second
line of state 1. It is again negotiable. Thus STEP1 is executed
for the second time by choosing a reduction, say {x\h(u,v)} .
Considering state 2 we obtain the new value of σ by
σρ = {z\gy}{x\h(u,v)} = {z\ gy,x\h(u,v)} , and with it the new
pair of literals
Xσ = P(h(u,v),f(gy),f(h(u,v))) and
Yσ = P(h(y,gy),f(gy),f(h(u,v))) ,
the difference of which is {{u,y}, {v,gy}} . Say {y\u} is
chosen in the present third round of STEP1 as reduction ρ .
For state 3 this yields
σρ = {z\gy,x\h(u,v)}{y\u} = {z\gu,x\ h(u,v),y\u} ,
Xσ = P(h(u,v),f(gu),f(h(u,v))) , and
Yσ = P(h(u,gu),f(gu),f(h(u,v))) , with the negotiable difference {{v,gu}} . This last difference is removed by execution
of STEP1 for the last time. Therefore the difference is empty,
i.e. no more negotiable, which causes $UNIF_1$ to enter STEP2,
and to output the final unifier shown in the last line of table
2. The unified literal is
Xσ = Yσ = P(h(u,gu),f(gu),f(h(u,gu))) .
        We are now going to prove that $UNIF_1$ behaves as
expected in general. In showing this, we shall appeal to the

following lemma relating the notions of difference and unification, whose intuitive content is that the difference between unifiable expressions is removable.

5.6.L. (**Negotiability lemma**) If X and Y are distinct expressions and σ unfies {X,Y} then DIFF(X,Y) is negotiable, and σ unifies each pair in DIFF(X,Y) .

Proof by induction on the maximal size k of X and Y .

If k=0 then at least one, say X , must be a variable, and the other, then, a constant or a variable different from X . In this case DIFF(X,Y) = {{X,Y}} obviously is negotiable, and obviously σ unifies every pair in DIFF(X,Y).

If k>0 then the assumption that σ unifies {X,Y} reduces the possibilities to the following two ones.

(a)   One, say X , is a variable that does not occur in Y .

(b)   The roots of X and Y are labeled with the same symbol and have the same number n of successor nodes with the corresponding subtrees $X_1,\ldots,X_n$ and $Y_1,\ldots,Y_n$.

In case (a), DIFF(X,Y) = {{X,Y}} and is obviously negotiable.

In case (b), DIFF(X,Y) = $DIFF(X_1,Y_1) \cup \ldots \cup DIFF(X_n,Y_n)$. Since σ is assumed to unify {X,Y} , this certainly is true also for $\{X_i,Y_i\}$, i=1,...,n . By the induction hypothesis we thus conclude that

(i) $DIFF(X_i,Y_i)$ is negotiable for any $i \in \{1,\ldots,n\}$ such that $X_i \neq Y_i$ (since X≠Y by assumption, there must be at least one such i), and

(ii) σ unifies each pair in $DIFF(X_i,Y_i)$, i=1,...,n . But (i) and (ii) is exactly what the lemma claims.   □

5.7.T. (**Unification theorem**) For any two terms or formulas without quantifiers X and Y , the following holds.

(i)   The unification algorithm $UNIF_1$, applied to X, Y, terminates after a finite number of steps.

(ii)   {X,Y} is unifiable iff $UNIF_1$ so indicates upon termination. Moreover, the substitution σ then available as output is a most general unifier of {X,Y} .

Proof. (i)   At each iteration within STEP1 of $UNIF_1$, another variable is eliminated from the expressions $X\sigma$, $Y\sigma$, hence STEP1 can be executed only a finite number of times.

(ii) The "only-if" case is immediately clear since $UNIF_1$ indicates that $\{X,Y\}$ is unifiable only if $DIFF(X\sigma,Y\sigma)$ is empty, i.e. only if σ in fact unifies $\{X,Y\}$. Thus only the "if" case remains to be demonstrated as follows.

We are going to show that if $\{X,Y\}$ is unifiable then the following proposition (a) remains true throughout the computation of $UNIF_1$ with X,Y as input.

(a)   For all unifiers τ of $\{X,Y\}$, $\tau = \sigma\tau$.

If (a) holds then for any unifier τ of $\{X,Y\}$, i.e. $X\tau = Y\tau$, we have $X(\sigma\tau) = Y(\sigma\tau)$, which by the definition of composition (5.2) means $(X\sigma)\tau = (Y\sigma)\tau$. Thus if (a) remains true throughout the computation, so does the following proposition.

(b)   For all unifiers τ of $\{X,Y\}$, τ unifies $\{X\sigma,Y\sigma\}$.

In order now to show (a) we observe that it is certainly true immediately after STEP0 since trivially $\tau = \varepsilon\tau$. Further if (a) – hence also (b) – is true before the execution of the "do" statement in STEP1 then it is true immediately after it, as we shall show now.

Let $\rho = \{x\backslash t\}$ denote the selected reduction. We have $x(\rho\tau) = (x\rho)\tau = t\tau$ by definition of composition and of ρ . By (b) it may be assumed that τ unifies $\{X\sigma,Y\sigma\}$, hence also $\{x,t\}$ by the Negotiability Lemma, thus $t\tau = x\tau$. Altogether this yields $x(\rho\tau) = x\tau$. $\rho\tau$ and τ agree not only at x , but at each variable since for $y{\neq}x$ obviously $y(\rho\tau) = (y\rho)\tau = y\tau$, i.e. $\tau = \rho\tau$ by definition . Thus given (a) we have $\tau = \sigma\tau = \sigma(\rho\tau) = (\sigma\rho)\tau$ by definition (see exercise E13). Hence when σ is replaced by $\sigma\rho$ in STEP1, (a) will still be true.

So (a) is preserved at each performance of STEP1; and this step is repeated as long as $DIFF(X\sigma,Y\sigma)$ is negotiable. The only way that $DIFF(X\sigma,Y\sigma)$ can fail to be negotiable is for it to be empty, by (b) and the Negotiability Lemma. Hence, when $UNIF_1$ finally leaves STEP1, (a) will be true and $DIFF(X^\sigma,Y^\sigma)$ will be empty. Therefore, $UNIF1$ in performing STEP2 will indicate that $\{X,Y\}$ is unifiable; and since (a) is still true it will be the case that σ is the most general unifier of $\{X,Y\}$. $\square$

The generalization of the unification algorithm for sets S with arbitrarily many elements is now straightforward. The empty set, i.e. $|S|=0$, is not unifiable, any singleton set, i.e. $|S|=1$, has ε as its most general unifier, and the case $|S|=2$ has just been completed. For $|S|>2$, UNIF_1 has to be modified to simply consider all pairs $\{X,Y\}\subseteq S$ rather than a single one as before. The details are left to the reader as an exercise (see E15 in section 8). With this generalization we may note the following corollary.

5.8.C.   If a set of expressions is unifiable then there exists a most general unifier for it. $\square$

A further generalization is the task to unify not only a single set, but any number of sets $S_1,\ldots,S_n$ with $n>1$. We restrict the discussion of this case to the special case where each S_i contains only two elements, i.e. $S_i = \{X_i,Y_i\}$, $i=1,\ldots,n$. In this case, we may consider an arbitrary n-ary symbol P which does not occur in any S_i . Obviously, σ is a most general unifier for each S_i , $i=1,\ldots,n$, iff σ is a most general unifier of the single pair $\{P(X_1,\ldots,X_n),\ P(Y_1,\ldots,Y_n)\}$. This reduces this case to the one for which UNIF_1 applies.

Often, however, the S_i will have to be unified one after the other. Also this task may be solved with UNIF_1 as follows. We unify S_1 obtaining a substitution σ_1 . Now assuming in an inductive way that we already have obtained a most general unifier σ_{n-1} unifying $S_1,\ldots,S_{n-1}$, we obtain σ_n unifying $S_1,\ldots,S_n$ by applying UNIF_1 to $\{X_n\sigma_{n-1},\ Y_n\sigma_{n-1}\}$ yielding a most general unifier σ (if it exists) since then, obviously $\sigma_n = \sigma_{n-1}\sigma$ holds (cf. the proof of the unification theorem).

UNIF$_1$ is not very efficient. It is even exponential in the worst case as the example $\{t_1,t_2\}$ with $t_1 = f(x_1,x_2,\ldots,x_n)$ and $t_2 = f(g(x_0,x_0),g(x_1,x_1),\ldots,g(x_{n-1},x_{n-1}))$ demonstrates. If $\rho_1 = \{x_1\backslash g(x_0,x_0)\}$ is selected in the first iteration then $t_1\rho_1 = f(g(x_0,x_0),x_2,\ldots,x_n)$. If $\rho_2 = \{x_2\backslash g(x_1,x_1)\}$ is selected in the second iteration, and so forth upto $\rho_n = \{x_n\backslash g(x_{n-1},x_{n-1})\}$ then

$t_1 \rho_1 \ldots \rho_n = f(g(x_0,x_0),g(g(x_0,x_0),g(x_0,x_0)),\ldots\}$ where the number of occurrences of g is exponential in n . Now note that the test for negotiability includes the so-called **occur-check** in which for {x,t} it has to be tested whether x occurs in t . Hence, the explosion of the terms in this example also blows up the time required for this occur-check and with it the time required by $UNIF_1$.

However, $UNIF_1$ may be improved to **linear** unification algorithms which will be discussed in section (IV.9). For the present chapter we content ourselves with this less efficient but simple version $UNIF_1$.

6.   THE CONNECTION CALCULUS

With all the tools developed in the present chapter we are now in the position to **lift** the connection method from the ground level to the first-order level, i.e. from propositional logic to first-order logic. As in propositional logic we will first accomplish this for formulas in normal form only. According to (4.5) this restriction, which simplifies matters considerably, does not cause any loss of generality. In view of efficiency, however, we have to be concerned with this restriction which will be on the agenda in chapter IV (see section IV.5).

The basic idea for lifting the connection method has already been illustrated at the beginning of the previous section with the formula KINDfather(john) $\rightarrow$ $\exists$xKINDx . In normal form it reads $\forall$john $\exists$x(KINDfather(john) $\rightarrow$ KINDx) . Since the prefix (i.e. the quantifiers) is determined by the matrix, we may drop it and will do so in most cases. Also we will mostly use the matrix representation. Thus the present example would be represented as the matrix
(E1) $\neg$KINDfather(john) KINDx
Now, it was suggested to first neglect all the terms in the literals of such a matrix and check the resulting fragment for complementarity. In the present case this fragment consists of $\neg$KIND KIND which certainly is complementary. In this affirmative case, we check in a second step whether the terms which correspond to each other in the original matrix via the connec-

tions establishing the complementarity of the fragment, whether these corresponding terms then are unifiable. In the present example there is only one such connection which relates the terms father(john) and x . The substition {x\ father(john)} obviously unifies them thus providing a complementary instance ¬KINDfather(john) KINDfather(john) of the given matrix which by (3.13) proves that (E1) in fact is a theorem.

In general, any such connection {P,¬P} - like {KIND, ¬KIND} in the present example - would relate n pairs of terms for any $n > 0$, which are determined by the corresponding pair of literals {$Ps_1...s_n$, ¬$Pt_1...t_n$} in the original matrix to yield {s_1,t_1},...,{s_n,t_n} - in the present example we have n=1, s_1=x, and t_1 = father(john) .

In practice, these two steps mentioned before are actually performed with each selected connection separately as the next example E2 demonstrates which is the formula ∀c∃xy(Px ∧ Qy → Pfy ∧ Qgc) . Its proof is displayed in figure 1 the way which has been used in section (II.4). In fact, we will now proceed in complete analogy with the development in that section. Therefore it is warmly recommended that the reader makes sure that he/she remembers its details which thus have not to be repeated here.

After an initializing step we consider the first matrix in the deduction of figure 1. One of its clauses has been selected to start with which is illustrated with the vertical arrow. The braces represent the empty substitution which is considered at this starting point. Now a literal is selected in the distinguished clause. Since there is only a single one this must be [1]Px . Ignoring any terms we look for an occurrence of P which is Pfy in the second clause relating the terms x and fy . Thus in order to make this a propositional connection these two terms have to be unified which yields the substition {x\fy} shown in the second matrix of figure 1. Everything else there is exactly as in propositional logic described in section (II.4), thus completing the first deduction step.

For the second deduction step, the literal Qgc is the only possible choice from the clause distinguished by the vertical arrow. In the same way as before with P , [1]Qy is selected, now relating the two terms gc and y . But note that

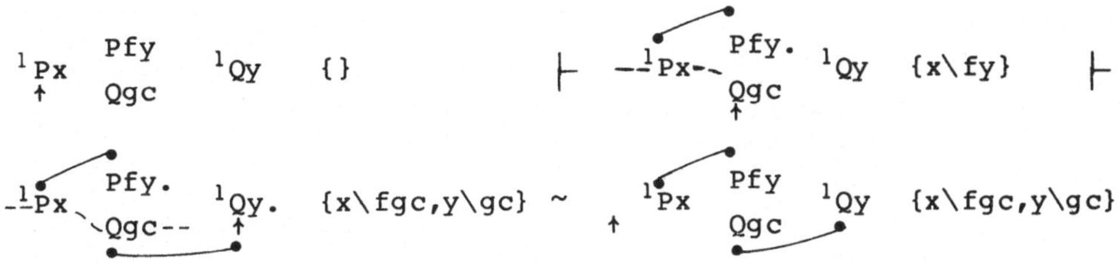

Figure 1. A connection deduction for E2

we already have restricted the variables with the previous substition. Hence, actually we have to unify {gc,y}{x\fy} now
which obviously yields the new substitution {y\gc} . The composition {x\fy}{y\gc} = {x\fgc,y\gc} then apparently unfies
both pairs of terms considered so far. With this we have ar-
rived at the situation illustrated with the third matrix in
figure 1.

Since extension (as the previous kind of deduction
steps has been called in II.4) is no more possible we may now
apply reduction (see II.4) as illustrated with the last matrix.
This now has a terminal structure thus finishing the proof.

The reader will have noticed that this works exactly
as on the ground level except for the additionally required
unifications. A further difference will now be illustrated
with the next example (E3) which informally states that everyone has a grandfather since everyone has a father:

(E3) $\forall u \exists a Fau \land \forall xyz(Fzy \land Fyx \rightarrow GFzx) \rightarrow \forall b \exists v GFvb$

Note that the usage of constants and variables in this formulas does not violate our denotational conventions which becomes clearer if the formula is transformed into its normal
form

(E3) $\forall ab \exists xyzuv(\neg Fau \lor (Fzy \land Fyx \land \neg GFzx) \lor GFvb)$

A deduction for this matrix is presented in figure 2. In this
presentation all occurring variables are decorated with an index, either with $._1$ or with $._2$. To understand the reason for
that we remind the reader of our version of Herbrand's theorem

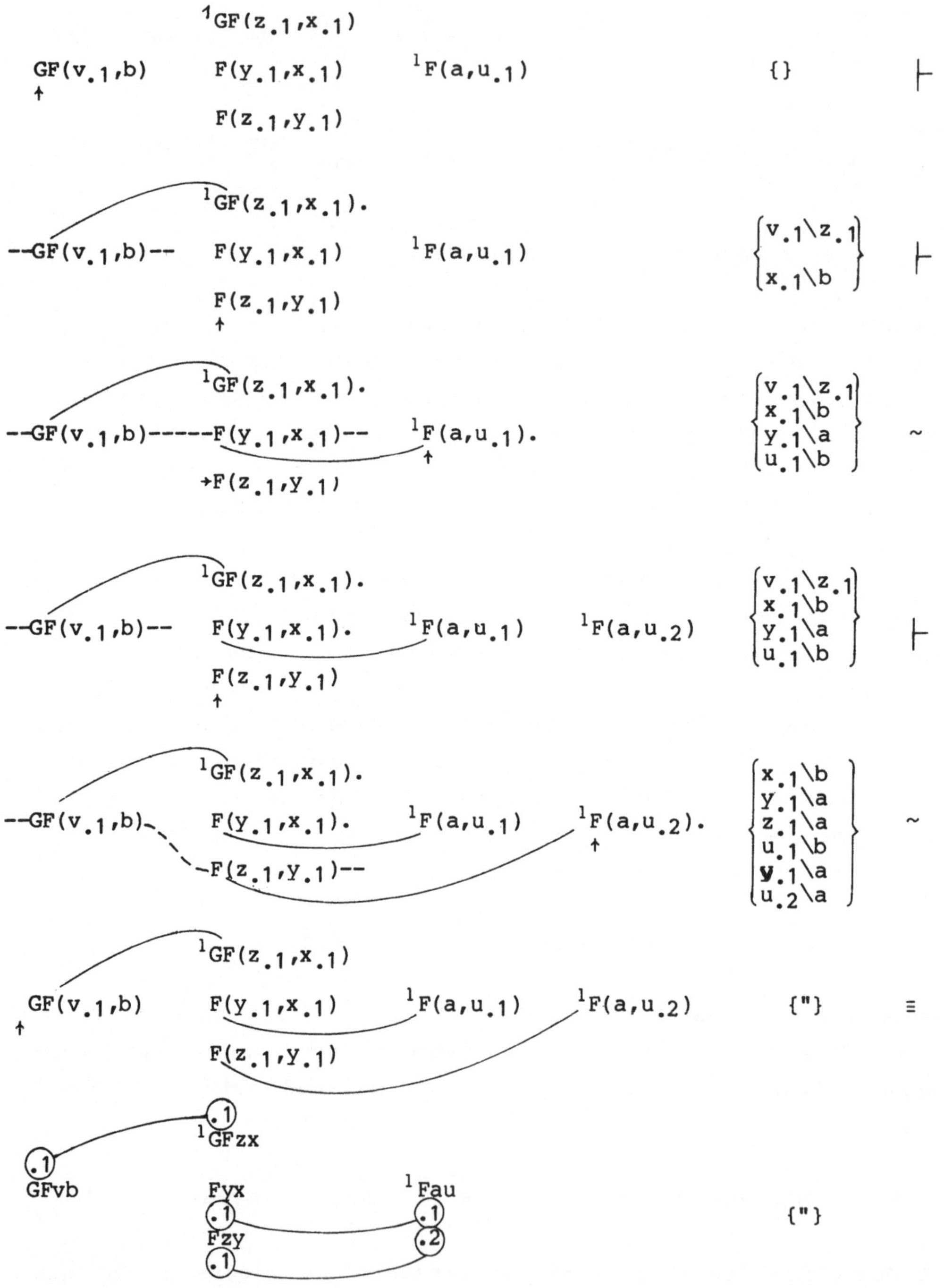

$${}^1GF(z_{.1},x_{.1})$$

$$GF(v_{.1},b) \qquad F(y_{.1},x_{.1}) \qquad {}^1F(a,u_{.1}) \qquad\qquad \{\} \qquad \vdash$$

$$F(z_{.1},y_{.1})$$

$$--GF(v_{.1},b)-- \quad {}^1GF(z_{.1},x_{.1}). \qquad F(y_{.1},x_{.1}) \qquad {}^1F(a,u_{.1}) \qquad \left\{\begin{matrix} v_{.1}\backslash z_{.1} \\ x_{.1}\backslash b \end{matrix}\right\} \vdash$$

$$F(z_{.1},y_{.1})$$

$$--GF(v_{.1},b)-----F(y_{.1},x_{.1})-- \quad {}^1GF(z_{.1},x_{.1}). \qquad {}^1F(a,u_{.1}). \qquad \left\{\begin{matrix} v_{.1}\backslash z_{.1} \\ x_{.1}\backslash b \\ y_{.1}\backslash a \\ u_{.1}\backslash b \end{matrix}\right\} \sim$$

$$\rightarrow F(z_{.1},y_{.1})$$

$$--GF(v_{.1},b)-- \quad {}^1GF(z_{.1},x_{.1}). \qquad F(y_{.1},x_{.1}). \qquad {}^1F(a,u_{.1}) \qquad {}^1F(a,u_{.2}) \qquad \left\{\begin{matrix} v_{.1}\backslash z_{.1} \\ x_{.1}\backslash b \\ y_{.1}\backslash a \\ u_{.1}\backslash b \end{matrix}\right\} \vdash$$

$$F(z_{.1},y_{.1})$$

$$--GF(v_{.1},b)- \quad {}^1GF(z_{.1},x_{.1}). \qquad F(y_{.1},x_{.1}). \qquad {}^1F(a,u_{.1}) \qquad {}^1F(a,u_{.2}). \qquad \left\{\begin{matrix} x_{.1}\backslash b \\ y_{.1}\backslash a \\ z_{.1}\backslash a \\ u_{.1}\backslash b \\ \mathbf{y}_{.1}\backslash a \\ u_{.2}\backslash a \end{matrix}\right\} \sim$$

$$-F(z_{.1},y_{.1})--$$

$$GF(v_{.1},b) \quad {}^1GF(z_{.1},x_{.1}) \qquad F(y_{.1},x_{.1}) \qquad {}^1F(a,u_{.1}) \qquad {}^1F(a,u_{.2}) \qquad \{"\} \qquad \equiv$$

$$F(z_{.1},y_{.1})$$

$${}^1GFzx \;\text{(.1)}$$

$$GFvb \;\text{(.1)} \qquad Fyx \;\text{(.1)} \qquad {}^1Fau \;\text{(.1)} \qquad\qquad \{"\}$$

$$Fzy \;\text{(.1)} \qquad \text{(.2)}$$

Figure 2. A connection deduction for E3

which allows for a complementary **compound** instance of (E3) to demonstrate its validity; in other words, it may be necessary to consider **more than one** copies of the matrix in order to obtain a proof, and this actually happens with (E3) as we shall see in a moment. The indices now serve for the distinction of such different copies; $_{.1}$ refers to the first, $_{.2}$ to second copy, etc. Note that for formulas in normal form there are no different copies of constants.

Now, the deduction in figure 2 starts with an extension, and proceeds with an extension followed by a reduction, similar as in figure 1 with (E2). But at this point, i.e. with the structure illustrated in the fourth line of the deduction, there is no way to proceed on a single copy. Namely, the two connections are not yet spanning, and the only potential connection which would yield the spanning property cannot be unified. Recall that we must find a substitution that unifies all connections which means that the substitution determined thus far has to be applied before testing for unifiability. In detail, this gives

$$\{F(z_{.1}, y_{.2}), F(a, u_{.1})\} \; \{v_{.1}\backslash z_{.1}, x_{.1}\backslash b, y_{.1}\backslash a, u_{.1}\backslash b\} = \{F(z_{.1}, a), F(a, b)\}$$

. Since a and b denote two different constants, unification must fail for this pair of literals.

There is no other way out of this conflict than considering a second copy of the matrix (E3). For reasons of space only one clause of this second copy is shown in the figure, viz. $\{^1 F(a, u_{.2})\}$. With this additional clause the proof can now be completed by an extension followed by reduction.

Not only on paper but also in the computer memory, the explicit generation of further copies of a matrix may require plenty of space. Hence it is worthwhile to notice rightaway that this explicit generation is not actually required as may be seen from the last two lines in figure 2. Rather we may shift the information given by the indices from the variables to the endpoints of the connection, without any loss of information as shown over there.

It is felt that with these tree examples the reader might have obtained a good feel for the nature of the connection method. In the remaining part of the present section this informal description will be associated with the corresponding

formalism and its justification. We begin with the generalization of some familiar concepts.

6.1.D. For any formula F (not necessarily in normal form) a
multiplicity μ is a function which assigns to each node r in
F , that is the root of a subformula of the form $\exists x_1 \ldots x_n$ F'
for some F' in F , a natural number $\mu(r) > 1$. F together
with μ will often be written in the form F^μ . $\Box$

The multiplicity μ determines the number of copies of an
existentially quantified subformula to be considered. μ is
undefined for any formula without existential quantifiers. For
(E3) in its normal form above there is exactly one existential
quantifier hence μ must be a constant function. In view of
the deduction of figure 2 for it, which needs exactly two
copies, μ might assign the value 2 to the corresponding node.

6.2.D. A (**first-order**) **path through** any formula F (not
necessarily in normal form) is a set of (occurrences of) literals in F defined inductively by (p1) through (p4).
(p1)   If $F = L^r$ for a literal L then   {F}   is the only
path through F .
(p2)   If $F = \vee(F_1,\ldots,F_n)$, n>0 , then for any path p_i
through F_i , i=1,\ldots,n , $\bigcup_{i=1}^{n} p_i$ is a path through F .
(p3)   If $F = \wedge(F_1,\ldots,F_n)$, n>0 , then any path p_i
through F_i , $i \in \{1,\ldots,n\}$, is a path through F .
(p4)   If $F = \exists x_1 \ldots x_n\ F_0$ or $F = \forall c_1 \ldots c_n\ F_0$ then any
path through F_0 is a path through F .

An **indexed path** $p.i$, with i>1 , **through** F in
Skolem normal form is a (first-order) path through F with
each of its elements L^r indexed by   i , written as
$L^r.i$ and denoting the literal
$L^r\{x\backslash x.i|$ variable x occurs in L} .

For any formula F in Skolem normal form with multi-
plicity μ , a **path through** F^μ is a set $\bigcup_{i=1}^{\mu(r)} (p_i).i$
where r denotes the node associated with the only existential
quantifier in F , and where p_i denotes any path through F
which then is indexed by i ; unless F does not contain any
existential quantifier in which case the matrix of F is treated as a propositional matrix.

     With the adjective **partial** associated with the previous concepts we refer to their subsets.   ◻

Note the distinction between the propositional paths as defined in (3.1) and the present first-order paths. The latter ignore the quantifiers (6.2.p4) while the former cannot look beyond any quantifier (3.1.p1). We shall simply speak of **paths** whenever it is clear from the context which kind is meant.

     Any index encodes a distinct copy of the formula. Hence, with the compound instances in (3.13) in mind, a path through F^μ is a path through the disjunction of all different copies where each copy may be traversed on its own path. For instance, consider (E3) with multiplicity 2. Say, the path $(p_1)_{.1}$ through the first copy is $\{GF(v_{.1},b),\ F(y_{.1},x_{.1}),\ {}^1F(a,u_{.1})\}$ and the path $(p_2)_{.2}$ through the second copy is $\{GF(v_{.2},b),\ {}^1GF(z_{.2},x_{.2}),\ {}^1F(a,u_{.2})\}$; then the union $(p_1)_{.1} \cup (p_2)_{.2}$ of these two sets is a path through $(E3)^2$.

6.3.D. A (**first-order**) **connection** in a Skolem normal form formula F^μ is a 2-element subset of a path through F^μ of the form $\{(Ps_1 \ldots s_n)_{.i}\ ,\ ({}^1Pt_1 \ldots t_n)_{.j}\}$.

     A set of connections in F^μ is called **spanning** if each path through F^μ contains at least one of these connections.   ◻

The last matrix of figure 2 displays three such connections with the indices encircled at their ends. Note that these connections are spanning for $(E3)^2$.

     With all this new terminology Herbrand's theorem (3.13) may be restated for normal form formulas in the following way.

6.4.C. A formula F in Skolem normal form is valid iff for some (constant) multiplicity μ there is a spanning set U of connections in F^μ and a substitution σ such that $u\sigma$ is a (propositionally) complementary pair of literals for any $u \in U$.

     Proof. With the relevant definition in mind it is clear that this is but a different way of expressing (3.13). In particular note that the number of instances in the

compound instance addressed in (3.13) here is encoded by way
of μ . $\square$

At this point we should pause for a moment in our course of
lifting matters to the first-order level, and compare (6.4)
with the main theorem (II.3.4) on the ground level. Both characterize validity via the existence of a spanning set of connections, the difference being that on the ground level this
provides a full charactization while on the first-order level
in addition a multiplicity μ and a substitution σ is re-
quired.With this observation and with the informal description
at the beginning of the present section it is straightforward
to lift the connection calculus previously defined in (II.4.2)
and (II.4.3). Namely, all which has to be done is to provide
for more than one copies of a matrix via μ and additionally
carry along σ , everything else being exactly as before.

6.5.D. A matrix **structured in view of the linear normal form
connection method for first-order logic** is a matrix F in
normal form paired with a structure S defined below; if the
kind of deduction is clear from the context, the pair (F,S)
will be simply called a **structured matrix** .

If F does not contain an existential quantifier then
S is exactly as in the propositional case, given by (II.4.2);
otherwise the structure S is a quadrupel $(\alpha, \beta, \gamma, \sigma)$ of functions defined by (i) through (iv).

(i) α is an integer function on some of the clauses in F
indexed by natural numbers, i.e. $\alpha(c_{.i}){=}n{>}1$ for some clauses
$c \in F$ and for some natural numbers $i, n{>}1$. Let F_1^S denote the
domain of α , shortly written F_1 if S is clear.

(ii) β is a boolean function on the set of occurrences of
indexed literals in F_1 , i.e. $\beta(L^r_{.i}) \in \{0,1\}$ for any
literal $L^r \in c$ for some $c \in F$ such that $c_{.i}{\in} F_1$. Let
$(c_{.i})_j = \{L^r_{.i} \mid L^r \in c,\ c_{.i} \in F_1 ,\ \text{and } \beta(L^r_{.i}) = j\}$.

(iii) γ is defined on some subset $F_1' \subseteq F_1 \setminus \{d_{.j}\}$ for
$d_{.j} \in F_1$ with $\alpha(d_{.j}) > \alpha(e_{.k})$ for any other $e_{.k}{\in}F_1$,
such that $\gamma(c_{.i})$ is an occurrence of an indexed literal
$L^r_{.i}$ with $L^r \in c$ and $\beta(L^r_{.i}) = 0$, i.e.
$\gamma(c_{.i}) = L^r_{.i} \in (c_{.i})_0 \subseteq c_{.i} \in F_1' \subseteq F_1$. The set

$\{L^r_{.i} \mid \gamma(c_{.i}) = L^r_{.i} \ , \ c_{.i} \in F'_1 \ , \ \text{and } i > 1\}$ is called the **active path** p^S_a , or shortly p_a , in F structured by S .

(iv) σ is a (variable) substitution; whenever $(x_{.i})\sigma$ is defined, x is variable occurring in F and $(x_{.i})\sigma$ is a term over indexed variables and function symbols occurring in F . $\square$

The figures 1 and 2 illustrate this concept of a structured matrix. Besides the indices, α, β, γ are exactly as on the ground level; hence, if the reader feels a need for some more explanation w.r.t. these then the digestion after (II.4.2) should be consulted once more. The index is $_{.1}$ in all literals and clauses in the figures 1 and 2 except for the literal or clause $^1F(a,u_{.2})$ where it is $_{.2}$. The substitutions are shown at the end of each line in the figures 1 and 2.

6.6.D. All the following concepts are introduced **in view of the linear normal form connection method for first-order logic;** by convention, this extra specification will never be mentioned if it is clear by the context.

For matrices without any existential quantifiers all the concepts are provided by (II.4.3); hence, in the following we may restrict the case to matrices with existential quantifiers.

For any two structured matrices (F,S) and $(\tilde{F},\tilde{S})$, we say that $(\tilde{F},\tilde{S})$ **is obtained from** (F,S) **by extension** if $F = \tilde{F}$ and $S = (\alpha,\beta,\gamma,\sigma)$ is related to $\tilde{S} = (\alpha,\tilde{\beta},\tilde{\gamma},\tilde{\sigma})$ in the way described in (i) through (v).

(i) There is a unique clause $d_{.i}$ such that $\alpha(d_{.i}) \geq \alpha(e_{.j})$ for any $e_{.j} \in F_1$ (the domain of α).

(ii) The domain $\tilde{F}'_1$ of $\tilde{\gamma}$ is $F'_1 \cup \{d_{.i}\}$ for $d_{.i}$ from (i), (and F'_1 the domain of γ), and we have $\beta(\tilde{\gamma}(d_{.i})) = 1$ and $\gamma = \tilde{\gamma}$ on F'_1 .

(iii) $\tilde{F}_1 = F_1 \cup \{e_{.j}\}$ where $e_{.j} \notin F_1$; further $e_{.j}$ is required to contain a literal $L_{.j}$ such that for some substitution τ and for some indexed literal $K_{.k}$ from the active path $\tilde{p}_a$ of $(\tilde{F},\tilde{S})$, $\{L_{.j},K_{.k}\}\sigma\tau$ is complementary; finally, $j=1$ or $e_{.(j-1)} \in F_1$ must be satisfied. For $e_{.j}$ we have $\alpha(e_{.j}) = \alpha(d_{.i})+1$.

(iv)   For any $L_{.j} \in e_{.j}$, $\tilde{\beta}(L_{.j}) \in \{0,1\}$ such that the following holds. $(e_{.j})\tilde{o} \neq \emptyset$; further if $(K_{.k})\tilde{\sigma} = (L_{.j})\tilde{\sigma}$ for some $^1K_{.k} \in \tilde{p}_a$ then $\tilde{\beta}(L_{.j}) = 0$; conversely, there is a substitution τ such that for any $L_{.j} \in e_{.j}$ with $\tilde{\beta}(L_{.j}) = 0$, there is a $^1K_{.k} \in \tilde{p}a$ with $(K_{.k})\sigma\tau = (L_{.j})\sigma\tau$; in fact, if τ denotes the most general unifier of all the pairs $\{(K_{.k})\sigma , (L_{.j})\sigma\}$ considered just before then $\tilde{\sigma} = \sigma\tau$.

(v) $\tilde{\beta}(\tilde{\gamma}(d_{.i})) = 0$ for $d_{.i}$ from (i); for any $L_{.i} \in d_{.i}$ with $L \neq \tilde{\gamma}(d_{.i})$, $\tilde{\beta}(L_{.i}) = \beta(L_{.i})$; $\tilde{\beta} = \beta$ also on any literal from $F_1 \setminus \{d_{.i}\}$.

    If $\tilde{\beta}(L_{.j}) = 0$ for all $L_{.j} \in e_{.j}$, the clause from (iii), then we say $(\tilde{\tilde{F}},\tilde{\tilde{S}})$ **is obtained from** (F,S) **by extension followed by truncation** if in addition $\tilde{F} = \tilde{\tilde{F}}$ and $\tilde{S}$ is related to $\tilde{\tilde{S}} = (\tilde{\tilde{\alpha}},\tilde{\tilde{\beta}},\tilde{\tilde{\gamma}},\tilde{\tilde{\sigma}})$ the way described in (vi) through (viii).

(vi)   The domain $\tilde{\tilde{F}}_1$ of $\tilde{\tilde{\alpha}}$ is empty if $(c_{.k})\tilde{o} = c_{.k}$ (recall 6.5.ii for the index o) for any $c_{.k} \in \tilde{F}_1$; otherwise, $\tilde{\tilde{F}}_1 = \{c_{.k} \in \tilde{F}_1 \mid \tilde{\alpha}(c_{.k}) < \tilde{\alpha}(e'_{.1})\}$ where $e'_{.1}$ is determined by $e'_{.1} \neq (e'_{.1})\tilde{o}$ and $(c_{.k}) = (c_{.k})\tilde{o}$ for any $c_{.k}$ with $\tilde{\alpha}(c_{.k}) > \tilde{\alpha}(e'_{.1})$. $\tilde{\tilde{\alpha}}(c_{.k}) = \tilde{\alpha}(c_{.k})$ for any $c_{.k} \in \tilde{\tilde{F}}_1$.

(vii) $\tilde{\tilde{\beta}}(L_{.k}) = \tilde{\beta}(L_{.k})$ for any $L_{.k} \in c_{.k}$ with $c_{.k} \in \tilde{\tilde{F}}_1$.

    The domain $\tilde{\tilde{F}}_1'$ of $\tilde{\tilde{\gamma}}$ is $\tilde{F}_1 \setminus ((\tilde{F}_1 \setminus \tilde{\tilde{F}}_1) \cup \{e'_{.1}\})$, where $e'_{.1}$ is as in (vi); $\tilde{\tilde{\gamma}}(c_{.k}) = \tilde{\gamma}(c_{.k})$ for any $c_{.k} \in \tilde{\tilde{F}}_1'$.

(viii) $\tilde{\tilde{\sigma}} = \tilde{\sigma}$.

    We say that $(\tilde{F},\tilde{S})$ **is obtained from** (F,S) **by separation** if $F = \tilde{F}$ and S is related to $\tilde{S}$ in the way described in (i) above and (ix), (x), and (xi) below.

(ix)   For no clause $c \in F$, there is an index k such that $c_{.k} \notin F_1$, $c_{.(k-1)} \in F_1$ or $k=1$, a literal $K \in \mathbf{\ell}$, a literal $L_{.1} \in p_a \cup \{M_{.i}\}$, and a substitution τ , such that $\{K_{.k},L_{.1}\}\sigma\tau$ is complementary, where $M_{.i}$ denotes some literal in $d_{.i}$ from (i) and p_a denotes the active path in (F,S) .

(x) $\tilde{F}_1 = F_1 \cup \{e_{.j}\}$ for any $e_{.j} \notin F_1$ with $e_{.(j-1)} \in F_1$ or $j=1$; $\tilde{\alpha}(e_{.j}) = \tilde{\alpha}(d_{.i})+1$, and $\tilde{\alpha}(c_{.k}) = \alpha(c_{.k})$ for any $c_{.k} \in F_1$.

(xi)   For any $L_{.j} \in e_{.j}$, $\tilde{\beta}(L_{.j}) = 1$; for any $K_{.k} \in c_{.k}$ with $c_{.k} \in F_1$, $\tilde{\beta}(K_{.k}) = 0$. The domain $\tilde{F}_1'$ of $\tilde{\gamma}$ is empty. $\tilde{\sigma} = \varepsilon$ (the empty substitution).

Any structure S_0 with $F_1 = \emptyset$ is called **terminal** , for any matrix F . Likewise, a structure S_1 is called **initial** if F_1 contains a single clause $c_{.1}$ with $\beta(L_{.1}) = 1$ for all its literals $L_{.1}$, and if for its substitution $\sigma_1 = \varepsilon$ holds. If S_0 is a terminal structure with its substitution $\sigma_0 = \varepsilon$, and if S_1 is an initial structure, then we say that (F,S_1) **is obtained from** (F,S_0) **by an initial step** .

The transition from (F,S) to $(F,\tilde{S})$ by an initial step, by extension, by extension followed by truncation, or by separation is called a **connection inference** , in symbols $(F,S) \vdash_c (F,\tilde{S})$. If no confusion may arise, simply $\vdash$ will be used rather than $\vdash_c$. A sequence of connection inferences $(F,S_1) \vdash (F,S_2) \vdash \ldots \vdash (F,S_n)$, $n>1$, is called a **connection deduction of** (F,S_n) **from** (F,S_1) . A connection deduction of the form $(F,S_0) \vdash (F,S_1) \vdash^+ (F,S_n)$ or of the form $(\{\emptyset\},S_0)$ is called a **connection proof of** F , if S_0 is a terminal structure with a substitution $\sigma_0 = \varepsilon$, S_1 is an initial and S_n a terminal structure. F is called **deducible** or **derivable** , in symbols $\vdash F$, if there is a connection proof of F . This completes the definition of the **connection calculus** . $\square$

The figures 1 and 2 show connection proofs of E2 and E3, respectively, with the same conventions as those mentioned after (II.4.3), and the reader is encouraged to match the precise definitions with these illustrated instances.

This completes the formalization of the connection method and we are left to provide its justification.

6.7.T. For any normal form formula F , $\vdash F$ iff F has a complementary compound instance.

Proof. "Only-if" case. In this case we assume that there is a connection proof of F of the form $(F,S_0) \vdash (F,S_1) \vdash \ldots \vdash (F,S_n)$ with $n>1$. Let μ denote the largest index occurring in any S_i, $1<i<n$. Let σ_n denote the substitution in S_n . Let τ denote a substitution such that for $\sigma = \sigma_n\tau$ the formula $(F_{.1} \vee \ldots \vee F_{.\mu})\sigma$ is a compound instance of F .

Because of our analogue treatment of the ground level in (II.4.3) and the first-order level in (6.6) it is now obvious (and formally proved by a straightforward induction on n) that the deduction of F may be simulated by a ground level deduction of $(F_{.1} \lor \dots \lor F_{.\mu})\sigma$ with corresponding inferences. Note that it may happen that the latter deduction has fewer steps than the former one since a comparison of (II.4.3.iv) and (6.6.iv) shows that $\tilde{\beta}$ might have the value 0 for less literals in $e_{.j}$ on the first-order level than on the ground level which leaves extra subgoals to be solved on the first-order level. Besides this difference and the difference in the substitutions which, of course, are not present on the ground level, both deductions are even identical. By (II.5.4), then, $(F_{.1} \lor \dots \lor F_{.\mu})\sigma$ is complementary.

"If" case. In this case, we may assume a complementary compound instance of the form $(F_{.1} \lor \dots \lor F_{.\mu})\sigma$ of F , hence, by (II.5.4) a ground level deduction of it, which, for the same reason as before, again may be simulated by a corresponding first-order level deduction of F^μ , this time with exactly the same number of inferences. The straightforward inductions, here again on n , are left to the reader (see E16 in section 8). □

6.8.C. The connection calculus is complete and consistent.

Proof. This is an immediate consequence of (6.7) together with (3.13). □

6.9.L. The inference relation ⊢ in the connection calculus in general is not confluent.

Proof. Consider the matrix $\begin{smallmatrix} Px \\ \neg Py \end{smallmatrix}$ $\neg Pa$ Qa $\neg Qa$. If the initial structure S_1 is chosen such that $\alpha_1(\{Px, \neg Py\}) = 1$ then obviously an infinite deduction may be generated which never may be terminated with a terminal structure. However, if the initial structure S_1' is chosen such that $\alpha_1(\{Qa\}) = 1$ then a proof is obtained in one further step. Hence, confluency does not hold. □

6.10.L. The inference relation $\vdash$ in the connection calculus in general is not bounded.

Proof. Consider S_1 as in the previous proof.

7.   ALGORITHMIC ASPECTS

The connection calculus, as introduced in the previous section, provides only the frame for the development of proof procedures for first-order logic since such a procedure, of course, is expected to be deterministic while for the connection calculus at each step in the search for a deduction there may be several choices how to proceed. In the present section we shall therefore describe one of the simplest such deterministic procedures which will be called CP_1^1 . As before, its application will be restricted to formulas in normal form. Additionally, we may assume the formulas to contain an existential quantifier since otherwise they may be regarded as propositional formulas (recall the discussion at the beginning of section II.1) for which CP_1^O from (II.6.12) applies.

Apparently, the main issue in the development of CP_1^1 is the appropriate treatment of the choices just mentioned before. Therefore let us first consider where such choices may arise.

First, there are as many different initial steps as there are clauses in the given formula. Let us call this the **first kind of choice** for the present discussion.

In the definition of extension in (6.6), $\tilde{\gamma}(d_{.i})$ denotes any literal L in $d_{.i}$ such that $\beta(L) = 1$ (see 6.6.ii). Hence, there may be more than one literals to be selected, a further kind of choice. This one, however, differs from the previousone in the following aspect. The first kind of choice is **relevant** in the sense that an inappropriate choice may fail to eventually lead to a proof even if one exists. The proof of(6.9) mentioned an example for this possibility. In se, this senthe new kind of choice of the literal here in fact is irrelevant because all the literals of a selected clause will eventually be processed (i.e. their value under β changed to zero) in a successfull proof, independently of the sequence which this happens (see exercise E18 in section 8). Therefore, we shall ignore in the following this kind of choice. We should, however, keep in mind that this ignorance might affect efficiency, as the following example demonstrates. Starting with Pb in the matrix

$$
\begin{array}{cc}
 & \neg Pa \\
Px & \\
 & Qx \\
Pb & \\
 & \neg Qy
\end{array}
$$

would immediately signal a failure while this is not the case when starting with Px .

The next kind of choice occurs in the selection of $e_{.j}$ as described in (6.6.iii), which will be called the **second** kind of choice. The **third** kind of choice derives from the fact that (6.6.iv) may hold for more than one selected $\tilde{\sigma}$ as the following trivial example demonstrates. Both,

$$
{}^1\!\!\!\underset{\uparrow}{Pa} \quad \begin{array}{c} Px \\ Py \end{array} \quad \vdash \quad --{}^1Pa-- \quad \begin{array}{c} \overset{\frown}{Px.} \\ \underset{\uparrow}{Py} \end{array} \quad \{x\backslash a\} \qquad \text{and}
$$

$$
{}^1\!\!\!\underset{\uparrow}{Pa} \quad \begin{array}{c} Px \\ Py \end{array} \quad \vdash \quad --{}^1Pa-- \quad \begin{array}{c} Px. \\ \underset{\uparrow}{Py.} \end{array} \quad \{x\backslash a, y\backslash a\} \ ,
$$

are correct extensions. Thus to a certain degree there is a choice w.r.t. the number of literals left unsolved (i.e. having the value 1 under $\tilde{\beta}$).

The final kind of choice is given in (6.6.x) defining the selected clause for continuation in a separation step. This kind, however, may be subsumed under the first kind of choice because of the following lemma.

7.1.L. For any connection proof of F there is a connection proof of F without separations and with no more deduction steps.

Proof. Let $(F,S_0) \vdash \ldots \vdash (F,S_{k-1}) \vdash (F,S_k) \vdash \ldots \vdash (F,S_n)$ denote the connection proof in question. We are done if none of its steps is a separation. Otherwise, assume that k is the smallest index such that $(F,S_k) \vdash \ldots \vdash (F,S_n)$ does not contain a separation step, i.e. $(F,S_{k-1}) \vdash (F,S_k)$ must be a separation step. It is now easy to see that $(F,S_0) \vdash (F,S_k) \vdash \ldots \vdash (F,S_n)$ may be changed to a correct proof of F simply by changing the involved indices appropriately, which induction proof is left to the reader as an exercise (see E17 in section 8). $\Box$

So, essentially the envisaged proof procedure CP_1^1 must deal with 3 kinds of choices, the first kind of which occurs once at the initial step while the other two occur again and again in the search for a proof. Such a phenomenon is well familiar in the field of intellectics, and it certainly would be helpful for the reader if he had some acquaintance with the general techniques and notions in this context, such as **search-space, and/or trees, breadth-first** or **depth-first search** , **back-tracking** , etc. (see $[\text{Nil}]$ for a good introduction). Here, we must confine ourselves with the following few remarks.

In our case, for any formula F the search space contains the unique node labeled by (F,S_0) where S_0 is the terminal structure with which we start off. If F has n clauses then any non-trivial deduction starts with one out of n possible initial steps, according to the first kind of choice. This may be illustrated in the form of a tree as in figure 3 where each node represents a structured matrix which may be derived from (F,S_0) .

Say, we are looking for the proof represented by nodes of the form Ⓧ . There are two possible extremes to search for this proof. One is to process **all** the successor nodes of (F,S_0) , and then **all** their successor nodes, and so on which is **breadth-first search** . The other is, first to process one branch, say the one illustrated by the boxes $\Box$, which is **depth-first search** . With both methods we face serious problems. The first one tends to quickly exhaust the computational resources while the second one might exhaust the resources even on a single branch since we know that there are branches with infinite length (see the example in the proof of 6.9.). Hence, in our case we need something smarter. For CP_1^1 it will be a simple combination of both kinds of search.

Recall that any proof will require a certain number of copies of F which has been encoded by our index. Hence we may first try whether a proof is possible with one copy, then with two, three, and so on. CP_1^1 will do this in an exhaustive way.

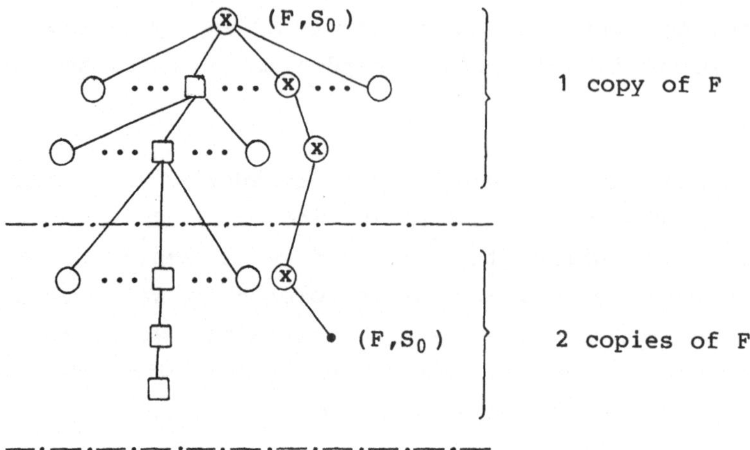

Figure 3. The search-tree for CP_1^1

Therefore, in a global view with respect to copies it will proceed in a breadth-first manner. This is indicated in the picture with the two horizontal lines. Each such line is not crossed before all nodes above it have been processed.

On the other hand, the nodes between two such lines are processed in a depth-first way. As soon as a node has been processed which lies immediately above the lower one of the two, the information necessary to continue the search on this branch will be stored (on the stack NEXTi1 in algorithm 7.2. below), to be resumed not before all other nodes above this line have been processed. For all other nodes between such two lines, one out of all alternative successors is selected, while the others are put aside for later consideration (on stacks ALTj, one for each kind of choices, i.e. j=1,2,3).

It is obvious, that such a simple arrangement guarantees that the proof will eventually be detected, provided that it exists and that the resources are not exhausted before a successful termination. But we will also see that this arrangement still is much too redundant for the more sophisticated applications for which we will discuss more selective **backtracking** facilities as those realized by the stacks mentioned above (see section IV.11).

    With these preliminaries we are now prepared for the
presentation of a proof procedure for first-order logic. It
should be regarded as an extended version of algorithm
(II.6.14), lifted to the first-order level. Therefore, all notations will be used in analogy with (II.6.14).

7.2.A. The **connection procedure** CP_1^1 for first-order logic
applicable to any formula F in normal form. WAIT, ALT1, ALT2,
ALT3, NEXTi, and NEXTi1, for $i=1,11,111,\ldots$, all denote stacks.
All other denotations follow the conventions used in this book.
STEP0. If F does not contain an existential quantifier then
apply CP_1^0 from (II.6.12).
STEP1. [**Initialization**]
$i \leftarrow 1$; $D \leftarrow F._1$; $\sigma \leftarrow \varepsilon$; $p \leftarrow \emptyset$;
WAIT, ALT1, ALT2, ALT3, NEXT1, NEXT11 $\leftarrow$ NIL ;
STEP2. [**Selection of start clause**]
select an enumeration for the clauses of D , say $c_1,\ldots,c_m$;
for $j=m,\ldots,2$ do ALT1 $\leftarrow$ push(ALT1,c_j) ; $c \leftarrow c_1$; $D \leftarrow D\backslash c$;
STEP3. [**Selection of subgoal**]
select a literal $L \in c$; $c \leftarrow c\backslash L$;
if $c \neq \emptyset$ then WAIT $\leftarrow$ push(WAIT,(c,D,σ,p)) ; $p \leftarrow p \cup \{L\}$;
STEP4. [**Selection of clause for extension**]
$k \leftarrow i+1$;
NEXTk $\leftarrow$ push(NEXTk,$(L,D,\sigma,p,$WAIT$)$) ;
select an enumeration, say $d_1,\ldots,d_m$, of all those clauses
from D such that $\{L_j,K_j\}\sigma$ is a unifiable connection,
for some $K_j \in d_j$ and some $L_j \in p$, $j=1,\ldots,m$;
if $m=0$ then goto STEP8;
for $j=m,\ldots,2$ do ALT2 $\leftarrow$ push(ALT2,$(L,d_j,D,\sigma,p,$WAIT$)$) ; $c \leftarrow d_1$;
STEP5. [**Selection of extension**]
$D \leftarrow D\backslash c$;
select an enumeration, say $e_1,\ldots,e_m$, on all those subsets
of c such that $(\{^1L\} \cup e_j)\sigma$ is unifiable with a most general unifier τ_j where $\tau_j \neq \tau_j'$ for $j \neq j'$ is required;
for $j=m,\ldots,2$ do ALT3 $\leftarrow$ push(Alt3,$(c,e_j,D,\sigma,\tau_j,p,$WAIT$)$);
STEP6. [**Extension**]
$c \leftarrow c\backslash e_1$; $\sigma \leftarrow \sigma\tau_1$; if $c \neq \emptyset$ then goto STEP3 ;
STEP7. [**Truncation**]
if WAIT = NIL then return "valid";
(WAIT,(c,D,σ,p)) $\leftarrow$ pop(WAIT) ; goto STEP3 ;

STEP8. [**Alternative extension**]
if ALT3 $\neq$ NIL then (ALT3,(c,e_1,D,σ,τ_1,p,WAIT)) $\leftarrow$ pop(ALT3) and
goto STEP6 ;
STEP9. [**Alternative clause for extension**]
if ALT2 $\neq$ NIL   then (ALT2,(L,c,D,σ,p,WAIT)) $\leftarrow$ pop(Alt2) and
goto STEP5 ;
STEP10. [**Alternative start clause**]
if ALT1 $\neq$ NIL then
$\ulcorner$(ALT1,c) $\leftarrow$ pop(ALT1) ; D $\leftarrow$ $F_{.i}\backslash$c ; σ $\leftarrow$ ε ; p $\leftarrow$ $\emptyset$; goto STEP3;
STEP11. [**Increase of index**]
if NEXTi = NIL then i $\leftarrow$ i+1 ;
(NEXTi,(L,D,σ,p,WAIT)) $\leftarrow$ pop(NEXTi) ; D $\leftarrow$ $DUF_{.i}$; goto STEP4;
END $\square$

In this algorithmic presentation α,β, and γ are encoded in an
implicit way as in (II.6.14) which is best seen with an exam-
ple. Let us consider the deduction of (E2) as shown in figure 1.

     After STEP2, we assume D = $\{c_1,c_2,c_3\}$ with
$c_1 = \{^1Px_{.1}\}$, $c_2 = \{Pfy_{.1},Qgc\}$, and $c_3 = \{^1Qy_{.1}\}$. The selection of c_1 and of its literal L = $^1Px_{.1}$ corresponds to setting $\alpha(c_1)$ = 1, β(L) = 0, and $\gamma(c_1)$ = L . In STEP4,
$d_1 = \{Pfy_{.1},Qgc\}$ is the only choice with $\tau_1 = \{x_{.1}\backslash y_{.1}\}$. The
assignment D $\leftarrow$ D$\backslash$c in STEP5 corresponds to setting $\alpha(c_2)$ = 2,
while c $\leftarrow$ c$\backslash e_1$ is the analogue for setting $\beta(Pfy)$ = 0 . At
this point, CP_1^1 continues with STEP3, executes STEP4 through
STEP7 where it successfully terminates.

     The reader may convince himself that with any other
start clause the process is similiar, hence, all the stacks are
filled with redundant information, thus illustrating that CP_1^1
certainly might be improved considerably as mentioned before
(see section IV.11). In comparison with SP , however, there
seems to be a substantial improvement due mainly to unification
used in CP_1^1 in the place of the fixed enumeration of the
terms in SP . The reader is encouraged to test this behavior
with further examples, such as (E3) from figure 2, or (II.1.9)
which is the normal form of our very first example (I.1.2) in
this book (see E19).

So, finally we have achieved the development of a moderately efficient proof procedure which is able to prove such formulas in an automatic way. Theoretically, it works for any theorem which is stated in the following corollary.

7.3.C. A formula F is valid iff CP_1^1 , with input F , terminates after a finite number of steps, returning "valid".

Proof. Since CP_1^1 is nothing else than the algorithmic realization of the connection calculus, checking all possible deductions in an exhaustive way, this result follows immediately from (6.8).   □

For practice, however, a lot of further improvement would be desirable. As an outlook for the next chapter we mention some of the possibilities.

(i)   In contrast to CP_1^0 , for simplicity we have not incorporated any reductions as defined in (II.6.11) into CP_1^1 . The point is that their inclusion is not as trivial as on the ground level since their application depends on the actual substitution σ . Hence, any change of σ may change the possible reductions which shows that reductions have to be encountered for throughout the whole proof process. Also, this potentially introduces a further kind of choice by which we choose to extend σ **in order to** be able to apply a reduction. Since such a choice may cause a failure later on this in turn would require a new stack for backtracking.

(ii) CP_1^0 itself may be improved substantially. In particular, it would be preferable to generalize it to arbitrary formulas, not necessarily in normal form, since by the transformation to normal form redundancy may be introduced. (See section IV.5).

(iii) We have mentioned already at the end of section 5 that our unification algorithm $UNIF_1$ may be improved considerably. (See section IV.9.)

(iv)   The weakest part in CP_1^1 is its stupid selection and backtracking mechanism which may be improved considerably even without giving up the criterion of completeness. (See section IV.11).

These and other possibilities for improvement will be discussed in the next chapter. But we should mention already here that this is still a wide field for further research, in particular w.r.t. (iv).

8.   EXERCISES

(E1)   According to (1.3) a quantified matrix in normal form represents a class of formulas in normal form. Generalize this notion of a quantified matrix such that any formula is represented in a natural way by some quantified matrix.

Hints: If a formula $\tilde{F}$ is represented by such a quantified matrix F , and if $\tilde{F}'$ is the result of deleting all quantifiers in $\tilde{F}$, and F' the result of deleting all sets of variables and sets of constants representing quantifiers from F then $\tilde{F}'$ is represented by F' in the sense of (I.1.3). As with the formulas, prefixes have to be allowed to label any submatrices as in $\{^{\{c\}}\{Pc\} \cup {}^{\{x\}}\{Pfx\} , {}^{\{y\}}\{^1Py\}\}$ which represents the formula (F1) from section 1. Those prefixes are lists of alternating sets of variables and sets of constants such as $\{c_1,\ldots,c_{n_1}\}\{x_1,\ldots,x_{n_2}\}\{b_1,\ldots,b_{n_3}\}$ ... . Giving a number of examples will be helpful for providing the final inductive definition.

(E2)   Give the details of the proof for (1.5).

(E3)   As an alternative to (2.2), define τ therein in a set-theoretic way as in (II.2.2) for the quantified matrices from (E1).

(E4)   Consider the theorem, known from plane geometry, that any isosceles triangle has two equal angles. Introduce predicates and give a formula F with them that formalizes this statement. After deleting the universal quantifiers from F, define an interpretation which relates the resulting formula to a particular isosceles triangle, and calculate its truth value. Do the same for other theorems from number theory, group theory, etc.

(E5)   Formulate and prove the deduction theorem (see II.2.5) for first-order logic.

(E6)   With the hints in the paragraph preceding (3.7) inductively define an enumeration of **T** , the set of terms.

(E7)   Apply the standard connection procedure from (3.7)
with the enumeration of **T** from (E6) to several examples such
as those in the figures 1 and 2 for which the test in STEP1
should be carried out with CP_1^0 from (II.6.12).

(E8)   For several formulas apply (4.1) transforming them
into normal form.

(E9)   Give the proof for (4.2).

(E10)   Complete the proof of the only-if case of the
lemma (4.3).

(E11)   Give the proof for (4.4) following the hints in the
text after (4.4).

(E12)   Prove that $(E\sigma)\tau = E(\sigma\tau)$.

(E13)   For the composition of substitions prove the following
two properties:
(i) $\varepsilon\sigma = \sigma\varepsilon = \sigma$, i.e. ε is an identity element.
(ii) $(\rho\sigma)\tau = \rho(\tau\sigma)$, i.e. composition is associative. Hence,
the substitutions form an algebraic system known as a **monoid** .
Give an example for which $\sigma\tau \neq \tau\sigma$.

(E14)   Apply $UNIF_1$ to the pair of terms
$\{f(x,f(g(z),f(u,y)))$, $f(g(y),f(y,f(z,g(u))))\}$.

(E15)   Generalize $UNIF_1$ to sets of expressions with arbitrarily many elements and prove the corresponding unification
theorem.

(E16)   Give the details of the inductions left out in the
proof of (6.7).

(E17)   Complete the proof of (7.1) as indicated there.

(E18)   Prove that it is irrelevant for the result of CP_1^1 which
literal is selected in STEP2 of (7.2).

(E19)   Apply CP_1^1 to some valid formulas such as (II.1.9) and
the matrix in figure 2.

9.   BIBLIOGRAPHICAL AND HISTORICAL REMARKS

For any bibliographical or historical details on first-order
logic the reader is referred to standard textbooks of mathematical logic (such as [He1]). Our way of proving the Skolem-
Herbrand-Gödel theorem essentially is the same as the standard
way of proving the consistency and completeness of first-order
formal systems (if one does not follow Henkin's proof). This
standard proof appears in the literature in a number of variants. For instance, [Sc4] and [Lo4] contain such proofs. In
comparison with both of these proofs, however, our proof yields
a more general result, since the standard procedure SP admits
any complementary formula as an axiom in STEP1 of (3.7). It
seems that it is only Herbrand himself who took an approach of
the same generality [Her]. In particular, the usual form of
Herbrand's theorem for ATP is our **special** case (3.13), further restricted to formulas in normal form. (3.13) itself has
been recently proved in a different way, and used by Andrews in
[An2]. Our proof was first given in the sections 2 and 3 of
[Bi5].

The convenience of the normal form for mechanical processing was first noted in [DaP].

Unification was first considered by Herbrand in section 2.4 in chapter V of his thesis [Her] and, 3 decades later,
by Prawitz in [Pr1]. It become well-known after Robinson in
[Ro1] brought it into an elegant algorithmic form for use within his resolution principle. Our presentation follows very
closely the excellent treatment in [Ro3] which contains a
slightly improved version of unification obtained independently
by Robinson [Ro3] and by Huet [Hu1].

The connection calculus explicitly has not been published before; if we take for granted the well-known lifting
technique, however, it is implicitly contained in [B11]. Its
basic ideas already appear in [BiS]. More recently, Andrews has
taken a similar approach in [An1], centered around the concept
of **general matings** [An2]. Its relationship with the
connection method has been explained in [B14].

Chapter IV

Variants and improvements

For one and a half decades the field of ATP has been dominated by **resolution** . Not mentioning resolution in the first three out of five chapters, as we did in this book, could therefore be misinterpreted as a provocation. The real reason for this kind of treatment, however, is the fact that with the connection method at hand resolution may be explained in an elegant way, which is carried out in the first section of the present chapter. It even turns out in section 2 that a certain linear refinement of resolution differs from the connection method in representational details only. Hence, the contents of the previous chapters is actually not so far from resolution as it might have appeared.

Nevertheless, the approach to ATP via the connection method has provided an insight into the nature of theorem proving to an extent which was never achieved before within resolution theory. One of the justifications for this claim can be found in the sections 4 through 6 where different refinements of resolution are unified in a combined improvement of the connection method, which turns out to be uniformly better than the known resolution refinements, and in particular applies to arbitrary formulas, not only those in normal form. This part is preceded by a discussion of the problem of comparing the performance of different proof procedures in section 3.

So far, these variants and improvements are concerned with the propositional features of proof procedures only. In the remaining sections of this chapter we develop improvements based on first-order, that is, non-propositional features. This includes the discussion of **natural deduction systems** for first-order logic and their relation with the connection method. Based on such a natural deduction system an alternative for skolemization and improved versions of unifications are provided, in particular one version which includes splitting by need. The chapter is concluded with an informal description of a connection procedure CP^1 which incorporates all these and further improvements, and thus summarizes all our major results.

For the more advanced material in this chapter, the reader is expected to have reached the level of insight into theorem proving as provided by the previous chapters. This allows a somewhat more concise way of presentation, which is necessary to meet the given space-limitations and to avoid burying the main ideas under a mess of details.

1.   RESOLUTION

The connection calculus is but one among several other logical calculi. In contrast to all others, however, it enjoys the unique feature that the formula to be proved is never changed throughout the whole proof. Rather the relevant information, gathered in the course of a proof, is accumulated within an additional structure in a way which is most economic from a computational point of view.

Other logical calculi are more or less closely related to our natural way of reasoning, and thus are less appropriate for computational purposes. One such natural rule of reasoning is the well-known **modus ponens** which has been mentioned already in chapter I : Given F and $F{\rightarrow}G$, we may infer G . It has been generalized to the so-called **cut rule** : Given $F{\vee}E$ and $\neg F{\vee}G$, we may infer $E{\vee}G$, for any formulas $E,F,$ and G among which E or G might be empty. Note that in the special case where E is in fact empty, the cut rule is identical with modus ponens (remember the conventions from II.1.3).

Now, **resolution** is closely related to this cut rule. On the ground level, i.e. in propositional logic, it is even identical with the cut rule provided F is restricted to literals. On the general level, i.e. in first-order logic, the relation is a little more complicated. Roughly speaking, from $L{\vee}E$ and $\neg L'{\vee}G$ we may infer $E'{\vee}G'$ by resolution where L and L' are unifiable literals with a most general unifier σ, for which $E\sigma = E'$ and $G\sigma = G'$.

Despite this close relationship, the usage of the cut rule and of resolution is opposite in the sense that the cut rule is used in generative type calculi while the resolution calculus - like the connection calculus - is of the recognition type (see II.5.2. for these notions). We will later see that there is an even closer relationship between resolution and the connection calculus in comparison with which the relationship with the cut rule appears to be superficial. In particular, Herbrand's theorem (III.3.13) will serve again as the key tool for establishing the resolution calculus as it did for the connection calculus.

At this point, we meet the conflict which has already been mentioned in the preface and in section II.1 (before 1.4) in this book, namely the conflict between our way of establishing the validity of a formula F in an **affirmative** manner and the more popular way of doing the same by **refutation** , i.e. by showing that the negation $\neg F$ is contradictory. One of the potential historical reasons for the prevailing preference for refutation procedures lies in the form of the cut rule which would have to be applied to a formula of the form $D \wedge (F \vee E) \wedge (\neg F \vee G)$ resulting in $D \wedge (F \vee E) \wedge (\neg F \vee G) \wedge (E \vee G)$. Obviously, the appropriate normal form for such formulas is the **conjunctive** one. However, the natural normal form of mathematical statements rather is the **disjunctive** one since these tend to be of the form $H_1 \wedge \ldots \wedge H_n \rightarrow G$ (cf. the formula I.1.2) which is equivalent with $\neg H_1 \vee \ldots \vee \neg H_n \vee G$, clearly a formula of a disjunctive nature. By negating such a formula, we obtain $H_1 \wedge \ldots \wedge H_n \wedge \neg G$ which is of a conjunctive nature right away, and thus in a form appropriate for the cut rule, without much further manipulation like transformation to the opposite normal form. Therefore people quite naturally tended to think in terms of negated formulas since the cut rule has played a dominant role in mathematical logic for decades.

Note, however, that this is a purely psychological explanation. There is **no** single mathematical argument in favour of refutations (vs. affirmations). In particular, there is, of course, also an "affirmative cut rule", known as **consensus rule** [DuN], which from $D \vee (F \wedge E) \vee (\neg F \wedge G)$ infers $D \vee (F \wedge E) \vee (\neg F \wedge G) \vee (E \wedge G)$, thus dealing right away with formulas of the natural disjunctive nature. Thus resolution could as well be established as an affirmative calculus. Of course, we are not going to commit such a heresy. Rather our set-theoretical representation of formulas allows to completely ignore this issue for the following reason.

Resolution is defined for formulas in normal form. Set-theoretically these are represented by quantified matrices of the form $\{c_1,\ldots,c_m\}$ $\{x_1,\ldots,x_n\}$ F_o where F_o is a set of clauses, i.e. of sets of literals (recall III.1.1). In the positive representation, which we prefer in this book, such a matrix represents a formula $\forall c_1\ldots c_m \exists x_1\ldots x_n \tilde{F}_o$, where $\tilde{F}_o$ is in disjunctive normal form (recall III.1.3). In view of the literature on resolution, however, the reader now has to think in terms of the negative representation in which such a matrix represents a formula $\exists c_1\ldots c_m \forall x_1\ldots x_n \tilde{F}_0$ where $\tilde{F}_0$ is in conjunctive normal form. Hence, by working with ma-trices, which are the same for both views (III.1.5), rather than with formulas we may avoid any conflict since everyone may think of his own preferred interpretation (see E1 in section 12). This leads us to the following definition.

1.1.D. For any literal, clause or matrix C , C' is called a **variant of** C if there exists a substitution $\rho = \{x_1\backslash y_1,\ldots, x_n\backslash y_n\}$ such that $C = C'\rho$, where the y_i all are vari-ables, for $i = 1,\ldots,n$, and $n \geqslant 0$.

For any (quantifier-free, first-order) matrix F in normal form and any clause c , we say $F \cup \{c\}$ **is obtained from F by a resolution inference** or simply **by resolution** , in symbols $F \vdash_r F \cup \{c\}$, if there exist clauses c_i, c_i', d_i, i=0,1 , a literal L and a substitution σ , satisfying the following properties.

(r1) $c_0, c_1 \in F$, called the **parent clauses** ;

(r2) c_i' is a variant of c_i , i=0,1 ;

(r3) c_0' and c_1' have no variables in common;

(r4) $d_i \subseteq c_i'$, i=0,1 ;

(r5) $d_0 \cup {}^1 d_1 = d_0 \cup \{{}^1 K \mid K \in d_1\}$ is unifiable, with most ge-neral unifier σ ;

(r6) $c = ((c_0'\backslash d_0) \cup (c_1'\backslash d_1))\sigma$, called the **resolvent** ;

(r7)   F does not contain a variant of c .

Whenever no confusion may arise, we simply use $\vdash$ instead of $\vdash_r$.

A sequence of resolution inferences $F_1 \vdash \ldots \vdash F_n$, $n \geqslant 1$, is called a **resolution deduction of** F_n **from** F_1 . Such a deduction is called a **resolution proof of** F_1 , if the empty clause $\emptyset$ is contained in F_n . F is called **deducible** or **derivable** , in symbols $\vdash$ F , if there is a resolution proof of F . $\square$

Apparently, variants of clauses are obtained simply by substituting variables for variables; for instance, $\{Puy,Qw\}$ is a variant of $\{Pxy,Qz\}$. Let us then consider an example of a resolution inference, viz.

$$\begin{array}{c} Pfy \\ Qgc \end{array} \quad {}^1Px \quad {}^1Qy \quad \vdash \quad \begin{array}{c} Pfy \\ Qgc \end{array} \quad {}^1Px \quad {}^1Qy \quad Qgc$$

Here, $c_0 = c_0' = \{Pfy,Qgc\}$ and $c_1 = c_1' = \{{}^1Px\}$. Further, $d_0 = \{Pfy\}$ and $d_1 = \{{}^1Px\}$, hence $d_0 \cup {}^1d_1 = \{Pfy,Px\}$ with $\sigma = \{x\backslash fy\}$. With the following inference, we even obtain a proof of the initial matrix.

$$\begin{array}{c} Pfy \\ Qgc \end{array} \quad {}^1Px \quad {}^1Qy \quad Qgc \quad \vdash \quad \begin{array}{c} Pfy \\ Qgc \end{array} \quad {}^1Py \quad {}^1Qy \quad Qgc \quad \emptyset$$

Here, $c_0 = c_0' = d_0 = \{Qy\}$ and $c_1 = c_1' = d_1 = \{Qgc\}$, hence $d_0 \cup {}^1d_1 = \{{}^1Qy,{}^1Qgc\}$ with $\sigma = \{y\backslash gc\}$.

It is awkward to rephrase all the clauses from the left side of a resolution inference again on its right side in the display of a deduction. Therefore, in practice, only the parent clauses and the resolvent of an inference are displayed such that the previous proof would be displayed in the form, as shown in figure 1 . Let us call this the **non-linear** format to be distinguished from the **linear** one considered before. For an appropriate assessment of resolution w.r.t. its computational qualities however, it is important to keep in mind that the linear format is more adequate since it displays the whole matrix which has to be taken into consideration (and thus stored in the computer memory) at any step of the deduction.

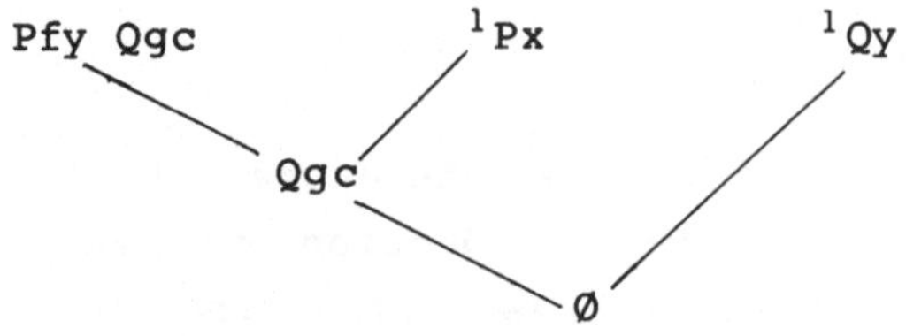

Figure 1. A resolution proof displayed in the non-linear
           format

Therefore we shall make use of both kinds of representations,
often even at the same time.

        In the non-linear format the previous deduction has
the form of a tree. This actually is not the case in general,
which is demonstrated with the following resolution proof.

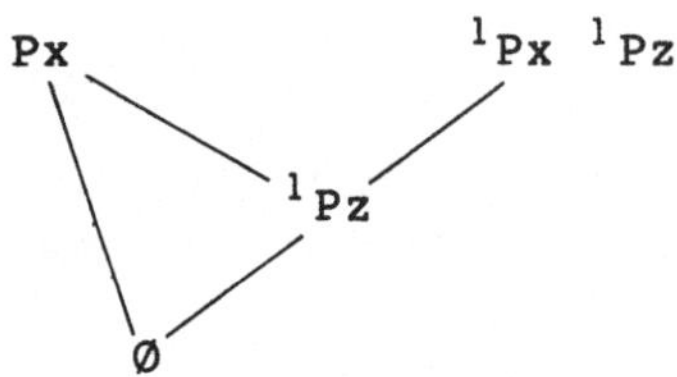

However, it may be regarded as a binary tree from which identical subtrees (like the Px here) are displayed only once.
With this interpretation it makes sense to use the tree terminology like branch, leave, etc. It also makes sense to speak
of the **deduction of the clause** at the root of such a deduction tree. Note that from the initial matrix in the last
example we could have derived the empty clause even in a
single step, similarly as in the following proof.

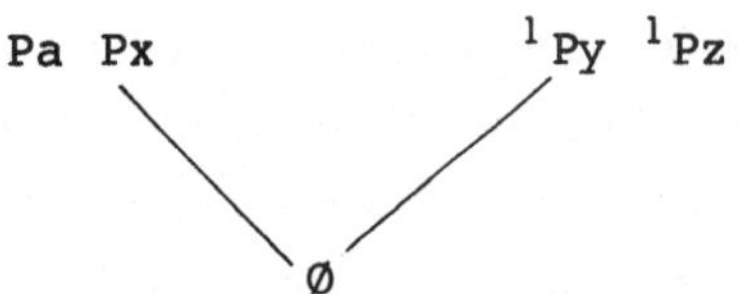

Here, $d_0 \cup {}^1 d_1 = \{Pa, Px, Py, Pz\}$ with $\sigma = \{x \backslash a, y \backslash a, z \backslash a\}$. In practice, an inference of this kind often is separated into 3 parts, the unification of $\{Pa, Px\}$ called **factoring** with the **factor** $\{Pa\}$, the factoring of $\{\neg Py, \neg Pz\}$ to yield the factor $\{\neg Py\}$, and, finally, the resolution inference restricted to singletons d_0 and d_1 .

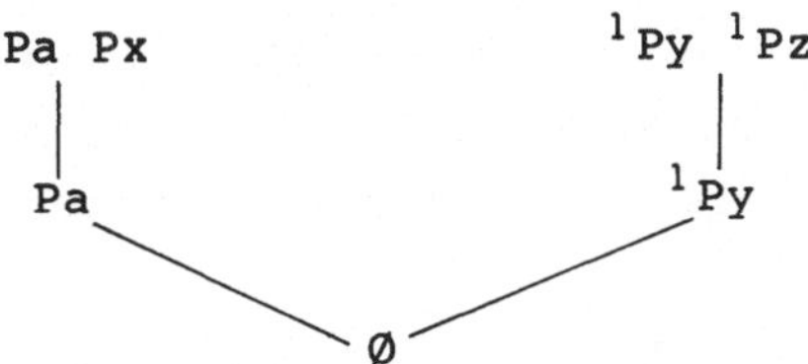

The reader is encouraged to study further examples (see E2 in section 12), in particular those considered for the connection calculus. For instance, the comparsion of the resolution proof in figure 1 above with the connection proof in figure 1 of section (III.6) of the same matrix suggests that a resolution step corresponds to establishing one (or more) connections with the connection method. The completeness and consistency proof for resolution, which we are now going to discuss, will in fact also clarify this correspondence between these two methods.

1.2.T. [**Completeness of resolution**] If F is a valid formula in normal form then there exists a resolution proof of the matrix of F .

Proof. By (III.3.13), the validity of F implies the existence of a complementary compound instance E of F . In other words, if F_0 denotes the matrix of F , there are, for some $n > 0$, $n+1$ matrices $F_0, \ldots, F_n$ which are variants of F_0 with pairwise no variables in common, and a substitution σ, such that $E = G\sigma$ for $G = F_0 \cup \ldots \cup F_n$ is complementary. In particular, this means that the set of all propositional connections in E is spanning for E , and is of the form $U\sigma$ where U is a set of connections in G . With $D = \emptyset$ we may assume that $G = F_0 \cup F_1 \cup \ldots \cup F_n \cup D$. Further let $E' = E$, and $\{L_1, \ldots, L_m\}$ denote the set of all unnegated literals in the connections of $U\sigma$.

We shall now prove by induction on m that if $U\sigma$ is
spanning for a subset $E' \subseteq E$, hence also for E , and contains
all propositional connections of the form $\{L_i, {}^1L_i\}$,
i=1,...,m , in E' then there is a resolution proof of $F_0 \cup D$.
Because of the previous initializations this then provides the
proof for the theorem.

If m = 0 , which means $U\sigma = \emptyset$, then there must be
no paths through E since $U\sigma$ is spanning for E ; hence,
$\emptyset \in E$, and thus also $\emptyset \in G$, which in turn implies $\emptyset \in F_0 \cup D$.
In this case, then, $F_0 \cup D$ is a trivial resolution proof of
itself.

To prove the induction step, we show that if $U\sigma$ is
spanning for $E' \subseteq E$, hence also for E , containing all propositional connections of the form $\{L_i, {}^1L_i\}$, i=1,...,m-1,
from E' and if there is no clause in E' containing both L_m
and ${}^1L_m$, then there is a resolution proof of $F_0 \cup D$. We
prove this by induction on the number k of pairs $\{L_m, {}^1L_m\}$
in $U\sigma$.

From (II.6.6) we already know that tautologies may be
deleted. In the present case, however, a slightly more general
result, given below in (1.3), has to be applied to be able to
delete any clauses form E' containing both L_m and ${}^1L_m$,
without affecting any of our present asumptions.

The base case with k=0 , then, obviously is settled by
the hypothesis for the induction on m . Thus we may now assume
k>0 .

Consider any propositional connection u of the form
$\{{}^0L_m, {}^1L_m\}$ from $U\sigma$. We have ${}^iL_m \in c_i'\sigma$ for some
$c_i' \in G$, for i=0,1 and $c_0' \neq c_1'$. If $c_i' \in F_{j_i}$ with
$0 < j_i \leqslant n$ then let c_i denote the corresponding variant clause
in F_0 , i=0,1 . Let $d_i = \{K \mid K \in c_i',\ K\sigma = {}^iL_m\}$, i=0,1 .
Of course, $d_0 \cup {}^1d_1$ is unifiable with some most general unifier τ such that for some substitution ρ we have $\sigma = \tau\rho$.
Finally, let $c = ((c_0' \diagdown d_0) \cup (c_1' \diagdown d_1))\tau$. By construction it is
obvious from (1.1) that c is a correct resolvent with the
parent clauses $c_i \in F_0 \cup D$, i=0,1 . Note that this is true even
for the case where c_0' and c_1' might contain common variables
since then we could use an appropriate different variant c_1''
(rather than c_1') with no variables in common with c_0' , and
an appropriate τ' such that $((c_0' \diagdown d_0) \cup (c_1'' \diagdown d_1))\tau' = c$.

Let $V = \{\{K_0^b, K_1^c\} \mid \{K_0^b, K_1^{ci}\} \in U$, $i \in \{0,1\}\}$, where the positions of the literals are indicated in a natural way by the names of the clauses in which they occur (cf. section III.1). Further let $\tilde{U} = (U \smallsetminus \{u\}) \cup V$, $\tilde{D} = D \cup \{c\}$, $\tilde{G} = F_0 \cup ... \cup F_n \cup \tilde{D}$, $\tilde{E} = \tilde{G}\sigma$, and $\tilde{E}' = E' \cup \{c\sigma\}$. Note that, by the definition of d_i above and because of the previous elimination of tautologies, $c\sigma$ does not contain L_m or ^1L_m . This, in particular implies that there are $k-1$ connections of the form $\{L_m, {}^1L_m\}$ in $\tilde{U}$ .Therefore, we shall have completed the whole proof, once we have shown that all present assumptions on U and E' also hold for $\tilde{U}$ and $\tilde{E}'$; since, by the hypothesis of the induction on k , we then have a resolution proof of $F_0 \cup \tilde{D}$ which, together with the previous resolution inference, gives a proof of $F_0 \cup D$ as requested. Hence, we are now going to prove these assumptions.

We see immediately, that no clause in $\tilde{E}'$ contains both L_m and ^1L_m since this holds for E', and $c\sigma$ does not contain any of these literals as we have just seen. It is also clear by the definition of $\tilde{U}$ and $\tilde{E}'$ that $\tilde{U}\sigma$ contains all propositional connections of the form $\{L_j, {}^1L_j\}$, $j=1,...,m-1$, based on the assumption that this is true for U and E' . Hence, the only assumption left to be established is that $\tilde{U}\sigma$ is spanning for $\tilde{E}'$, provided that this is true for $U\sigma$ and E' , which will now be settled.

If $c=\emptyset$ then $\tilde{U}\sigma$ is trivially spanning for $\tilde{E}'$ since there is no path through $\tilde{E}'$ in this case (in which the desired resolution proof of $F_0 \cup D$ is actually completed). Hence, let $c \neq \emptyset$. Further, let p' be any path through $\tilde{E}'$, let $K^c = p' \cap (c\sigma)$, $p = p' \smallsetminus \{K^c\}$, and $p'' = p \smallsetminus (p \cap (c_0{}'\sigma \cup c_1{}'\sigma))$. Without restricting generality, we may assume $K \in c_0{}'\sigma$ and $L_m \in c_0{}'\sigma$ by using appropriate notation (recall that we had $\sigma = \tau\rho$ above); hence, we may distinguish the following two cases (i) and (ii).

(i) $\{L_m^{c_0}, {}^1L_m^{c_1}\} \subseteq p'$ (see figure 2). Since $p'' \cup \{K^{c_0}, {}^1L_m^{c_1}\}$ is a path through E' , and thus contains a connection from $U\sigma$ by assumption, the same must be true for p' w.r.t. $\tilde{U}\sigma$, because it contains just one more literal, viz. $L_m^{c_0}$, and K^c instead of K^{c_0} but both paired with the same literals ^1K in $\tilde{U}\sigma$.

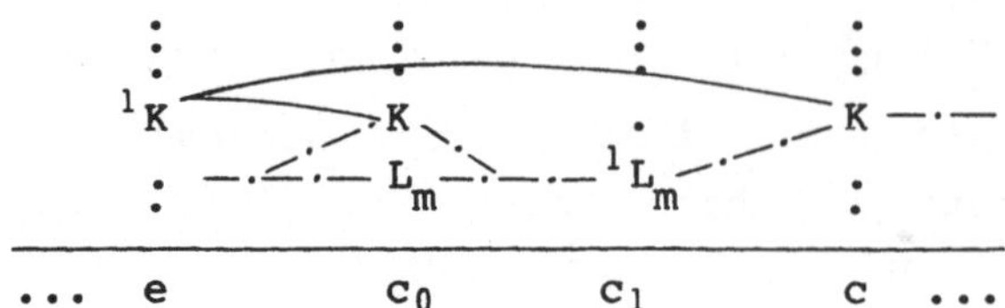

Figure 2. The case $\{L_m^{c_0}, {}^1L_m^{c_1}\} \subseteq p'$

(ii) $\{L_m^{c_0}, {}^1L_m^{c_1}\} \not\subseteq p'$. In this case, by definition of $\tilde{U}\sigma$, each connection from $U\sigma$ contained in p - and there is at least one by assumption - is also contained in   p' = p∪{K^c} and in $\tilde{U}\sigma$.

Thus, in any case p' contains a connection from $\tilde{U}\sigma$, for any path p' through $\tilde{E}'$ wich means that $\tilde{U}\sigma$ is spanning for $\tilde{E}'$ (and then also for $\tilde{E}$).   □

1.3.L. If, for any matrix F in normal form and for any set U of propositional connections from F , a clause c∈F contains L and ^{1}L for some literal L , and for all clauses d and e in F   with   d≠e , $\{L^c,{}^1L^d\} \in U$ and $\{{}^1L^c,L^e\} \in U$ implies $\{L^e,{}^1L^d\} \in U$ then U is spanning for F iff U∖V is spanning for F∖{c} where $V = \{\{K^c,{}^1K^b\} \in U \,|\, b \in F\}$.

Proof. The proof is the same as the one for (II.6.6) except that the connections taken into consideration have to be restricted to those in U or in U∖V , thus substituting "complementary" by "spanning". The details are left to the reader as an exercise.   □

Note that the condition in (1.3) which states some kind of a transitivity property must not be weakened since otherwise the lemma might not be true as the following example demonstrates:

$$K \qquad \begin{matrix} K \\ {}^1K \end{matrix} \qquad {}^1K$$

In reviewing now the whole completeness proof for resolution given above, the reader, who is familiar with the usual completeness proof, will notice that our proof does not make use of the so-called **lifting lemma** . Rather it consists in a straightforward inductive process in the course of which the elements of a spanning set of connections, provided by our version of Herbrands theorem, are "resolved away" one by one, including those generated in this process. Again, it is our basic notion of complementarity which has made possible such an elegant proof without this global lifting tool. Of course, there is the lifting involved in our proof, too. But it may be handled locally (with the substitutions σ and τ above), so that this proof and its restriction to the ground level (see [B10]), do not really differ very much.

Moreover, in one direction this proof relates resolution with the connection method; but before we discuss this relationship, we now show the consistency of resolution, again in a way providing at the same time the other direction of this relationship. The following lemma serves for this purpose.

1.4.L. For any resolution deduction Δ of a clause c from a matrix F there exists a resolution deduction Δ' of c from a matrix F' such that
(i)   each clause in F' is a variant of a clause in F , and
(ii)   for any variable x occurring in any clause d of Δ', viewed in the non-linear format, there exists a unique branch $B = (d_1,\ldots,d_k)$ in Δ' with $d_k = c$ and $d_i = d$ for some $i \in \{1,\ldots,k\}$, such that x occurs in each clause d_j with $1 \leq j \leq i$, but does not occur in any clause e of Δ' which is not in B .

Proof by induction on the length l of Δ . If $l=0$ then in view of the non-linear format there is only a single node in Δ , viz. $c \in F$, which trivially satisfies (i) and (ii).

Otherwise, if $l>0$ then c is the result of a resolution step with some parent clauses c_0 and c_1 which are derived from F by some deductions Δ_0 and Δ_1 . For those we may assume that the lemma holds, by the induction hypothesis. But it still may be that it does not hold for Δ , which may happen in the following two cases.

(1)   There are branches B_i in Δ_i , $i=0,1$, with common variables.

(2)   There is a variable occuring in c   which does not occur in c_i , $i=0,1$.

In the first case (1), let us assume that x   occurs in B_0 and B_1 . By y   we denote some variable which does not occur in Δ . In each clause of B_1 (but not of B_0), x   is substituted by y . As a result of this substitution previously identical subtrees in Δ may become different; but it is obvious (by a trivial inductive argument) that the resulting deduction of c still is a correct resolution deduction.

If (1) does not hold (anymore) but (2) applies then say x occurs in c but neither in c_0 nor in c_1 which may well happen in a resolution inference. It may be assumed that x does not occur in any clause of Δ different from c since otherwise it might be substituted by some new variable y in all such clauses. But in this case there is at least one parent clause, say c_1 , containing a variable x' which either via the variant c_1' in the terminology of (1.1) or via the substitution σ (or both) is substituted by x . In the unique branch B   in Δ_1 , all clauses of which contain x' , this variable is substituted by x .   □

For instance, if Δ denotes the resolution proof of {{Px} , {^{1}Py,^{1}Pz}} given above then Δ' would read

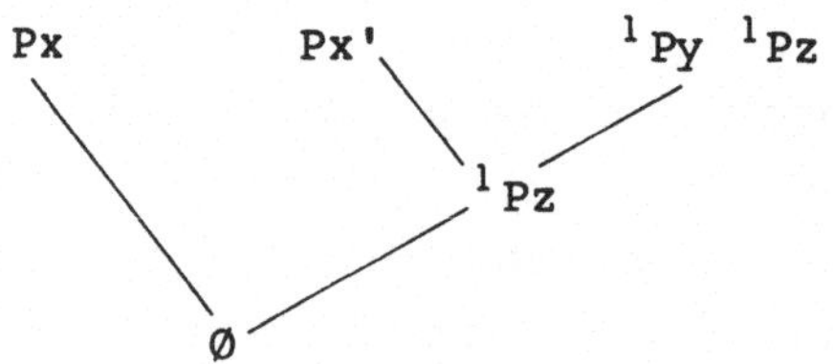

1.5.T. [**Consistency of resolution**] A formula F   in normal form is valid if there exists a resolution proof of its matrix F_0 .

Proof. By (1.4) we may assume that the resolution proof is a deduction Δ' of Ø from F' which satisfies (i) and (ii) from the previous lemma. For such a deduction we obviously may assume that, in the notation of (1.1), $c_i = c_i'$ for any resolution inference in Δ' .

Let $B = (e_0,...,e_k)$ denote any branch in Δ' where $e_0 \in F'$ and $e_k = \emptyset$. Further let τ_j denote the most general unifier for the resolution inference, the resolvent of which is e_j , restricted to the variables occuring in e_{j-1} , for $j=1,...,k$, and let $\tau = \tau_1\tau_2...\tau_k$. If $B_1,...,B_m$ are all the different branches in Δ' then we thus obtain substitutions $\sigma_1,...,\sigma_m$, the domain of which is pairwise disjoint (because of ii). Hence, $\sigma = \sigma_1 \cup ... \cup \sigma_m$ is a well-defined substitution for variables which occur in F' .

If we can prove that $F'\sigma$ is complementary then the theorem follows immediately. Namely, simply by adding a set F'' of variants of clauses of F_0 to F' we can achieve $F' \cup F'' = F_0 \cup F_1 \cup ... \cup F_n$ for some $n \geqslant 0$ such that $F_1,...,F_n$ are variants of F_0 . Hence, by Herbrands theorem (III.3.13), F is valid since $(F_0 \cup ... \cup F_n)\sigma$ now is a complementary compound instance of F .

In order to show that $F'\sigma$ is complementary - the only assertion left over - we prove by induction on the length l of $\Delta' = G_0 \vdash ... \vdash G_l$ with $G_0 = F'$ and $\emptyset \in G_l$, that for each matrix G_i , $G_i\sigma$ is complementary, $i=0,...,l$.

For G_l this trivially holds since there is no path through $G_l\sigma$ because of $\emptyset \in G_l\sigma$. Hence, by the induction hypothesis, we may assume that this holds for $G_1,...,G_l$, and we claim that it holds for G_0 . To show this we consider the inference $G_0 \vdash G_1$. For this inference we apply all the notations from (1.1). Thus, in particular, we have $c_i = c_i' \in G_0$, $i=0,1$, and $G_1 = G_0 \cup \{c\}$. Let $d_0\sigma = \{L\}$, hence $d_1\sigma = \{^1L\}$, and consider any path p through G_0 . We have to show that p is complementary. This trivially true if $L^{c_i} \in p$ for $i=0,1$. But otherwise, there must be some literal $K \neq {}^1L$ with $K^{c_i} \in c_i\sigma$ and $K^{c_i} \in p$ for $i \in \{0,1\}$. Since then $p \cup \{K^c\}$ is a path through $G_1\sigma$ by the definition of c in (1.1), and thus is complementary by assumption, it is obvious that p , which contains the same literals, must also be complementary. $\square$

1.6.C. A formula in normal form is valid iff there exists a resolution proof of its matrix.

Proof. This combines (1.4) and (1.5). $\square$

As we mentioned before our proof for this result has been chosen to reveal the relationship between resolution and the connection method since otherwise consistency (but not completeness as we noted above) could have been established in a more direct way (see theorem 2.6.3 in $[Lo4]$).

Let us first explore the "consistency direction" which for any formula with matrix F_0 takes a resolution proof $\Delta' = G_0 \vdash \ldots \vdash G_1$ for granted (using all the notations from the previous proof). This proof may be used to constructively define a spanning set U_0 of connections in $F_0 \cup \ldots \cup F_n$, following the induction of the proof. Namely, we take the empty set of connections for G_1 , and thus assuming that such a set, say U_1 , has already been obtained for G_1 , we let U_0 consist of all connections from G_1 , which do not contain a literal K^c from the resultant c , together with all the connections from $\{\{K,K'\} \mid K \in d_0$ and $K' \in d_1\}$, and finally all those connections from which the connections in U_1 containing some K^c are "inherited". For instance, $\{^1K^e,K^c\}$ is inherited from $\{^1K^e,K^{c_0}\}$ in this sense in the figure 1 above (see 2.2 in $[B10]$ for a precise definition and exercise (E3) in section 12).

This construction not only yields a spanning set of connections in G_0 , hence also in $F_0 \cup \ldots \cup F_n$. But also any of these connections is related to one (or more) resolution inferences $G_i \vdash G_{i+1}$, $0 \leqslant i \leqslant 1$, via that inheritance relation; more precisely, a connection is related to an inference whenever the connection is inherited in a transitive way from some connection of the set $\{\{K,K'\} \mid K \in d_0$ and $K' \in d_1\}$ for this inference, the set of connections **resolved upon** in it.

Conversely, in the completeness proof we started with a spanning set U of connections in $F_0 \cup \ldots \cup F_n$, and obtained a resolution proof by resolving upon all of them and their inherited ones (except the ones with literals in tautologies). Thus, altogether we have a pairwise correspondence between the connections in some spanning set in $F_0 \cup \ldots \cup F_n$ on the one side, and the resolution inferences on the other side. As we know from chapter II and III (in particular see III.6.7), each step in the connection method encounters a number of additional connections in $F_0 \cup \ldots \cup F_n$ until a span-

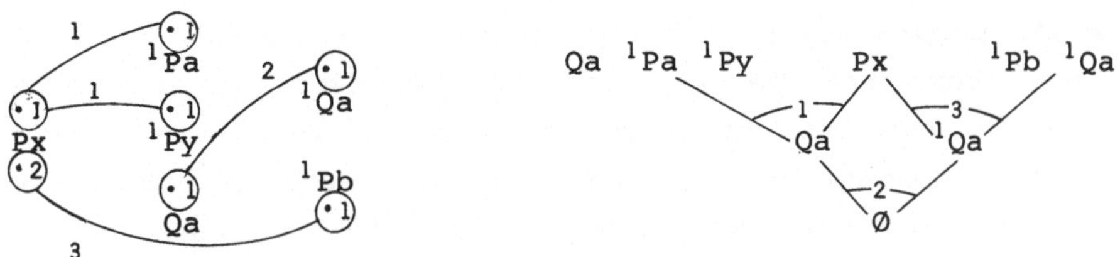

Figure 3. A connection proof and a resolution proof.

ning set has been compiled which in turn now relates the connection inferences via those connections with resolution inferences. In the discussion of (1.1) above, the reader has been
encouraged to note this relation between the connection proof
in figure 1 of section (III.6) and the corresponding resolution
proof in figure 1 above. Figure 3 here demonstrates this relation explicitly. It comprises the connection proof into one
copy of the matrix by numbering the connection encountered in
the steps 1, 2, and 3. These numbers appear again in the related resolution inferences.

As we will see later in the next section this relation
may be generally so close that, for proving any given formula,
one method may simulate the other even step by step. Will this
mean that it does not really matter which one we prefer ? Certainly not, neither from a quantitative point of view, which
will be discussed in the subsequent sections, nor from a didac-
tic point of view which we find particularly important.

Namely, we have learned that in order to obtain a
proof for a formula in one way or the other a global structure
has to be detected in it, viz. a spanning set of connections.
Our treatment in the chapters II and III (but also that in the
subsequent sections) hopefully has convinced the reader that
this structure best is explored with the formula as a whole in
mind (or in the computer memory). In contrast to that resolution breaks the formula into parts (the resolvents) such that
our attention tends to become focused on such isolated parts
rather than on the global structure of the proof. Locally, to
put it in other words, resolution is easily understood since

it is a simple and intuitive proof rule (which partially explains its popularity); globally, however, the connection method is much more transparent such that improvements or strategies come to the mind much easier than for resolution, which also will be demonstrated in the subsequent sections. Before we turn to the next one, we simply note the following trivial observation on resolution.

1.7.T. Resolution as an inference relation, restricted to valid formulas, is confluent.

   Proof. Note that all clauses of the matrix in the premise also appear in the conclusion. Also only a finite number of distinct clauses, which are not variants of each other, may be generated; thus, by (r7) in (1.1) there are no deductions with infinite length. With these two facts the theorem is obvious.   □

2.   LINEAR RESOLUTION AND THE CONNECTION METHOD

Computational experience with the basic form of resolution, as defined in the previous section, has shown very early that unguided generation of resolvents for practical examples quickly exhausts the computational resources, in particular the available storage, before the desired proof could be obtained. Much efforts have therefore been invested in the development of so-called **refinements** of resolution. They all have in common that at any stage of the attempted proof they guide the selection of the next resolution inference under more global aspects than are available in the basic form.

   In this and the subsequent sections, three different, and in a way representative kinds of such refinements will be briefly discussed and compared with the connection method. In all three cases the comparison will show that an analogue refinement may easily be achieved for the connection method with an even better and more easily understandable result. This situation in fact holds in general. Therefore there is good reason to ignore the many other refinements of resolution, which have appeared in the literature (see [Lo4]), within this book, and rather concentrate on improvements of the connection method.

        As we know from the previous section, the selection of
a resolution inference to proceed with corresponds to the
selection of connections in the connection method, which basically is a ground level problem (recall our parallel treatment
in the chapters II and III). Therefore, the basic ideas of any
of these resolution refinements may well be explained on the
ground level without the extra-complications arising from the
first-order features such as substitutions, instances etc. The
reader should keep in mind that these are treated exactly as
before.

        With these preliminaries we now turn our attention to
the so-called **linear** refinements of resolution. Actually we
are going to introduce its basic form as a simple representational variant of the connection method. Relying on the solid
formal grounds built in the previous chapters we may use now an
informal and intuitive way of presentation.

        Recall the connection deduction for the matrix called
E in figure 1 within section (II.4). Exactly the same deduction will now be presented once more in figure 4, but in a
different way explained in detail now.

        First, all the occurring matrices are displayed in a
top-down rather than left-to-right fashion. Resolution, as we
know, works with the negated formula, hence the matrix represents a conjunction of clauses which are listed top-down in
accordance with our conventions and those of resolution. In the
affirmative representation, preferred within this book, a
matrix represents a disjunction of clauses, and is thus listed
from left to right. Properly, the way of listing therefore
differs which, however, should not cause any trouble for the
reader once he is aware of it.

        Now, the initial matrix is encoded here by adding the
start clause, here ^{1}LK , below the matrix with its literals
in a certain sequence. The right-most literal in it, here K,
and any clause containing its complement, here M^{1}K is selected, and the first connection inference is performed. Instead of
using pointers and the dotted line as in figure (II.1) the
same information in the second matrix is now encoded as a
clause-like structure, called a **chain** , viz. ^{1}L[K]M . It
contains the literals from the start clause in the   same

```
    L              L              L
   ¹M             ¹M             ¹M
     M ¹K            M ¹K            M ¹K
   ¹L  K    ⊢     ¹L  K    ⊢     ¹L  K    ⊢
   ¹L  K          ¹L [K] M        ¹L [K][M]


    L              L              L
   ¹M             ¹M             ¹M
     M ¹K            M ¹K            M ¹K
   ¹L  K    ⊢     ¹L  K    ⊢     ¹L  K
   ¹L             [¹L]            ∅
```

Figure 4. A different representation of the connection proof
         from figure (II.1)

sequence, with the selected literal K bracketed, which
encodes its belonging to the active path. To the right of this
bracketed literal all literals from the selected clause except
¹K are listed in a certain sequence. Here, there is only
one, viz. M .

    With the right-most literal in this chain, viz. M , we
proceed as with K before which gives ¹L[K][M] , saying that
the active path contains K and M . Since there is no unbracketed literal at the right end of the last chain, we cancel
bracketed literals at the right end (first [M], then [K])
until the right-most literal is unbracketed, viz. ¹L . This
literal is processed as K and M before yielding the chain
[¹L] which disappears by cancelation as before. The resultant
empty chain indicates the sucessful termination of the proof.

    The key message of this description is that the struc-
tures of the connection proof may be encoded in the form of
chains which are lists of bracketed and unbracketed literals.
The description itself has been given already in terms of this
new encoding. Note, however, that we still talk of connection
proofs as defined in chapter II.

Now, obviously the deduction in figure 4 may be represented in a less redundant way shown in figure 5. This representation avoids the redundant repetition of the whole

1.	L	given
2.	$\neg M$	given
3.	M^1K	given
4.	$^1L\ K$	given and selected as start chain
5.	$^1L[K]M$	extension with 3.
6.	$^1L[K][M]$	extension with 2.
7.	^1L	truncation
8.	$[^1L]$	extension with 1.
9.	$\square$	truncation

Figure 5. A linear resolution refutation for the matrix from
         figure 3.

matrix at each step by simply listing it once, with the start clause at the end, and by adding the intermediate chains one by one. Again note that we are still dealing with the connection proof, but in a different representation.

By definition, any connection proof in a representation as in figure 4 for the purposes of this book will be called a **c-linear resolution refutation** (or **proof**). The term "refutation" is preferred in the resolution terminology since the negation of the theorem is proved inconsistent. The term "linear" is understood immediately by a look to figure 6 which shows the refutation from figure 4 in the non-linear format used earlier, together with the general structure of such a linear resolution proof. This structure consists of a **linearly** sequenced binary tree in which any right parent may be either a given clause or may be identical with an ancester of the corresponding left parent as indicated with the dashed line. The "c" in c-linear reminds of the connection method as its origin since there are a few minor differences in comparison with traditional linear resolution [Lo4], discussed in some detail in [B11].

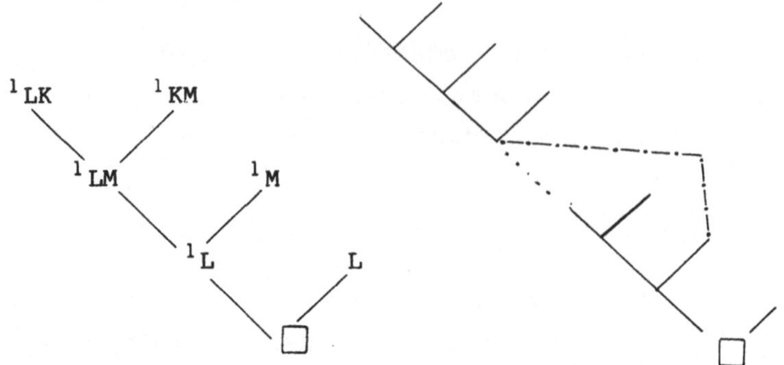

Figure 6. Linear resolution: special case and general form

According to this definition, c-linear resolution differs from the connection method only w.r.t. its representation. This justifies the informality of this definition w.r.t its details since the form of representation is an implementational issue rather one of the method's nature. In view of such an implementation, the connection method, because of this representational difference, even has a small advantage over c-linear resolution since the structures (α,β,γ) defined in (II.4.2) need less storage than the corresponding chains except if these are realized by exactly those structures which certainly is a possibility. Therefore, there is no reason to spend any more time on the discussion of c-linear resolution and its many different variants known from the literature. We mention that these variants and their relations are discussed in Loveland's book [Lo4] in great detail, in case the reader would like to know more about them.

We, however, continue to rely on the representation form of the connection method. Incidentally, the linearity of the reasoning is manifested in it as well, namely in its active paths, and the reader should review the figures 1 and 2 once more under this aspect.

3.   ON PERFORMANCE EVALUATION

The introduction of resolution quite naturally has led us to the question whether resolution is preferable to the connection method or not. The position taken within this book clearly favors the connection method. But is this preference based on ideological or rational grounds ? Of course, we claim that there are convincing rational arguments for it.

These arguments are of two different kinds. One is the kind of arguments which have been given at the end of section 1 saying that the connection method provides a clearer view of the global problem of generating a proof for a theorem, and thus supports the development of refinements. While this is of a qualitative (or psychological) nature the other kind of arguments is a quantitative one, for instance saying that the connection method needs a little less storage space than the c-linear resolution method as defined in the last section, which has been discussed there.

It is this quantitative aspect which we are now going to discuss in general terms. The reason for this discussion is the fact that such quantitative evaluation of the performance of theorem provers is quite a complicated thing, such that it will be helpful to have a clearer view of what we mean by quantitatively better or improved methods.

In principle, the performance may be measured either by experience with running systems or by mathematical analysis. In the former case one would compare the relative performance of implementations of different methods on a number of samples.

Such comparison heavily involves judgements, however. We have to judge which quantity should be used for measuring the performance, like CPU-time, space-requirements, a combination of both, or something else. Even if at best the implementations are done on the same machine and in the same programming language, a rare case indeed, any of these quantities may be questioned whether they adequately reflect the method's quality. This applies also for more sophisticated measures such as the **penetrance** and the **effective branching factor** which are in use in intellectics, i.e. artificial intelligence (see [Nil], section 2.6).

Often it happens that a theorem prover TP1 performs much better on an example F1 than a different one TP2 which may even be unable to prove F1, while on another example F2 their relative performance is quite the opposite. Hence, if this happens among the selected test examples then this obviously calls for further judgement which again might be questionable. Since for any of these judgements there is relatively little experience in the current state of the art of building and testing theorem provers, any such experimental comparisons at present should be taken with much caution, though at the same time, just in order to acquire more such experience, it should definitively be regarded as a valuable contribution. Work of this kind can be found in [WiM] and [MOW].

Under these circumstances it is not surprising that the present techniques of a mathematical analysis, the other possibility of measuring performance, are rather limited as well, a point which will be discussed now. For such an analysis, what we would need is a realistic mathematical model of the binary relation which captures the natural and practically relevant meaning of the term "better than" w.r.t. proof procedures. It therefore seems to be a good idea to begin with making a little more precise this natural meaning of "better than".

Naturally, we would assume that the procedures are not responsible for any effects due to a particular implementation or to the internal performance of a particular machine. In other words, it will be assumed that they are all coded in exactly the same way and with exactly the same machine. However, in a finite world it should certainly be taken into account that the resources w.r.t. time and memory, say r, are limited with limitations varying within a certain range $R = \{r \mid r1 < r < r2\}$.

Now, if a comparison of two procedures TP1 and TP2 shows that for any $r \in R$, TP2 is able to prove any theorem proved by TP1 then clearly TP2 would be regarded as better than or equally good as TP1 (w.r.t. R), say TP1 < TP2 . In this case we shall say that TP2 is **uniformly** better than TP1 , suppressing the equality case for simplicity.

As we mentioned above one has to encounter also a non-uniform behaviour. That this may happen is seen by considering the following extreme situation. It is a common experience that smarter programs often become more complicated. Now,

assume we design a marvelous procedure   TP1   which, however,
has become so complicated that its code exhausts all the
available memory and thus is not even able to prove a single
theorem. No doubt that we would regard it as worthless, and
rather prefer a simpler procedure   TP2   which leaves room for
working space. With this example the reader may think of less
extreme cases and gradually approach them to the extreme, to
see that non-uniform affects may in fact occur.

In order to cover such cases we have to make a judgement on theorems, say j(F). Further, let   PR1(r)   and   PR2(r)
respectively denote the set of theorems proved by   TP1 and TP2.
"TP2 is better than TP1" would then naturally have to be expressed by saying that the amount of theorems in   PR2(r)   counted with their judged value is greater than that in PR1(r) , or
formally , $\sum_{F \in PR1(r)} j(F) < \sum_{F \in PR2(r)} j(F)$, for any $r \in R$, where
Σ , $<$ would have to be defined in some appropriate way. Clear-
ly, this is too complicated to be feasible which shows that the
best we can expect is a treatment of the uniform case. Unfortunately, even this one seems to be too complicated for mathematical treatment because of the range R. Therefore, in the literature we only find the idealized **average-case** and **worst-
case** treatment, as well as the **simulation technique** , wich
are briefly discussed below. But we hope to have demonstrated
with the previous discussion that any of these idealized
treatments in fact may be far from reality, thus their results
should be taken with similar caution as in the case of experimental comparisons.

In the average-case and worst-case treatment, the
inputs of the considered procedures, i.e. the formulas in our
case, are measured by some quantity, mostly by their size
which in the case of formulas naturally would be their length.
The performance of the procedures is then measured by their
complexity which is the quantity of resources required for
processing inputs of a given size. If this complexity is taken
as the maximum complexity over all inputs of given sizen then
it is referred to as **worst-case complexity** , otherwise if it
is taken as the average complexity over all inputs of given
size then it is referred to as **expected complexity** . If the

resources restricted to the required computing time or to the required memory space then we speak of **time** or **space** complexity, respectively.

Let us now consider the simple case of restricting the analysis to worst-case time complexity of resolution for propositional logic only. Moreover, for any formula F this complexity, as a further approximation is measured by the length of the shortest resolution proof for F which certainly provides a lower bound on the time required to **find any** proof for F . The reader should really be aware of the drastic restrictions imposed on this case, in order to adequately appreciate the dimension of the problem of a mathematical analysis of theorem proving procedures. Even in this presumably simple case the solution is **not** known to date because the problem has turned out to be a really hard one. We only know a lower bound for this complexity for the (further) restricted case of **regular** resolution by a result of Tseitin [Tse]which has further been explored in [Gal] and [B-A]. This lower bound is 2^{cn} where n is the number of literals in the given formula and c is some positive constant.

In regular resolution the same literal must not be resolved upon more than once in any branch of the deriviation (in the non-linear format), a restriction which mainly is of a theoretical interest. Experience indicates that regular resolution proofs are not longer than unrestricted resolution proofs [Sc1]; therefore it is conjectured by most experts that the same lower bounds apply to unrestricted resolution. If this conjecture would be true this would mean that for any (arbitrarily large) n>0 there are propositional formulas with n literals such that any resolution proof for them requires more than 2^{cn} distinct clauses. The search for obtaining such a proof would then require even more steps, of course. We speak of an **exponential** behavior in such a case.

Exponential behavior is regarded to be computationally infeasible [Co1] since 2^n grows tremendously with growing n . Based on these considerations many people have drawn the premature conclusion that theorem proving itself is computationally infeasible. Such a conclusion is premature because (i) worst-case analysis may be totally misleading in view of practical cases (see below), (ii) so far the conjecture has not been proven correct, (iii) resolution will probably not be the best which can be achieved, (iv) in particular, a future deductive system very likely will work with more tools than simply with a complete deductive rule like resolution or the connection rule, to mention the main arguments.

The problem with the average case treatment is that, as a prerequisite, we need a probability distribution of the inputs for its application (see [AHU], p. 92). Such an actual distribution may be hard to obtain, in particular in the case of theorems. In [Gol], a variety of such distributions has been assumed for propositional logic, and the resultant expected time complexity for the **Davis-Putnam procedure** [DaP] has been derived. This is a proof procedure related in a certain way with regular resolution [Gal]. These results are much more encouraging than the previous worst-case ones. For instance with one of these distributions the number of steps required on the average to obtain a proof is $c \cdot r \cdot n^2$, where c is some constant, r is the number of distinct atoms and n the number of clauses in the formula, which certainly is tractable on the computers of today.

Unfortunately, little can be said on how realistic these distributivity assumptions are. Further it has to be noted that things become much more complicated on the first-order level, particularly by the fact that according to Herbrand's theorem (III.3.13) not only a single instance but possibly many instances have to be encountered in a proof of a given formula. Therefore it seems that, in a sober judgement of all these mathematical complexity results, their message for reality seems to be little more than saying that theorem proving in fact is a hard activity but its prospects for practical applications are not hopeless, a view which also is supported by the experience with running systems.

The simulation technique for the comparison of different proof procedures is of particular interest for us. Assume that we intend to apply it to two procedures TP1 and TP2. We must be able to isolate units of their computations which are regarded as steps such that there is some relation between the steps of TP1 and those of TP2 which may (at least approximately) be quantified.

For instance, remember the relation between the connection method and c-linear resolution discussed in the previous section. We have seen that both may simulate each others' behaviour if we relate the step of setting a further connection in the connection method with the corresponding step of resolving in c-linear resolution. We also have seen that the execution of a single step in the connection method requires somewhat less computational resources than that in c-linear resolution. Otherwise, the simulation is one-one, i.e. for any connection deduction there is a c-linear resolution deduction with the same number of steps and vice versa. Under these circumstances we clearly can say that the connection method is uniformly better than c-linear resolution in the sense described further above, in fact for arbitrary ranges R .

Unfortunately, the situation will be more complicated in most situations. For instance, in the following two sections we will have to compare two procedures TP1 and TP2 where each step of TP2 will require more resources than TP1 while TP2 will never need more and often less steps than TP1 in a simulation. Since the extra-costs for the execution of each step appear to be rather cheap on existing computers we will approximately regard it as negligible, and thus may regard TP2 as approximately uniformly better than TP1. If in addition the experimental results support this view then the chances are good that we are moving in the right direction.

In conclusion, we may say that to date there is no safe way of evaluating a method's performance. However, experiments **combined** with theoretical considerations of the kind discussed before probably provide helpful information for the direction of further research.

4.   CONNECTION GRAPH RESOLUTION AND THE CONNECTION METHOD

Resolution as defined in section 1 has no mechanism preventing that an inference which already has been carried out, will be repeated once more in exactly the same way. It seems to be obvious that such repetitions are completely redundant. Developing this thought a little further, one would also feel that

It is waste of efforts to resolve upon connections inherited from connections which already have been resolved upon. This is illustrated with the following example (using integers for denoting positions).

$$
{}^{1}L^{1}\ \overset{\frown}{}L^{2}\ {}^{1}K^{3}\quad \vdash \quad {}^{1}L^{1}\ \overset{\frown}{}L^{2}\ {}^{1}K^{3}\ K^{4}\quad \vdash \quad {}^{1}L^{1}\ \overset{\frown}{}L^{2}\ {}^{1}K^{3}\ K^{4}\ L^{5}
$$

Here, in the first step it is resolved upon the connection $\{{}^{1}L^{1},L^{2}\}$. From this connection the connection $\{{}^{1}L^{1},L^{5}\}$ is inherited in the second step resolving upon $\{K^{2},{}^{1}K^{3}\}$. Now the feeling expressed above would say that after the second step none of the following connections should be subject for resolving upon them: $\{{}^{1}L^{1},L^{2}\}$ and $\{K^{2},{}^{1}K^{3}\}$, since both have already been processed, but also $\{{}^{1}L^{1},L^{5}\}$, since this is inherited from one which already has been processed, viz. $\{{}^{1}L^{1},L^{2}\}$. And in fact resolving upon the only remaining connection $\{{}^{1}K^{3},K^{4}\}$ results in a successful proof.

This leads us to the question whether this does hold in general, and if so, how one could prevent such redundant inferences. Given the illustration with the arcs representing connections, we easily see that the latter can be solved simply by deleting arcs after resolving upon them. Thus the previous two steps would now be visualized by

$$
{}^{1}L^{1}\ \overset{\frown}{}L^{2}\ {}^{1}K^{3}\quad \vdash \quad {}^{1}L^{1}\ L^{2}\ {}^{1}K^{3}\ K^{4}\quad \vdash \quad {}^{1}L^{1}\ L^{2}\ {}^{1}K^{3}\ K^{4}\ L^{5}
$$

This is a correct **connection graph resolution** deduction. The underlying inference rule, shortly denoted by **cg-resolution** , is a powerful tool, in particular if it is combined with a sharpened form of the reduction rules from section (II.6). For instance, the pure literal elimination introduced in (II.6.3) in its sharpened form (see [B10]) would consider L^{2} to be pure after the first step, thus causing the deletion of the clause $\{L^{2},K^{2}\}$ such that the process would be forced to resolve upon the only remaining connection $\{{}^{1}K^{3},K^{4}\}$ already in the second step, resulting in the shortest possible proof.

This intuitive introduction suggests that cg-resolution is as resolution except that in addition a given set of connections in the premise generates a set of inherited connections which in particular does not contain that one which has been resolved upon. As simple and intuitive this might appear, the details are decidedly non-trivial. For this reason the definition of a cg-resolution inference will be given for the ground level only, as we already said in section 2. With the definition (1.1) of resolution as a guideline, the reader should then have no problems to lift it to the first-order level (see exercise E4 in section 12).

4.1.D. For any two connection graphs (F,W) and $(F \cup \{c\}, \widetilde{W})$, we say $(F \cup \{c\}, \widetilde{W})$ **is obtained from** (F,W) **by a cg-resolution inference** or simply **by cg-resolution** , in symbols $(F,W) \vdash_{cgr} (F \cup \{c\}, \widetilde{W})$, if F is a matrix in normal form and c a set of literals, such that there exist clauses c_0, c_1, and a literal L, satisfying the following properties.

(c1) $c_0, c_1 \in F$, called the **parent clauses** ;

(c2) $w = \{L^{c_0}, {}^1L^{c_1}\} \in W$ the **resolved connection** ;

(c3) $c = (c_0 \setminus \{L\}) \cup (c_1 \setminus \{{}^1L\})$

(c4) $\widetilde{W} = (W \setminus \{w\}) \cup V$,   where V is the set of connections $\{{}^1K^d, {}^0K^c\}$ with $d \in F \setminus \{c_0, c_1\}$ such that $\{{}^1K^d, {}^0K^{c_i}\} \in W$ holds for some $i \in \{0,1\}$, unless it holds that ${}^0K \in c_0$, ${}^0K \in c_1$, and $\{{}^1K^e \mid e \in F \setminus \{c_0, c_1\}$ and $\{{}^1K^e, {}^0K^{c_j}\} \in W\}$ is a subset of $\{{}^1K^e \mid e \in F \setminus \{c_0, c_1\}$ and $\{{}^1K^e, {}^0K^{c_k}\} \in W\}$ for $k = (j+1) \bmod 2$ and some $j \in \{0,1\}$, in which case the condition $\{{}^1K^d, {}^0K^{c_i}\} \in W$ is strengthened by restricting i to $i=j$. $\square$

Without the phrase beginning with "unless" in (c4), we obtain a slightly weaker and considerably simpler form which is recommended for consideration in a first approach. The reader is expected to match it with the two inferences in the deduction given before.

In its full form cg-resolution ignores even more redundant connections than those discussed above which further restricts the number of possibilities in the search space for a proof. Specifically, there are two kinds of such redundancies having been eliminated. One is shown by figure 7 which illus-

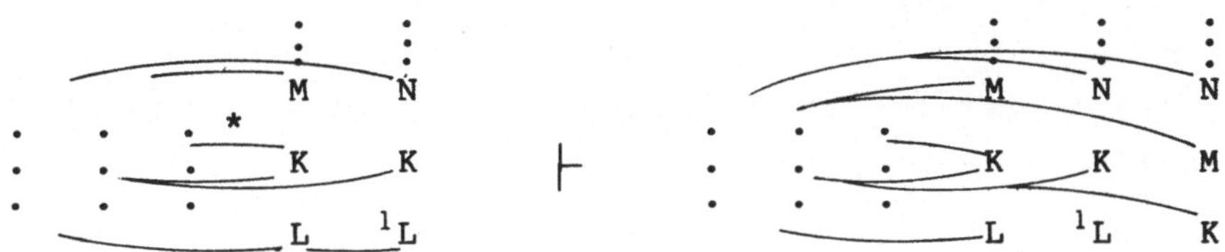

Figure 7. A cg-resolution inference

trates a cg-resolution step. There, the conditions in the unless-phrase of (c4) are apparently satisfied for K with the consequence that there is no connection with a literal in the resolvent inherited from the connection marked with an asterix.

The other kind of redundancy occurs in cases where the resolvent is a tautology and is illustrated by figure 8.

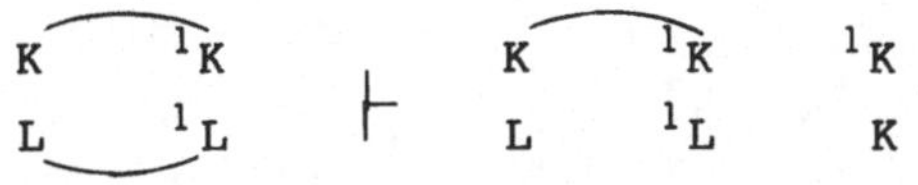

Figure 8. The case of tautological resolvents

Note that there are no connections with literals in the resolvent as one might expect.

For both kinds it is certainly not obvious that we are in fact dealing with redundancies. This can be seen only on the grounds of the proof for the following two theorems.

4.2.T. [**Completeness of cg-resolution**] If   F   is a valid formula in normal form and W the set of all its connections, then there exists a cg-resolution proof of the connection graph (F,W) .

4.3.T. [**Consistency of cg-resolution**] If there exists a cg-resolution proof of a connection graph (F,W) for a formula in normal form then F is valid.

The proofs for these two theorems go exactly as the respective ones for resolution in (1.2) and (1.5). It is left to the reader as an exercise to check this in all details (see E5 in section 12).   □

It is clear that cg-resolution can compete with resolution only if it also enjoys the property of confluence, for resolution shown in (1.7) by a trivial argument. Unfortunately, for cg-resolution this is a decidedly non-trivial problem which so far has not been solved. Figure 9 shows a kind of complication which may happen with cg-resolution. We see that after two steps the original connection graph identically appears again, except for positional denotations. Hence, the same two steps may be repeated infinitely many times. Consequently, without some proviso, confluency does not even hold. However, most people believe that the following conjecture eventually might be proved.

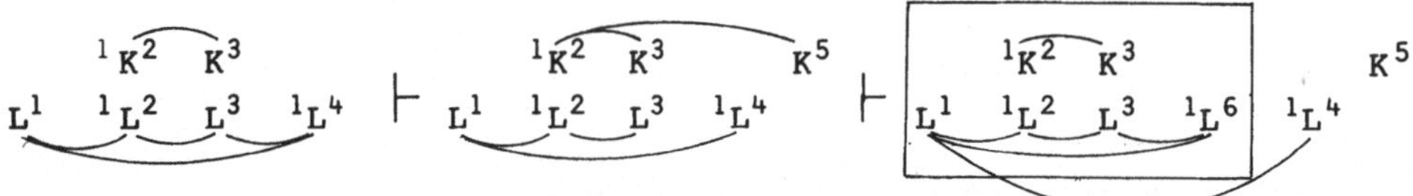

Figure 9. A potentially infinite cg-resolution deduction

Confluency conjecture for cg-resolution . cg-resolution, restricted to valid formulas, is confluent provided that in any deduction each connection has a finite chance to be resolved.

The complicated nature of cg-resolution, which makes it un-intuitive in the details, is one major disadvantage. Another one is the extra-storage required for keeping track of all connections, which is enormous as experimental experience demonstrates. Therefore, let us have a closer look to these and other features in comparison with the connection method.

In particular we ask whether the connection procedure CP_1^O from (II.6.14) in a certain sense may simulate a cg-resolution deduction with the same number of steps. For that purpose consider the following example.

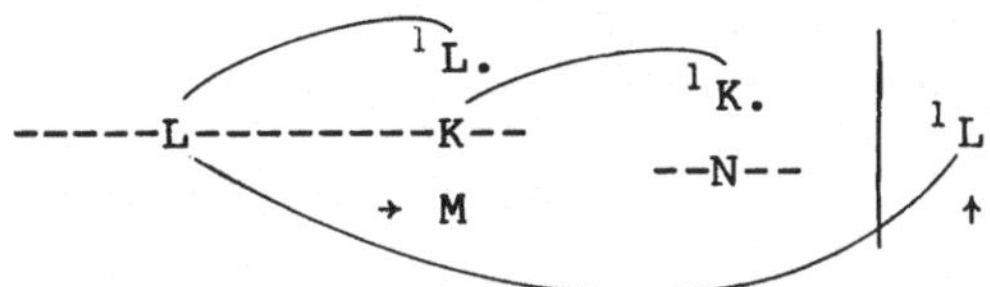

It shows a situation in a run of (II.6.14) using the representation which has been introduced in section (II.4) (cf. figures 1 and 2 there). In addition, a vertical line has been inserted to visualize the application of line 7 in (II.6.14). Apparently, CP_1^O should notice at such a situation that the matrix is complementary since all paths contain the last connection $\{L,^1L\}$. But unfortunately it does not since it is designed to empty the stack WAIT which at this point has an entry containing the literal M. Now note, that this simple example only demonstrates the effect as such. We leave it to the reader to extend the example such that the occurrence of this effect cannot be avoided by any reductions (see II.6.11) and causes arbitrarily many more steps to be performed by CP_1^O.

If the corresponding deduction is performed with cg-resolution then this effect does not appear.

This shows that the version CP_1^O cannot simulate this cg-resolution proof with 3 steps. But one immediately feels that this is due to the present **version** of the connection method rather than to the method itself. And in fact we are now going to discuss the version CP_2^O of the connection method, presented in table 1 from which this redundancy of CP_1^O has been eliminated.

Table 1. The connection procedure CP_2^o

```
 0: D←F; WAIT←NIL;                          ⎫ initialisation
 1: p←∅; i←0; SC←∅;                         ⎭
 2: select a clause c from the matrix D;    ⎫ selection of
    D←D∖c;                                  ⎬ initial structure
 3: select a iteral L from c; c←c\L;        ⎫
    if c≠∅ then                             ⎪
    WAIT←push(WAIT,('sg',i,(c,p,D)));       ⎬ preparation of
    i←i+1; p←p∪{(L,i)};                     ⎪ inference
 4: if D=∅ then return 'invalid';           ⎭ unsuccessful exit
 5: if there is no clause d∈D such that      ⎫
    ¹L∈d then                               ⎪
 6: ⌈if there is no clause d∈D such that     ⎬ separation
      ¹K∈d for some (K,j)∈p  then            ⎪
      ⌈WAIT←NIL; goto 1;⌉                    ⎭
 7:  else ⌈select c from D such that         ⎫
            ¹K∈c for some (K,j)∈p;           ⎪
            WAIT←push(WAIT,('dm',i,NIL));⌉⌉  ⎪
 8: else select c from D such that           ⎪
    ¹L∈c;                                    ⎪
 9: D←D∖c;                                   ⎬ execution of
10: c←c√¹L;                                  ⎪ extension
    for all literals K such that             ⎪
    ¹K∈c and (K,j)∈p for some j do           ⎪
    ⌈c←c√¹K; select j such that (K,j)∈p;      ⎪
     WAIT←push(WAIT,('sc',i,{j}));⌉           ⎪
11: if c≠∅ then goto 3;                       ⎭
12: if WAIT=NIL then return 'valid';        ⎭ successful exit
```

```
13: if the label of top WAIT is 'sg' then
      if i = index of top of WAIT then
       (WAIT,(label,index,(c,p,D)))←pop(WAIT);
       if SC≠∅ then
       ⌈SC←SC∪{j|j>i};
        WAIT←push(WAIT,('sc',i,SC)); SC←∅;
       else (WAIT,(label,i,(c,p,D))←pop(WAIT);
       goto 3;⌉
14: if the label of top of WAIT is 'sc' then
     ⌈(WAIT,(label,i,SC'))←pop(WAIT);
      SC←SC∪SC'; goto 12;⌉
15: if the label of top of WAIT is 'dm' then
     ⌈SC←SC\{j|j>index of top of WAIT};
      while index of top of WAIT > maximum of SC do
      (WAIT,item)←pop(WAIT);⌉
      goto 12;
```

}truncation

END

Comments

CP_2^0 applies to any propositional formula F in normal form
testing whether it is complementary. The presentation is structured exactly as (II.6.14), and uses the same conventions and
denotations. The entries on the stack WAIT are structured in
the form (label,index,value), where the labels distinguish
entries of the type 'sg' for **subgoal** , 'sc' for **set of connections** , and 'dm' for **ditchmarker** .

First note that CP_2^O contains literally everything from CP_1^O , thus is a pure extension of CP_1^O . In fact, if we apply CP_2^O to the previous example, then up to the third clause we obtain the same picture as the one given further above. At this point the value of p is {(L,1),(K,2),(N,3)} and the only entry in WAIT is

('sg',1,({M} ,{(L,1)},{{^{1}K,N},{L}})) .

In line 7, the algorithm now selects the clause {^{1}L} since (L,1)$\in$p , and pushes a ditchmarker indexed by 3, in order to encode the occurrence of this particular situation illustrated by the vertical line after the 3rd clause in the previous picture. In line 10 the connection from ^{1}L in the 4th clause to L in the 1st clause is stored on WAIT, encoded as ('sc',3,{1}) , and in this particular case transferred immediately afterwards, viz. in line 14, into SC, encoded as {1} . Since the index of both entries in WAIT is now greater or equal than the maximal element in SC, which is 1, both are simply removed in line 15, thus terminating this run successfully in line 12.

Two versions of a somewhat more complicated example are given in figure 10. In the first version the process terminates successfully after arrival at the 6th clause by removing all entries from WAIT. Because of the single additional connection, in the second version the literal K6 on WAIT cannot be disregarded, hence the process correctly terminates with failure. The reader is encouraged to hand-simulate a run of CP_2^O for these two examples (see E6 in section 12).

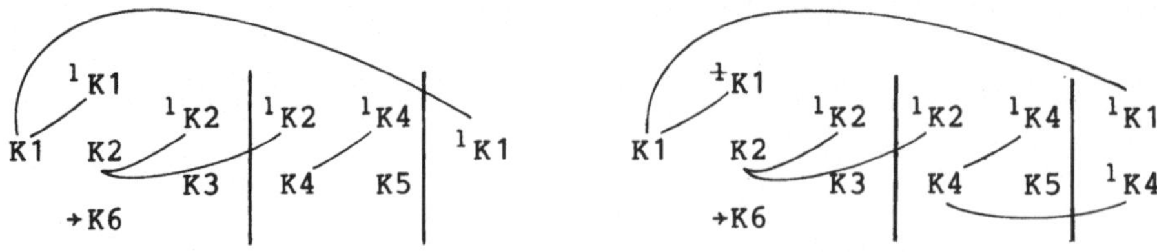

Figure 10. Two slightly differing examples

After these examples we are prepared to turn our attention to the general situation, illustrated by figure 11 and subject of the following theorem.

4.4.T. For any propositional matrix F in normal form, the connection procedure CP_2^o terminates, and it returns "valid" iff F in fact is valid.

Proof. For CP_1^o the same statement was proved in (II.6.13). Now, the only crucial additional feature of CP_2^o is given by line 14 where subgoals in contrast to CP_1^o are simply deleted. Hence, completeness, i.e. the if-case, is a trivial consequence of (II.6.13). Consistency, i.e. the only-if-case, is a little more difficult to show which goes as follows.

We consider the situation upon arrival at the while-statement in line 14 in a run of CP_2^o with any matrix F as input. Let W denote the set of connections considered up to this point by execution of the lines 8 - 10 except those which have been deleted from WAIT by previous executions of the while-statement in line 15. Let B denote the set of paths through F which are proved complementary by W . This situation is illustrated in figure 11.

$K_1,...,K_n$ are literals in p , not necessarily all. K_i , $0 < i < n$, denotes the rightmost literal which is connected with a literal beyond the ditch determined by the ditchmarker 'dm' that is currently being considered in the if-condition of line 15 and visualized by the right vertical line. The left vertical line visualizes the next 'dm' on WAIT or the end of the matrix if there is none. j is restricted by $i < j < n$. M_j is any literal in the clause c_j' on WAIT remaining from c_j . The reader might note that the two examples in figure 10 and the one further above all are special cases of this general situation.

Now, let q denote any path through F , which would have been tested explicitly for complementarity if the while-loop in line 15 would not be executed in the present situation. Our claim is that q already belongs to B . In order to see this let q' be obtained from q by replacing the literal $q \cap c_j$ in q by the literal K_j, for j = i+1,...,n. By construction, we have $q' \in B$ and the connection $w \in W$, which pro-

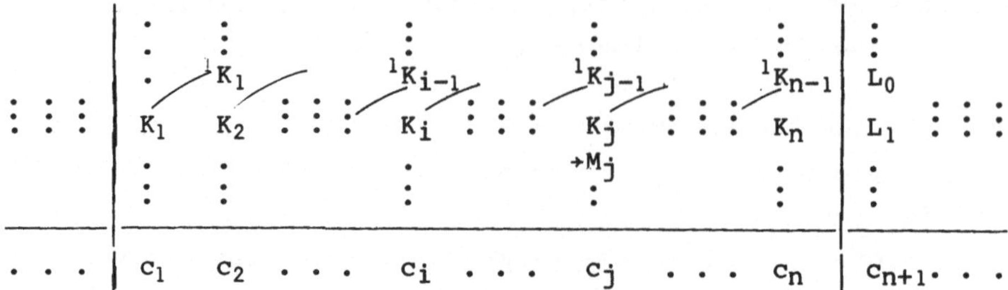

Figure 11. The connection graph (F,W)

vides the complementarity of q' , cannot contain any of the literals $K_{i+1},\ldots,K_n$. Thus, w must be also contained in q , and we have $q \in B$. Abandoning the explicit test of q for complementarity, as done by line 15, is therefore a   sound action.   □

For the comparison of CP_2^O with CP_1^O now the discussion at the end of the previous section applies. Namely, if we remember from section (II.6) that the information represented by WAIT may actually be encoded in an efficient way via α,β,γ given there together with a similar encoding of the additional features of CP_2^O the the difference in the requirements for executing a step in CP_1^O and in CP_2^O is really negligible in practice. On the other hand, the examples in this section have demonstrated that CP_2^O in a simulation of CP_1^O may need less, even remarkably less steps than CP_1^O . Therefore approximately we regard CP_2^O as uniformly better than CP_1^O .

Having achieved this improvement of the connection method we may resume the discussion concerning the comparison with cg-resolution which actually led us to CP_2^O . In a sense, cg-resolution and CP_2^O are hard to compare since cg-resolution has much more freedom in sequencing its steps than has CP_2^O . This kind of freedom may be worthless, however. More important is the question whether the simulation of CP_1^O for some input by corresponding steps of cg-resolution or, conversely, the simulation by CP_2^O of a sequence of steps by cg-resolution, which is such that it may in fact be realized by CP_2^O , shows any differences in the **number** of steps. The **conjecture** is that it does not, and section 5 in $[B11]$ provides good arguments that it holds. Because of the complicated nature of cg-resolution, however, a complete proof for it seems to be far away.

Assume this conjecture indeed holds, then CP_2^O offers a remarkable advantage over cg-resolution. Namely its storage requirements are similar to those of CP_1^O (hence also to those of linear resolution). It is easy to see that they are linear in the size of the input matrix (see lemma 4.4. in $[B11]$). cg-resolution in contrast to that is awfully storage consuming, as experienced by running systems, because at any time it has to store a set of original or generated connections which is quadratic in the size of the input matrix extended by all generated clauses. In other words, CP_2^O seems to combine the storage advantages of linear resolution with the running time advantages of cg-resolution.

Exactly in the same way as we lifted CP_1^O to obtain CP_1^1 given in (III.7.2) we are now in the position to do the same with CP_2^O to obtain a procedure CP_2^1 which is left out for reasons of space. Further, an actual implementation of CP_2^1 would have to integrate the reduction rules from section (II.6) which point will be further discussed not before CP_2^O will have been further enhanced in the next section.

5.   A CONNECTION PROCEDURE FOR ARBITRARY MATRICES

Except for the standard procedure SP from (III.3.7), all proof procedures discussed up to this point are applicable to matrices in normal form only. Although we have learned in section (III.4) that this does not mean a restiction of generality, in practice the use of normal form has serious disadvantages. The reason lies in the redundancy which is introduced into the matrix by the transformation to normal form given in (III.4.1). Specifically, its step 3 requires each formula of

the form A∧(B∨C) to be replaced by (A∧B)∨(A∧C) which produces a second copy of each of the literals in A .

     For instance, the formula $(\forall x\ \overbrace{Px\ \to\ Pa}) \wedge (\forall y\ \overbrace{Py\ \to\ Pb})$
is recognized as a theorem simply on the basis of the two
inserted connections since according to (III.6.2) it has exactly the two paths {¬Px,Pa} and {¬Py,Pb} . But the transformation to normal form produces a matrix with twice (i.e. 2^1) as
many literals which may require 3 times as many proof steps
with the connection method. The following matrix shows the
situation after the 3rd step.

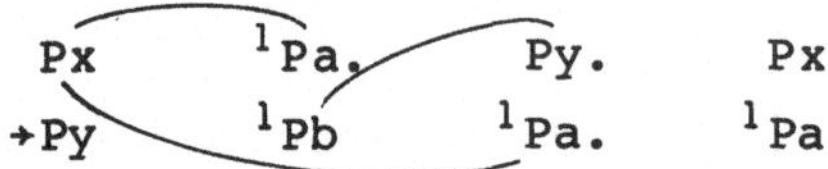

$$
\begin{array}{llll}
Px & {}^{1}Pa. & Py. & Px \\
\to Py & {}^{1}Pb & {}^{1}Pa. & {}^{1}Pa
\end{array}
$$

If we add to the same formula another conjunct $(\forall z\ \overbrace{Pz\ \to\ Pc})$,
then the resultant matrix in normal form will have even 4 times
(i.e. 2^2) as many literals, and so on. In other words, there
are cases for which the transformation to normal form causes an
exponential increase of the length of the matrix, the increase
of the search space for a proof being even worse.

     Moreover, such cases are among those arising in prac-
tice. For instance, the simple mathematical theorem saying
that "if F is a function and R and S are subsets of the
domain of F , then the image under F of the union of R and
S is the union of the images of R and S under F", after
eliminating definitions may be expressed by a formula with 20
literals which by transformation to normal form expands to a
matrix with 104 literals, as shown in figure 1 of [An2]. A
further point of similar importance is the fact that in the
expanded matrix the basic logical structure of the theorem is
no longer apparent.

     This leads us naturally to the question whether the
connection method may be generalized to arbitrary matrices.
Remember for this purpose that our version of Herbrand's theorem (III.3.13) has been proved for formulas in Skolem normal
form, which are obtained from arbitrary formulas by the trans-
formational steps 0, 1, and 2 (but not 3) in (III.4.1). Therefore it is strong enough that, once we have a ground-level
connection procedure for arbitrary matrices, this may be lift-

ed to the first-order level exactly as CP_1^O has been lifted in section (III.7) to obtain CP_1 . Such a procedure, called CP_3^O , may be found in table 2.

Admittedly, its size is frightening at first sight. But note that again CP_3^O is a pure extension of CP_2^O , as CP_2^O has been a pure extension of CP_1^O . Hence, essentially CP_3^O behaves like CP_1^O but with the additional features incorporated into CP_2^O . Therefore, we only have to pay our attention to the added lines of code which take care of the nested structure of a general matrix as defined in (II.1.1).

Let us first apply CP_3^O or, properly speaking, its lifted version CP_3^1 to the matrix, {{{¬Px,Pa} , {¬Py,Pb}}} of the formula considered at the beginning of the present section. Since there is only a single clause in this matrix, CP_3^O has no choice in line 2. c now contains two matrices from which say {¬Px,Pa} is selected for C and {¬Py,Pb} pushed on WAIT in line 3. Since C is not a literal as it would be in a normal form matrix, CP_3^O notes this by pushing a levelmarker on WAIT. Apparently, CP_3^O notes in this way every second '{' of the matrix along any branch in its tree-structure.

With D = {¬Px,Pa} , CP_3^O returns to line 2 , selects the clause say ¬Px in line 2 and its only literal in line 3. Of course, we have now to think in terms of the lifted version CP_3^1 of CP_3^O to find the clause Pa and the substitution σ = {x\a} such that L = (¬Px)σ and ^1L = (Pa)σ , in line 8 . D=∅ by line 9 and c=∅ by line 10 , thus from line 11 CP_3^O goes to line 12. From there it arrives at line 16, returns to line 12, pops the subgoal {¬Py,Pb} from WAIT, and processes it exactly as the one before.

As we see, CP_3^O may ignore a lot of the code from such a simple example, and appropriately locates the two required connections. But, of course, this ignored code is not redundant in general. In particular, there is this other new feature of potentially redundant subgoals, labeled 'prsg', which is illustrated with the matrix {{M,Q}, {{^{1}M,^{1}Q},L}, {^{1}L}}, visualized in the 2-dimensional display as follows.

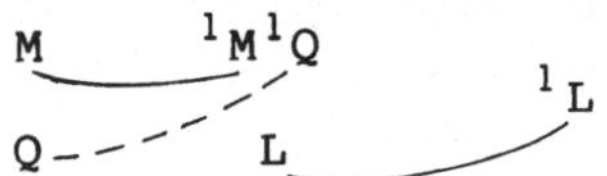

Table 2. The connection procedure CP_3^o


```
 0: D←F; WAIT←NIL;
    WAIT←push(WAIT,('lm',0,NIL));
 1: p←∅; i←0; SC←∅; PRSG←∅; E←∅;
 2: select a clause c from the matrix D; D←D\c;
    for all literals K such that
    ¹K∈c and (K,j)∈p for some j do
    ⌈c←c\¹K; select j such that (K,j)∈p;
     WAIT←push(WAIT,('sc',i+1,{j}))⌋ ;
    if c=∅ then goto 12;
 3: select a matrix C from c; c←c\{C};
    if there exists (k,B)∈PRSG such that
    k<i and B∪C is complementary then
    ⌈if c≠∅ then goto 3 else goto 12⌉ ;
    if c≠∅ then WAIT←push(WAIT,('sg',i,(c,p,D)));
    if SC≠∅ then
    ⌈SC←SC\{j|j>i}; WAIT←push(WAIT,('sc',i+1,SC)); SC←∅⌉ ;
    if PRSG≠∅ then
    ⌈PRSG←PRSG\{(k,B)|k>i};
    ⌈WAIT←push(WAIT,('prsg',i+1,PRSG)); PRSG←∅⌉ ;
    if C is not a literal then
    ⌈WAIT←push(WAIT,('lm',i,NIL)); D←C∪D; goto 2⌉ ;
    i←i+1; L←C; p←p∪{(L,i)};
 4: if D=∅ then return 'invalid';
 5: if there is no clause d∈D such that ¹L occurs in d then
 6:  if there is no clause d∈D such that
    ¹K occurs in d for some (K,j)∈p then
    ⌈while the label of top of WAIT is not 'lm' do
     (WAIT,value)←pop(WAIT); goto 1⌉
 7:  else  select c from D such that
    ¹K occurs in c for some (K,j)∈p;
     WAIT←push(WAIT,('dm',i,NIL))⌉⌉
 8: else select c from D such that ¹L occurs in c;
 9: D←D\c;
10: if ¹L occurs in c then
    select a matrix C∈c such that ¹L occurs in C
    else select a matric C∈c such that
        ¹K occurs in C for some (K,j)∈p;
    c←c\{C};
    for all literals K such that
    ¹K∈c or ¹K=C , and (K,j)∈p for some j do
    ⌈c←c\¹K; select j such that (K,j)∈p;
     WAIT←push(WAIT,('sc',i,{j}))⌉ ;
11: if C is a literal then
```

```
      ⌈if E≠∅ then
       ⌈WAIT←push(WAIT,('prsg',i,{(0,E)})); E←∅⌉ ;
        if c≠∅ then goto 3 else goto 12⌉ ;
       if c≠∅ then ⌈WAIT←push(WAIT,('sg',i,(c,p,D)));
                   WAIT←push(WAIT,('lm',i,NIL))⌉ ;
       if ¹L occurs in C then
       select a clause c from C such that ¹L occurs in c
       else select a clause c from C such that
            ¹K occurs in c for some (K,j)∈p;
       E←C∖c; D←DUE; goto 10;
12:  if WAIT=NIL then return 'valid';
13:  if the label of top of WAIT is 'sg' then
     ⌈if i = index of top of WAIT then
      ⌈(WAIT,(label,index,(c,p,D)))←pop(WAIT);
       if SC≠∅ then
       ⌈SC←SC∖{j|j>i};
        WAIT←push(WAIT,('sc',i,SC)); SC←∅⌉ ;
       if PRSG≠∅ then
       ⌈PRSG←PRSG∖{(k,B)|k>i};
        WAIT←push(WAIT,('prsg',i,PRSG)); PRSG←∅⌉⌉
      else(WAIT,(label,i,(c,p,D)))←pop(WAIT);
      goto 3⌉ ;
14:  if the label of top of WAIT is 'sc' then
     ⌈(WAIT,(label,i,SC'))←pop(WAIT);
      SC←SC∪SC'; goto 12⌉ ;
15:  if the label of top of WAIT is 'dm' then
     ⌈SC←SC∖{j|j > index of top of WAIT};
      while index of top of WAIT > maximum of SC
            and label of top of WAIT ≠ 'lm' do
      (WAIT,value)←pop(WAIT)⌉ ;
      goto 12;
16:  if the label of top of WAIT is 'lm' then
     ⌈(WAIT,(label,i,value))←pop(WAIT); goto 12⌉ ;
17:  if the label of top of WAIT is 'prsg' then
     ⌈SC←SC∖{j|j > index of top of WAIT}; m←max(SC∪{0});
      for each (k,B)∈ value of top of WAIT do
      if m>k then replace k by m in (k,B);
      (WAIT,(label,i,PRSG'))←pop(WAIT);
      PRSG←PRSG∪PRSG'⌉ ; goto 12;
END
```

Comments

CP_3^o applies to any propositional formula F , testing whether
it is complementary. The presentation is structured exactly as
CP_2^o in table 1 in section 4, and uses the same conventions and
denotations. Additional labels are 'lm' for 'levelmarker' and
'prsg' for 'potentially redundant subgoal'.

According to the definition of a path (III.6.2), any path through this matrix containing ^1M must also contain ^1Q . Hence, when the connection $\{M,^1M\}$ is located, then ^1Q is memorized by CP_3^O as the value of E labeled by 'prsg' on WAIT in line 11. Later when the subgoal Q is considered in line 3, it has not to be processed further since in line 3 B C = $\{Q,^1Q\}$ is complementary, illustrated by the dashed connection in the picture above, which clearly shows that the path $\{Q,^1M,^1Q,^1L\}$ is complementary. Of course, we could have handled Q also as a usual subgoal. But then L would appear as a subgoal for a second time, and its solution redundantly would have to be elaborated once more, which might be not as cheap as in the present example.

This deletion of subgoals cannot be allowed in an unrestricted way, however, which is demonstrated by two selected counterexamples in figure 12. In the first one, none of the subgoals Q may be deleted since $\{Q,N,L,^1M\}$ and $\{^1N,Q,L,^1M\}$ obviously are non-complementary paths. In this case it is the connection $\{M,^1M\}$ with ^1M from the last clause which causes this restriction. Similarly for the second one, where the Q in the first clause must not be deleted because of the path $\{Q,N,N\}$ while that in the second clause in fact is redundant. Here it is the connection $\{^1N,N\}$ with N in the last clause which must be observed. Figure 13 shows two further examples in which all subgoals are redundant. In general, the following holds expressed in the terminology suggested by these illustrations.

5.1.L. Exactly those subgoals are redundant which are to the rightmost left end among all connections with a right end below or to the right of the right end of the dashed connections.

The proof is left to the reader as exercise E8 in section 12 .   □

For reasons of space, we also must leave out the proof of the following theorem.

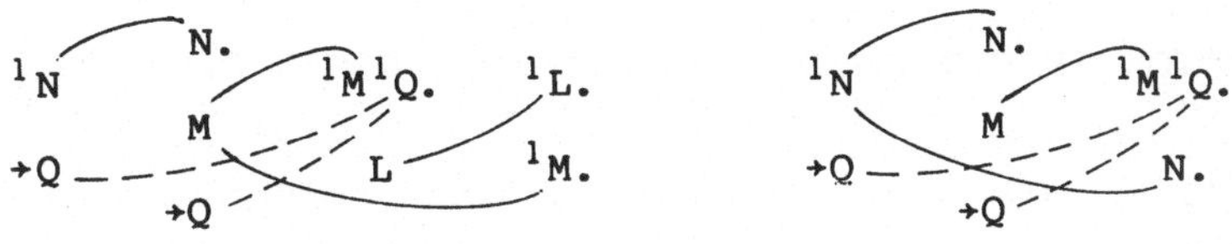

Figure 12. Restriction for subgoal deletion

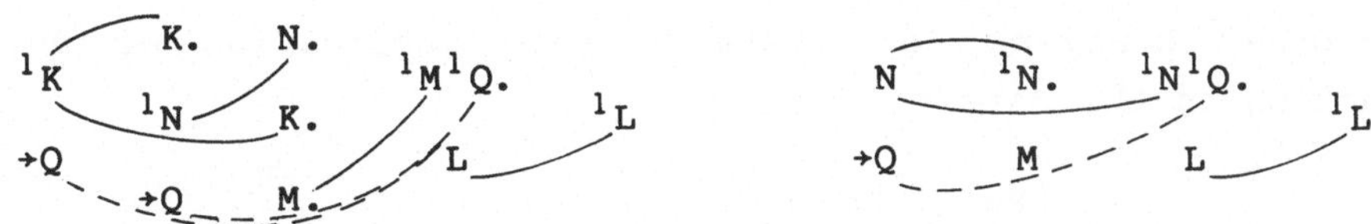

Figure 13. Examples for redundant subgoals

5.2.T. For any propositional matrix F , the connection procedure CP_3^O terminates, and it returns "valid" iff F in fact
is valid.   □

The proof may be found in [Hö2] (see also [HöB]) . Further it
is mentioned that CP_3^O has been implemented by Hörnig and
tested with many examples.

    In comparison with CP_2^O , the increase of the resources
required to perform any step of CP_3^O may be expressed by a
small constant factor. In the approximation determined by
ignoring this factor, we may thus say that CP_3^O is uniformly
better than CP_2^O since it avoids the redundancy resulting from
the transformation to normal form.

    As a final remark, note that CP_3^O defines a logical
calculus just as CP_1^O or resolution has determined one. The
obvious difference lies in the fact that the underlying logical
rule may be expressed only in a rather complicated way. But
this seems to be the necessary price to be payed for enhanced
performance.

6.   REDUCTION, FACTORIZATION, AND TAUTOLOGICAL CIRCUITS

In section (II.6) we have introduced the reductions MULT, PURE, TAUT, SUBS, and UNIT. They have been left out from all our procedures in order to keep these simple enough for the reader's understanding. In actual implementations they definitively have to be taken into consideration in order to speed up the proofs.

On the first-order level their application does require some care, however. For instance, the application of UNIT-reduction to the matrix

$$Pa \quad \begin{matrix} {}^{1}Px & Pb \\ {}^{1}Pb & Px \end{matrix}$$

does imply the need for the substitution $\sigma = \{x\backslash a\}$, yielding ${}^{1}Pb \begin{matrix} Pb \\ Pa \end{matrix}$ and , by a second application, Pa . This shows that UNIT-reduction, whenever its application implies a change in the substitution σ , has to be treated as an option among other possibilities, and therefore the procedure possibly has to consider later backtracking to another option. For instance, in the present example such an alternative option would be to consider the connection shown in

$$\begin{matrix} {}^{1}Px & Pb \\ & & Pa \\ {}^{1}Pb & Px \end{matrix}$$

with $\sigma = \{x\backslash b\}$. Apparently, it is now possible to apply MULT-reduction without a further change of σ which immediately completes the proof in this case.

This discussion applies in exactly the same way to all other reductions thus demonstrating that on the first-order level reductions cannot be applied in a preprocessing step without further consideration, rather they have to be integrated into the proof procedure in a dynamic way. One possibility is to apply them only if this can be done without any change

of σ which, however, requires to provide for their application at any point in the process. But even then we have to take
into account the case where in fact a further instance of that
part of the matrix is needed for obtaining the proof which is
deleted by reduction in the actual instance (see figure 2 in
section III.6 for an example). Hence such a part can be disregarded only within the actual instance.

In fact, the simplest solution seems to be an integra-
tion of the reductions into the connection calculus. This
means that we disregard within an extension step any clause
which under the actual substitution σ contains a pure literal (w.r.t. the remaining clauses including further instances),
or contains two complementary literals, or is subsumed by any
other clause. It also means that we reconsider MULT-reduction
under the actual substitution σ in the clause under actual
consideration which reduces subgoals in this clause to a single
one that may even have been processed already and thus does not
need any further consideration at all. Finally, under this
dynamic solution we would prefer unit clauses (and two-element
clauses as a second choice) for extension whenever they are
among the actual options.

In fact, dynamically there are two further reductions,
that is, factorization and avoidance of tautological circuits,
which are discussed in the remaining part of this section. For
their justification the following result will be useful which
is of interest in its own right and is due to Prawitz.

6.1.T. For any propositional matrix F , containing two
clauses c_0, c_1 with $^0L \in c_0$ and $^1L \in c_1$, F is complementary iff
both, $F_0 = (F \diagdown \{c_0, c_1\}) \cup \{\{^0L\}\} \cup \{c_1 \diagdown \{^1L\}\}$ and
$F_1 = (F \diagdown \{c_0, c_1\}) \cup \{\{^1L\}\} \cup \{c_0 \diagdown \{^0L\}\}$ are complementary.

Proof. Figure 14 illustrates the general case of this
theorem which says that only a subset of the set of all paths
has to be proved complementary in order to prove the complementarity of the whole matrix. This subset for instance contains the path illustrated with the full line, but not the one
illustrated by the dashed line.

Since the "only-if"-case is trivial, let us assume
that F_0, F_1 are complementary, and that p is any path

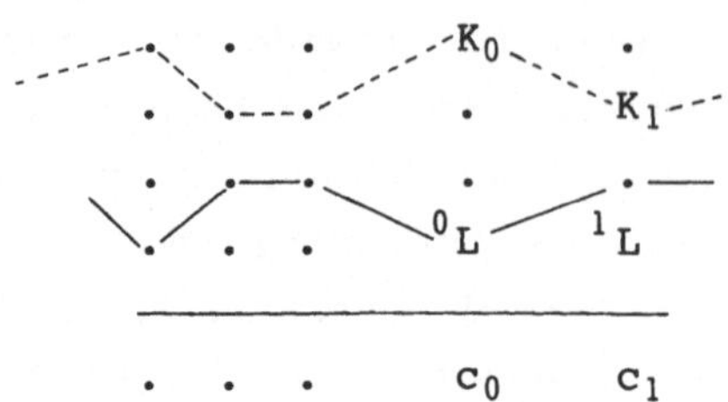

Figure 14. Prawitz' matrix reduction

through F . For p we have to show complementarity. Because
of the present assumption, the only non-trivial case is when,
for $K_i = p \cap c_i$, we have $K_i \neq {}^iL$, i=0,1 .   Since $(p \smallsetminus K_i^{c_i}) \cup {}^iL^{c_i}$
is a path through F_i, i=0,1 , both these paths are comple-
mentary by assumption, and thus each contains a connection
$u_i = \{{}^0M_i^{d_0i}, {}^1M_i^{d_1i}\}$. If ${}^iL^{c_i} \in u_i$, say ${}^iL^{c_i} = {}^iM_i^{d_ii}$, i=0,1,
then $\{{}^0M_1^{d_01}, {}^1M_0^{d_10}\}$ is a connection contained in p; otherwise
we obviously have $u_j \subseteq p$ for some $j \in \{0,1\}$. Hence in any case
p contains a connection, and thus is complementary.   □

This result provides another complete and consistent logical
rule for proving validity, which is $F \vdash F_0, F_1$ with the notation from (6.1). It is called **matrix reduction** in [Pr3]. Note
that F_0 and F_1 , both are strictly smaller than F , so that
an iterative application (to each of F_0 and F_1 separately)
eventually will lead to matrices, which contain the empty
clause Ø and thus are trivially complementary.

        Unfortunately, the explicit application of this rule is
even more redundant than resolution since $F \smallsetminus \{c_0, c_1\}$ occurs
in **both** subgoals F_0 and F_1 thus expanding the memory space
at each step. This can be partially avoided by structure sharing (see [SaC]). The connection method, however, offers a much
clearer solution since the basic advantage of matrix reduction
may be easily integrated into it with little additional cost.
This solution is equivalent with the avoidance of tautological
circuits to be discussed now.
        Consider the connection proof

The dashed and the dotted connection are not part of the proof. The dashed one has been added to illustrate the simplest case of a tautological circuit which here consists of this dashed connection $\{L,^1L\}$ together with the connection $\{K,^1K\}$. Along these two connections we may travel from the first clause to the second one and, on a **different** route, back to the first one. The general case involves more than just two clauses, with the crucial feature that no occurrence of a literal is involved in more than one connection of the circuit. The following example illustrates the case with three clauses and three connections.

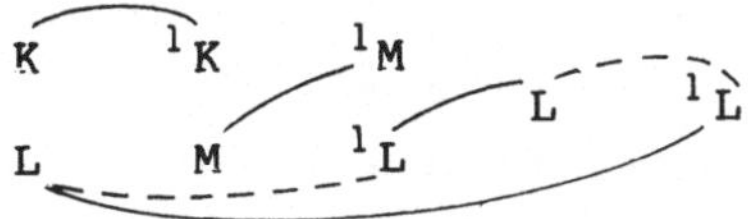

In both cases, apparently there is a much simpler proof with the dotted connection, and (6.1) enables us to avoid the more complicated one.

For instance, consider the first example and call it F . Further let its first two clauses be c_0 and c_1 . Then we have the situation dealt with in (6.1) with exactly the same notations. The theorem now says that any path through F containing K and ^{1}K is of the kind illustrated by the dashed path in figure 14 which has not to be checked for complementarity. On the other hand, the connection calculus, by extension via the connection $\{K,^1K\}$, examines exactly these paths, thus performs a redundant action with this step. The redundancy is removed by avoiding the step in such a situation. The following theorem states that this situation is characterized by the property that the clause c_1 selected for extension, such as $\{^1K,^1L\}$ in the first and $\{^1M,^1L\}$, in the second example, contains a literal ^{1}L where L occurs in a clause c_0 considered before, but this occurrence being no element of the active path. For making precise this informal description, we need once more the details and notations of the definition of a structured matrix and of extension for which the reader is referred to (II.4.2) and (II.4.3).

6.2.T. [CIRCUIT] Without affecting completeness or consistency of the connection calculus, extension $(F,S) \vdash (F,\tilde{S})$ may be restricted by the following requirement. The clause c_1 selected for extension (according to II.4.3.iii where c_1 is denoted by e) via a literal K in the active path $\tilde{p}_a$ (denoted by L in II.4.3.ii) does not contain a literal ^1L with $L \notin \tilde{p}_a$ satisfying the following property for $S = (\alpha,\beta,\gamma)$.

(*)   There is a clause c_0 in the domain of α such that $L \in c_0$.

Proof. Whenever there is a literal ^1L in the selected clause c_1 such that (*) holds then the set B of paths through F , checked for complementarity at this extension step, is given by $B = \{p \mid \tilde{p}_a \cup \{N\} \subseteq p$, $N \in c_1$, $\tilde{\beta}(N)=0\}$, using notation from (II.4.3). If F_0 and F_1 are defined as in (6.1), then none of the paths in B is one through any of these. Thus, by (6.1), the extension step in fact is redundant and may be avoided.   □

The following example - due to K.M. Hörnig (private communication) - shows that the condition $L \notin \tilde{p}_a$ in (*) cannot be deleted.

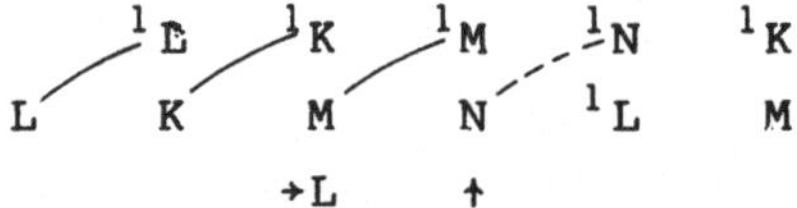

Extension via the dashed connection is now excluded since (*) applies. Apparently, the process would stop with failure after one further step. But the matrix is in fact complementary as shows a run respecting **both** conditions in (*):

Let us assume that the connection calculus is restricted as in (6.2) and applied to the first of the present examples. We assume it selects K in $\{K,L\}$ as before. But now there is no appropriate clause for extension. Thus separation may be applied, which withdraws the clause $\{K,L\}$ from further consideration. In the remaining matrix ^1K is now pure, and thus $\{^1K,^1L\}$ may be ignored as well. The rest is treated in one step by locating the dotted connection. Similarly for the second example.

A related result on deleting tautological circuits has been given in [B10]. In contrast to (6.2), which provides a dynamic avoidance of circuits, the result in [B10] is given in form of a reduction rule (like PURE for instance).

In resolution the feature corresponding to this avoidance of circuits is the avoidance of tautological resolvents. Namely, resolving on all but one of the connections of such a circuit results in a tautological resolvent; that is why we call them **tautological** circuits. We are now turning our attention to another feature which also is well-known in resolution and is called **factorization** .

Consider the matrix $\begin{smallmatrix} K & ^1K & ^1L \\ L & L & L \end{smallmatrix}$. After the connection calculus has located the connection $\{K,^1K\}$ it is left with two identical subgoals L . The following theorem says that the right one of these two subgoals may be safely ignored relying on the solution for the left one. Hence explicitly only the dotted connection must be considered which implicitely also takes care of the dashed connection. In more complicated examples, this feature may save much more than processing just a single connection.

6.3.D. $(F,S) \vdash (\tilde{F},S)$ is called **extension with factorization** if the two structured matrices (F,S) and $(\tilde{F},S)$ are related as described for extension in (II.4.3) except that the requirement "For any $L \in e$, $\tilde{\beta}(L) = 0$ iff $^1L \in \tilde{p}_a$" in (iv) there is substituted by the following requirement.

(**)   For any $L \in e$, $\tilde{\beta}(L) = 0$ iff $^1L \in \tilde{p}_a$ or there is a clause c_0 in the domain of α such that $L \in c_0$, $\beta(L) = 1$, and $\gamma(c_0) \neq L$. $\Box$

6.4.T. $\lceil$FACTORIZATION$\rceil$ Building factorization into the connection calculus (with or without the circuit feature) the way described in (6.3) does not affect its completeness and consistency.

Proof. By (**) more subgoals may be deleted than with usual extension. If this in fact happens then F contains two clauses of the form $c_0 = c_0' \cup \{L\}$ and $c_1 = c_1' \{L\}$. It does not affect validity, if we substitute these two clauses by the single, but non-normal form clause $\{\{c_0',c_1'\},L\}$ (cf. E5 in II.7), which combines the two subgoals into one. If we project the structure S into this new matrix it becomes obvious that the subgoal L in c_0 may play the role of this common subgoal. $\qquad\qquad\square$

With the features $\overset{c}{\text{CIRUIT}}$ and FACTORIZATION built into the connection calculus, for instance, we obtain the following piece of a proof.

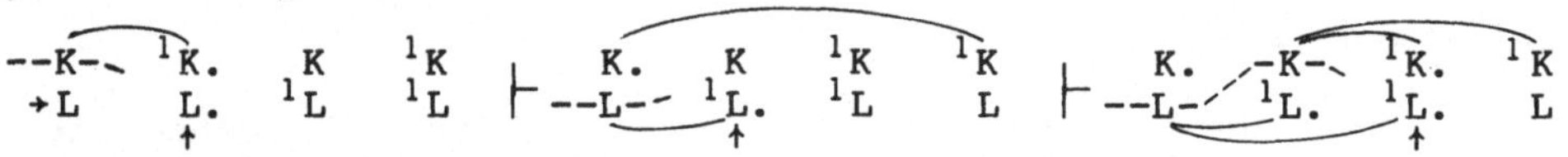

```
   ___                        _______________
 --K-⌐ ¹K.   K   ¹K      K.   K    ¹K    ¹K        K.  ⌐-K-⌐ ¹K.  ¹K
 →L    L.  ¹L  ¹L   ├ --L-- ¹L.  ¹L     L    ├ --L-⌐ ¹L.  ¹L.    L
       ↑                    ↑                           ↑
```

We have treated only the case of normal form matrices for these two features. For the generalization to arbitrary matrices, which requires some care, the reader is referred to $\lceil$HÖB$\rceil$. The lifting of these features to the first-order level is straightforward indeed; but note that we may or may not allow a change of the substitution σ for their application as discussed in similar context at the beginning of this section.

As we have seen above, whenever FACTORIZATION applies then there is a common factor in two separate clauses. The converse of this statement, however, is not true which means that there are cases of separate clauses with common factors which are not covered by FACTORIZATION. For instance, consider the following proof.

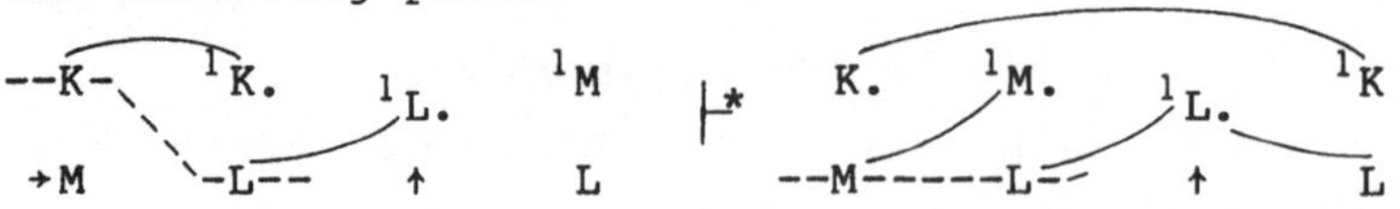

```
   ___
 --K-⌐  ¹K.    ¹L.    ¹M      ├*    K.    ¹M.    ¹L.      ¹K
 →M    `-L--    ↑     L           --M-----L--    ↑        L
```

It solves the subgoal L twice in exactly the same way. In [Sh1], Shostak has generalized FACTORIZATION (within a linear resolution setting) to cover such cases as well. The idea is, to simply memorize solved subgoals so that a second occurrence may be easily noticed. The details are not trivial, however, since the phenomena described in (5.1) have to be taken into consideration.

Even with Shostaks generalization, the phenomenon of common factors is not exhausted as the following example demonstrates.

The dotted connection is useless to take into consideration since it leads to a subgoal, K , which already is on the agenda, that is, within the active path. In general, we have the following result.

6.5.T. Without affecting completeness or consistency of the connection calculus, extension may be restricted such that the clause selected for extension does not contain a literal which already occurs in the active path.

The proof goes similar as the one for (6.4), and is left to the reader as an exercise (see E11 in section 12).   □

All these partial solutions to the phenomenon of a common factor in two different clauses are special cases of the most general solution which first eliminates such factors by iterated application of the distributivity law $\{c \cup \{L\}, d \cup \{L\}\}$ $\vdash \{\{c,d\},\{L\}\}$ and then applies the non-normal form procedure CP_3^o (with the CIRUIT feature added) from the previous section.

The problem is that on the general level the common factors are not known in advance without predetermining to some extent the global substitution σ . Therefore, the most promising solution seems to be one which allows this application of the distributivity law at any point in the connection proof. This requires the description of the distributivity law for structured matrices in the form $(F,S) \vdash_d (F',S')$ where F' is obtained from F by multiplying out one common factor the way given in the previous paragraph and S' is a structure on F' corresponding to S on F. Note that F' is strictly smaller than F. At present such a solution does not exist in a running system, therefore experience has yet to show whether it is practicable.

From experience with many examples it is hard to believe that there are propositional formulas for which the connection method with such a smart solution of factorization still requires an exponential number of proof steps, as the people working in complexity theory believe (the conjecture is that NP ≠ coNP holds; see [CoR]). A further discussion of this side-remark, however, would lead us away from the topic of this book. We only want to make the point with it that this material might be of considerable relevance for some key problems in theoretical computer science.

Not only from such a theoretical point of view, but also in view of the realization of a real smart proof machine based on the connection method there is still a wide field open for further research, even on the ground level. For instance, the most appropriate data-structure for representing formulas, which allows a quick execution of each single step, seems not to have been found so far. We, however, now turn our attention to potential improvements of **first-order features** , that are features which have no significance on the ground level.

7.   LOGICAL CALCULI OF NATURAL DEDUCTION

Over the last hundred years many different calculi for first-order logic have been developed. This development started with the famous Begriffsschrift by Frege [Fre], and later led to so-called Hilbert-type calculi in which valid formulas are derived from a sequence of basic logical formulas by means of a few forms of inference [HiA]. Gentzen called these **logistic** calculi in [Ge1] and argued there that they are "rather far

removed from the forms of deduction used in practice in mathematical proofs". Gentzen's intention, therefore, was "to set up
a formal system which comes as close as possible to actual
reasoning". For this purpose, he very carefully studied actual
mathematical proofs (see II.1 in [Ge1], and §4 in [Ge2]), and
came up with his famous calculus of natural deduction, denoted
by NK with N for "natural" and K for "classical", that is,
"klassisch" in German.

Our interest in such natural calculi from the point of
view of ATP arises from the following two aspects. First of
all, it is certainly not a satisfactory imagination that a
running proof machine simply outputs **true** as the result of a
completed proof. Rather we would prefer it to print on request
the whole proof in a form which can be well understood by anyone familiar with natural logical reasoning; or, in case of
failure, we would like to see where the natural chain of
reasoning actually fails. The most important step towards such
a goal certainly consists in establishing the formal connection
between, say, a connection proof and a natural deduction proof,
which will come along as a corollary in section (10.6).

On the other hand, a number of technical variants have
been derived from NK which, due to their extremely lucid structure allow a deep insight into the nature of proofs. In fact,
it was the author's study of such a formal system which eventually resulted in the connection calculus. For its potential
further improvement, an intimate knowledge of these systems
still seems to be indispensable.

In the present section, we will therefore introduce
such a formal system denoted by GS which is to remind of Gentzen and Schütte. In order to point out the extent to which it
still may be regarded as a "natural" deduction system, we
first present Gentzen's NK from [Ge1] adapted to our terminology. We do so also because NK is still to be regarded as the
most natural calculus for first-order reasoning.

The essential novelty of NK is its deductions starting
from **assumptions** (as in natural reasoning) rather than from
basic logical propositions as in the Hilbert-type calculi, or
logistic calculi as Gentzen calls them. These **assumption**

formulas or formulas of the form $A \lor \neg A$ (**tertium non datur**) are placed at the leaves of the **derivation tree** while the formula to be proved occurs at its root. The nodes of the tree are related according to the **inference figure schemes** or rules listed in table 3, which are briefly discussed now (for any further details see Gentzen's own beautiful text).

Table 3. The inference figure schemes of NK

$$
\wedge\text{-I} \qquad \frac{A \quad B}{A \wedge B}
\qquad\qquad
\wedge\text{-E} \qquad \frac{A \wedge B}{A} \quad \frac{A \wedge B}{B}
$$

$$
\lor\text{-I} \qquad \frac{A}{A \lor B} \quad \frac{B}{A \lor B}
\qquad\qquad
\lor\text{-E} \qquad \frac{A \lor B \quad \overset{[A]}{C} \quad \overset{[B]}{C}}{C}
$$

$$
\forall\text{-I*)} \qquad \frac{F}{\forall c\, F}
\qquad\qquad
\forall\text{-E} \qquad \frac{\forall x F}{F\{x\backslash t\}}
$$

$$
\exists\text{-I} \qquad \frac{F\{x\backslash t\}}{\exists x F}
\qquad\qquad
\exists\text{-E*)} \qquad \frac{\exists c F \quad \overset{[F]}{C}}{C}
$$

$$
\to\text{-I} \qquad \frac{\overset{[A]}{B}}{A \to B}
\qquad\qquad
\to\text{-E} \qquad \frac{A \quad A \to B}{B}
$$

$$
\neg\text{-I} \qquad \frac{\overset{[A]}{F}}{\neg A}
\qquad\qquad
\neg\text{-E} \qquad \frac{A \quad \neg A}{F} \quad \frac{F}{D}
$$

*) Such inferences are subject to a variable condition (cf. 7.1)

For each logical symbol there is both a rule for its introduction (I) and for its elimination (E). For instance, $\wedge$-I thus introduces the symbol $\wedge$ while $\wedge$-E eliminates it. The presentation as figures in the plane had been chosen to visualize the tree-structure. In the previous parts in this book we have preferred the linear presentation with the meta-symbol $\vdash$ for the inference relation. Thus, for instance, we also could write $\wedge$-I in the form $A,B \vdash A\wedge B$.

The bracketed formulas refer to assumption formulas of the derivation which is best illustrated with an example. The derivation in figure 15 (adapted from II.4 in [Ge1]) uses two such assumptions labeled by 1 and 2. These two labels reoccur as indices in the inferences $\exists\text{-}E_1$ and $\rightarrow\text{-}I_2$ in order to show explicitly which assumption formula is actually used in each of these inferences. Hence, the instance of $\exists\text{-}E$ in this example uses $\forall b\ Pab$ as an assumption. While its premise $\forall b\exists x\ Pxb$ depends on this assumption, the same is no more the case for its conclusion which only depends on the assumption $\exists x\ \forall b\ Pxb$, which becomes clear by the corresponding natural proof in figure 15.

This natural text, adapted from (II.1.2) in [Ge1], demonstrates the naturalness of NK, as do the other examples in Gentzen's text. In fact, it should not be too difficult to design a system which automatically produces such a text from a given derivation in NK, the converse being somewhat more difficult, of course. Hence the natural communication with a

$$
\cfrac{
\cfrac{
\exists a\ \forall y\ Pay \qquad
\cfrac{
\cfrac{
\cfrac{
\cfrac{\forall y\ \overset{1}{Pay}}{Pab}
}{\exists x\ Pxb}
}{\forall b\ \exists x\ Pxb}
}{\exists x\ Pxb}
}{\forall b\ \exists x\ Pxb}
}{\exists a\ \forall y\ Pay \rightarrow \forall b\ \exists x\ Pxb}
\qquad
\begin{array}{l}
\forall\text{-}E \\[4pt]
\exists\text{-}I \\[4pt]
\forall\text{-}I \\[4pt]
\exists\text{-}E_1 \\[4pt]
\rightarrow\text{-}I_2
\end{array}
$$

"Suppose there is an a such that for all y Pay holds (assumption 2). Let a be such an a (assumption 1). Then for all y Pay holds. Now let b be an arbitrary object. Then Pab holds ($\forall$-E). Thus there is an x, viz. a, such that Pxb holds. Since b was arbitrary, our result therefore holds for all objects, i.e. for all b there is an x such that Pxb holds ($\forall$-I and $\exists$-E$_1$). This yields our assertion ($\rightarrow$-I$_2$)."

Figure 15. A derivation in NK and a corresponding natural proof

theorem prover seems to be feasible, once we have understood
the precise relationship between an NK-proof and a connection
proof. This task will be divided into two parts, the first one
being settled in the rest of this section with the description
of the correspondence between NK and the system GS to be introduced now.

Technically, the representation of the dependence of formulas
in an NK-derivation, also called **D-formulas** , from assumptions $A_1,\ldots,A_n$ turned out to be somewhat awkward. In that
respect logistic calculi are more appropriate. Gentzen himself
noticed this, and he pointed out the possibilities of convert-
ing an NK-derivation into a closely related logistic one, among
which is this: "We replace a D-formula B, which depends on the
assumption formulas $A_1,\ldots,A_n,$ by the new formula
$A_1 \wedge \ldots \wedge A_n \to B$. This we do with all D-formulas." (see III.1
in [Ge1]).

We have to note, however, that the use of the symbols
$\wedge$ and $\to$ by this procedure actually takes place at the meta-
level of the formal language. Strictly speaking, they therefore should be considered as new symbols necessitating additional inference rules. But, of course, the logical meaning of
these symbols remains the same on any level of language; hence,
the rules would be the same as before. Based on this observation Schütte [Sc4] merged the two levels by neglecting the
distinction between the symbols $\wedge$, $\to$ on the basic and on the
meta-level which provided remarkable technical improvement.

In addition, Schütte dropped the redundant elimination
rules and restricted the tertium-non-datur to literals. With
all these modifications applied to NK and with the subsequent
adaption to the first-order language used within this book we
easily arrive at the following calculus GS for first-order
logic.

7.1.D. Inductive definition of the derivability relation $\vdash$
for GS.
(ax)   We have $\vdash v(G_1,Pt_1\ldots t_n,G_2,\neg Pt_1\ldots t_n,G_3)$, that
is, all formulas of this kind, which are called **axioms** , are
derivable. Here and in the following rules the occurrence of

the formulas G_i , i=1,2,3 , is optional.

($\wedge$)   From $\vdash$ $v(G_1,F_i,G_2)$ for i=1,...,n with n>2 , we may infer $\vdash$ $v(G_1,\wedge(F_1,...,F_n),G_2)$

($\forall$)   From $\vdash$ $v(G_1,F,G_2)$ we may infer $\vdash$ $v(G_1,\forall c_1...c_nF, G_2)$, provided that the c_i , i=1,...,n with n>1 , do not occur in G_1,G_2 .

($\exists$)   From $\vdash$ $v(G_1,F\{x_1\backslash t_1,...,x_n\backslash t_n\}$, $\exists x_1...x_nF,G_2)$ we may infer $\vdash$ $v(G_1,\exists x_1...x_nF,G_2)$, where the occurrence of $\exists x_1...x_nF$ in the premise is optional and where n>1 . None of the variables or constants in t_i, i=1,...,n , is bound by some quantifier in F . $\square$

Perhaps it is helpful to remind the reader once again of our conventions from (II.1.3) and (III.1.4) w.r.t. formulas which we are still using, of course. Hence $Lv\neg L$, $L\rightarrow LvG_3$, (G_1vL) v $(L\rightarrow G_3)$, all are axioms in the sense of (ax). This shows that the axioms are instances of the tertium-non-datur for literals possibly with additional disjunctive parts.

Further we have a single rule for each of the 3 symbols $\wedge,\forall$, and $\exists$, that is, 3 rather than the 15 rules as in NK. The rule ($\wedge$) apparently is a variant of $\wedge$-I in NK with an arbitrary number of arguments and possibly with additional disjunctive parts.

In a similar way, the rule ($\forall$) is related to $\forall$-I in NK, and an example of its application is shown in figure 16. In ($\forall$) we have spelled out the **variable condition** which ensures that the objects denoted by c_i, i=1,...,n , are in fact completely arbitrary. The reader may easily grasp the natural idea behind this condition by neglecting it in a faulty "derivation" of $\forall x\exists a$ x<a $\rightarrow$ $\exists y\forall b$ b<y from the axiom b<a $\rightarrow$ b<a which formula obviously is not valid (see exercise E12 in section 12).

Finally, the rule ($\exists$) corresponds to $\exists$-I in NK. Its application again is demonstrated in figure 16. Incidentally, this derivation as a whole corresponds to that in figure 15. The steps, one by one, correspond to each other, except for the last one $\rightarrow$-I_2 in figure 15 which is taken care of in GS by carrying the assumptions as premises in all formulas. This correspondence is further discussed below.

$$
\begin{aligned}
Pab &\rightarrow Pab & \text{(ax)} \\
\forall y\ Pay &\rightarrow Pab & (\exists\,) \\
\forall y\ Pay &\rightarrow \exists x\ Pxb & (\exists\,) \\
\forall y\ Pay &\rightarrow \forall b\,\exists x\ Pxb & (\forall) \\
\exists a\forall y\ Pay &\rightarrow \forall b\,\exists x\ Pxb & (\forall)
\end{aligned}
$$

Figure 16. A derivation in GS of the formula from figure 15

There is also a close relationship with the standard procedure SP from (III.3.7), since step 3 in SP generates the inverse of an instance of ($\forall$) or ($\exists$). Hence the recognition-type calculus SP may be viewed as the inverse of the generative-type calculus GS except that SP has a more general axiom property, viz. propositional complementarity, for which reason there is no inverse to rule ($\wedge$). This relationship provides the following result.

7.2.C. The calculus GS is consistent and complete.

   Proof. Consistency is an immediate consequence of (III.4.4ii), (III.3.6), and (III.3.2). Completeness follows from completeness of SP shown in (III.3.11), since for any valid formula F a run of SP yields a derivation which can be easily extended to a derivation of F within GS by appropriate insertions of instances of ($\wedge$) which preserves validity by (III.4.4.ii). $\square$

As we said further above the relationship between NK-proofs and connection proofs will be established in two parts, the intermediate role being played by GS-proofs and their relation with connection proofs being explored in the subsequent sections. For the relationship of NK-proofs and GS-proofs we have described how GS has been developed out of NK. With this description at hand it is an easy exercise to set up a procedure which generates from a given proof in NK with no occurrence of rule $\rightarrow$-E , the **modus ponens** , a corresponding proof in GS (see E14 in section 12; the elimination of the modus ponens from any NK-proof may be achieved with the procedure from the proof of Gentzen's Hauptsatz [Ge1]).

   The converse is a little more demanding, but still

rather straightforward. Here we give just a brief outline of such a procedure leaving its details again to the reader (see E15 in section 12). Thus we assume we are given a formula F and a derivation Δ of F within GS . We are looking for a procedure, say ND, which generates from F and Δ a natural deduction Δ' of F within NK. As an example, we are considering the formula and derivation in figure 16 in comparison with the derivation in figure 15 to be generated.

During the process ND has to store a set **H** of hypotheses. Initially (and after termination), **H** is empty. But whenever F turns out to be of the form A→B then A is added to **H** , B is assigned to F as its new value, and a corresponding instance of rule →-I is added to Δ' . In our example, this generates the last inference →-I$_2$ in figure 15.

ND now considers the last inference in (the actual value of) Δ and distinguishes the two cases determined by whether this inference affects a formula part currently in F or one in **H** . For instance, the last inference in figure 16 introduces the ∃a in the premise which at this stage already is in **H** . In both cases, this inference together with the entries in **H** and F determines the next step(s) in Δ' . In the present case, for instance, there is exactly one rule in NK which in its inverse direction allows the deletion of an existential quantifier in a hypothesis, viz. ∃-E . Thus the next step in Δ' turns out to be ∃-E$_1$ as in figure 15. This causes the only entry in **H** to be substituted by the new hypothesis ∀yPay . In Δ the last step may now be deleted by ND .

After this deletion the actual last step in Δ this time affects F . Again, it uniquely determines the next step ∀-I in figure 15. In the same way the next step ∃-I is obtained. Note here that the given derivation Δ (even in general) also provides the term t to be substituted for x in ∃-I . The same is true in the case of rule ∀-E , an instance of which is generated by ND in the last step for the present example which also empties **H** .

With this informal description we think it is now rather obvious how the precise details of ND may be completed by a careful case-analysis. It also shows once again how closely related the two systems NK and GS actually are. For this close relationship GS may well be regarded as a **natural** deduction system which at the same time is logistic in Gentzen's sense. Its main technical advantage lies in its restriction to only 3 rules of inference which enables a deeper insight into the structure of natural proofs (represented by GS-proofs) as we will see in the next section.

As a final remark, we notice that ND actually makes a distinction between the formulas $A \to B$ and $\neg A \vee B$ since in a natural proof the intention behind the two is of course different. For this reason we have kept the implication sign in many examples of this book. In an actual implementation one would do the same for the benefit of ND (and thus of the user); but the theorem prover would not notice the distinction (except perhaps for strategical purposes).

8.   AN ALTERNATIVE FOR SKOLEMIZATION

The connection calculus, which was introduced in section III.6, applies for formulas in Skolem normal form only. At this point, if we speak of the connection calculus, we may actually have in mind a version which incorporates all the improvements discussed in earlier sections of the present chapter. Still, such an improved version is subject to that restriction as well since all these improvements are of a propositional nature only.

From section III.4 we know that this restriction actually is of little harm since via skolemization any formula may be easily transformed into Skolem normal form. Traditional experts in ATP might even question whether there is any harm at all.

In order to exhibit one disadvantage of skolemization, we consider the formula $\exists x_1 \ldots x_m \, \forall c \, P(c, \ldots, c)$, where P is an n-ary predicate. Thus the length of this formula is about m+n . Skolemization yields the formula $\exists x_1 \ldots x_m \, P(f x_1 \ldots x_m, \ldots, f x_1 \ldots x_m)$, the length of which is about $m + n \cdot m$. This shows that skolemization may increase the length of the formula

ula quadratically. There is an increase for all (non-trivial) formulas, though not always of such an extreme extent. Even if we would neglect the additional storage space, the resultant effect on the time required for the (often many) unifications to be carried out in a proof might add up to a quantity where it begins to make sense to worry about.

Apart from this technical point, skolemization apparently destroys part of the natural structure of the formula which is of disadvantage at least in an interactive theorem proving system. These two reasons might be regarded as a motivation for attempting an alternate solution. After successful completion of this attempt we will see in the rest of this chapter that our alternative solution provides us even with further advantages mentioned later.

A natural starting point for such an attempt is the system GS from the previous section (or its inverse form SP from III.3.7), since there is nothing like skolemization in it so that something else must take over its role.

Consider the theorem $\exists x(Px \lor \forall c \exists y(Py \lor \neg Pc))$. Its skolemized form is $\exists x \exists y(Px \lor \overline{Py} \lor \neg Pfx)$, where the single connection provides the proof. Apparently, the connection $\{Px, \neg Pfx\}$ cannot be used for a proof with multiplicity 1 since, with no substitution can x and fx ever be unified. This is different in the original formula where the corresponding connection $\{Px, \neg Pc\}$ would become complementary by the substitution $\{x \backslash c\}$. There must be something else in GS , then, which prevents this substitution in some other way. In fact, it is the variable condition in rule $(\forall)$ of (7.1) which serves exactly for this purpose. Namely, while

$$Px \lor Pc \lor \neg Pc \;\vdash\; Px \lor \exists y(Py \lor \neg Pc) \;\vdash\; Px \lor \forall c \exists y(Py \lor \neg Pc)$$
$$\vdash\; \exists x(Px \lor \forall c \exists y(Py \lor \neg Pc))$$

is a correct deduction in GS , the same is not true for

$$Pc \lor Py \lor \neg Pc \;\vdash\; Pc \lor \exists y(Py \lor \neg Pc) \;\vdash\; Pc \lor \forall c \exists y(Py \lor \neg Pc)$$
$$\vdash\; \exists x(Px \lor \forall c \exists y(Py \lor \neg Pc)),$$

since after the second step the constant c does occur "free" in Pc thus violating (∀) . All this applies in the same way to the theorem $\exists x \forall c \exists y (Px \vee Pyv \neg Pc)$, but now with respect to the condition from (∃) in (7.1), which the reader should quickly check.

Even from this simple example we may immediately derive a general **rule** : Whenever in a formula of the form $\exists xF$, F contains a subformula of the form $\forall cF_0$, then the term substituted for x must not contain the constant c since otherwise one of the conditions in 7.1 would be violated. If we do not worry for the moment for further details (such as multiplicity other than 1) then it seems that we may apply the connection calculus to un-skolemized formulas as before except for respecting such a rule, which will turn out to be true.

For instance, the dashed connections in $\exists x (Pxv \forall c \exists y (Py \vee \neg Pc))$ and $\exists x \forall c \exists y (Px \vee Pyv \neg Pc)$ give rise to substitutions which violate the rule, while the full connections do provide the proof. Similarly, $\forall c \exists x (Qcx \rightarrow Qxc)$ represents a correct proof while $\exists x \forall c (Qcx \rightarrow Qxc)$ does not, all in accordance with correct logic.

In its present form, the rule would require an awkward testing. Namely, consider the formula $\exists x \forall c \exists y (Px \vee Qcv (\neg Py \wedge \neg Qy))$. Only after considering the full connection, the chain c-y-x would show that the dashed connection violates the rule (with multiplicity 1), since c is substituted for y hence also for x . This looks frightening since in general such chains may be arbitrarily long. But there is an elegant technical solution, allowing an easy and fast test, which will now be introduced.

Informally, in cases like in the last example we have $\exists x < \forall c$, or shortly x < c , where < denotes the tree ordering of the formula. In case of a substitution $\{x \backslash c\}$ we let c <· x with a further partial ordering <· , which expresses our rule above in negative form, saying that, since c has been substituted for x , x < c must **not** be the case, that is, c <· x must be compatible with < . For all dashed connections above, this compatibility is **not** satified, rather we have both, x < c and c <· x . This may be regarded as a cycle x < c <· x in the transitive closure, say ◁ , of < U<· . Hence in this representation, checking the rule means testing for cycles, even in the general case which will now be treated in a precise way.

8.1.D. The descendance (or ancestry) relation in a formula tree (see I.1.2) will be denoted by $<$, or sometimes by $<_F$, where F denotes the formula. This partial ordering will be called the **tree ordering** of F . By convention, this relation will often be represented by the pairs of labels associated with the tree nodes rather than by the nodes themselves. The root always is the least element w.r.t. $<$.

For any substitution σ substituting terms for variables, an equivalence relation $\sim$ and a relation $<\cdot$ (sometimes also denoted by $\sim_\sigma$ and $<\cdot_\sigma$, resp.) is defined as follows.

(r1)   If $x\backslash y \in \sigma$ then $x \sim y$ holds.

(r2)   If $x\backslash t \in \sigma$ and t is no variable, then $y <\cdot x$ holds for any variable y occurring in t and $c <\cdot x$ holds for any constant c occurring in t .

(r3) $\sim$ fulfils the requirements of an equivalence relation; further if $x \sim y$ and $c <\cdot x$ hold then also $c <\cdot y$ holds.

By $\triangleleft$ we denote the transitive closure of the union of the relations $<$ and $<\cdot$. $\square$

The formula $\exists x\ \forall c\ \exists y\ (\overline{Pxc} \lor \neg Pyy)$ illustrates why we introduced the relation $\sim$. Namely, if we introduce a Skolem term fx instead of c then fx cannot be unified with y since this would actually result in a unification with x because x and y have to be unified as well. The same effect is achieved here by (r3) which from $x \sim y$ and $c <\cdot y$ implies $c <\cdot x$, thus leading to a cycle.

The formula $\exists x\ \forall c\ (\overline{Pfc} \lor \neg Px)$ similarly illustrates why $c <\cdot x$ is taken in (r2) for any constant in a term (here fc). For the case of a variable the same is illustrated by the formula $\exists x\ \forall c\ \exists y\ (\overline{P(fy,c)} \lor \neg P(x,y))$ where (r2) yields $c <\cdot y <\cdot x$ again leading to a cycle.

In this form now it appears to be quite obvious that skolemization may be replaced by these relations from (8.1).

However, they have been presented so far in a much too simplified form, so that their complete definition will require substantially more formalism.

Remember from section III.6 that possibly several copies of the formula are needed for a connection proof. For that purpose we have introduced the notion of a multiplicity for formulas (see III.6.1). While this definition was given for arbitrary formulas, its further use in section III.6 was actually restricted to formulas in Skolem normal form. If we want to get rid of skolemization then we have to remove this restriction, as will be done now.

8.2.D. Let F^μ be a formula with multiplicity μ , and $\Omega(F)$ denote the set of its positions or nodes. Then the set of its **indexed nodes** $\Omega(F^\mu)$ is a set of pairs (r,κ) , or shortly r^κ such that the following holds.

(i1) $r\in\Omega(F)$, r is a node in F

(i2)   If the set $\{r_1,\ldots,r_n\} \subseteq \Omega(F)$, $n>0$, contains all positions r_i in F such that $r_1 < r_2 < \ldots < r_n < r$ and for all i $F_{:r_i} = \exists x_{i1}\ldots x_{in_i} F_i$ holds for some F_i and some x_{ij} $j=1,\ldots,n_i$, then we have $\kappa = j_1 \cdot j_2 \cdots \cdot j_n$ and $1 \le j_i \le \mu(r_i)$ for $i=1,\ldots,n$.

For instance, consider for F the formula $\exists x^{r1}\forall c(L^r \vee \exists y^{r2} K p)$, and let $\mu(r1) = 2$ and $\mu(r2) = 3$. Let us first consider the node r , where we find the literal L , and ask for its possible indices. Obviously, there is exactly one position, viz. r1, in F such that the outermost symbol of the subformula in F with root r1 (remember the notation $F_{:r1}$ from II.1.2) is an existential quantifier. Since its multiplicity $\mu(r1)$ is 2 , we have to consider exactly 2 copies of L , that is, the two indexed nodes $(r,1)$ and $(r,2)$ for r . The node p in addition lies in the scope of the quantifier at position r2 with multiplicity 3; therefore each of the 2 copies deriving from r1 once more splits into 3 copies, which gives the altogether 6 indexed nodes $(p,1.1)$, $(p,1.2)$, $(p,1.3)$, $(p,2.1)$, $(p,2.2)$, and $(p,2.3)$.

When we are talking of different copies this appeals to the readers imagination only, since the calculus never con-

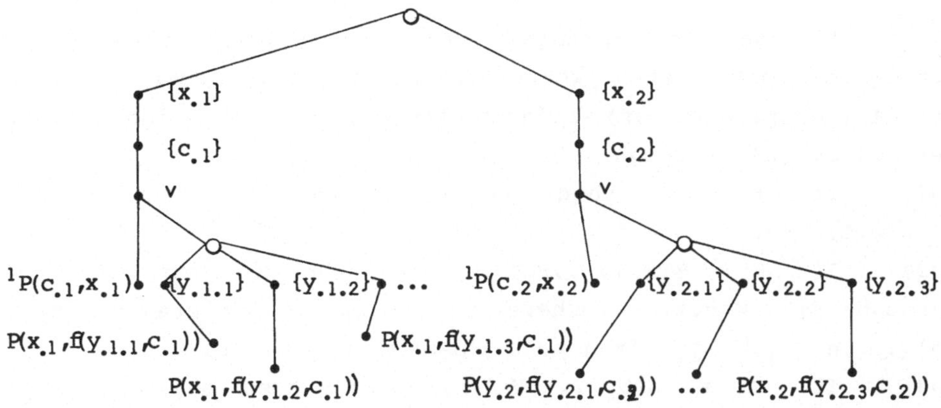

Figure 17. The explicit formula tree for an indexed formula

siders such different copies explicitly as we already know from
section III.6 (cf. figure 2 there). Nevertheless it is sometimes very helpful for the reader to think in terms of explicit copies. For illustration the previous formula F^μ is
presented in figure 17 with specified literals (L specified
as ^1Pcx and K as Px,fyc), and the copies shown explicitly
as far as space allowed to do so. For exhibiting the copies
extra nodes (the little circles) have been introduced. They
may well be interpreted as disjunctive nodes which becomes
clear by noticing that such different copies in GS are realized by rule ($\exists$) with an v as outermost symbol. With this
interpretation the following concepts are in fact obvious.

8.3.D.   For F^μ as before the tree ordering $<_{F^\mu}$, or
shortly < , is defined by:
$r1_{.\kappa_1} < r2_{.\kappa_2}$ iff $r1 < r2$ and $\kappa1.\kappa = \kappa2$ for some κ .
        For any literal L^r in F^μ and for any index κ
with $r_{.\kappa} \in \Omega(F^\mu)$, the set of indexed positions in F^μ , the
indexed literal $L_{.\kappa}$ is the literal $L\sigma$ where σ contains
all substitutions $z\backslash z_{.\kappa_1}$ satisfying the following property.
        z is a variable or a constant occurring in L and
quantified at some position r1 with $r1_{.\kappa_1} \in \Omega(F^\mu)$ and
$r1_{.\kappa_1} < r_{.\kappa}$.

A **path** p **through** F^μ is a path through F^μ w.r.t. the empty index, where p **w.r.t.** (any) **index** κ is a set of (occurrences of) indexed literals in F inductively defined by (p1) through (p5).

(p1)   If $F = L^r$ then $\{L_{.\kappa}\}$ is the only path through F w.r.t. κ .

(p2)   If $F = \vee(F_1,\ldots,F_n)$, $n>0$, then for any path p_i through $F_i^{\mu_i}$ w.r.t. κ , where μ_i is μ restricted to F_i , $i=1,\ldots,n$, $\bigcup_{i=1}^{n} p_i$ is a path through F^μ w.r.t. κ .

(p3)   If $F = \wedge(F_1,\ldots,F_n)$, $n>0$, then any path p_i through $F_i^{\mu_i}$ w.r.t. κ , where μ_i is μ restricted to F_i , $i \in \{1,\ldots,n\}$, is a path through F^μ w.r.t. κ .

(p4)   If $F = \exists^r x_1 \ldots x_n F_0$ with $\mu(r) = m$, then for any path p_i through $F_0^{\mu_0}$ w.r.t. $\kappa.i$, for $i=1,\ldots,m$, where μ_0 is μ restricted to F_0 , $\bigcup_{i=1}^{m} p_i$ is a path through F_0 w.r.t. κ.

(p5)   If $F = \forall c_1 \ldots c_n F_0$ then any path p through $F_0^{\mu_0}$ w.r.t. κ is a path through F^μ w.r.t. κ .

A **connection** in a formula F^μ is a 2-element subset of a path through F^μ of the form
$$\{(Ps_1 \ldots s_n)^{r0}_{.\kappa 0} \, , \, (^1Pt_1 \ldots t_n)^{r1}_{.\kappa 1}\} \, .$$

A set of connections in F^μ is called **spanning** if each path through F^μ contains at least one of these connections.   □

The generalized tree ordering $<$ is illustrated by figure 17 which also shows several indexed literals. The notions of paths, connections and spanning sets of connections are straightforward generalizations of those notions for the restricted case of Skolem normal form formulas defined in (III.6.2) and (III.6.3).

The definition of the relations $\sim$, $<\cdot$ and $\triangleleft$ in (8.1) for any substitution does not exclude the case of indexed variables and constants. Therefore we may now assume that $\triangleleft$ is defined also for the general case, which, at last, enables us to express our rule above in precise terms and to relate it with skolemization.

8.4.T. For any formula F , let $c_1,\ldots,c_n$ denote all different constants occurring in the closure of F (see

III.4.1.STEP0) and $\sigma = \{c_i \backslash f_i x_1 \ldots x_{m_i} \mid i=1,\ldots,n\}$ denote the substitution for skolemization of the closure of F (see III.4.1. STEP1) yielding formula $\tilde{F}$ in Skolem normal form, with the inverse substitution $\sigma^{-1} = \{f_i x_1 \ldots x_{m_i} \backslash c_i \mid i=1,\ldots,n\}$. Further let μ be a multiplicity for F (hence also for $\tilde{F}$) , U a spanning set of connections in F , and $\tilde{U}$ the corresponding set of connections in F with $\tilde{U} = U\sigma$. Finally let the two substitutions ρ and τ be related by $\rho = \tau\sigma^{-1}$, hence $\tau = \rho\sigma$ (recall III.5.2 for the composition of substitutions).

τ is a substitution such that $u\tau$ is a (propositionally) complementary pair of literals for any $u \in \tilde{U}$ iff

ρ is a substitution such that u is a complementary pair of literals for any $u \in U$ and the relation $\lhd$ determined by ρ and F^μ has no cycles.

With the motivation given at the beginning of this section the straightforward proof should be obvious, and thus is left to the reader as an exercise (see E16 in section 12).   □

From (III.6.4) we know that the left side in the iff-statement actually characterizes the validity of $\tilde{F}$, hence of F by (III.4.5). Thus this theorem provides a new characterization of validity which now applies for arbitrary formulas.

8.5.C. A formula F is valid iff

for some multiplicity μ there is a spanning set U of connections in F^μ and a substitution σ such that $u\sigma$ is a complementary pair of literals for any $u \in U$ and the relation $\lhd$ determined by σ and F^μ has no cycles.   □

In this characterization of validity the role of the Skolem functions has equivalently been taken over by the relation $<\cdot$ (together with the test for cycles in the resulting relation $\lhd$). In the motivation from the beginning of this section we have already illustrated the idea behind $<\cdot$ in terms of derivations in GS which may now be formalized in the following fact.

8.6.T. For any formula F , with μ , U , σ as in (8.5), there is a derivation Δ of F in GS such that for any pair

c, x (possibly with indices), for which c <· x holds, there
is a uniquely determined $\forall$-inference introducing $\forall$c which is
below (that is closer to the root of Δ) a uniquely determined $\exists$-inference of the form   v(G$_1$, G{...,x \ xσ,...} ,
$\exists$...x... G, G$_2$) $\vdash$ (G$_1$, $\exists$...x...G ,G$_2$) .   □

In other words, <·   encodes information about the **sequence**
of inferences in a corresponding derivation of F within GS.
Via (8.4), which relates <·   with Skolem functions, the same
can be said for Skolem functions. In fact such a derivation Δ
can even be constructed with the information given by F, μ, U,
and σ . At this point, however, we leave out further details
for this construction as they will be given in a more general
setting in section 10. As a preparation for this even more
complicated treatment exercise E17 in section 12 would be very
helpful.

   Altogether we thus have worked out an alternate technique instead of Skolem functions which applies to any original
formula to be proved, and thus does not suffer from the two
disadvantages mentioned at the beginning of this section. In
addition, it offers the advantage of an immediate relation with
a deduction in GS, as we have just described, which in turn is
closely related to a natural deduction as we know already
from section 7. But there are further advantages to be discussed in the following two sections.

9.   LINEAR UNIFICATION

In the present section we resume the discussion on unification
from section (III.5), and at the same time point out a close
relationship with the material of the previous section.
   Recall from the end of (III.5) that algorithm UNIF$_1$
in the worst case required exponential running time which was
demonstrated with the two terms $t_1 = f(x_1,...,x_n)$ and
$t_2 = f(g(x_0,x_0),...,g(x_{n-1},x_{n-1}))$. Even the mere writing
up of the final unifying substition is exponential since t in
$\{x_n \setminus t\}$ obviously contains $\sum_{i=1}^{n} 2^i$ occurrences of g . Both

can be substantially improved, however, as will be explained
now.

A more efficient and in fact linear representation of
unifiers can be achieved rightaway by considering sequences of
unifiers such as $\rho_1\rho_2\ldots\rho_n$ with $\rho_i = \{x_i\backslash g(x_{i-1},x_{i-1})\}$,
$i=1,\ldots,n$, in the previous example and by preventing the
actual computation of these compositions. But note for this
example that any different sequence w.r.t. the variables would
result in a worse representation. Therefore we are left with
the problem of how such an optimal sequence can be easily
achieved, which will also be solved by the subsequent algorithm.

As in (III.5) the discussion is restricted to the case
of the unification of a **single** set of **two** terms since the
generalizations mentioned at the end of (III.5) are then
straightforward. Also, our discussion will be rather informal
since a complete formal treatment would fill a whole chapter
(see the references in section 13).

Now, we have pointed out already at the end of (III.5)
that the problem with $UNIF_1$ lies in the so-called **occur-
check** checking for occurrences of variables in terms, so that
a smarter solution would have to keep track of such occurrences in a more clever way. One such solution in fact starts with
a different representation of terms as **directed acyclic
graphs** , shortly **dags** , rather than trees. In such dags common
subterms are represented by a single subgraph.

For instance, in the pair $\{f(x,gy,x)$, $f(gy,gx,ga)\}$
the subterms x and gy both occur more than once. Its corresponding labeled dag representation, then, is the following
one.

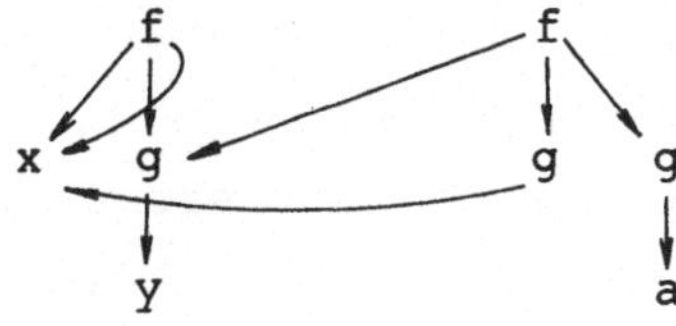

All tree notions from (I.1.2) are still meaningful for dags.

Any substitution σ naturally determines an equivalence relation $\sim$ on the set of nodes of such a dag. It will
be illustrated by connecting two equivalent nodes with an

undirected edge in the dag, as shown in the following example
for its mgu {x\gy} {y\gz} .

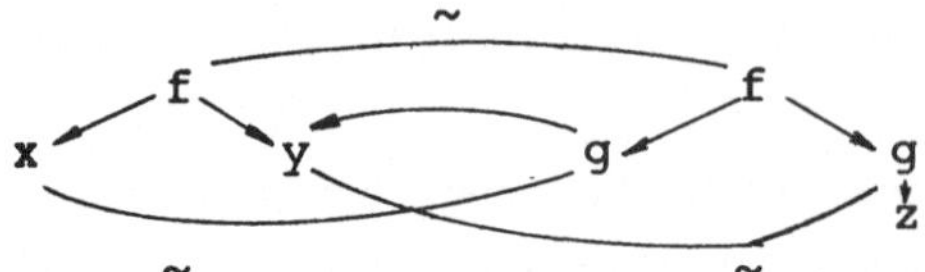

If σ is the mgu of the two terms represented by the dag we
will call ~ the **mgu-equivalence** .
        It is now obvious that an mgu-equivalence ~ must
satisfy the following two properties (i) and (ii).
(i)   Two nodes labeled with the same function symbols are
equivalent under ~ iff their corresponding successors are
pairwise equivalent under ~ .
(ii)   No equivalence class determined by ~ does contain
two nodes labeled with distinct function symbols.
        The partial ordering < given by a dag (where roots
are always least elements) naturally infers a binary relation
◁ on the equivalence classes determined by ~ by defining
$[ft_1 \ldots t_n]_\sim$ ◁ $[t_i]_\sim$ for any $i \in \{1, \ldots, n\}$. With this relation
the mgu-equivalences can now be characterized.

9.1.T. An equivalence relation ~ on the nodes of a dag
satisfying (i) and (ii) is an mgu-equivalence iff
        ◁ is a partial ordering (i.e. ◁ has no cycles).
        For the proof see exercise (E18) in section 12.   □

This theorem in some form provides the basis for all known
efficient unification algorithms. The essence of any such
algorithm may be described as follows. The roots of the two
given terms of course have to be equivalent. From there the
equivalence is **propagated** to the successor nodes according
to (i) which corresponds to the definition of DIFF for
$UNIF_1$ in (III.5.3). This propagation continues but with a
preference for smaller equivalence classes w.r.t. ◁ by which
precaution cycles may be automatically detected. Whenever one
of the pair of equivalent nodes is labeled with a variable x
the other is the root of subterm t with no arrow pointing

from some node in t to x (the case of a cycle) then {x\t}
is the next in the sequence of substitutions which finally
will represent the mgu. The latter action was called reduction
in (III.5.4). So the steps themselves are actually very similar to those in $UNIF_1$ the basic difference lying in the
sequence in which they are carried out.

Table 4 shows the details of an algorithm of that kind
with a worked example shown in figure 18. Both the algorithm
and the example are due to Paterson and Wegman [PaW] for which
reason we call the algorithm $UNIF_{PW}$. Its details are now
discussed in the form of comments to the snapshots (1) through
(5) shown in figure 18.

The given terms are   e(fv,guv) and e(fw,g(w,hxy)) .
Their dag is shown in (1) with the roots already connected.

At this point $UNIF_{PW}$ may encounter any function
node. Although in practice one would implement a preference
for nodes close to the root, let us, just for illustration of
the general case, do quite the opposite and select the node
labeled with h . Now, after the first line in the procedure
FINISH , the pointer of this node which, say, is denoted by
the number 1, will point to itself. This is illustrated in (2)
by labeling h with this value.

An important feature of FINISH is that it does not
consider h any further until all its ancestors have been
processed and deleted which will not happen before (3). This
feature realizes the preference for smaller equivalence classes
w.r.t. ◁ mentioned above. Thus FINISH is applied recursively once more, now to the predecessor, say 2 (labeled by g) of
node 1. There, the same happens as with node 1, and with another call of FINISH , applied to the predecessor, say 3 (labeled
by e), of node 2, the edge shown in (1) is finally taken into
account as the current value of {p,q} , with p=r=3. q is made
to point to r ; in other words, q is put into the equivalence
class [r] .

Now, the edge {p,q} may be propagated to the successors of its nodes which includes the deletion of {p,q} , and
of p and q and their outgoing arcs. The result illustrated in
snapshot (2).

Since the call FINISH(3) has thus been finished, the

Table 4. The unification algorithm UNIF$_{PW}$

Comment: UNIF$_{PW}$ tests {s,t} for unifiability.
represent {s,t} as a dag; σ←NIL;
if there is only a single root then return σ ;
create an undirected edge connecting the two roots;
while there is a node r labeled with a function symbol do
FINISH(r);
while there is a node r labeled with a variable do
FINISH(r);
return σ ;

procedure FINISH(r);
if pointer(r) is defined then return 'fail:loop' else
pointer(r)←r ;
create new stack-variable WAIT and WAIT←NIL;
WAIT←push(WAIT,r);
while WAIT≠NIL do
⌈p←pop(WAIT);
 if r and p are labeled with different function symbols then
 return 'fail:clash';
 while p has some predecessor q do FINISH(q);
 while there is an undirected edge {p,q} do
 ⌈if pointer(q) is undefined then pointer(q)←r;
  if pointer(q)≠r then return 'fail:loop';
  delete the undirected edge {p,q} ;
  WAIT←push(WAIT,q)⌉ ;
 if p≠r then
 ⌈if p is labeled with a variable then σ←σ{p\t$_r$} where t$_r$
  denotes the term with root r in the dag;
  if p is labeled with a function symbol and has n successors then
  for i=1,...,n do create an undirected edge connecting the
  i-th successor of r and of p ;

  delete p and the directed arcs out of p⌉⌉;
delete r and the directed arcs out of r ;
END

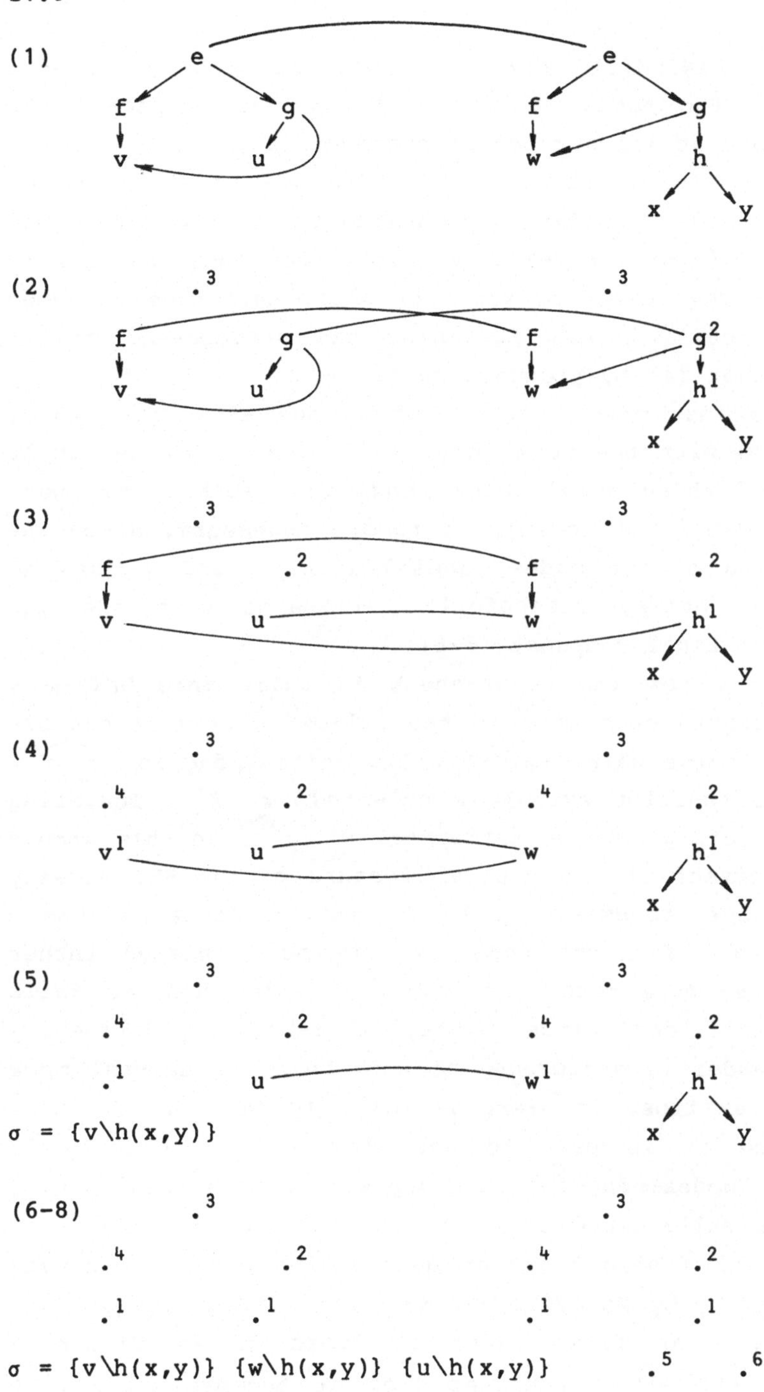

(1)

(2)

(3)

(4)

(5)

$\sigma = \{v\backslash h(x,y)\}$

(6-8)

$\sigma = \{v\backslash h(x,y)\}\ \{w\backslash h(x,y)\}\ \{u\backslash h(x,y)\}$

Figure 18. A run of UNIF_{PM}

processing of FINISH(2) may be resumed. As before, the edge connecting the two nodes labeled with g is propagated to their successors as illustrated in snapshot (3).

Finally, the first call of FINISH may be continued by traveling from node 1 to the node labeled by v along the connecting edge. This node receives a pointer to 1 and the edge is deleted. After the temporary visit on WAIT, this node is named p , and r=1 still holds. Finishing the predecessor of p leads to snapshot (4) by propagation as before.

In the last phase v, w, and u, one after the other, are now unified with the term hxy with root r , the result of the first of these steps being shown in snapshot (5). Note that an occur-check, of course, is nomore necessary. Since the final processing of the nodes labeled with x and y has no effect anymore, $UNIF_{PM}$ sucessfully terminates with the mgu σ shown in the final snapshot (6-8).

The way, how the occur-check is built into $UNIF_{PW}$, will be illustrated once more in the following trivial example of the non-unifiable pair {x,fx} . Its initial dag is $x \quad f$, and the single function symbol is selected $x \quad f^1$. Traveling along the connecting edge we arrive at $x^1 \quad f^1$. In this simple example, the effect of the crucial feature of FINISH, already pointed out above, becomes very lucid. Namely, since x has a predecessor, viz. f , the node x is not finished rather FINISH is called once more with node f which however fails with output 'fail:loop' since pointer (1) is already defined.

The reader is encouraged to work this way several more examples such as those in exercise (E19) in section 12. After such experience it is easy to see that $UNIF_{PM}$ actually is linear in the "nodes+edges" of the dag w.r.t. both running time and space, basically since each node is finished only once.

There is a second linear unification algorithm developed independently by Martelli and Montanari [MaM]; let us thus call it $UNIF_{MM}$. At first sight it looks rather different from $UNIF_{PW}$; but after a closer look it becomes clear that both methods are based on the same crucial idea represented by (9.1). However, $UNIF_{MM}$ uses a different data-structure since the authors observed that a suitable sequence of unifications may be obtained by a simple count of variable occurrences. While the details of $UNIF_{MM}$ (see $[MaM]$) appear to be a little less intuitive than those of $UNIF_{PM}$, for which reason we preferred the detailed presentation of $UNIF_{PM}$, it is important to note that for a possible implementation this clever counting technique provides $UNIF_{MM}$ with a practical advantage over $UNIF_{PM}$ as has been experienced by extensive implementational comparisons (see $[TWi]$).

In order to give the reader at least an idea of $UNIF_{MM}$'s behavior, we are now going to discuss its application to the same example as the one in figure 18, which is illustrated in figure 19. There, snapshot (1) shows the initial configuration consisting of the given pair of literals, and for each occurring variable the initial empty substitution in the form of an equation. For each of these substitutions the attached index represents the number of occurrences of this variable in the given terms.

The first actions simply consist in the propagation of the equivalence relation to the successors exactly as in $UNIF_{PW}$ (or in $UNIF_1$), leading to the situation shown in (3-4), where the numbering of the snapshots is such that corresponding configurations in the figures 18 and 19 have the same numbers.

In the step leading to snapshot (5) the equivalence between v and w (selected arbitrarily among the 3 choices) is worked into the second line by combining the two last substitutions into a single one as the union of the left and the right sides. At the same time a new index is calculated as the sum of the two previous indices minus the two occurrences of u and v just considered, that is, (2+2)-2=2. The same happens in the next step with the calculation (1+2)-2=1. Similarly in the next step except that now the second term is not a variable, in which case this term is added as a new element to the set on the right side of the unique equation which contains the first term as a variable in the set on the left side. This again includes the calculation of a new index which in this case simply consists of subtracting 1 for the single occurrence of v which has been taken care of during this step.

(1)   {{e(fv,guv) , e(fw,gw(hxy))}}
        $\{x\}_1 = \emptyset$, $\{y\}_1 = \emptyset$, $\{u\}_1 = \emptyset$, $\{v\}_2 = \emptyset$, $\{w\}_2 = \emptyset$,

(2)   {{fv,fw} , {guv,gw(hxy)}}
        $\{x\}_1 = \emptyset$, $\{y\}_1 = \emptyset$, $\{u\}_1 = \emptyset$, $\{v\}_2 = \emptyset$, $\{w\}_2 = \emptyset$,

(3-4)   {{v,w} , {u,w} , {v,hxy}}
        $\{x\}_1 = \emptyset$, $\{y\}_1 = \emptyset$, $\{u\}_1 = \emptyset$, $\{v\}_2 = \emptyset$, $\{w\}_2 = \emptyset$,

(5)   {{u,w} , {v,hxy}}
        $\{x\}_1 = \emptyset$, $\{y\}_1 = \emptyset$, $\{u\}_1 = \emptyset$, $\{v,w\}_2 = \emptyset$,

(6)   {{v,hxy}}
        $\{x\}_1 = \emptyset$, $\{y\}_1 = \emptyset$, $\{u,v,w\}_1 = \emptyset$,

(7) $\emptyset$
        $\{x\}_1 = \emptyset$, $\{y\}_1 = \emptyset$, $\{u,v,w\}_0 = \{hxy\}$

(8) $\emptyset$
        $\{x\}_0 = \emptyset$, $\{y\}_0 = \emptyset$,
        $\sigma = \{u\backslash hxy, v\backslash hxy, w\backslash hxy\}$

Figure 19. $UNIF_{MM}$ applied to the example of figure 18

        The first line has now become empty. As an immediate
consequence of (9.1) for unifiable terms there must be in this
case at least one equation in the second line with an index
zero, which is then selected. If its right side contains more
than one term, all these terms are taken into the first line
for unification as with the initial terms, and this equation
is canceled in the second line. Otherwise a new element for the
final list of substitutions may be read from this equation as
shown in snapshot (8). Note that in such a case the occurrences
of variables in the term are taken care of in the indices of
the respective equations in the second line. Since in the
present example the first line is now empty and the second line
contains only trivial substitutions, $UNIF_{MM}$ successfully
terminates with the final σ as mgu.

We conclude the present section by pointing out the relationship of these methods with the alternative for Skolem functions from the previous section. For this purpose, consider the formula $\exists x \forall c \exists y(p(fy,c) \lor \neg P(x,y))$.

Without Skolem functions, the unification must respect the relation $x<c$ as described in the previous section. Hence the dag representing the two literals would therefore include $x<c$ as an additional arrow pointing from c to x as shown in

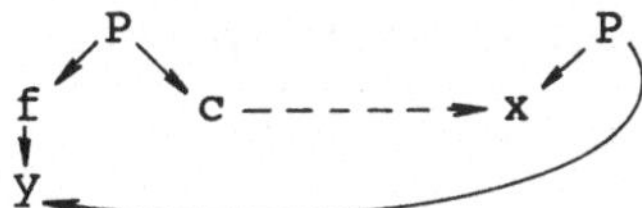

On the other hand, the introduction of a Skolem function cx instead of the constant c yields two literals which are represented by exactly the same dag. It is obvious that this is in fact true in general, which shows that the treatment with the relation $<$ is actually the more direct way, since it avoids the introduction of the Skolem terms into the formula. Otherwise unification may be treated in both approaches in exactly the same way which becomes apparent in a comparison of (8.5) and (9.1) since the crucial criterion w.r.t. unification for both is the non-existence of cycles. In the following section, this treatment with $<$ will now be extended to include what is called splitting.

10.   SPLITTING BY NEED

If we ask a warehouse-clerk or a data-base system for 2 items it1 and it2 whether they are available, say $AVit1 \land AVit2$, this question most likely will be split into 2 parts to be treated independently. This is just a trivial application of a powerful tool used all-over in any kind of problem solving. Therefore it is a necessity to make this tool available within the connection method.

Let us just use this trivial application for a first illustration, and consider the theorem
$\forall x\ AVx\ \rightarrow\ AVit1\ \land\ AVit2$. Without splitting the following

connection proof will be obtained:

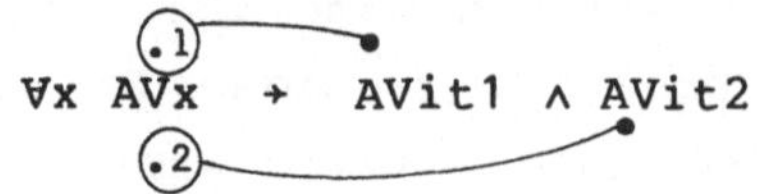

$$\forall x \ A V x \quad \rightarrow \quad A V i t 1 \ \wedge \ A V i t 2$$

With splitting the 2 questions are solved independently, first
$\forall x \ AVx \ \rightarrow \ \overline{AVit1} \ [\ \wedge AVit2]$ thus ignoring the second item, then
$\forall x \ AVx \ \rightarrow \ [AVit1 \ \wedge] \ \underline{AVit2}$ ignoring the first item. Since both
actions can certainly be performed on a single copy of the
formula, this second proof with splitting is adequately represented as

$$\forall x \ AVx \ \rightarrow \ AVit1 \ \wedge \ AVit2$$

This proof is simpler than the previous one in so far as the
multiplicity involved is 1 rather than 2 as in the first proof
(recall from section III.6 that by convention the connection
indices are deleted if they are all 1). This appears like a
ridiculous difference, having 1 rather than 2. But recall that
this actually means that implicitly a second copy of the quantified formula has to be taken into consideration.

In this simplest possible example the implicit second
copy actually has no further effect. But consider the following theorem with just one more literal, and each literal a
little more complicated:

$\exists x \ (\exists y \ Payx \ \wedge \ \exists z \ Pbzx) \ \vee \ (\exists u \ \neg Puuc \ \wedge \ \exists v \ \neg Pvbd).$

It already contains a first connection in an attempted connec-
tion proof yielding the substitution $\sigma = \{u \setminus a, \ y \setminus a, \ x \setminus c\}$.
Without splitting the second literal $\neg Pvbd$ would not be com-
plementary to $Payx$ in the active path under σ_1 . Therefore
we need a second copy of the first clause in order to be able
to continue this proof. One possibility for continuation is the
following one.

$\exists x \ (\exists y \ Payx \ \wedge \ \exists z \ Pbzx) \ \vee \ (\exists u \ \neg Puuc \ \wedge \ \exists v \ \neg Pvbd)$

In contrast to the first example, here the new index does indeed have an effect since the literal $Pbzx$ implicitly occurs

twice as a subgoal namely as $(Pbzx)_{.1.1}$ and as $(Pbzx)_{.2.1}$, and both have to be solved in order to complete the proof (note that an index 1.2 instead of 2.1 does not work). If this formula, however,   is   split   into   4   subproblems ($\exists$x $\exists$y Payx v $\exists$u ¬Puuc , etc.) then none of the literals occurs as a subgoal more than once.

     This shows that splitting may in fact save time in obtaining a proof. In this very little example the savings are certainly marginal. But, of course, we may well think of arbitrarily more complicated cases, for instance, of the literal Pbzx in the formula above replaced by an arbitrarily large subformula. That is to say, splitting is in fact an important issue which cannot be ignored.

     Unfortunately, there is no simple general splitting rule. Only in the special case of a formula F containing a subformula $G_1 \wedge G_2$ (recall from III.1.4 that - is not part of our proper formula language) with no variable occurring both in G_1 and in G_2 , we can say without any restriction that F is valid iff $F\{G_1 \wedge G_2 \setminus G_i\}$ is valid for i=1,2 , which allows to prove these 2 formulas independently. But even for our previous example this rule could not be applied since the variable x occurs in both literals Payx and Pbzx . Any attempt to generalize the rule (e.g., by allowing the occurrence of a variable in the same argument of two literals G_1 and G_2 as in our example) may be easily rejected by an appropriate counterexample (e.g. by the formula
$\exists$x $\exists$w($\exists$y Payxw v $\exists$z Pbzwx) v   ... , resp.). In particular, there are simple examples, such as $\exists$x (Pxb $\wedge$ Pax) v ¬Pab , demonstrating that splitting in fact may lead to wrong "proofs".

     All this shows that splitting in general can only be achieved with a method which reacts in a flexible way to the particular structure of a given formula. The most elegant such approach seems to be the inclusion of splitting into the process of unification, a solution which will be presented now.

     Let us consider once more our simplest example from the beginning of the present section and illustrate with it the relation of splitting with the form of proofs in the system GS from (7.1). Apparently, splitting is nothing else than the inverse application of rule ($\wedge$) :

$$\forall x \ A\forall x \ \rightarrow \ A\forall it1 \wedge A\forall it2 \quad \models^{-1} \quad \forall x \ A\forall x \rightarrow A\forall it1 \ , \ \forall x \ A\forall x \rightarrow A\forall it2$$

More precisely, this means that in any derivation of the given
formula this instance of rule ($\wedge$) should be the last inference; in particular, then, this instance will occur below of
the instances of rule ($\exists$) which are associated with the quantifier $\forall x$.

Recall from section 8 (in particular, see 8.6 and the
discussion thereafter) that we successfully used a relation
$<\cdot$ in order to encode such information about the sequence of
inferences in an analog situation. It is therefore a natural
idea to extend the domain of $<\cdot$ to include instances of
$\wedge$-symbols in a formula. For instance we could write $\wedge <\cdot$ x
in order to express that in the previous example splitting is
applied first, that is, the corresponding $\wedge$-inference is
closer to the root of the derivation than any $\exists$-inference
which belongs to x .

In terms of the connection method the relation $\wedge<\cdot$ x
naturally will be introduced by need only. For instance, after
locating the second connection in

$$\forall x \ A\overline{\forall x \ \ \rightarrow \ \ A\forall it1 \wedge A}\forall it2 \ , \ \wedge <\cdot \ x$$

the clash between the 2 resulting substitutions $\{x\backslash it1\}$ and
$\{x\backslash it2\}$ can be avoided simply by adding $\wedge <\cdot$ x . This
extra-information liberalizes the case of failure by clash in
the unification process in a way which is determined by the
interpretation of $\wedge <\cdot$ x suggesting that in a GS-derivation
the corresponding inferences occur in the sequence determined
by $\lhd$ via $<$ and $<\cdot$ as in (8.1). With this interpretation in mind we see immediately that $\lhd$ still must not allow
any cycles. But this is only one of the requirements for $<\cdot$
which will now be presented in the following definition.

10.1.D. For any formula F with the set $\Omega(F)$ of its positions and for any such position $r \in \Omega(F)$, we let λr denote
the label at this position in the formula tree.

A formula F is called a **contracted** formula if for

any two positions r and q from $\Omega(F)$, such that q is a successor of r , the following 2 properties hold.

(c1) λr and λq are not of the same logical sort, that is, not both $\wedge$, nor both $\vee$, nor both (sets of) constants, nor both (sets of) variables.

(c2)   If $\lambda r = \wedge$ then q is not a (set of) variable(s).

   For any contracted formula F with multiplicity μ and for any binary relation $<\!\cdot$ on the set $\Omega(F^\mu)$ of indexed positions in F^μ , the transitive closure of $< \cup <\!\cdot$ is denoted by $\vartriangleleft$ (for $<$ see 8.3). Then $<\!\cdot$ is called a **skeleton ordering** if the conditions (s1), (s2), and (s3) hold.

(s1)   For any 2 indexed positions $r1_{.\kappa 1}$ and $r2_{.\kappa 2}$ from $\Omega(F^\mu)$, $r1_{.\kappa 1}$ $<\!\cdot$ $r2_{.\kappa 2}$ implies the properties (i), (ii), and (iii).

(i)   One of the following two possibilities holds.

(i.1)   There is some indexed node $r_{.\kappa}$ in F^μ , labeled with an $\vee$, such that $r1_{.\kappa 1}$ and $r2_{.\kappa 2}$ occur in different subtrees of $r_{.\kappa}$ w.r.t. $<$ (which implies $\kappa i = \kappa.\kappa i'$ for some $\kappa i'$, i=1,2).

(i.2)   There is some indexed node $r_{.\kappa}$ in F^μ , labeled with some variable x , that is, $x \in \lambda r$, such that $r_{.\kappa} < ri_{.\kappa i}$ and $\kappa i = \kappa.\kappa i'$ for some $\kappa i'$ with $\kappa 1' \neq \kappa 2'$ holds, for i=1,2 .

(ii)   The label of r1 is an $\wedge$ or a constant, and that of r2 is a variable, that is, $\lambda r1 = \wedge$ or $a \in \lambda r1$, and $x \in \lambda r2$, for some a and x .

(iii)   For no indexed position $r_{.\kappa}$ in F^μ ,
$r1_{.\kappa 1} <\!\cdot r_{.\kappa} < r2_{.\kappa 2}$ or $r1_{.\kappa 1} < r_{.\kappa} <\!\cdot r2_{.\kappa 2}$ holds, that is, $<\!\cdot$ in this sense is a minimal relation.

(s2) $\vartriangleleft$ has no cycles, that is, for no indexed position $r_{.\kappa}$ in F^μ , $r_{.\kappa} \vartriangleleft r_{.\kappa}$ holds.

(s3)   If for 2 indexed positions $ri_{.\kappa i} \in \Omega(F^\mu)$, i=1,2 , both r1 and r2 are labeled with variables and $\kappa i = \kappa.mi$ for some index κ and some number $mi \geqslant 1$ holds for i=1,2 , then $r1_{.\kappa 1} \vartriangleleft r2_{.\kappa 2}$ implies m1<m2.   □

For illustration, let us represent our previous simple example in the form of a labeled formula tree, shown in figure 20, similarly as in figure 1 in (III.1). There μ=const=1 , hence

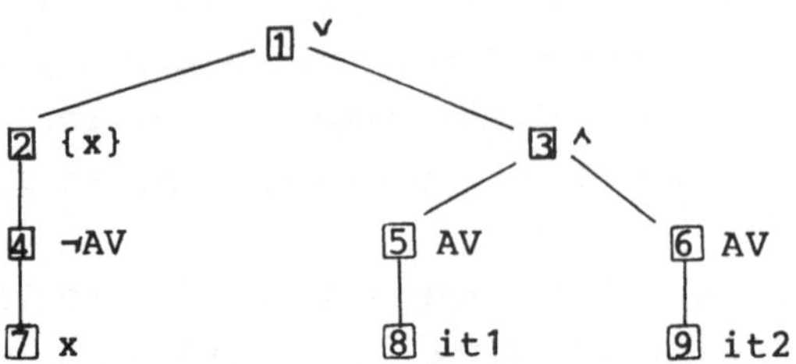

Figure 20.   ∀x AVx → AVit1 ∧ AVit2 represented as a tree

all indices are disregarded by convention. The positions or
nodes are denoted by numbers. The labels are attached to their
nodes. Thus, for instance, λ②ꞏ = {x} , that is, x ∈ λ② , which
identifies the position with x in the role of a quantifier.
This is to be distinguished from position ⑦ with λ⑦ = x ,
where x occurs as a variable.

     Now, the definition of a skeleton ordering has been
restricted to contracted formulas. This kind of normalization,
which is used for a simplified presentation only, by no means
is a serious restriction. Specifically, (c1) simply takes
serious the way of our formula definition (III.1.4), so that
F∧(G∧H) really is taken as ∧(F,G,H), or ∀x∀yF as ∀xyF .
(c2) can always be achieved by the transformation rule
III.4.4.iv (or viii), so that A ∧ ∀cB is transformed into
∀c(A∧B) . In contrast to other transformation rules, this one
has no effect whatsoever to any proof process.

     The condition (2) in the definition of a skeleton
ordering <ꞏ itself has been motivated already before (10.1).
So let us turn our attention to condition (1). For illustration
of (i.1) in it, recall that we used ∧ <ꞏ x in our example
which more precisely would have been expressed with positions
rather than labels, i.e. by ③ <ꞏ ② . Now it is obvious that
(i.1) in fact is satisfied for our example with r = ① . If we
recall the intention behind <ꞏ , which is to determine
sequences of GS-inferences, then a mere look to the form of the
rules in GS (7.1) explains the reason for (i), since only in
the two cases so described there is any choice at all w.r.t.
such a sequence (note the symbol   ∨   in all rules of GS   –

case i.1 - and the 2 copies of F in the premise of (∃) -
case i.2).

        The condition (ii) should be obvious since c <· x
or ∧ <· x are exactly the 2 types considered in all examples. And (iii) is not very important anyway since it is mere-
ly of a technical nature reducing the number of cases to be
distinguished in proofs. Similarly with condition (s3) which
only normalizes the way of numbering the indices.

        With this experience of a frightening definition ex-
pressing rather obvious ideas, we hope the reader is inclined
to enter even more messy formalism. The reason why it cannot be
avoided lies in the fact that for the sake of an efficient
method all aspects of proofs are concentrated within the structure of formulas. Once this barrier of formalism has been
surmounted, the ideas really appear to be quite simple. With
this encouragement (and warning) we plunge into the details of
a characterization of valid formulas which, like the one from
(8.5), applies to any formulas, but, in addition, will incorporate a most flexible form of splitting. We begin with the
first central notion.

10.2.D. A **skeleton** is a triple $(F^\mu, U, <·)$ where F^μ is a
formula F with multiplicity μ , U is a spanning and non-
empty set of connections in F^μ , and <· is a skeleton
ordering for the contracted F .   □

As will be seen below, a skeleton under certain conditions determines to a certain degree an GS-derivation of its formula,
hence it may actually be regarded as a "skeleton" of a derivation. The conditions under which this in fact is the case will
be captured in the following definition of a liberalized notion
of unifiability.

10.3.D. For any skeleton $(F^\mu, U, <·)$ the following concepts
are defined.

        U is called **locally consistent** if for each connec-
tion u ∈ U there is a substitution σ such that uσ is a
(propositionally) complementary pair of literals. For notational simplicity, we may think in the sequel of U as of such a
locally consistent set.

For any unordered pair of indexed occurrences of terms a function DIFF is defined inductively as follows.

(d1)   DIFF $\{(t,r1_{.\kappa 1}),(t,r2_{.\kappa 2})\} = \emptyset$.

(d2)   If $s = fs_1 s_2 \ldots s_n$ and $t = ft_1 t_2 \ldots t_n$ then DIFF $\{(s,r1_{.\kappa 1}),(t,r2_{.\kappa 2})\} = \bigcup_{i=1}^{n}$ DIFF $\{(s_i,r1_{.\kappa 1}),(t_i,r2_{.\kappa 2})\}$

(d3)   DIFF $\{(s,r1_{.\kappa 1}),(t,r2_{.\kappa 2})\} = \{\{(s,r1_{.\kappa 1}),(t,r2_{.\kappa 2})\}\}$ in any other case not covered by (d1) and (d2).

For any connection $u = \{(Ps_1 \ldots s_n)^{r1}_{.\kappa 1},(\neg Pt_1 \ldots t_n)^{r2}_{.\kappa 2}\}$ from U , DIFF(u) $= \bigcup_{i=1}^{n}$ DIFF $\{(s_i,r1_{.\kappa 1}),(t_i,r2_{.\kappa 2})\}$ where the terms are taken from the indexed literals as defined in 8.3. For the whole set U , DIFF(U) $= \bigcup_{u \in U}$ DIFF(u) .

For any $u \in U$, an "ignorance" function IGN_u determines a subset in DIFF(U) such that $\{(s,r1_{.\kappa 1}),(t,r2_{.\kappa 2})\} \in \text{IGN}_u(U)$ holds if for some indexed position $r_{.\kappa} \in \Omega(F^\mu)$, labeled with an $\wedge$, and for the indexed position $ro_{.\kappa o}$ of one of the literals in u the following conditions (i1), (i2) and (i3) are satisfied.

(i1) $r_{.\kappa} < ro_{.\kappa o}$.

(i2) $ro_{.\kappa o}$ and $r1_{.\kappa 1}$ occur in different subtrees of $r_{.\kappa}$.

(i3)   t is a variable x indexed with ι such that $x \in \lambda q_{.\iota}$ for some node $q_{.\iota} \in \Omega(F^\mu)$ with $r_{.\kappa} \vartriangleleft q_{.\iota}$.

Let $\text{PART}_u(U) = \text{DIFF}(U) \smallsetminus \text{IGN}_u(\text{DIFF}(U))$, for any $u \in U$; for such a set of pairs of indexed occurrences of terms a substitution is called a mgu if it is a mgu of the set of pairs of the terms themselves (without the indexed positions).

Then U is called **unifiable w.r.t. $<\cdot$** if for each $u \in U$ there is a mgu σ_u of $\text{PART}_u(U)$ such that the relation determined by σ_u according to 8.1 is a subrelation of $\vartriangleleft$.   □

If a set of connections is not locally consistent then unification is never possible, with or without splitting. Hence the restriction to a locally consistent U is not serious, but simplifies the situation.

The function DIFF is essentially the same as DIFF defined in (III.5.3) for unification. Therefore the only remaining difficult part of this definition is the one concerned with

the ignorance function which for any connection $u \in U$ determines a certain set of term-pairs. For its illustration our
previous example, shown in figure 20, will be used once more.

Recall its proof above with 2 connections and with
$\wedge <\cdot\ x$. Using the denotations for the nodes from figure 20,
the two connections are $u1 = \{\neg AVx^{\boxed{4}}, AVit1^{\boxed{5}}\}$ and $u2 = \{\neg AVx^{\boxed{4}},$
$AVit2^{\boxed{6}}\}$, and $\wedge <\cdot\ x$ more precisely reads $\boxed{3} <\cdot\ \boxed{2}$, where
the trivial indices are deleted by convention. Now, let us
consider IGN_{u1} for $DIFF(\{u1,u2\}) = \{\{x^{\boxed{4}},it1^{\boxed{5}}\},\{x^{\boxed{4}},it2^{\boxed{6}}\}\}$.
Starting from the 2 nodes of $u1$, i.e $\boxed{4}$ and $\boxed{5}$, suitable
candidates for $r_{.\kappa}$ are determined by moving towards the
root. Since there is only one $\wedge$, only $r_{.\kappa} = \boxed{3}$ is a possibility. We notice that (i1) then obviously holds with
$ro_{.\kappa o} = \boxed{5}$. (i2) is violated for $\{x^{\boxed{4}},it1^{\boxed{5}}\}$, but holds for
$\{x^{\boxed{4}},it2^{\boxed{6}}\}$ with $r1_{.\kappa 1} = \boxed{6}$, which also satisfies (i3) with
$q_{.1} = \boxed{2}$. Thus, we have $IGN_{u1} = \{\{x^{\boxed{4}},it2^{\boxed{6}}\}\}$. Similarly,
one obtains $IGN_{u2} = \{\{x^{\boxed{4}},it2^{\boxed{5}}\}\}$.

The central notion of unifiability w.r.t. $<\cdot$ in
(10.3) now says that unification has not to be done for all
connections in U at the same time (as we always did before),
rather the pairs of terms may be partitioned into subsets to be
unified independently. In our example, $PART_{u1}(\{u1,u2\}) =$
$\{\{x^{\boxed{4}},it2^{\boxed{5}}\}\}$ and $PART_{u2}(\{u1,u2\}) = \{\{x^{\boxed{4}},it1^{\boxed{6}}\}\}$ with an obvious unifier for each.

This illustrates that these notions capture exactly our
way of splitting as described further above. It is only the
generality which makes the definitions somewhat complicated. We
now can state the main result of this section.

10.4.T. A formula F is valid iff there exists a skeleton
$(F^{\mu},U,<\cdot)$ such that U is unifiable w.r.t. $<\cdot$.

Proof. If F , is valid then there is a GS-derivation
of F by (7.2) which determines a skeleton, as can be verified
by induction on the length of the derivation. Conversely,
a skeleton determines a GS-derivation-like structure as defined
in (10.5) below, which for U unifiable w.r.t. $<\cdot$,

again by induction on its length, turns out to be a derivation
of F , so that with (7.2) the theorem follows. The 2 inductions
in a sense are straightforward, but messy in their technical
details.   □

This theorem apparently is a refinement of our basic characterization of the valid formulas in Skolem normal form in
(III.6.4). Therefore the connection calculus, built upon
(III.6.4), has now a corresponding refinement with an additional "coordinate", viz. $<\cdot$, in its search space. Basically, connections are selected as before, one after the other
until a spanning set U is achieved. But whenever a unification fails for an additionally selected connection u , the
procedure now may also consider an extension of $<\cdot$ so that
unifiability is restored w.r.t. $<\cdot$.

For instance, let us illustrate this with our previous
example. We always start with $\mu=1$, $U=\emptyset$, $<\cdot=\emptyset$, and $\sigma=$NIL .
The first connection u1 is selected from which $\sigma = \{x\backslash it1\}$
is determined. The only other connection u2 requires a uni-
fier $\sigma2 = \{x\backslash it2\}$ which is not compatible with σ , however.
One possibility now is the extension of $<\cdot$ "by need" to include the pair $(\wedge,x)$ so that $\wedge <\cdot x$ holds. This possibility may quickly be determined from the formula tree according to our definitions above. After this the process continues
with 2 independent subcases, one with u1 and $\sigma1 = \sigma$ the
other with u2 and $\sigma2$. In the present example, in fact, it
terminates since $\{u1,u2\}$ is spanning.

We mention again that this possibility is not the only
one, since also the index may alternatively be increased as we
discussed at the beginning of this section. But with this
remark we touch on a matter of strategy which will be discussed
in the next section.

Of course, our example is too simple for demonstrating
the real power of this combination of unification and splitting by need, which rather requires big and complex problems.
Still rather trivial, but nevertheless instructive, is the
second formula from the beginning of this section, the proof

of which in the way just described is left to the reader as an exercise (see E20 in section 12 or [B13]).

As we already mentioned at the end of section 8, at the beginning of the present section and in the proof of (10.4), skeletons in fact encode in a concentrated form all information needed in order to write down a corresponding GS-derivation, stated as a corollary further below, which in turn determines a natural deduction as we discussed in section 7. Again, in their full generality, the details of the "decoding procedure" are messy, but for sake of completeness they will be given in the following definition.

10.5.D. Inductive definition of a (derivation-like structure which may be proved to be a) derivation Δ **generated by** a skeleton $(F^\mu, U, \lessdot)$ for which U is unifiable w.r.t. $\lessdot$.

First, we assume that F is in contracted form and explain the changes afterwards, which are necessary otherwise. Since our formula definition does not distinguish between F and $v(F)$, it may further be assumed that F is of the form $v(F_1, \ldots, F_m)$ with $1 \leqslant m$.

Let r_j denote the roots of F_j, $j=1, \ldots, m$. Since F is contracted, for the label $\kappa_j \neq v$ holds for $j=1, \ldots, m$.

Together with Δ , we inductively define an index κ_j for F_j and a multiplicity for each occurring existential quantifier. Initially, the index of F is the empty list NIL, and the multiplicity is 1 throughout.

Finally, the following assumption is simply a matter of appropriate notation and sequencing : There exist numbers n1, n2, n3, and n with $0 \leqslant n1 \leqslant n2 \leqslant n3 \leqslant n \leqslant m$ such that (i), (ii) and (iii) is satisfied.

(i)   For any r_j with $j \in \{1, \ldots, m\}$ we have $j \leqslant n$ iff r_j is "affected" by some connection in U , that is, there is some node $r \in \Omega(F^\mu)$ with $r_j \lessdot r$ and $\{K^r, L^q\} \in \mathcal{U}$ for some K,L, and q .

(ii)   For $j=1, \ldots, n1$, λk_j consists of constants, for $j=n1+1, \ldots, n2$, k_j consists of variables, and for $j=n2+1, \ldots, n3$, $\lambda k_j = \wedge$.

(iii)   Among all nodes $(r_i)._{\kappa_i}$, with $1 \leqslant i \leqslant n$, those with a subscript $j \leqslant n3$ are closest to the root w.r.t. $\vartriangleleft$, that is,

$(r_i)._{\kappa_i} \lhd (r_j)._{\kappa_j}$ never holds for such subscripts.

With all these assumptions the inductive definition consists of the following cases (a) through (e).

(a)   If F_i (initially F itself) has index κ_i and is of the form $\vee(F_{i1},\ldots,F_{ik})$ then $F_{i1},\ldots,F_{ik}$ in $\vee(F_{i1},\ldots,F_{ik},\ldots,F_m)$ all have index κ_i .

(b)   If n=0 then Δ consists of a single formula, F , which is an axiom since it contains a complementary connection. In the remaining cases we may assume n>0 .

(c)   If $0<n_1$ and $F_1 = \forall c_1 \ldots c_\kappa \, \tilde{F}_i$, and if $\tilde{\Delta}$ is a derivation for $\vee(\tilde{F}_1,F_2,\ldots,F_m)$, where $\tilde{F}_1$ has index κ_1 , then Δ consists of $\tilde{\Delta}$ extended by the inference $\vee(\tilde{F}_1,F_2,\ldots,F_m) \vdash \vee(F_1,\ldots,F_m)$.

(d)   Assume 0=n1<n2 and, for i=1,\ldots,n2 , $F_i = \exists^{(mi)} x_{i1}\ldots x_{ik_i} \, \tilde{F}_i$, and $\tilde{\Delta}$ is a derivation   for $\vee(\tilde{F}_1\sigma,F_1,\ldots,\tilde{F}_{n2}\sigma,F_{n2},F_{n2+1},\ldots,F_m)$. Here σ is the substitution for the variables $x_{11},\ldots,x_{n2k_{n2}}$ which unifies U w.r.t. <· (note iii above); the multiplicity m_i in F_i is increased by 1; the index of $\tilde{F}_i\sigma$ is $\kappa_i.m_i$ and that of F_i is κ_i . Then Δ consists of $\tilde{\Delta}$ extended by the n2 inferences $\vee(\tilde{F}_i\sigma,F_1,\ldots,\tilde{F}_{n2}\sigma,F_{n2},\ldots,F_m) \vdash$ $\vee(F_1,\ldots,F_{n2}\sigma,F_{n2},\ldots,F_m) \vdash \ldots \vdash \vee(F_1,\ldots,F_{n2},\ldots,F_m)$.

(e)   Assume 0=n1=n2<n3 , and, for i=1,\ldots,n3 , $F_i = \wedge(F_{i1},\ldots,F_{ik_i})$. By r_{ij} denote the root of F_{ij} which is indexed by k_i ; U and <· partitions into U_{ij} and <·$_{ij}$ determined by the subtrees with root r_{ij} . Then Δ is obtained from derivations Δ_{ij} of $\vee(F_{ij},F_{n3+1},\ldots,F_m)$, which exist by induction hypothesis for S_{ij} and <·$_{ij}$, together with n3 appropriate inferences according to rule (∧) in GS.

If F is not in contracted form then we obtain a derivation $\tilde{\Delta}$ of the contraction of F , as just explained, which can be easily transformed into a derivation of Δ (by splitting inferences into parts and by simple changes in their sequence).   □

10.6.C. For any skeleton $(F^\mu,U,<·)$ such that U is unifiable w.r.t. <· , Δ defined by (10.5) is in fact a GS-derivation of F which can be computed from the skeleton in time linear in the length of Δ .   □

11.   SUMMARY AND PROSPECTUS

At this point, it seems to be necessary to summarize all the
results achieved so far in view of an ultimate connection procedure, say CP^1 .

First recall the basic connection procedure CP^1_1 presented in (III.7.2). In the preceding sections of the present
chapter we have discussed a number of improvements of
isolated features of CP^1_1 . The procedure CP^1 , which we now
have in mind, is supposed to incorporate all these and even
more such improvements. Unfortunately, the formal description
of CP^1 even at a very high level of language would exceed the
frame of any book. Just recall the connection procedure CP^O_3
presented in table 2 within section 5 which only applies to
propositional formulas. It gives an idea of how complex CP^1
actually will be, as CP^O_3 in fact realizes only a rather small
isolated portion of CP^1 .

Therefore all we can do here is an informal description
of the main features of CP^1 . Its realization has to be left
to a major programming project which hopefully will be undertaken in the near future (a restricted version, realizing some
of the features discussed so far, does however exist already
[Mül]; see section V.7 for more details).

Let us begin with pointing out that CP^1 eventually
may deal with any first-order formula, not only with those in
normal form. This was discussed in section 5 restricted to the
ground level, resulting in CP^O_3 mentioned just before. However, CP^O_3 does not completely meet this goal even at the
ground level, since formulas containing the defined connectives
$\neg$, $\rightarrow$, and $\leftrightarrow$ need to be transformed according to the conventions in (II.1.3) in order for CP^O_3 to be applicable. In the
case of $\leftrightarrow$ this could be a real disadvantage since the transformation redundantly increases the formula; for instance $A \leftrightarrow A$
would become $(\neg A \vee A) \wedge (A \vee \neg A)$. But, of course, this redundancy
can be easily avoided by incorporating these conventions into
CP^O_3 rather than explicitly carrying out the transformations.
Such a version of CP^O_3 would come up with the proof $\overparen{A \leftrightarrow A}$ for
the previous example, where each of the two connections belongs
to one of the two directions of the implication sign. More

precisely, we have to extend the notion of a spanning set of connections (following those conventions) to cover such formulas directly, that is, without any such explicit transformation; and CP^0 has then to be adapted to this extended notion. From now on we may assume that CP_3^0 has undergone this relatively easy modification.

Even then, CP_3^0 does not yet incorporate all the features discussed in section 6 such as reductions, factorization and tautological circuits. A work which deals with an extension of CP_3^0 towards including all these features, say CP_4^0 , is given by [HöB]. It may well be expected that even such a version allows further improvements. Hence, the ground version CP^0 of CP^1 will be CP_4^0 or an improved version thereof.

Speaking in terms of the procedure CP_1^1 in (III.7.2) , such a ground version does not only apply in STEP0 for essentially propositional formulas, rather its main responsibility is for controlling the possible selections in STEP2 through STEP5. In comparison with CP_1^1 , these possible selections are much more restricted in the case of CP^0 , since many redundant selections are not considered by this enhanced versions. But otherwise, the basic structure of CP^1 is the same as that of CP_1^1 . It selects connections, thereby extending the global substitution σ , possibily backtracks to alternative selections, and does so until the selected set of connections turns out to be spanning. However, the fine structure of CP^1 will be much more complex than that of CP_1^1 , not only w.r.t. the ground level behavior, since it is expected to incorporate the following features.

One of these features is the sophisticated and faster unification technique discussed in the sections 9 and 10 which includes what we called splitting by need. Although locally this may increase the number of possible selections (since more pairs of literals may become unifiable), globally this technique also contributes to the reduction of the search space since a proof may potentially be attained with smaller indices.

In connection with the splitting technique we have to mention also the important operation of antiprenexing, illustrated with the following example.

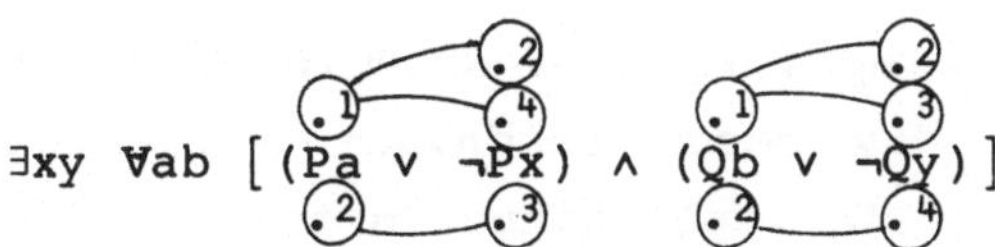

$$\exists xy\ \forall ab\ [\,(Pa\ \lor\ \neg Px)\ \land\ (Qb\ \lor\ \neg Qy)\,]$$

It is easy to see that the 6 connections in fact represent a connection proof. The proof apparently is rather complicated, and a simpler one actually does not exist with our previous techniques (including resolution).

From (III.4.4), however, we know that this formula is equivalent with

$$(\forall a Pa\ \lor\ \exists x \neg Px)\ \land\ (\forall b Qb\ \lor\ \exists y \neg Qy)$$

which obviously has a much simpler proof. The transformation from the first to the second version following the rules (iii) through (viii) in (III.4.4) is called **antiprenexing** . Its effect consists in diminuishing the scope of the quantifiers for which reason the resulting formula also is called in **miniscope form** .

Note in this connection that our transformation to normal form defined in (III.4.1), given the miniscope form of the previous example, would not produce the first form above but the formula $\forall ab\ \exists xy\ F_0$ for a certain F_0 . It is easy to see that for this difference this transformation avoids the complication of proofs which otherwise might occur. With this remark we refer to the discussion at the end of section (III.4).

In [Bi2] there is a theorem showing that antiprenexing often leads to simpler but never to more complicated proofs. Therefore this operation is mandatory for any proof procedure, hence in particular for CP^1 . However, one would like to see even a smarter solution which involves the associative, commutative and distributive laws for the boolean operations. This, however, leads to difficulties of the following kind.

The formula $\exists xy\ (Px\ \land\ Qy\ \land\ Rxy)$ is not really in miniscope form since it may be transformed either to $\exists x\ (Px\ \land\ \exists y(Qy\ \land\ Rxy))$ or to $\exists y\ (Qy\ \land\ \exists x(Px\ \land\ Rxy))$. If this is part of a more complicated theorem, it may well happen that one of these two alternatives leads to a simpler proof than the other. The same effect may be generated with the distribu-

tive law. Since it is impossible to detemine the better alternative in advance, a "by need" technique would again be the
appropriate solution as for splitting. In terms of our relation
< , introduced in section 8, this actually could be realized in
such a way that < is not fixed in advance by the tree-order-
ing of the given formula, rather < in some way would have to
represent the set of the tree-orderings of all possible miniscope forms of the given formula and by need the connection
proof would be able to make its appropriate selection w.r.t.
the simplest possible proof.

A further feature of CP^1 will be a more sophisticated
backtracking mechanism the need for which was already emphasized in (III.7). For illustration consider the following simple
example.

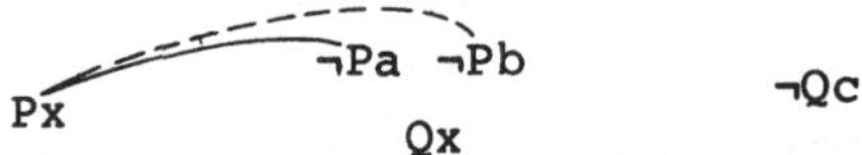

After selection of the left-most clause, a proof using the
fully-lined connection fails since the subgoal $Qx\{x\backslash a\}$ cannot be solved. CP_1^1 would now backtrack and try the alternative dashed connection. In contrast to that a **selective
backtracking technique** would prepare and carry along the
information such that this useless attempt would not be
considered anymore. Techniques of this kind have been studied
extensively by Bruynooghe and by Pereira for the special case
of Horn formulas [BrP], and more recently by Cox and
Pietrzykowski for the general case. It is clear that such
techniques have to be included in CP^1 .

The last feature of CP^1 , which we mention, is a more
sophisticated technique for increasing the indices in a more
selective way. Let us refer to that with the notion of **selective index increase technique** .

For illustration, let us consider the theorem
$\forall u\ \exists a\ Fau \land \forall xyz(Fzx \land Fyx \to GFzx) \to \forall b\ \exists v\ GFvb$ from section (III.6), which expresses the fact that anyone has a
grandfather (GF) where F denotes the relation "father-of".
Note that in accordance with our conventions the quantifiers
binding x, y, z, u, v are actually to be regarded as
existential quantifiers, since in matrix representation the

formula reads

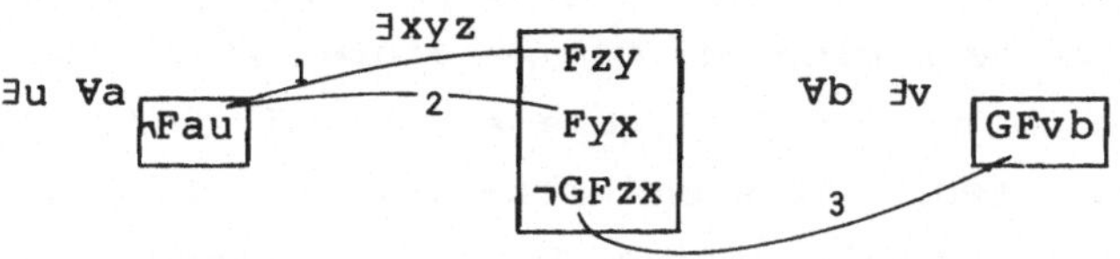

(recall the formula F1 after III.1.4 for this way of representation). The 3 connections, labeled with 1, 2, and 3, are
spanning, but for multiplicity μ = const = 1 they do not
provide a proof since the respective pairs of literals are not
unifiable. Since there are no further alternatives, the only
way to achieve the proof consists in considering a different
μ by increasing any of the indices (implicitly) attached to
the existential quantifiers.

A crude way of doing this would consist in trying each
possible increase in any sequence. Our example demonstrates
why a more sophisticated selection is needed. Namely, this
crude way might choose to increase the index attached to ∃v
while keeping the others fixed. Obviously, any work invested
into this attempt is wasted, since the only increase which
works is that of the index attached to ∃u . This shows that
we need some technique for selecting the appropriate quantifier such as ∃u in the present example.

Unfortunately, no work is known which would provide
any such selective technique. The reason probably is that this
problem in the prevailing resolution theory is even hard to be
clearly recognized. We hope that this situation will be
changed by the present book. Here we will just mention a few
ideas indicating the direction of further research.

For instance, let us consider any formula with a
spanning set of connections which, however, is not unifiable.
Then it is easy to see that unifiability cannot be established
by increasing the index of an existential quantifier, which
has in its scope only unit clauses with literals contained in
at most one of the connections. The quantifier ∃v above
satisfies this condition, and thus is of no use as we observed
before. It is conjectured that this statement even holds for
general clauses (not only unit clauses). With such a result,

even the quantifier $\exists xyz$ could be disregarded in the previous example, so that the only appropriate selection, viz. $\exists u$, would have been singled **out** , since this is the only quantifier which has in its scope a literal contained in more than one, viz. two, different connections. This demonstrates the potential power of results of such a nature, which makes them worthwhile for discovery.

The second source of information, which might be helpful for ruling out irrelevant index increases, are the terms to be unified via the set of connections. Specifically, an analysis of why the unification fails may prevent waste of efforts. For our previous example such an analysis may be illustrated in the following way.

$$
\begin{array}{ccccccc}
v & = & z & = & a & \neq & b \\
  &   &   & \nparallel & \lor &   & \| \\
  &   & y & = & u & = & x
\end{array}
$$

This illustrates all the unifications resulting from the 3 connections, and demonstrates their failure in the form of **conflicting cycles** . For instance, a = y = u < a   and a = y = u = x = b ≠ a , both are such conflicting cycles which have to be resolved (recall < from section 8) by increasing appropriate indices. Since v and **x** , both are not part of these two cycles, increasing the indices of the respective quantifiers $\exists v$ and $\exists x$ necessarily is useless, while there is a good chance with both y and u since they do occur in both cycles. In particular the first part of this statement obviously holds in general in the form that only those quantifiers are candidates for increase of their indices, the variables of which are part of such conflicting cycles. Again we believe that a careful study into this direction would provide more helpful results of such a kind.

In summary, we imagine that CP^1 will also incorporate a selective index increase technique which derives its benefit both from the information contained in the graph structure of the connections within the formula and from that contained in the resultant conflicting substitutions.

Now note that none of these features of CP^1 discuss-

ed so far is of a strategic nature. They all eliminate potential redundancies, and in that sense provide a proper improvement (in the sense of section 3). It seems to be rather un-
likely that there are **general** strategies, **not** supported by
structural properties like those discussed in the present
chapter, which provide a real improvement. In other words
strategic tools might have their value only in special applications or as intermediate substitutes for structural insights
which appear to be too complicated to be clarified (see also
section V.7).

   As a final point, we mention once more (cf. the end of
section III.3) that there are classes of formulas which are
decidable. It is clear that CP^1 for any such class may be
extended with little extra complications such that it behaves
like a decision procedure for any formula of such a class.
First steps into such a direction have been done in $[Fis]$.

   In summary, this envisaged procedure CP^1 would easily
compete with any existing theorem prover for fol (in the sense
of section 3), since it incorporates all their virtues without
sharing their drawbacks. Its only critical point is the man-
power required for its development and implementation, both, in
terms of quantity and quality. Namely, the reader may have
noted that all these features do affect each other, hence are
by no means independent. That is, theorem proving requires a
joint solution for so many different problems, for which reason
such a solution is so difficult to be achieved.

   The situation is not so bad, however, in particular if
we realize that even less demanding versions may well serve
for special needs; for instance, even CP^1_1 will provide
enough deductive power for a wide range of applications. CP^1
should therefore be regarded as something like an ultimate
goal.

   Apart from all these possible improvements any such
procedure may be specialized for particular applications or
extented to cover richer logics than fol, which is the topic of
the next chapter.

12.   EXERCISES

(E1)   The formula (E3) in section (III.6) has there been transformed into normal form (in the affirmative view). Now, negate (E3), put it in prenex form $\exists c_1 \ldots c_m \; \forall x_1 \ldots x_n \; \tilde{F}_0$ with $\tilde{F}_0$ in conjunctive normal form, and compare the two results, regarded in our set-theoretic view. Specify the results of this book which show that the noted difference between the affirmative and the negative representation actually holds in general. Test it with more examples.

(E2)   Give a resolution proof for (E3) in section (III.6) and compare it with the connection proof in figure 2 of section (III.6) the way we did with the figures 1 in the sections (IV.1) and (III.6), respectively. Do such a comparison for further examples.

(E3)   Sharpen the proof of (1.5) in the way indicated in the paragraphs after (1.6), in order to obtain the following form of (1.5):

A resolution proof of a matrix F_0 constructively determines a set U_0 of connections which are spanning for $F_0 \ldots F_n$, where F_i are variants of F_0 , $i=1,\ldots,n$.

(E4)   With the definition (1.1) of resolution as a guideline, lift the definition (4.1) of cg-resolution to the first-order level.

(E5)   Give the proofs for (4.2) and (4.3) on the first-order level by checking the details of the proofs for (1.2) and (1.5) for the special case of cg-resolution as defined in (E4).

(E6)   Apply CP_2^o from table 1 to the matrices in figure 10 of section 4, noting the history of the values of all variables. For comparison do the same with cg-resolution.

(E7)   Apply CP_3^o from table 2 to the matrices in figure 12 and 13, further to the matrices $\{\{L\},\{\{\{^1L,K,\{\{R,^1R\}\}\},^1Q\}\}$, $\{\{^1N,^1T\},\{N,\{\{M,Q\},\{P,R\}\}\},\{\{\{^1M,^1Q\}\},L\},\{^1L,\{\{^1P,^1R\}\}\},\{T\}\}$, noting in each case the history of the values of the variables.

(E8)   Give a proof for (5.1).

(E9)   Relying on the correctness of CP_2^O , give a proof
showing that CP_3^O is complete and consistent.

(E10)   Apply the connection calculus with the features CIRUIT
and FACTORIZATION to the full matrix in 3 variables (see
II.7.E7) and to other examples.

(E11)   Prove theorem (6.5).

(E12)   Give a "derivation" of the formula
$\forall x\ \exists a\ x{<}a\ \rightarrow\ \exists y\ \forall b\ b{<}y$ in GS which is correct except that it
violates the variable condition in ($\forall$). Give an interpretation
which demonstrates that the formula cannot be valid.

(E13)   Give a derivation of the two formulas
$P\ \lor\ Q{\land}R\ \rightarrow\ (P{\lor}Q)\ \land\ (P{\lor}R)$ and $\neg\exists x\ Px\ \rightarrow\ \forall c\ \neg Pc$ in both, NK and
GS. Translate the resulting NK-derivations into a natural text.

(E14)   Design (and possibly implement) a procedure which
generates from a given proof in NK a corresponding proof in GS.

(E15)   Following the outline given in section 7 of the procedure ND complete its details (possibly with an implementation)
such that it generates from any proof in GS a corresponding
proof in NK.

(E16)   Give the proof for theorem (8.4).

(E17)   Give a constructive proof for (8.6) which includes a
more precise identification of the 2 inferences mentioned
there.

(E18)   Give the proof for (9.1).

(E19)   Apply $UNIF_{PW}$ and $UNIF_{MM}$ by hand to the following
pairs of literals: $\{f(x,y,z),f(g(u,u),g(x,x),g(y,y))\}$

$\{f(u,x,y,z),f(gy,z,x,u)\}, \{f(x,y,z),f(gy,a,gb)\}$.

(E20)   Give a connection proof for the formula
$\exists x\ (\exists y\ Payx\ \wedge\ \exists z\ Pbzx)\ \vee\ (\exists u\ \neg Puuc\ \wedge\ \exists v\ \neg Pvbd)$ both with
splitting, based on and explained after (10.4), and without
splitting. In both cases, give the derivation in GS determined
by the resulting skeleton according to (10.5).   (The solution
is contained in [B13]).

13.   BIBLIOGRAPHICAL AND HISTROICAL REMARKS

The history of resolution is more complex than it is usually
described in the literature, which mentions J.A. Robinson as
its discoverer. Of course, there is no doubt that it was
Robinson in [Ro1] who developed resolution as a recognition
type proof calculus for first-order logic in a clear and
coherent way suitable for practical use. But the roots actually are rather widespread. In fact, it is correct to say that
all details combined within resolution were known before [Ro1].
Resolution as a propositional rule was well-known as Quine's
consensus rule [Qui] which in turn is just a variant of the
cut rule [Ge1], the generalized version of the famous **modus
ponens** . Dunham and North have used the consensus rule as a
recognition-type rule for theorem proving [DuN]. Although they
only treated the ground level, they clearly did so with the
possibility of generalization to the first-order level in mind.
For this generalization it is just unification which is needed.
Unification, however, has been first discovered by Herbrand
(see [Her], p. 148), and later it appears again in [Pr1]. Hence
Robinson's achievements consisted in putting all these scatter-
ed pieces together into a uniform and elegant calculus (cf.
[Ro3], p. 292).
        The linear refinement of resolution was introduced in-
dependently by Loveland in [Lo1] and [Lo2], by Luckham in
[Luc], and by Raphael in [Rap]. The representation of the line-
arity idea within the connection calculus first appears in
[B11].
        A general discussion of the comparison of proof proce-

dures similar to part of that in section 3 is contained in [Bi4]. Detailed comparisons of different proof procedures have been carried out in [Lo3], [Sc2], [B11], and others. In addition to the complexity oriented work referenced in the text we mention [CoR].

Connection graph resolution is due to Kowalski [Ko2]. The first consistency and completeness proof for it appears in [B10]. A proof for the confluence conjecture, first stated in [Ko2], has been attempted in [Br1], [SSi], and [B12]. But at present none of these attempts may be regarded as completed.

The procedure CP_2^o is published in [B11] . Hörnig has contributed to the development of CP_3^o which is an extension of another version published in [B11].

The reductions are well-known for many years; TAUT and SUBS, for instance, appear in [Qui] and MULT, PURE, and UNIT in [DuN]. Also factorization is familiar in resolution theory [Lo4]. Tautological circuits have been considered in various forms, as the **merge condition** in [An1], as the **tautology loops** in [Sic], as **loops** in [Sh1], and as **simple circuits** in [B10].

The alternative for skolemization has been developed in [Bi2], and extended in [BiS] for covering splitting by need and allowing for full antiprenexing. A different approach to a more flexible form of splitting has been taken in [TyB]. The idea of splitting itself appears in [Wan], [B11] and [Ern]. Further references are mentioned in [Lo4], p.103.

In additon to the linear unification algorithms from [PaW] and [MaM], we mention quasi-linear solutions presented in [Hu1] and [Bax].

Chapter V

Applications and extensions

In a well-balanced monograph on ATP the material treated so far
in the previous chapters would perhaps amount to $^1/_{10}$ of the
whole volume. In other words we would now have to proceed with
another 36 chapters which is obviously impossible. In other
words this book is not at all a well-balanced treatise rather
it is relatively detailed in topics discussed so far and is
short, to say the least, for the rest.

We will make an attempt in the present chapter to
briefly discuss at least most of the topics of major importance
with a particular emphasis on applications. But the reader
should keep in mind that a thorough treatment of the material
of each of the following sections might actually fill several
chapters if not even a whole book.

In view of such applications we may notice a general
need for systems behaving in a more intelligent way. More
knowledge and an enhanced reasoning capability, both seem to be
crucial features for such intelligent systems. For both issues
deductive systems may provide substantial contributions. While
this is evident in the latter case, we will discuss the use of
theorem provers for storage, processing and retrieval of knowledge in section 1.

More intelligent systems are bitterly needed for a
cheaper and more reliable way of software production. The role
of theorem provers in programming and problem solving is therefore briefly discussed in section 2. There, of course, we will
speak of logic programming. But we demonstrate it from the
viewpoint of the connection method rather than providing something like a real introduction to this wide field.

In any application of proof systems we are dealing with
special predicates which call for a special treatment. The
equality predicate is the most important example for which we
discuss a special handling embedded into the connection method

in section 3. But there are many other special predicates which may be treated in such a special way using rewrite rules or generalized unification. These will be the topic of section **4**, which also contains a short introduction into the famous Knuth-Bendix method.

Many mathematical theorems cannot be proved but with induction. In section 5 we show ways how to include induction into the connection method. Other mathematical theorems cannot even be naturally expressed in the first-order language used so far. We therefore show in section 6 how the connection method may be extended to include higher-order features, which, incidentally, provides an alternative for treating equality and induction.

Last not least in section 7 we discuss several issues which arise in actual implementations of proof systems, and briefly mention some of the major systems, which are in actual use, together with their achievements. This is followed by kind of an excuse in section 8 for omitting further topics of interest.

1.   STRUCTURING AND PROCESSING KNOWLEDGE

Storage, processing and retrieval of information is a central issue in current computer technology. There are the simple cases where a number of pieces of data have to be stored for later use. For instance, you might wish to check your money spending habits and for that reason store any expense over the period of a month. In this case your "data base" would consist simply of several numbers like 17.25, 3.50, 114.00, etcetera. Perhaps you might even wish to know when and for what purpose you spent your money in which case the data might be represented in the following way typical for what is called a data base.

Amount	Date	Purpose
17.25	1. Oct.	dinner
3.50	2. Oct.	subway ticket
114.00	2. Oct.	new book
⋮	⋮	⋮

At the other end of the spectrum there are information systems which require the storage of sophisticated knowledge with a complex structure. For instance, there are **expert systems** for medical diagnosis and therapy which store knowledge of medical doctors and to some extent are able to simulate their reasoning. Or there are systems for the automatic construction of programs which for that purpose store knowledge on problem domains, mathematical knowledge, knowledge about data structures, algorithms etcetera.

In practice, there is a tendency that for each application people invent their own theory of knowledge structure thus causing a lot of confusion and waste of ingenuity. Rather we should realize that the structure of any such knowledge is logical by nature. Hence logic may be used as a uniform and rather universal language for expressing knowledge of any kind.

For instance, in our first example we are actually talking about a unary relation which might be referred to by a unary predicate SPENT. The fact that the amount of 17.25 DM was spent thus is expressed by SPENT(17.25) (similarly we have SPENT(3.50), SPENT(114.00), etcetera). Recall that such syntactic items were called **literals** (see III.1.1) where 17.25 plays the role of a **constant** .

Note however that in the context of data bases a phrase like SPENT(17.25) contains more information than just the syntactic structure as a literal. First, SPENT is not meant to be interpreted by an arbitrary relation rather by a very particular one given by the **meaning** of the word "spent"; similarly for the constant 17.25. In other words, the literal is meant **together with a fixed interpretation** (i.e. the meaning) (recall III.2.1). Secondly, by storing SPENT(17.25) we also mean that this amount actually has been spent, that is, SPENT(17.25) under this paricular interpretation **is true** (III.2.2).

In a less trivial data base like that given by the table above we are still concerned with relations with a syntactic representation logically to be regarded as literals. In this example we might introduce the ternary predicate SPEND-REC (for "spending record") and thus would have SPEND-REC(17.25, 1.Oct., dinner) , etcetera. The arguments in

addition are   in   unary   relations   such   as
AMOUNT(17.25), DATE(1.Oct.), etcetera.

Thus we see that the entries in data bases represent
logical constructs such as literals. In this connection it is
important to note that the **intrinsic logical structure** of any
information is regarded as independent from the particular
representation. For studying the logical structure, as we did
in this book, the particular representation with strings of
symbols usually is preferred in logic texts. But even we partially departed from this tradition with our matrices for
reasons given in previous chapters and, of course, we still
dealt with logic, didn't we. The same applies here where we
noticed that each row in the previous table represents a
logical structure, viz. a literal. There are even several other
possible ways of representing logical structures such as
semantic networks (see [Nil]) to mention another important
one. Although all of these representational forms have their
particular value under special aspects such as implementation
etc. , their differences are unimportant from a logical point
of view. The same distinction between the **intrinsic structure**
on one side and the **forms of representation** on the other side
can be seen in number theory where, for instance, the fact that
13 is a prime number obviously is an intrinsic number theoretic
feature which is not affected by the way of representing this
number with binary digits, Roman letters, or any other means.

As long as we are dealing with data bases as simple as
the one in the previous table, it is of little help in practice
to be aware of its logical structure. For this reason many
experts in data base technology did not care very much about
logic. However, there is a clear trend towards the need for
storing information with a more and more complex logical structure in expert or even more general information systems which
implies the need for a lot more care in this respect. In the
remaining part of this section we want to illustrate that the
connection calculus introduced in the previous chapters may in
fact serve as a valuable tool for such complex **knowledge
bases** or **information systems** .

First let us explain the logical nature of a **query**
posed to such a knowledge base. For instance, if we ask in the

example above whether it is the fact that an amount of 17.25 was spent then this again would be expressed as the literal SPENT(17.25). In contrast to what has been said above for the **truth value** of this literal here, in the context of a query, the truth-value is unknown. Logically this means that we want to know this truth value under the assumption that all facts stored in the knowledge base are true. As we explained inform- ally in the Introduction after (I.1.2), or, more formally, by the deduction theorem (III.2.5), this is the same as asking whether the conjunction of all facts in the knowledge base implies the query, that is, whether

$$\text{SPENT}(17.25) \wedge \text{SPENT}(3.50) \wedge \ldots \rightarrow \text{SPENT}(17.25)$$

is a valid formula, which it is as the single connection, representing a connection proof, shows.

In the second version we might query for which purpose we have actually spent this amount, in other words, is there some purpose x such that for some date y, 17.25, y, and x are related by SPEND-REC, expressed formally by $\exists x \, \exists y \, \text{SPEND-REC}(17.25,\ y,\ x)$. Again the answer logically is obtained by a connection proof with one connection as before.

$$\text{SPEND-REC}(17.25,\ 1.\text{Oct.},\ \text{dinner}) \wedge \ldots \rightarrow$$
$$\exists x \, \exists y \, \text{SPEND-REC}(17.25,\ y,\ x)$$

Where however is the expected answer ? In order to see this we have to recall from chapter III that the spanning set U of connections of such a proof determines a most general unifier σ such that uσ is complementary for each u ∈ U . This sub- stitution, applied to the variable representing the questioned object, yields the answer, in general. Here, for instance, the variable in question is x to be substituted by "dinner", in order to have the same respective terms at each end of the connection; thus "dinner" is the appropriate answer.

Again we emphasize that in this simple type of data bases this answer, and the way to obtain it, is obvious even without any reference to logic and to the connection method. Our point is that with this insight into the logical background we have a general and efficient method at hand which, in contrast to any adhoc approaches, enables us to answer even very complex questions about complicated situations. For reasons of space it is never possible in a book to describe complicated situation in all details. Hence our next example, though being a little bit more complicated, will just give an idea of what we have in mind.

Figure 1 shows what might be fragments of a railway information system, namely three lines of a table with some information about departures of trains from the central station in Munich (i.e. München), thus representing a predicate DPRT-MNCH, 2 further explanatory statements, and the query for the departure time, given in american style, of a train to Garmisch. The quantifiers, for simplicity, are left out since they are all of the same kind, viz. existential. Also note that the first statement implicitly is contained in the table and thus is in fact redundant.

The answer for this query is obtained by the same general method illustrated with the previous example. Logically

Predicate	TIME	CATEG	#	DESTIN
⋮	⋮	⋮	⋮	⋮
DPRT-MNCH	14.50	TEE	80	Hamburg
DPRT-MNCH	14.51	IC	181	Garmisch
DPRT-MNCH	14.59	D	781	Salzburg
⋮	⋮	⋮	⋮	⋮

$$\text{DPRT-MNCH}(x,y,z,u) \rightarrow \text{TIME}(x) \wedge \text{CATEG}(y) \wedge \#(z) \wedge \text{DESTIN}(u)$$

$$\text{TIME}(v) \wedge (v>12.00) \rightarrow \text{AM-TIME}((v-12.00)\text{p.m.})$$

...

$$\text{Query for } w \text{ s.t. } \text{AM-TIME}(w) \wedge \text{DESTIN}(\text{Garmisch})$$

Figure 1. Fragments of a railway information system

this means that we have to prove that the entries $E_1,\ldots,E_n$ in the data-base imply the query QU , i.e. the formula $E_1\wedge\ldots\wedge E_n \to QU$ is claimed to be valid. It is easy to see that the **4** connections shown in the figure establish a connection proof for this claim with 2.51 p.m. substituted for w thus providing this value as the correct answer (as explained for the previous example).

This example may illustrate a number of other important points. First note that, of course, internally the correct connections may be recognized without explicitly composing the formula $E_1\wedge\ldots\wedge E_n \to QU$ (which might be huge). In fact, the connections not involving the query may be computed even **in advance** of any query since the **informational** part "$E_1\wedge\ldots\wedge E_n \to$" of this formula is fixed for any query. With current hardware technology it seems even possible to realize such a **preprocessed** informational part in fixed hardware with open "connector sockets" for plugging in the connection plugs from the query as illustrated with the 2 connections involving the query in figure 1.

We see in figure 1 three more such connector sockets which are useless for the present query but might be relevant for other queries such as the query $CATEG(w) \wedge TIME(14.50)$, questioning for the category of the train leaving at 14.50. The proof providing the answer for this question requires only 3 and in fact different connections thus illustrating that by "preprocessing the informational part" we do not mean **fixing** the internal part of the proof rather we mean preparing poten- tial alternatives for possible proofs.

Now imagine a real railway information system for whole of Germany (or even Europe) which is smart enough to provide the answers to the questions posed in real life to the officer at the information deck in the central station of München. Then it becomes obvious that the capability for reasoning as illus- trated with the previous trivial queries would have to be a crucial feature in such a system in particular for more complex questions. Namely, a system without such a reasoning component would have to store explicitly the answers to all possible questions in advance, which clearly is absolutely impossible.

In other words, there is a trade-off between the amount

of stored knowledge and the reasoning power w.r.t. the performance of such a system. For instance, although the second statement in figure 1 might be replaced by explicitly providing the
information about departure times in american style in a separate column AM-TIME within the table, this alternative would
require about a thousand more entries just for München. And
there are thousands of such "columns" for other possible questions. Thus it is obvious that the connection method offers a
technically much better solution.

As a final remark, we mention that the informational
part of such a smart information system would have to contain a
huge variety of knowledge. There are the pure **facts** as those
in table above. There are the statements expressing **specific**
knowledge about the topic in question ("for first class you
have to pay more than for second class"), but also general
world knowledge ("arriving at 3 a.m. in a little town may
cause you some troubles"). It would even have to contain uncer-
tain statements ("a TEE-train is more likely to arrive in time
than a D-train"), beliefs, assumptions and the like. Logic is
flexible enough for covering anything of this sort. But, of
course, here we have touched only one, viz. reasoning, among a
number of issues relevant in the context of such systems for
which the reader is referred to the literature on data base,
expert or knowledge systems.

2.   PROGRAMMING AND PROBLEM SOLVING

In any computer system one might naturally distinguish the 2
basic features captured by the terms **knowledge** and **algorithm** . We have touched upon the knowledge-side in the previous
section, and will now focus on the algorithmic aspects.

At first sight one might overlook the potential role of
logic with its deductive features for the wide field of programming, and it has in fact been overlooked in the first phase
of the short history of computer science. Only during the past
few years has the importance of logical tools for programming
been widely accepted for a variety of special applications.

The earliest such application is for proving the cor-

rectness of given algorithms, which is called **program verification** . In a different approach it has been attempted to
generate a proof of the logical decription of the stated
programming problem and extract an algorithm thereof which is
known as program synthesis. In a further approach programs are
actually written in the language of logic and executed in an
interpretive way by a theorem prover, which is called **logic
programming** . There are further applications, in particular the
one concerned with the **logic of programs** (modal, algorithmic,
dynamic, temporal, etc. logics) but those 3 are the ones which
we will briefly discuss in the present section, beginning with
logic programming .

Consider the well-known problem of computing the
factorial of a natural number. By definition, the factorial of
0 is 1, and whenever the factorial of x is y then the
factorial of x+1 is y·(x+1) . More formally this definition
reads

(f1)   fact 0 = 1

(f2) $\forall xy \left[\text{fact } x = y \;\rightarrow\; \text{fact } x+1 = y \cdot (x+1) \right]$

The problem is to compute, for any given input, the value of
the factorial of this input, determined by this definition.
Logically this may be expressed by asserting the existence of
such an appropriate output in the form of the following **goal**
statement

(fg) $\forall$ input $\exists$ output fact input = output

As a whole the problem is then captured by the formula

(**fact-progr**)   f1 $\wedge$ f2 $\rightarrow$ fg

that is, under the conjunction of the defining statements we
are claiming the goal statement.

This format is not specific for the factorial problem
rather it is quite a general one, given by

(**progr**) def1 $\wedge$ def2 $\wedge$ ... $\wedge$ defn $\rightarrow$ goal

where defi , i=1,...,n , are the **defining statements** while
goal is the **goal statement** . Even the queries as defined in
the previous section are exactly of this form in which special
case defi denotes a simple fact in the knowledge base,
i=1,...,n . W.r.t. this format the logic programming community
has adapted several conventions.

Developed within the refutation oriented resolution

environment (cf. IV.1), it considers the denial of the formula
(**progr**) rather than the formula itself, which is equivalent
with

(¬ **progr**)   def1 ∧ def2 ∧... ∧ defn ∧ ¬ goal.

Further, all the statements are restricted to Skolem normal
form (cf. III.4), that is, each statement is of the form
∃b1...bk ∀x1...xm qu-free-clause , where qu-free-clause is a
formula without quantifiers, and k,m⩾0 . Note that all the
statements in the denial of fact-progr are of that form since
¬ fg is equivalent with ∃ input ∀ output ¬ fact input = output
(III.1.4.c4). Since in this standard form quantifiers are
understood, they can be deleted. Thus the statements in such a
logic program are quantifier-free clauses.

In addition, these clause are restricted to **Horn
clauses** (II.1.8 and II.1.3.c4/5) of the form
K1 ∧ K2 ∧ ... ∧ Kl → L , where each Ki , i=1,...,l , and L
are unnegated literals, and l⩾0 . In fact, these clauses by
convention are written with the arrow pointing to the left
rather than to the right, and the conjunction symbols are
replaced by commas, thus resulting in L ← K1, K2, ..., Kl . In
this format the clauses for the factorial program read

(f1)   fact 0 = 1   ←

(f2)   fact x+1 = y·(x+1) ←   fact x = y

(fg)   ←   fact input = output

Note that for reasons of uniformity the arrow in (f1) is inserted although no literals occur on the right side. Similarly
for (fg) where the negation sign is expressed by the arrow
(cf. II.1.3.c5).

In general terms, a **logic program** is a set of Horn
clauses represented the way just described, with an empty left
side in the goal clause. According to our previous remark, a
data base query represented with these conventions is in fact a
logic program (see E3 in section 9). There is even a well-
defined programming language, called **PROLOG** [CKC], the programs of which essentially are such logic programs. Of course,
a logic program may as well be represented (positively) as a
matrix, the basic notion of this book. There, each clause
L ← K1,...,Kl appears as one of its columns in the form

$$\begin{array}{c} \neg L \\ K1 \\ \cdot \\ \cdot \\ \cdot \\ Kl \end{array}$$

with at most one negated literal, which by convention in this
context is written as the top-most element. Note how simple the
transformation between these 2 kinds of representations (in
both directions) actually is. Thus, the factorial program **in
matrix representation** reads

$\neg$ fact 0 = 1 $\neg$ fact x+1 = y$\cdot$(x+1)

____

                fact x = y   fact input = output

In order to emphasize the Horn clause form, a horizontal line
separates the negated literals (in each column at most one, in
general) from the unnegated ones.

     For given input such a logic program may be executed,
yielding the desired output, exactly in the same way as in the
previous section for answering queries, which consists in a
connection proof of the formula represented by the logic program (in one representation) or by the matrix (in the other).
For instance, let input = 1 in the present example then the
substitution resulting from the spanning set of connections in
the following connection proof

$\neg$ fact 0 = 1 $\neg$ fact x+1 = y$\cdot$(x+1)

____

                fact x = y   fact 1 = output

yields the value 1 for output , as will explained in a
moment.

     The way of carrying out such a proof has an analogy in
the way procedures are invocated in conventional programming
languages. In this **procedural interpretation of Horn clauses**
each clause B $\leftarrow$ A1,...,Al is interpreted as a **procedure
definition** , where B is the procedure **name** and A1,...,Al the
procedure **body** . If we start the proof shown above with the
literal in the goal clause then locating the right connection
in this analogy is interpreted as an **invocation** of the proce-

dure (f2), represented in the second column of the matrix. By
this invocation or instantiation x must be substituted such
that x+1=1 which gives x=0 ; similarly, we obtain y=output.
Solving the subgoal fact 0 = output in this instance of the
procedure body of (f2) in the same way leads to the left connection and the value 1 for output . Now the special way of
representing logic programs, as explained above, has been
chosen for no other reason than for illustrating exactly this
procedural analogy.

Of course, this interpretation does not affect at all
the nature of the execution process itself which is a proof as
we just noted. Since the matrix representation is so adequate
for representing connection proofs, as we demonstrated in all
chapters of this book, we will continue to use it also in the
context of logic programs, the difference to the conventional
logic programs in the case of Horn clauses being marginal
anyway as described above. The advantage of our preference lies
in the important fact that in the matrix representation we may
certainly handle non-Horn form problems as well as Horn ones
since the connection method applies to arbitrary formulas
(IV.5). Although the restriction to Horn clauses does not
restrict generality (III.4.5, and execise (E2) in section 9),
it does affect efficiency (cf. IV.5) as well as naturalness
since, of course, many problems naturally are expressed in
non-Horn form.

Let us now execute the factorial program for input = 2.

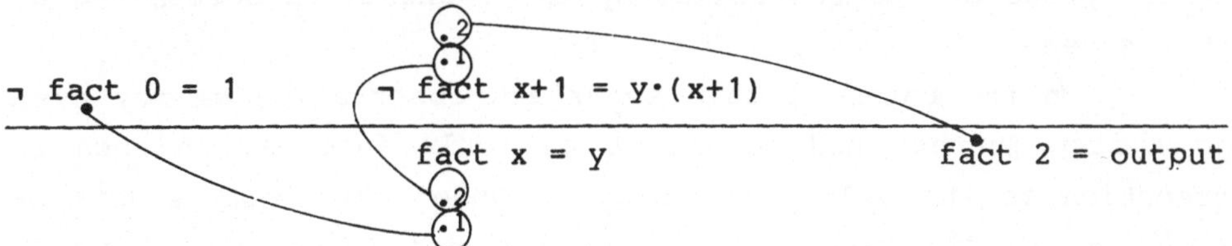

By a trivial induction proof on n we see that the proof for
arbitrary n>0 has the following form.

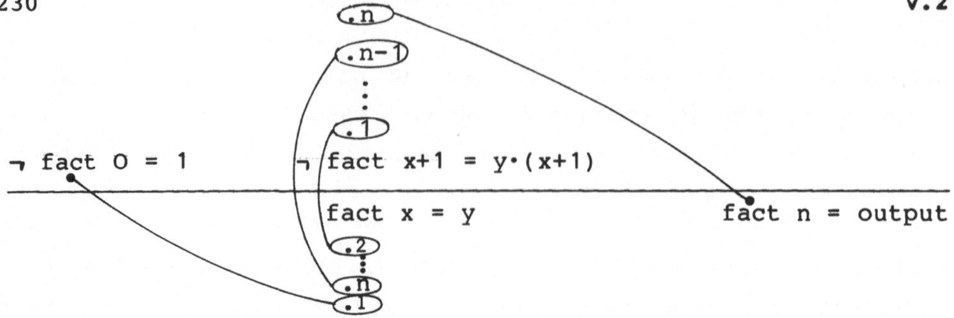

This may be abbreviated in the following self-explanatory form.

2.1.F.

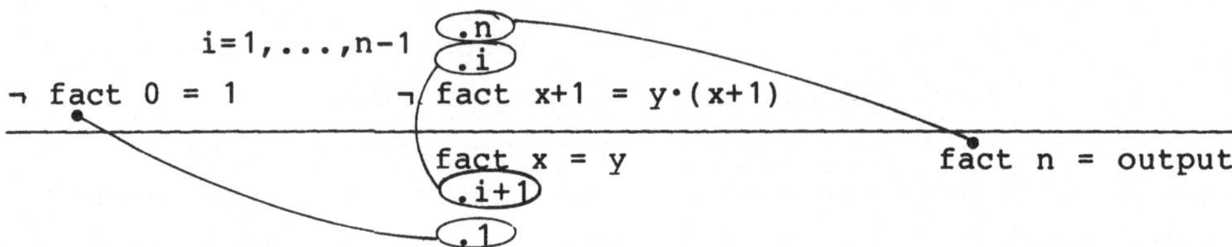

The point which we want to emphasize with this exercise is the following one. As we have seen the execution of a logic program consists in proving the validity of the representing matrix (or formula). In general, proving involves search thus is time- and space-consuming. But often it is easy, as in the present example, to recognize (even automatically) the general scheme of the proof for arbitrary input, which we call the **connection scheme** , as shown in the last picture. Once this scheme is available search is not necessary anymore since the execution of the proof may be controlled by the connections determined by this scheme.

On the basis of this important observation we may even go a step further and note that our only interest in such an execution is the value for output under the final substitution σ of the proof. Thus once the general proof scheme is known, the execution of the proof may in fact degenerate to simply calculating σ . Let us see how this works in the previous general proof. The left connection implies $x_{.1}\sigma = 0$ and $y_{.1}\sigma = 1$. With the (n-1)-fold connection in the middle we have $x_{.i+1}\sigma = (x_{.i}+1)\sigma$ and $y_{.i+1}\sigma = [y_{.i}\cdot(x_{.i}+1)]\sigma$, for $i=1,\ldots,n-1$. Finally, $output\sigma = [y_{.n}\cdot(x_{.n}+1)]\sigma$ via the right connection. Evidently, from there it is only a little step to the following algorithmic program which simulates these equations one by one.

```
x ← 0; y ← 1;
for i=1,...,n-1 do y ← y·(x+1) and x ← x+1;
output ← y·(x+1)
```

In other words, there is a very close relationship between an algorithmic program such as the previous one, and the corresponding general proof scheme further above. The execution of the algorithmic program may be regarded as a degenerated execution of a particular proof. In fact, this relationship is of quite a general nature and has been phrased by the illustrative equation

algorithm = logic + control

In the present example, the logic is the formula (fact-progr) in any representation such as the matrices above, and the control is the connection scheme shown in the last matrix above. The information provided by both may be transformed into the conventional form of an algorithm as just illustrated.

Under this view, the task of programming splits into the following 3 subtasks.

(**logic**)   Provide a suitable logical formalization of the problem to be programmed.

(**control**) Generate a connection scheme for this logical formalization which serves as a proof scheme for arbitrary input.

(**algor**)   Transform the algorithmic content provided by the formalization and the scheme into efficient code.

At present, for none of these 3 tasks there are well-developed and feasible methods. This is amazing as far as the last 2 are concerned since there is some evidence that it is relatively easy to develop such automatic methods which apply for a wide range of problems of practical importance. However, in the traditional computer science community the interest in logic has been emerging only recently, and in the logic programming community efficiency is certainly a secondary issue. With the details of our previous discussion we have attempted to inspire the development of such methods.

The first of these tasks is certainly the most difficult one since it is often the case that a natural problem specification is far from such a suitable logical formalization.
Not only is it generally a difficult task to formalize a natural specification which often is even ambiguous and incomplete;
but even if a specification is given in a logical form it may
still be far from being suitable as the following logic program
demonstrates which naturally specifies the problem of determining the maximal element m_0 or output in an ordered set S_0 .

(**max-progr**)   MAX(S,m) $\leftarrow$ $m \in S \wedge S < m$

$\leftarrow$ MAX(S_0,m_0)

where $S < m$ abbreviates $m' \in S \rightarrow m' < m$ (note that we are already
at a loss with the restriction to Horn clauses). In matrix
representation, according to the transformation explained
further above, this problem reads

$$\neg \ \dot{\text{MAX}}(S,m)$$
$$\rule{10cm}{0.4pt}$$
$$m \in S \qquad\qquad\qquad \dot{\text{MAX}}(S_0,\text{output})$$
$$S < m$$

For simplicity let us assume that the 2 predicates $\in$ and $<$
are **built into** the proof system in the sense that for given
m and S the system may evaluate the truth-value of $m \in S$ and
$S < m$ which in the latter case obviously requires as many comparisons (i.e. evaluations of $m' < m$) as there are elements in
S . Then the only algorithm suggested by this logical description and the single possible connection would exhaustively test
for each element m in S_0 whether $S_0 < m$ holds, not a very
efficient maximum algorithm, indeed. In this sense, (**max-
progr**) is not a suitable formalization. The generation of a
more suitable one falls into this task labeled (**logic**) above.
A method for solving this task has been suggested in $\lceil$Bi8$\rceil$ and
is further studied in the LOPS-project $\lceil$BiH$\rceil$. Here is not the
place to go into any details of this system. We just want to
point out that a theorem prover plays an important role in
LOPS, as it might be expected since without **reasoning** (that
is what theorem provers actually are supposed to do) such a
task may never be carried out.

Thus in our suggested approach to the construction of
programs which is in the tradition of **program synthesis** and

is characterized by the 3 subtasks (**logic**), (**control**), and
(**algor**) above, a deductive component (i.e. a theorem prover)
is essential at a number of places in the whole process. Some
occur within (**logic**) as we mentioned just before and, obviously it is required for the generation of connection schemes
in (**control**). In addition, the issue of efficiency in practice may often be ignored such as in preliminary or experimental programs, in which cases the subtasks (**control**) and
(**algor**) may be replaced completely by a theorem prover interpreting the logic program.

This approach to programming, also termed **predicative
programming** , offers many attractive prospects. It certainly is
the only approach which covers the process of programming as a
whole, and even in a uniform way. It allows support by the
machine for solving (**logic**) in a way which is close to the
human way of reasoning (recall that logic is an abstracted form
of **human** logic), and which is not burdened by the messy
details entering with the controlling features (present in all
conventional programming languages). It, finally, suggests the
complete automation of the messy tasks (**control**) and
(**algor**) which seems to be feasible for practical problems.

Nevertheless it is a fact that traditional programmers
like all people coddle their own habits even if they are bad
and costly ones as has become evident in the ever deepening
software crisis. Therefore they favor the use of theorem
provers for **program verification** . We will not discuss any
details of this approach since we argue that it is not a very
promising one anyway.

Its underlying paradigm requires the programmer to
provide both, a complete formal specification and the program
with no other support for the programming process in between
than an occasional indication by the **verifier** that the pieces
of code match the intentions as expressed in the specification,
apparently not a very constructive support indeed. Moreover the
logic required for such verifiers has to cope with time and
thus is intrinsically more complicated than the one for the
synthesis approach which has to deal with (time-independent)
facts only. Hence the bottleneck of any of these approaches,
which still is theorem proving, in the verification approach is

burdened with an even heavier load. Therefore the synthesis
approach is not only more natural but, in a fair comparison
based on an equal amount of automation, appears to be even more
realistic.

Goad in a further approach [Goa] uses the fact mentioned above, that proofs may be regarded as descriptions of computations, for the **automatic transformation** towards more efficient or more specialized ones which seems to be particularly
promising w.r.t. feasibility in the very near future (and which
has been suggested much earlier in [Bi3], section 11).

The headings of this section pair programming with
problem solving. Indeed, it is evident that any kind of a
(rational) problem may be modeled as a programming problem.
Consequently all what we said on programming at the same time
applies to general problem solving with the computer.

3.   THE CONNECTION METHOD WITH EQUALITY

At various places in this book such as in the sections (I.1),
(II.2), and in the previous 2 sections we have seen that in ATP
we are dealing with formulas of the form $AX1 \wedge AX2 \wedge \ldots \wedge AXn \rightarrow T$
where the AXi, $i=1,\ldots,n$, according to the respective field
of applications are called **axioms** , **data base entries** , **hypotheses** , etc. and where T is the actual **theorem** , **query** , or
claim in question. In particular in mathematics it often occurs
that a relation or function is so familiar that no mathematician would ever be aware of its defining axioms but rather
would evaluate the relation or function right away following
"built-in" rules. In the maximum example from the previous section we have already encountered 2 such relations, viz. $\in$ and
$<$; the most significant instance in this context, however, is
the equality relation $=$.

For example, if we know that Pa holds and a ist the
same as b, i.e. $a=b$, then anyone immediately concludes that Pb
holds as well without any explicit reference to any particular
axioms defining the equality predicate, rather by application
of the "built-in" substitution rule about equality saying that
"equals may be substituted for equals". For the connection

calculus in its present form, however, this implication, viz. $Pa \wedge a=b \to Pb$, certainly is not a valid formula, since no such special knowledge about $=$ is built into it (note that we use the familiar infix notation $a=b$ rather than something strange like $=(a,b)$ or even $P_=(a,b)$ according to (III.1.4.c8). Rather we have to characterize the nature of this relation by axioms, as we do in the following definition.

3.1.D.   The **axioms of equality** are

(eq1) $\forall x \quad x=x$

(eq2) $\forall x_1 \ldots x_n y_1 \ldots y_n (x_1=y_1 \wedge \ldots \wedge x_1=y_n \to fx_1 \ldots x_n=fy_1 \ldots y_n)$
          for any n-ary function symbol f and for $n > 0$

(eq3) $\forall x_1 \ldots x_n y_1 \ldots y_n (x_1=y_1 \wedge \ldots \wedge x_1=y_n \to (Px_1 \ldots x_n \to Py_1 \ldots y_n))$

          for any n-ary predicate symbol P and for $n > 0$ $\square$

Note that there are as many instances of the **substitutivity axioms** (eq2) and (eq3) as there are function and predicate symbols. With such an instance of (eq3) as a hypothesis the previous formula can now actually be proved with the connection method as the following matrix demonstrates where the familiar notation $a \neq b$ is used instead of $\neg a=b$.

3.2.F.

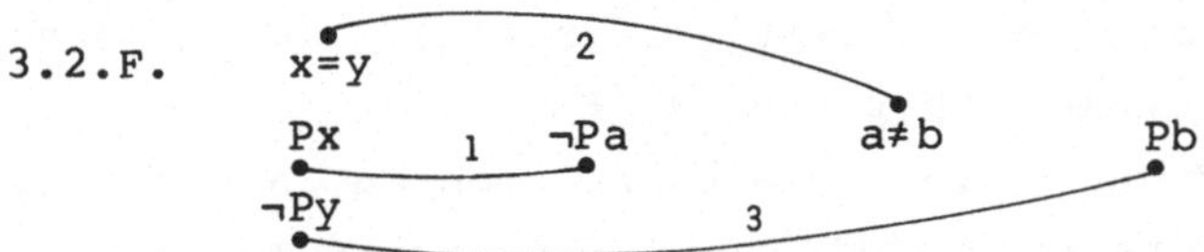

In other words, the connection method of course can deal with equality as with any other relation via its axioms but the way it does this appears to be awkward in comparison with the mathematician's approach, according to which we would rather expect a connection proof of the following kind.

3.3.F. $\neg Pa \qquad a \neq b \qquad Pb$

It illustrates the idea that the connected literals are complementary because of the associated assumption $a=b$. Although (3.3) certainly is more concise and more natural than (3.2), the logical meaning of this new kind of connection with an **associated** assumption obviously is the one given by (3.2).

That is, (3.3) is to be regarded as an abbreviated and less redundant version of (3.2), which is visualized in the pictures by attaching equal numbers to the respective (parts of) connections. We call these parts **association arcs** or **association connections** . The instance of (eq3) in (3.2) has degenerated in (3.3) to a single **association node** . The analogue abbreviation for the case of (eq2) is shown in a single picture, this time with 2 associated assumptions.

3.4.F.

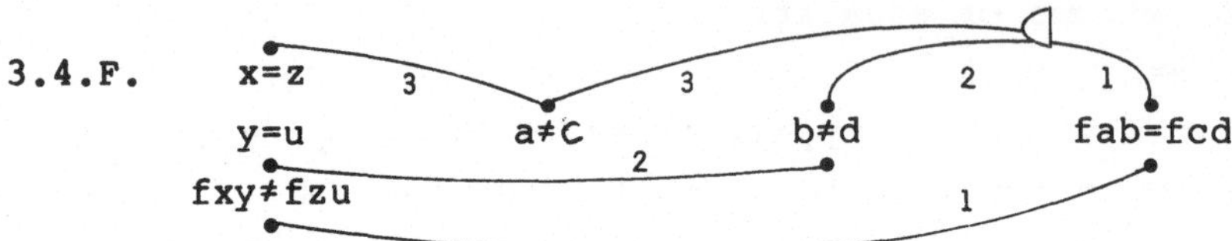

With these illustrations in mind it is straightforward to build equality into the connection method with such new kinds of connections, as we will do now.

3.5.D. The following concepts are defined for a formula F possibly with a multiplicity μ (for simplicity μ and any indices necessary for the general case are suppressed since their inclusion is obvious).

An **eq-literal** (L,e) is a literal L of the form $s=t$ associated with a set $e = \{s_1 \neq t_1,\ldots,s_n \neq t_n\}$, $n \geqslant 0$, such that $\{L\} \cup e \subseteq p$ for some path p through F .

An **eq-connection** (u,e) is a connection u associated with a set e as before such that $u \cup e \subseteq p$ for some path p through F .

An eq-literal (L,e) is called **valid** if there is a substitution $\tau = \tau_1 \ldots \tau_m$ with $\tau_i \in \bigcup_{j=1}^{n} \{s_j \backslash t_j, t_j \backslash s_j\}$,$i=1,\ldots,m$, $i=1,\ldots,m$, $m \geqslant 0$, such that $\{s,t\}\tau$ is a singleton set.

An eq-connection (u,e) is called **complementary** if there is a substitution τ as before such that $u\tau$ is a (propositionally) complementary connection.

A path p through a formula F is said to **contain** an eq-literal (L,e) or an eq-connection (u,e) if $\{L\} \cup e \subseteq p$ or $u \cup e \subseteq p$, respectively.

A set of eq-literals and eq-connections is called **spanning** for F if each path through F contains at least one element from this set.

F   is called   **eq-valid**   if there exist instances
E1,...,En, n>0 , of the equality axioms such that E1∧...∧En → F
is valid.   □

The eq-connection shown in (3.3) is complementary since
{¬Pa, Pb} {a\b} = {¬Pb, Pb} (note that these are substitutions
of the general type as defined in III.1.6). It is also spanning
for this formula since there is only a single path containing
all its literals. Similarly, (3.4) shows an eq-literal which is
valid and spanning. As a further example the formula consisting
of the single literal a=a trivially is a valid eq-literal which
also is spanning, thus illustrating the incorporation within
(3.5) of the **reflexivity** axiom (eq1) from (3.1) above. Similarly, Pa ¬Pa shows a trivially complementary and spanning
eq-connection, that is, these new concepts include the old
ones, as a special case. As a corollary to the version
(III.6.4) of Herbrand's theorem we obtain the following result
(as a preparation for it exercise E5 in section 9 is recommended).

3.6.C. A formula F in Skolem normal form is eq-valid iff
for some (constant) multiplicity μ there is a spanning set W
of eq-literals and eq-connections in $F^μ$ and a (variable)
substitution σ such that for any element w ∈ W , wσ is valid
if it is an eq-literal and is complementary if it is an eq-connection.

     Proof. If F is eq-valid then by definition E1∧...∧ En→F
is valid which formula may be transformed into Skolem normal
form simply by transforming it appropriately into prenex normal
form. Thus, according to (III.6.4) there is a multiplicity μ ,
a spanning set U of connections and a substitution σ such
that uσ is complementary for any u ∈ U . As illustrated with
the examples (3.2), (3.3), and (3.4) above all connections in
U with literals in E_i, i ∈ {1,...,n} , can (inductively) be
replaced by appropriate eq-literals and eq-connections yielding
a set W such that the right side of the corollary holds.

     Conversely, if the right side of the corollary holds
then by the inverse process each eq-literal or eq-connection

(inductively) may be taken care of by connections containing literals of an appropriate instance of an equality axiom, after which process (III.6.4) can be applied to infer that F is eq-valid.   □

We have stated (3.6) as a corollary of (III.6.4). Of course, we could have stated and proved analogue results by starting from the more general versions (IV.8.5) or (IV.10.4) of Herbrand's theorem which is left to the reader as an exercise (see E6 in section 9).

As throughout this book, our main interest in a result like the previous one is its computational application. For that purpose once more note the similarity of (3.6) and (III.6.4) which suggests that for matrices in normal form we may develop a **connection calculus with equality** from (3.6) in an analogue way as the connection calculus defined in (III.6.5) and (III.6.6) has been developed from (III.6.4). In fact this is a straightforward although lengthy exercise which, as far as the formal details are concerned, is left to the reader (see E7 in section 9). Here we give an outline of this development under the assumption that the reader is now familiar with the basic features of the connection calculus as defined in section (III.6).

The essential difference between (III.6.4) and (3.6) is the fact that in the latter case a path (through the given formula) may be "finished" not only by locating a connection which under the actual substitution σ is complementary but also by complementary eq-connections and valid eq-literals (under σ). Hence this additional feature is actually all what we have to build into the connection calculus. It is immediately clear that the necessary changes affect the definition of **extension** only. So let us recall extension and outline the changes.

In figure 2 we illustrate an extension step in a rather abstracted form by just indicating the active paths p_a and $\tilde{p}_a$ as dashed lines threading literals, the clause d with the literal N selected for extension of the active path p_a at this step, and the clause e with at least one literal L such that $\{L,K\}\tilde{\sigma}$ is complementary for some K in the active path and for an appropriate substitution $\tilde{\sigma}$ (for the precise details recall III.6.6). The changes for inclusion of equality will now be explained in reference of the notation in this figure.

```
              *.  L                              *.  L.
p_a--K----M-- N   H    |--    p̃_a--K----M----N--  H
              *   *                              *   *
              *   *                              *   *

              d   e                              d   e
```

Figure 2. Abstract structure of an extension step

According to (3.5), literals which are inequalities may play a special role (in associated sets). Therefore let $p_{\neq}$ and $\tilde{p}_{\neq}$ denote the subsets of all such inequalities in p_a and $\tilde{p}_a$, respectively. Then the literal L in e may recieve a dot (illustrating β-value 0) for exactly the same reason of $\{L,K\}\tilde{\sigma}$ being complementary as before. But now there may also be other reasons listed under (1) trough (4).

(1) $(\{L,K\},\tilde{p}_{\neq})\tilde{\sigma}$ is a complementary eq-connection.

(2) $(L,\tilde{p}_{\neq})\tilde{\sigma}$ is a valid eq-literal.

(3)   L is an inequality such that $(\{K,M\}, \tilde{p}_{\neq} \cup \{L\})\tilde{\sigma}$ is a complementary eq-connection.

(4)   L is an inequality such that $(M,\tilde{p}_{\neq} \cup \{L\})\tilde{\sigma}$ is a valid eq-literal.

Of course, L is to be regarded as a dummy literal which represents all literals in e satisfiying any of these 4 properties, and similarly for K and M representing any 2 literals in $\tilde{p}_a$ with the respective properties. $\tilde{\sigma}$ plays the analogue role to the one before.

In addition to all these kinds of extension we allow the case in which none of the literals in e is qualified to recieve a dot for the previous reasons but e contains an inequality literal H by which the active path $\tilde{p}_a$ is extended in the next step. Such an extension of $\tilde{p}_a$ in some sense is to be regarded as a neutral action.

An instance of such an extension (to be followed by

reduction) is shown in figure 3 which is the last step in a
4-step deduction of this formula (not counting the initial step
and the subsequent reduction). Note the step preceding that
shown in the figure which is allowed in this way (else permit-

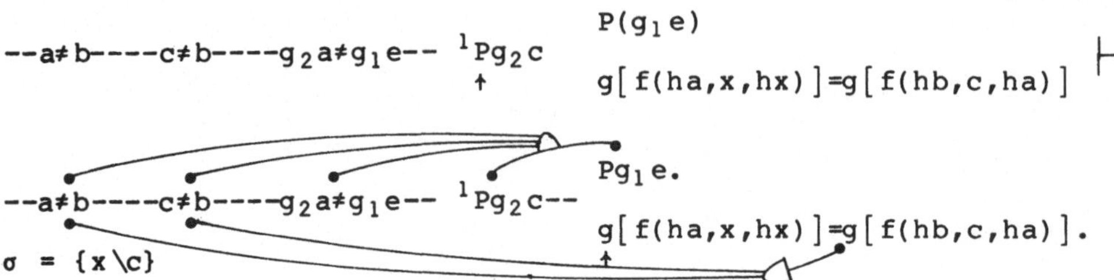

Figure 3. An extension step with equality

ted in an initial step or in truncation only) since all previous steps are such neutral actions.

     As for the illustrated extension itself, the calculus
locates a complementary eq-connection and a valid eq-literal.
In both cases the associated set of inequalities is determined
by need as indicated by the following description of the
process carried out during execution of this step.

     It recognizes the connection $\{^1Pg_2c, Pg_1e\}$ but unifi-
cation fails. Therefore in $p_{\neq}$ it determines a literal such
that one of its 2 terms has g_2 (or g_1) as outermost symbol
which yields $g_2a{\neq}g_1e$. Since g_1e occurs in Pg_1e we let
$\tau_1 = \{g_1e \setminus g_2a\}$ and   associate   this   literal   with
$\{^1Pg_2c,Pg_1e\}\tau_1 = \{^1Pg_2c,Pg_2a\}$ which, however, is still not
complementary. As before $p_{\neq}$ is scanned for another literal
with terms c (or a) yielding $c{\neq}b$ and thus $\tau_2 = \{c\setminus b\}$. Also
this literal is   associated   with $\{^1Pg_2c,Pg_1e\}\tau_1\tau_2$ =
$\{^1Pg_2b,Pg_2a\}$. The same process repeated once more gives
$\tau_3 = \{b\setminus a\}$ and   associates   the   literal $a{\neq}b$ with
$\{^1Pg_2c,Pg_1e\}\tau_1\tau_2\tau_3 = \{^1Pg_2a,Pg_2a\}$ which apparently is now
complementary, so that pg_1e may receive its dot.

     The second literal is an equality. It is true in gener-
al that in such a case we may restrict our attention to the
question whether it is valid as an eq-literal associated with
$p_{\neq}$ (since an eq-connection in this case might be interpreted
as an eq-literal). So we try unification which gives $\sigma = \{x\setminus c\}$
but otherwise fails for the subterms a,b and c,a, thus initiat-

ing the association of $a \neq b$ and $c \neq b$ with the substitution $\tau_1\tau_2 = \{a \backslash b\}\{b \backslash c\}$. As a result we obtain a valid eq-literal since apparently
$$\{g[f(ha,x,hx)],g[f(hb,c,ha)]\}\sigma\tau_1\tau_2 = \{g[f(hc,c,hc)]\} \ .$$

Admittedly, this description glosses over a number of subtle details. But it should be clear that these details can be filled in by a more comprehensive treatment. Such a treatment has been carried out by Digricoli in [Di2] with the flavor of what we have in mind. Unfortunately his treatment is carried out within the less transparent resolution setting where the details are much more complicated. Therefore we must leave the reader with the task of filling out the subtle algorithmic details, possibly adapted from [Di2] (see also exercise E8 in section 9).

We should mention that in resolution theory equality is handled by **paramodulation** [RoW]. The basic idea is the same as the one carried out here for the connection calculus: several resolution steps involving equality axioms are **abbreviated** by a single **macro-step** called paramodulation where the equality axioms are no more visible, as we **abbreviated** several connections by a single **macro-connection** called eq-connection. In fact the correspondence is again a rather close one. However, while our extension is a rather global action associating inequalities by need, resolution with paramodulation would try many stupid substitutions in a locally oriented way which is blind for the structure of the formula as a whole. These insights leave not the slightest doubt that in comparable implementations of both approaches the connection method with equality will be superior in its performance in comparison with resolution with paramodulation (cf. section 7).

When we say "comparable" this may (or may not) include the need for carrying out the development of a connection calculus with equality on the basis of any of the enhanced versions discussed in chapter IV rather than on that of (III.6.6). Note in this connection that (3.6) is not restricted to normal form formulas. The ultimate goal would be the incorporation into CP^1 envisaged in section (IV.11).

Our example in figure 3 has been taken from [Di1] where it is proved by paramodulation and by Digricoli's RUE-resolu-

tion which might ease the comparison of the 3 methods by the
interested reader.

4.   REWRITE RULES AND GENERALIZED UNIFICATION

At the beginning of the previous section we mentioned equality
as one out of a number of special relations or functions which
are handled by humans in some built-in way rather than by
explicit reference to the defining axioms. The question thus
arises whether the approach taken in the previous section
w.r.t. equality might be useful in other contexts as well. As a
further example we therefore consider here the so-called **word-
problem** in **group theory** .

4.1.D. A **group** is a mathematical structure with 3 special
functions or operators e (nullary), $^-$ (unary), and $\cdot$ (binary)
which satisfy the following 3 axioms.

(g1) $\forall x$ $e \cdot x = x$ (left identity)
(g2) $\forall y$ $y^- \cdot y = e$ (left inverse)
(g3) $\forall uvw$ $(u \cdot v) \cdot w = u \cdot (v \cdot w)$ (associativity) $\Box$

The word-problem then is the problem to decide for arbitrary
terms s and t   built exclusively with these three operators
whether or not   s=t is a consequence of the group (and equality) axioms. Thus this problem is just a theorem proving problem
of a very special kind, and as such can certainly be solved
with the connection method with equality. For instance, an eq-
connection proof for $s = (a^- \cdot a) \cdot b$ and $t = (e \cdot a^-) \cdot (a \cdot b)$ is the
following one (where for simplicity quantifiers are now deleted
as usual).

$$e \cdot x \neq x \qquad y^- \cdot y \neq e \qquad (u \cdot v) \cdot w \neq u \cdot (v \cdot w) \qquad (a^- \cdot a) \cdot b = (e \cdot a^-) \cdot (a \cdot b)$$

The problem of finding such a proof, however, is by far not
trivial in general. Namely, recall that the association arcs
actually reflect a sequence of substitutions which in the pre-
sent case may be chosen as $\sigma \tau_1 \tau_2$ where $\sigma = \{x \backslash a^-, u \backslash a^-, v \backslash a, w \backslash b\}$,

$\tau_1 = \{e \cdot a^- \backslash a^-\}$, and $\tau_2 = \{a^- \cdot (a \cdot b) \backslash (a^- \cdot a) \cdot b\}$.

The difficulties in finding such a proof arise from the fact that each term in the conclusion may have several subterms which match with different terms in the axioms. For instance, consider $(a^- \cdot a) \cdot b$ which as a whole matches with $(u \cdot v) \cdot w$. However, there is also the possible match of its subterm $a^- \cdot a$ with $y^- \cdot y$. There are further, less direct matches such as that of $(a^- \cdot b) \cdot b$ with $u \cdot (v \cdot w)$ via $e \cdot x \neq x$. Thus finding the correct proof may actually involve a lot of search. Could it be avoided ?

A first possibility towards such a goal might be a fixed **direction** of the substitution determined by the axioms. For instance, with σ defined above the axiom $e \cdot x \neq x$ may be used as $\tau_1 = \{e \cdot a^- \backslash a^-\}$ as we did before but also as $\tau_1' = \{a^- \backslash e \cdot a^-\}$ according to (3.5). Our preference certainly would be for the direction realized by τ_1 (rather then τ_1') since τ_1 obviously simplifies matters, an action which in equational theorem proving is known as **demodulation** . Hence we could restrict the τ_i in such a way that, for instance, the left side in any of the 3 group axioms always is substituted by the right one, and never the other way around. Adopting standard notation from this special field of rewriting, from now on in this section we write $s \rightarrow t$ rather than $s \backslash t$. Thus we use

(rg1) $e \cdot x \;\rightarrow\; x$

(rg2) $x^- \cdot x \;\rightarrow\; e$

(rg3) $(u \cdot v) \cdot w \;\rightarrow\; u \cdot (v \cdot w)$

Such substitutions are also called **rewrite rules** , and a collection of them is known as a **term rewriting system** . Rewriting a term t with a rule $s_1 \rightarrow s_2$ to obtain t' , in symbols $t \rightarrow t'$, means $t' = t\{s_1\sigma \backslash s_2\sigma\}$ in our previous substitutional notation, for some variable substitution σ . Note that rewriting a term in a formula as the one further above is just another way of representing the information contained in a respective association connection. For instance, the association connection labeled with 1 in the eq-connection proof above could be expressed in this new notation as $(e \cdot a^-) \cdot (a \cdot b) \rightarrow a^- \cdot (a \cdot b)$ rewriting the left term by means of (rg1).

We now return to our question concerning the elimina-

tion of search which by fixing the direction of the substitutions certainly is not fully settled. In particular, we have
already seen above that it may well happen that in a given term
there may be several subterms matching the left side of rewrite
rules (e.g. $(a^-\cdot a)\cdot b$ matches the left side of both, rg2
and rg3). Thus if we select one, we may fail afterwards hence
making back-ups necessary. For instance, in our example we
might rewrite $(a^-\cdot a)\cdot b \to e\cdot b \to b$ by means of rg2 and
rg1, and $(e\cdot a^-)\cdot(a\cdot b) \to a^-\cdot(a\cdot b)$. In both cases,
the last term is **irreducible** , that is, none of the rules can
be applied anymore. Moreover, these 2 terms are different and
it is intuitively clear (and holds in general) that a proof is
established in this form once we are able to rewrite the given
terms to 2 **identical** terms like with $(a^-\cdot a)\cdot b \to a^-\cdot(a\cdot b)$ and
$(e\cdot a^-)\cdot(a\cdot b) \to a^-\cdot(a\cdot b)$ representing our eq-connection proof
above.

Thus back-ups seem to be unavoidable and strictly
speaking, they in fact cannot be avoided. But we may **short-
cut** the necessary detour which is illustrated in the following
picture.

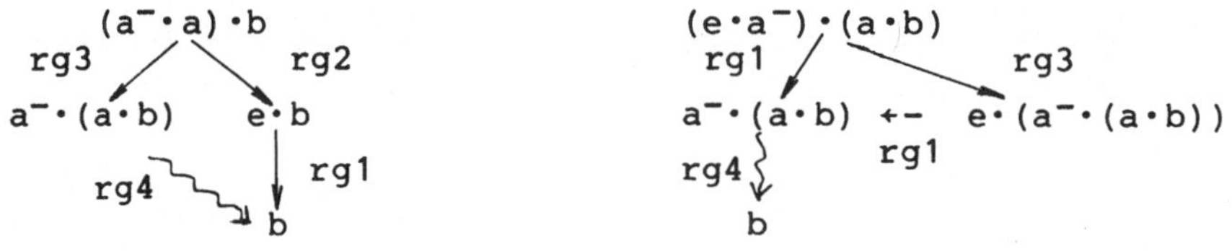

<pre>
        (a⁻·a)·b   (e·a⁻)·(a·b)
   rg3 /   \ rg2   rg1 /   \ rg3
 a⁻·(a·b)   e·b   a⁻·(a·b) ←– e·(a⁻·(a·b))
      rg4 ⤳ | rg1   rg4 ⤳   rg1
           ↘ ↓   ↓
              b   b
</pre>

There we show all possible ways of rewriting our 2 given terms,
and "avoid" any back-ups by short-cutting the detour with the
use of the new rule

(rg4) $y^-\cdot(y\cdot w) \to w$

The essential idea, due to Knuth and Bendix [KnB], is now the
observation that such an additional rule may be figured out by
applying the previous rules to themselves, denoted by **superposition** . This is shown in the following diagram.

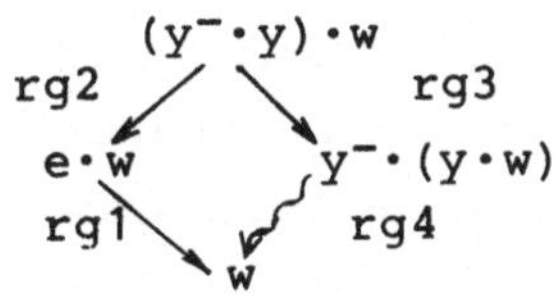

Obviously, the topmost term $(y^-\cdot y)\cdot w$ is the left side $y^-\cdot y$ of (rg2) **superposed** on the left side $(u\cdot v)\cdot w$ of (rg3). This iterative process of superposing rules on other rules including the newly created ones may generate a number of such rules, and eventually saturate with a final set of rules which is **complete** in the following sense: Any 2 terms s and t can be **reduced** by rewriting to 2 uniquely determined irreducible terms s_0 and t_0 such that s=t is a consequence of the axioms iff s_0 and t_0 are identical.

For the case of free groups without relations one such **complete set of reductions** is the following set of rules.

(rg1)	$e\cdot x \rightarrow x$	(rg6)	$e^- \rightarrow e$
(rg2)	$x^-\cdot x \rightarrow e$	(rg7)	$x^{--} \rightarrow x$
(rg3)	$(x\cdot y)\cdot z \rightarrow x\cdot(y\cdot z)$	(rg8)	$x\cdot x^- \rightarrow e$
(rg4)	$x^-\cdot(x\cdot y) \rightarrow y$	(rg9)	$x\cdot(x^-\cdot y) \rightarrow y$
(rg5)	$x\cdot e \rightarrow x$	(rg10)	$(x\cdot y)^- \rightarrow y^-\cdot x^-$

Note that the terms on the left side are never simpler (e.g. in the sense of the sum of the depth of the leaves in the term tree, as defined in II.1.2) than those on the right side, for which reason we can be sure that the iterative application of these rules to any pair of terms eventually **terminates** . This is also expressed as the fact that complete sets of reductions have the unique and finite **termination property** .

In summary, the rewrite rules approach may be stated as follows. For special and often used sets of axioms, usually characterizing well-known theories such as group theory, ring theory and the like, it is attempted to generate from these axioms a complete set of reductions with a well-defined procedure known as the **Knuth-Bendix completion algorithm** . If this attempt succeeds then, in order to decide whether 2 terms s and t are equal under these axioms, this can be achieved by iteratively applying these rules to s and t in any sequence. If upon (guaranteed) termination of these reductions the final 2 terms are identical then s and t are in fact equal, otherwise they are not.

Note that this approach can be applied not only for proving equalities s=t but also for deciding the equality of s and t under any other circumstances. For instance, we might want to prove the formula $P(e \cdot a, b \cdot y^-) \rightarrow P(x,e)$ in group theory where apparently the test for equality of the 2 pairs of terms $e \cdot a, x$ and $b \cdot y^-, e$ for some substitution σ occurs as a subproblem within the unificational part. For this reason the rewrite rules approach often is also viewed as a **generalized unification** approach where the reduction process is incorporated into the unification process.

There is a busy literature on rewrite rules and generalized unification. The attraction derives from the alluring prospect that inefficient search (necessary in traditional ATP) might be replaced by efficient computation. But upon closer inspection we notice the following major draw-backs.

Perhaps the least serious (but most obvious) disadvantage of this approach is the requirement that the proof system must, for each distinct set of axioms, store a separate set of rules, and retrieve upon a special application the adequate one. The great variety of rules and methods which appeared in the literature is certainly confusing for people who still are the ones having to design such a system.

Further, we should mention that the rewrite rules approach has theoretical limitations such as non-termination of the Knuth-Bendix algorithm and non-existence of a complete set of reductions in certain cases which, however, might be only of an academic interest.

But our main concern is expressed in the critical question whether it is actually true that the rewrite rules approach is more efficient than a comparably smart traditional ATP system based on the connection method. First recall, what we demonstrated above, that the application of a rewrite rule is just another form of representation of the same process which in the eq-connection method is illustrated with an association connection. Thus we can focus on the more specific

question whether or not the introduction of short-cutting rules
replacing back-ups, as we explained above, in fact offers a
measurable advantage in the average number of steps required
for practical cases.

That this is by far not obvious can be seen in the
diagram for our worked example further above. Namely, if the
theorem prover happens to do the right thing, viz. application
of (rg3) to the left and (rg1) to the right term, it may finish
its task after these 2 steps. Not so the rewriting system which
has to proceed with 2 further applications of (rg4) in order to
obtain the irreducible term b on both sides. In other words,
the rewriting system has to pay a price for the elimination of
back-ups. If on the other side of a smart ATP system we imagine
that the rules (i.e. the connections) are applied in an intelligent way guided by the structure of the 2 given terms in a
"by-need" way then it is certainly a real open question which
approach might be the more efficient one on the long range.

The most likely future development might consist in a
convergence of both approaches where the knowledge gathered for
special sets of axioms is used as an additional meta-level
guidance for the actions of a connection system (cf. [BuW]).
This expectation is based on the insight that from the point of
view of the connection method a complete set of reductions may
be regarded simply as an encoding of a deterministic control
for the actions of the prover.

5.   THE CONNECTION METHOD WITH INDUCTION

Induction is such a fundamental tool in human reasoning that
any theorem prover without the capability for inductive reasoning would have to be considered as a torso. In particular for
the application of theorem proving in programming induction
becomes crucial since most programs and data structures by
their nature are recursive constructs, and recursion essentially is inversed induction.

However, well-known logical results seem to suggest
that in the presence of induction theorem proving is no more a
realistic enterprise a view which, besides the exhausting

difficulties in building efficient theorem provers even without
induction, has long discouraged the incorporation of this vital
tool. In contrast to that the results of experiments with
running systems coping with induction are promising indeed.
Thus motivated let us see how induction could be built into the
connection method.

Let us first restrict our attention to statements on
natural numbers, such as the factorial program from section 2.
In this special case our first-order language, defined in
(III.1.1) includes the familiar special functions 0 (nullary),
+1 (unary), +, x, etc. (binary), which we use in the familiar
mathematical way. Induction may then be expressed in the
following way.

5.1.F. $F\{a\backslash 0\} \wedge \forall x(F\{a\backslash x\} \rightarrow F\{a\backslash x+1\}) \rightarrow \forall a F$

In words, this says that, if the formula F holds for 0 and
if it holds for x+1 whenever it holds for x , then F holds
for any natural number a which obviously expresses the usual
induction principle on natural numbers.

Our first idea might be to use (5.1) in an axiomatic
way in a natural deduction system like GS in (IV.7.1). For
this purpose we would simply extend the set of axioms in GS by
formulas essentially of the form (5.1), specifically by
$\vdash v(G_1, \neg F\{a\backslash 0\}, G_2, \exists x(F\{a\backslash x\} \wedge \neg F\{a\backslash x+1\}), G_3, \forall a F, G_4)$
as one possible generalization. With such an extended system in
mind one would have to infer the necessary changes for the
connection method, for instance introduce some kind of an
induction connection as we introduced an eq-connection in section 3. So far no one has pursued this idea any further.

Alternatively, (5.1) might be used in the form of an
inference scheme (cf. those in IV.7.1) as follows.

(IND)   From $\vdash v(G_1, F\{a\backslash 0\}, G_2)$

         and $\vdash v(G^1, F \rightarrow F\{a\backslash a+1\}, G^2)$

         infer $\vdash v(G_1, F, G_2)$

         where a must not occur in G_i, i=1,2 .

In a restricted application of (IND) one might think of proving

the premises by the connection method without induction. Let us
illustrate this by the simple example where F is the formula
0+a=a . Of course, we have to supply the defining properties
for + which are $\forall x(x+0=x)$ and $\forall yz\left[y+(z+1) = (y+z)+1\right]$.
With these definitions we easily obtain an eq-connection proof
for each of the two premises in (IND) for this case.

5.2.F. $\forall x(x+0=x)\wedge\forall yz\left[y+(z+1)=(y+z)+1\right] \rightarrow 0+0=0$

$\forall x(x+0=x)\wedge\forall yz\left[y+(z+1)=(y+z)+1\right] \rightarrow (0+a=a\rightarrow 0+(a+1)=a+1)$

Here the eq-connection in the second proof encodes the natural
equality proof $0+(a+1) = (0+a)+1 = a+1$ where the numbers refer to the respective association arcs. By (IND) we may thus
infer the formula

5.3.F. $\forall x(x+0=x)\wedge\forall yz\left[y+(z+1)=(y+z)+1\right] \rightarrow 0+a=a$

     In terms of theorem proving we would have to think in
the opposite direction. In order to prove a formula like the
one in (5.3) we have first to determine both, the part F in
it for which the induction is to be carried out (viz. 0+a=a in
5.3), and the induction variable a . With this information the
2 premises in (IND) are uniquely determined by the given formula. Their proofs thus can be attempted by the connection
method.

     Having established the validity of a formula like (5.3)
we may then add its conclusion in quantified form, that is the
formula $\forall u(0+u=u)$ in the present case, to the set of axioms,
which implied it, as a **lemma** . This enlarged set of axioms may
then be used in subsequent proofs. For instance, in an induction proof establishing commutativity of + , i.e. a+b=b+a ,
our previous result contributes to establishing the **base case**
as shown in the following proof.

x+0=x $\wedge$ y+(z+1)=(y+z)+1 $\wedge$ 0+u=u $\rightarrow$ 0+b=b+0

In practice many induction proofs may be established in this
simple way. Nevertheless this approach certainly has limitations. Suppose we want to prove a+b=b+a ; how could we know in
advance that we first have to prove 0+a=a and add it to the

axioms ?

        Well, in this special and similar cases one may apply a
"by-need" kind of solution. Namely, determining, as described
before, the two premises for the formula
$x+0=x \;\wedge\; y+(z+1)=(y+z)+1 \;\rightarrow\; a+b=b+a$ requires in particular a
proof of $x+0=x \;\wedge\; y+(z+1)=(y+z)+1 \;\rightarrow\; 0+b=b+0$ when   a   is chosen as the induction variable. This formula may then again be
tried by induction if the connection method alone fails.

        Even with such an additional feature this approach
still has limitations since it is well known that the **cut
rule** (or modus ponens) cannot be eliminated in the presence of
induction. In a generalized form the cut rule is the following
inference scheme.

(C)   From $\vdash$ $v(G_1,F,G_2)$ and $\vdash$ $v(G_3,\neg F,G_4)$
           infer $\vdash$ $v(G_1,G_2,G_3,G_4)$

For theorem proving the presence of this rule apparently is
destructive since for a given conclusion there is not the
slightest indication about   F   and   ¬F   to be inserted in the
premises, which forces us to leave the cut rule out from consideration within ATP. It is not clear how serious the limitations caused by this deletion actually are in practice. Nevertheless we might wish to find an alternative solution for over-
coming these limitations. For this purpose we have the following proposal.

        In order to explain this proposal we must get an idea
why the cut rule can be eliminated in the absence of induction
but not in its presence. Consider the following cut in matrix
representation.

$$\neg L \quad L \qquad \genfrac{}{}{0pt}{}{\neg L}{K} \quad L \quad -K \qquad\qquad \vdash \qquad\qquad \neg L \quad K \quad L \quad \neg K$$

For each of the 3 matrices we have added a connection proof
with the important feature that the connection proof for the
conclusion may be obtained in a straightforward way from those
for the premises. One simply has to "connect" (as illustrated
by the dashed line) each connection ending in a literal of the
left occurrence of the cut formula with each connection ending
in the corresponding literal in the right occurrence of the cut

formula, each resulting in a new connection for the conclusion;
while any connection in the premises with no literal in the cut
formulas (e.g. {K,¬K}) is carried over to the conclusion
without any change. This observation is written down in the
following lemma.

5.4.L. There is an algorithm by which 2 sets V_1,V_2 of connections for the premises F_1,F_2 of a cut are transformed to a
set V of connections for its conclusion F , such that V_i
is spanning for F_i, i=1,2 , iff V is spanning for F .
        The details of the algorithm and of the proof (by in-
duction) are left to the reader (see E11 in section 9).   □

In the sense of this result the cut rule does not increase the
deductive power of the connection method, and thus it may be
deleted without restricting generality.
        In the presence of induction, however, we cannot obtain
such a result simply because we have not defined how connection
proofs for the premises of an induction inference are to be
transformed to connection proofs of its conclusion. In fact, in
traditional calculi there is no such transformation at all,
hence also no cut elimination. This is different for the connection method where such a transformation may be defined if we
allow **connection schemes** as in (2.1). Such a connection
scheme for the formula (5.3) is shown as follows.

5.5.F.   x+0=x ∧ y+(z+1)=(y+z)+1 → 0+a=a

                                                i=1,...,a

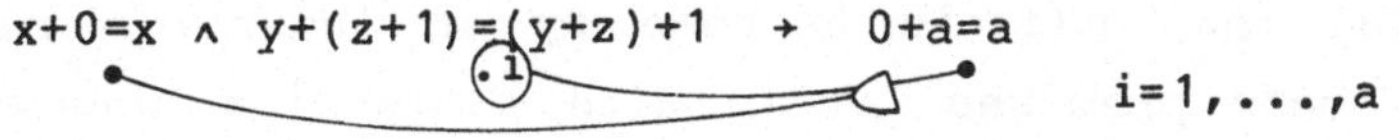

This scheme incorporates all the association arcs of the   a
instances of the second formula in (5.2) and the one connection
in the first formula which is illustrated for   a=2   in the
following picture.

5.6.F.   x+0=x ∧ y+(z+1)=(y+z)+1 → 0+0=0

         x+0=x ∧ y+(z+1)=(y+z)+1 → (0+0=0→0+(0+1)=0+1)

         x+0=x ∧ y+(z+1)=(y+z)+1 → (0+1=1 → 0+(1+1)=1+1)

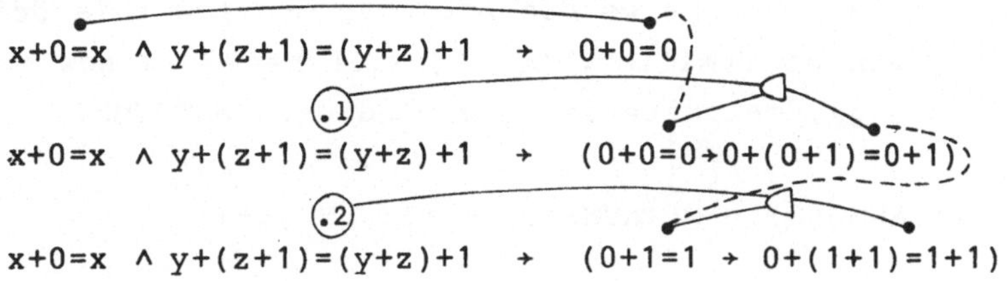

By "connecting" respective ends of arcs (as illustrated by the dashed lines) which, become loose ends when this induction proof, where each induction step is carried out explicitly, is condensed to the form given in (5.5), we obtain the connection scheme of (5.5).

This indicates a general method how to obtain from a connection proof of each of the 2 premises of an induction inference a connection proof for the conclusion. Note that this method works even in the case of a quantified induction variable (like a in 5.5) since the scope of the quantifier may be extended to cover the respective parts of the connection scheme. If we now generalize the algorithm mentioned in (5.4) and indicated before (5.4) then one can actually prove a lemma which is exactly as (5.4) but concerned with connection schemes rather than sets of connections.

With such a result we may then characterize valid formulas even in the presence of induction in an analogue way as in (3.6) for the case of equality, and on the basis of such a result develop a **connection calculus with equality and induction** in the way as we did several times in this book. With such a calculus a formula like the one in (5.5) would be proved simply by locating the connection scheme shown in (5.5). Moreover such a calculus would apply for arbitrary formulas which can be proved in number theory.

As an aside this approach is of interest also for proof theory. It has the same effect (of providing cut elimination) as replacing the induction scheme by an induction rule with infinitely many premises [Sc3]. With connection schemes, however, we are given a **finite** encoding of the same information.

All what we did in this section for the case of natural numbers can be applied to any other data structure (such as lists, stacks, trees, etc.) in an analogue way. Any such data structure, namely, is defined in some inductive way. For the case of natural numbers we did not even mention this definition since they are so familiar. But it will be added now for showing the analogy, characterizing a predicate NATNUMB.

5.6.D. $NATNUMB(0) \wedge NATNUMB(a) \rightarrow NATNUMB(a+1)$

For lists of natural numbers, e.g., the analogue definition is

5.7.D.   LIST(nil) $\wedge$ LIST(a) $\wedge$ NATNUMB(b) $\to$ LIST(b.a)

Apparently, induction on natural numbers in any form like (5.1) or (IND) simply mirrors this definition (5.6). Hence from (5.7) we easily obtain an induction scheme on lists in analogy with (IND).

(IND_{LIST}) From $\vdash$ $(G_1, F\{a\backslash nil\}, G_2)$
                   and $\vdash$ $(G_1, F \to F\{a\backslash b.a\}, G_2)$
                   infer $\vdash$ (G_1, F, G_2)
                   where   a   must not occur in G_i, i=1,2 .

Such a scheme is called a **structural** induction scheme. Obviously, it can be used exactly as (IND), thus leading to a connection calculus with induction on lists. And what we did for lists can be done in the same way for any other recursively defined data structure.

We might also notice at this point that at the same time we have introduced data types into logic via those predicates NATNUMB and LIST. This way we may distinguish objects of different types even in quantified formulas such as
$\forall c(NATNUMB(c) \to F)$ or $\exists x(LIST(x) \wedge F)$
often abbreviated as
$\forall c \in NATNUMB(F)$ or $\exists x \in LIST(F)$, respectively.
Note that in accordance with our natural unterstanding we have used implication in connection with all-quantification but conjunction in connection with existential quantification.

Logicians call first-order logic with such different types or sorts of objects also **sorted logic** . As we have just seen logically there is not much difference. For practice, however, **typing** is a very important tool which may considerably enhance the preformance of proof systems since respecting the types of constants and variables possibly excludes many connections which otherwise would have to be taken into consideration. Incidentally, this kind of typing is to be distinguished from the types in higher-order logic to be discussed in the next section.

6.   THE CONNECTION METHOD IN HIGHER-ORDER LOGIC

First-order logic is so rich that with sufficiently strong
axioms practically all of mathematics can be formalized in it.
Specifically this is true for Zermelo-Fraenkel set theory on
which most of mathematics can be built. From the point of
naturalness, however, first-order logic has certainly limitations which are felt in many applications.

For instance, assume that we want to make the statement
that the predicate MULTBYTWO defined as MULTBYTWO$(x,y) \leftrightarrow x \cdot 2 = y$
is a function. Then, in accordance with our discussion in sec-
tion (I.1.1), the most natural formalization of this statement
would be FUNCT(MULTBYTWO) where FUNCT is a predicate which
applies to objects intended to represent functions. Hence FUNCT
would be characterized by
FUNCT$(P) \leftrightarrow \forall xyz(P(x,y) \wedge P(x,z) \rightarrow y=z)$ according to the familiar characterization of functions. Thus we are actually talking
about a predicate, viz. FUNCT, the argument of which is itself
a predicate, viz. MULTBYTWO or P . Apparently, predicates taking predicates as arguments are not possible in first-order
logic.

Going a step further we might want to express that
there exists a function P satisfying a certain property PROP,
which formally would read $\exists P(\text{FUNCT}(P) \wedge \text{PROP}(P))$. And, of
course, such a statement might be just part of a larger for-
mula. In other words, there is a natural need for considering
predicates of a **higher type** , that is, predicates which take
predicates as arguments, and for allowing quantification over
such predicates. **Higher-order logic** is the natural generalization of first-order logic developed in order to provide such
means.

Such a generalization must be done with care in order
to avoid inconsistencies caused, for example, by predicates
which apply to themselves. One way to cope with this problem is
by introducing **types** for the distinction of predicates
providing the exclusion of self-application. There is the basic
type o **of objects** . A binary predicate supposed to take
objects as arguments, such as MULTBYTWO above, is then said to

be of the type predicate-applied-to-object-object, which is abbreviated simply by (o,o). In the case of three arguments we would have obtained (o,o,o), and so on, with the special case () of zero arguments, which is to be regarded as the type of formulas. In this way we can proceed to higher types. For instance, FUNCT is a predicate taking one argument of the type (o,o), thus its type will be ((o,o)) with one more pair of parentheses, which altogether illustrates the following definition.

6.1.D. Inductive definition of **types** , denoted by α,β,γ .
(t1)   o is a type (the type of objects).
(t2)   If $\alpha_1,\ldots,\alpha_n$, $n>0$, are types then $(\alpha_1,\ldots,\alpha_n)$ is a type.   □

Because of this approach via types the higher-order logic, which we discuss in the sequel, is also called **(simple) type theory** and was originated by Russel [Rus]. Note that the types considered at the end of the previous section from the present point of view all are object types. Therefore in order to include the distinction discussed there, we would have to split the object type o into a number of distinct object types $o_1,o_2,\ldots,o_m$ for some $m>1$, which for simplicity will not be considered in the following.

        Now we turn our attention to the language of higher-order logic which, roughly speaking, consists of formulas built as in first-order logic except that predicates, arguments, quantified variables and constants, all may be of a higher type. In the course of making this more precise we encounter the need of talking about a predicate such as MULTBYTWO above without having introduced such a nice name for it by an explicit definition as the one at the beginning of this section. Church's **λ-notation** is a convenient tool for this purpose by which MULTBYTWO, for instance, may equivalently be named as $\lambda xy(x\cdot 2=y)$. Thus we write the symbol λ followed by a list of arguments, which in turn is followed by the defining body. Such a term $\lambda x_1\ldots x_n\ F$ may be read "the set of all tuples $x_1\ldots x_n$ such that F " . The arguments for a so-defined predicate are written behind the term as usual like in

$\lambda xy(x \cdot 2 = y)(3,6)$, often written with auxiliary brackets as $[\lambda xy(x \cdot 2 = y)](3,6)$. With such arguments the term may actually be evaluated yielding $3 \cdot 2 = 6$ in the present example an operation which is called **λ-conversion** .

With these preliminaries we are now prepared for the following definition.

6.2.D. Inductive definition of **terms** (of any type) where the terms of type () are also called **formulas** . The underlying alphabets are $\mathbf{V}^\alpha$ (variables of type α), $\mathbf{C}^\alpha$ (constants of type α), for any type α , and $\mathbf{F}$ (functions of arity $\geqslant 1$). For simplicity we omit the distinction of occurrences and other such subtleties.

(t1)   Every variable x^α or constant c^α of type α is a term of type α .

(t2)   If f is an n-ary function symbol and $t_1^o, \ldots, t_n^o$ are terms of type o then $ft_1^o \ldots t_n^o$ is a term of type o .

(t3)   If $s^{(\alpha_1, \ldots, \alpha_n)}$ is a term of type $(\alpha_1, \ldots, \alpha_n)$ and $t_i^{\alpha_i}$ is a term of type α_i for $i=1, \ldots, n$, $n>0$, then $s^{(\alpha_1, \ldots, \alpha_n)}(t_1^{\alpha_1}, \ldots, t_n^{\alpha_n})$ is a formula.

(t4)   If F is a formula of the form $s^{(\alpha_1, \ldots, \alpha_n)}(t_1^{\alpha_1}, \ldots, t_n^{\alpha_n})$ with a variable or constant s then $\neg F$ is a formula, denoted also by ^1F , and both F and $\neg F$ are called **literals** .

(t5)   If F and G are formulas then $F \vee G$ and $F \wedge G$ also are formulas.

(t6)   If F is a formula then $\exists x^\alpha F$ and $\forall c^\alpha F$ also are formulas.

(t7)   If F is a formula then $\lambda z_1^{\alpha_1} \ldots z_n^{\alpha_n} F$ is a term of type $(\alpha_1, \ldots, \alpha_n)$. $\square$

Note how much more complicated this language actually is, since even large formulas via (t7) may be used as terms in the definition (t3) of literals, a loop in the definition of formulas for which there is no analogue in the first-order case. Because of these complications we have left out several minor details in order not to obscure the important features. An interested reader will be able to adapt these details from the definitions (III.1.1) and (III.1.4) keeping in mind that (6.2) is to be a strict generalization of the first-order case. Such an adaption is taken for granted also for all our conventions concerning formulas. We just have to add the convention that a formula of the form $\neg[\lambda z_1 \ldots z_n \ F](t_1,\ldots,t_n)$ means $[\lambda z_1 \ldots z_n \ \neg F](t_1,\ldots,t_n)$. Further we note that formulas again may be viewed as set-theoretic constructs which may be displayed as matrices in the plane.

We skip the difficult subject of semantics of our language of higher-order logic referring the reader to § 12 in [Sc4]. Rather we give a purely syntactical characterization of the valid formulas, or better to say theorems, by generalizing the formal system GS from section (IV.7.1) to higher-order logic, denoting the resulting system by GS^m .

6.3.D. Inductive definition of the derivability relation $\vdash$ for GS^m (with optional formulas G_1, G_2, G_3).

(ax) $\quad \vdash \ v(G_1, \ s^\alpha(t_1^{\alpha 1},\ldots,t_n^{\alpha n}), \ G_2, \ \neg s^\alpha(t_1^{\alpha 1},\ldots,t_n^{\alpha n}), \ G_3)$, where s^α is a variable or constant of type $\alpha = (\alpha_1,\ldots,\alpha_n)$ for $n > 0$.

($\wedge$) $\quad$ From $\vdash \ v(G_1, F_i, G_2)$ for $i=1,\ldots,n$ with $n > 2$, we may infer $\vdash \ v(G_1, \wedge(F_1,\ldots,F_n), G_2)$.

($\forall$) $\quad$ From $\vdash \ v(G_1, F, G_2)$ we may infer $\vdash \ v(G_1, \forall c_1^{\alpha 1}\ldots c_n^{\alpha n}F, G_2)$, provided that the c_i, $i=1,\ldots,n$ with $n > 1$, do not occur in G_1, G_2 .

($\exists$) $\quad$ From $\vdash \ v(G_1, F\{x_1^{\alpha 1}\backslash t_1^{\alpha 1},\ldots,x_n^{\alpha n}\backslash t_n^{\alpha n}\} , \ \exists x_1^{\alpha 1}\ldots x_n^{\alpha n}F, G_2)$ we may infer $\vdash \ v(G_1, \exists x_1^{\alpha 1}\ldots x_n^{\alpha n}F, G_2)$ where the occurrence of $\exists x_1^{\alpha 1}\ldots x_n^{\alpha n}F$ in the premise is optional and $n > 1$.

(λ) $\quad$ From $\vdash \ v(G_1, F\{z_1^{\alpha 1}\backslash t_1^{\alpha 1},\ldots,z_n^{\alpha n}\backslash t_n^{\alpha n}\}, G_2)$ we may infer $\vdash \ v(G_1, [\lambda z_1^{\alpha 1}\ldots z_n^{\alpha n}F](t_1^{\alpha 1},\ldots,t_n^{\alpha n}), G_2)$. $\qquad\qquad$ $\square$

The upper index m in GS^m refers to the maximal **order** which is envisaged. Here by the **order of a type** we mean the maximal depth of the nodes in its tree-structure (II.1.2). Thus (o,o) as well as () are of order 2, ((o),o,o) of order 3, and so on. A formula is **of order** m if the maximal order of the types of the quantified variables and constants is m . In GS^m all formulas are restricted to those of order m .

For practice, the most important special case is **second-order logic** (except for first-order logic, of course) where we may quantify over predicates the arguments of which are of the object type, as in the examples above. Other examples will follow further below.

GS^m has nothing like a cut rule which is possible without restricting generality (see theorem 12.4. in [Sc4]). This is important in view of ATP as we noted in the previous section.

Now we remind the reader that GS from (IV.7.1) or its inverse (recognition-type) form SP , the standard procedure from (III.3.7), have provided the basis for all the versions of Herbrand's theorem given so far in this book. This fact together with the close relationship between GS and GS^m hopefully gives the reader some convincing intuition for our claim saying that all these versions may be generalized to higher-order logic in a way which intuitively is straightforward but is cruel in its technical details. In the sequel we are now going to state the generalization of version (III.6.4), but for obvious reasons cannot carry out the proof.

We have to proceed as several times before in this book (for comparison section III.6 is recommended). That means that we first have to capture the notion of a path through the formulas in consideration. For simplicity we restrict these formulas (as in III.6.4) to Skolem normal form, that is to formulas of the form $\forall c_1^{\alpha_1} \ldots c_m^{\alpha_m}\ \exists x_1^{\beta_1} \ldots x_n^{\beta_n}\ F$ where F does not contain any quantifiers. Then paths are defined as in (III.6.2) with the following additional specification.

(p5)   If $F = [\lambda z_1^{\gamma_1} \ldots z_k^{\gamma_k}\ F_0]\ (t_1^{\gamma_1}, \ldots, t_k^{\gamma_k})$ then any path through $F_0\{z_1^{\gamma_1}\backslash t_1^{\gamma_1}, \ldots, z_k^{\gamma_k}\backslash t_k^{\gamma_k}\}$ is a path through F .

The formula $[\lambda z^{()}(z^{()} \vee {}^1K)]((K{\wedge}L){\vee}{}^1L)$ illustrates the necessity of substituting the terms in F_0 before determining its paths since by rule (λ) in (6.3) it actually represents the formula $(K{\wedge}L) \vee {}^1L \vee {}^1K$. With the basic notion of paths through formulas in Skolem normal form with multiplicity μ at hand, **connections** and **spanning** sets of connections are defined as in (III.6.3). So we may state a version of Herbrand's theorem for higher-order logic as follows.

6.4.T. A formula $\forall c_1^{\alpha 1}\ldots c_m^{\alpha m}\ \exists x_1^{\beta 1}\ldots x_n^{\beta n}\ F$ of higher-order logic in Skolem normal form is a theorem, that is derivable in GS^m , iff for some (constant) multiplicity μ there is a substitution ρ on the variables $x_i^{\beta i}$ with $\beta_i{\neq}o$, a spanning set U of connections in $(F^\mu)\rho$, and a substitution σ on the variables $x_i^{\beta i}$ with $\beta_i{=}o$, $i{=}1,\ldots,n$, such that $u\sigma$ is a (propositionally) complementary pair of literals for any $u \in U$. $\square$

The reason for separating the required substitution in (6.4) into a first- and higher-order part σ and ρ is illustrated with the formula $\forall c\forall P\ \exists x^{(o)}\exists y\ [\lambda z^{(o)}(z^{(o)} \vee Py)]\ (x^{(o)}(c))$. Note that we omit types whenever they are clear by the context or by the notation. In this formula without a substitution ρ it is difficult for the reader to recognize any connection at all. But with $\rho = \{x^{(o)}\backslash\lambda z_1^o(\neg Pz_1^o)\}$ we obtain the matrix $[\lambda z^{(o)}(z^{(o)} \vee Py)](\lambda z_1^o(\neg Pz_1^o)(c))$ which after 2 λ-conversions (carried out in any order) reads $\neg Pc \vee Py$ so that we obtain a proof with $\sigma = \{y\backslash c\}$. Keep in mind that this rewriting is just done for the readers understanding while a system might be programmed to locate this connection within the given formula, a view which we have taken throughout the book.

Since Skolem functions, of course, are not meaningful for higher types our restriction to Skolem normal form formulas in (6.4) does in fact restrict generality. If we wanted a characterization of all theorems we would have to proceed as in section (IV.8), and thus generalize (IV.8.5) rather than (III.6.4). Splitting might then be incorporated in analogy with the material in section (IV.10) thus yielding a generalized version of (IV.10.4).

We now turn our attention to the use of (6.4) as the theoretical basis for a connection calculus for higher-order logic. Namely it is known [Go2] that the **unification** problem (see III.5) is undecidable in second-order, hence a fortiori in higher-order logic. In other words, an algorithm deciding unifiability and possibly generating a most general unifier, as described in (III.5) for the case of first-order logic, does not exist in higher-order logic.

But recall that theorem proving in first-order logic is an undecidable problem as well, yet we can prove theorems. Similarly here, were there are procedures which are semi-decision procedures in the sense that they might generate a unifying substitution or might run forever, depending on the given input. The best such unification procedures are presented in chapter 3 of [Hu1].

Once we have unification available, it is easy to generalize any version of the connection calculus to the higher-order level, since all its other features are very much the same on any level. Only λ-conversion has to be taken care of appropriately.

A few examples showing theorems from second-order logic, together with appropriate substitutions and spanning sets of connections, demonstrate that in practice matters are far less complicated than one might expect from the previous abstract and general treatment. They show at the same time that equality, induction and other notions on the second-order level may be incorporated in an elegant way.

First we define equality over objects of type o as $EQ = \lambda xy \; \forall P(Px \rightarrow Py)$, and write $t1=t2$ rather than $EQ(t1,t2)$ as usual. We claim that the predicate so defined is reflexive, symmetric, and transitive.

For reflexivity we claim that $\forall a(a=a)$ is a theorem. After replacing $=$ by its definition, advancing the quantifier in order to bring the formula into Skolem normal form, and performing λ-conversion for sake of readability we obtain

$$\forall a \; \forall P \; (\overline{Pa} \rightarrow \overline{Pa})$$

The single connection establishes the proof without any further substitution.

For commutativity we claim that $\forall ab(a=b \rightarrow b=a)$ which yields as before

$$\forall ab \ \forall P \ \exists X \ \left[(Xa \rightarrow Xb) \rightarrow (Pb \rightarrow Pa) \right] \ , \ \rho = \{X \backslash \lambda z \neg Pz\}$$

Note that the all-quantified constant P of type (o), i.e.
second-order predicate, from the definition of EQ above, by
the negation implicitly involved on the left side of the implication actually becomes a existentially quantified predicate
variable, by convention denoted by X,Y, or Z . Obviously, the
2 connections are spanning, and ρ makes them complementary.

The proof for transitivity, i.e. for $a=b \wedge b=c \rightarrow a=c$,
is better displayed in the matrix representation.

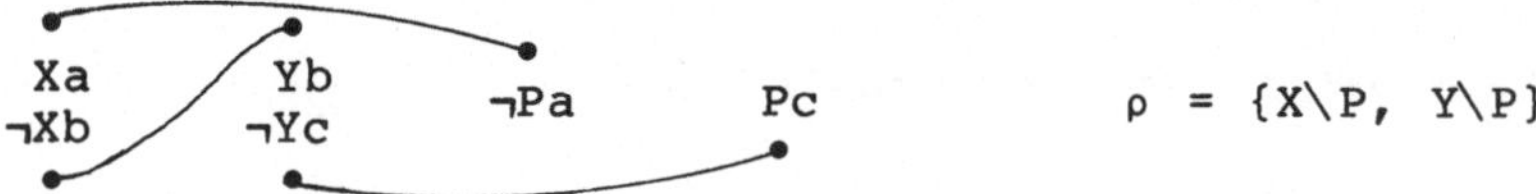

The first-order proof for $Pa \wedge a=b \rightarrow Pb$ given in (3.2), and
with an eq-connection in (3.3), here in second-order logic as a
matrix reads

which is as simple as the eq-proof in (3.3), in fact even
easier to be understood, since the eq-connections are certainly
less intuitive than the regular connections used here. This
shows how simple and natural proofs may be on the second-order
level, an experience which can be made with many other examples. In fact, one may notice that the predicate EQ in some
sense has the form of a rewrite rule.

Similarly as equality, we may also incorporate induction within second-order logic by introducing a predicate NAT
characterizing the natural numbers (see VI.3 in $\left[\text{He1}\right]$, e.g.):

$$NAT = \lambda z \forall P \left[P0 \wedge \forall x (Px \rightarrow P(x+1)) \rightarrow Pz \right]$$

This in an explicit definition in contrast to the implicit one
given for NATNUMB in (5.6). But of course NAT may now be used
as a data type exactly as NATNUMB before. Further the induction
proofs from section 5 may now be carried out in the form of
regular connection proofs in second-order logic.

As a final example we mention inequalities where $<$
may be defined [ERa] by

$$< \; = \; \lambda xy \; \forall P\left[Py \wedge \forall z(P(z+1) \rightarrow Pz) \rightarrow Px\right]$$

which allows to obtain short proofs for formulas involving this
special predicate $<$.

In conclusion, our feeling is that, although higher-
order logic in its full generality seems to be far too complicated for a feasible mechanization, the addition of restricted
higher-order features to first-order provers might enhance both
power and efficiency with only slightly more complications, as
demonstrated with the previous examples.

7.   ASPECTS OF ACTUAL IMPLEMENTATIONS

The field of ATP is one of the rare actual examples of intensive and fruitful cooperation of **theory** and **practice** which
might in fact be the deeper reason for the remarkable progress
achieved by relatively few people within a quarter of a century. Nevertheless there are lively discussions constantly going
on about the right balance between these two points of view
which only proves the closeness of their contact within the ATP
community. ·Since the pages left in this book for treating the
practical side does by no means reflect its importance, it is
necessary to correct the misleading conclusion possibly drawn
from this disproportion in mere numbers of pages.

Very often implementations are pioneers for the theoretical development. For instance, the idea of carrying out
proofs on essentially a single copy of the given formula, which
is now realized in a complete theoretical treatment within the
present book, actually has been anticipated in practice by
several implementations such as the one described in [BM1] or
the system NIUTP to be discussed further below. In fact this
and other ideas of the connection method heve been realized to
some extent in programs written by the author and his students
many years ago (see [Bi2] and [BiS]). Similarly with the idea
of simplification by rewriting which, under the name of demodulation, may be found in [WRC], years before rewriting became

popular. These and other such experiences clearly underline the importance of implementations.

Often it has even been stated that the ultimate test for any ATP method must be the machine, and the present author strongly supports this view, if it is taken in a well-defined sense. But as with any simplified slogan, also this one may (and in fact has) lead to unfortunate judgements. Namely, it might easily be interpreted such that any theoretical proposal will not be noticed unless it produces some spectacular results through an implementation. Such an attitude would be as stupid as one which ignores the value of experimental work. Obviously the success of an implementation may depend from a number of circumstances some of which are of a more organisational nature and are more often than not hard to realize for someone having a brilliant idea. Often it is also possible to predict beyond any doubt the favorable impact of a new method for practice in advance of any implementation, just on the basis of theoretical insight.

Thus implementations, on the one side, are of an invaluable help for pioneering, testing, and enhancing proof methods. On the other side progress would be limited if these experiences would not be worked up in theory which in turn provides insight and stimulates new practical attempts.

After these preliminary remarks we are now going to discuss a few general issues about implementations of proof systems before we mention several such systems in actual use. We begin with the issue of **strategies** .

Towards the end of section (IV.11) we have expressed doubts w.r.t. the value of **general** strategies for theorem proving in **pure** logic except if they are explored as substitutes for otherwise too complex structural insight. With actual implementations, however, we emphasize specialization rather than generality, and the expectation of hints for further structural insights is one of the major motivations for such experiments. Therefore strategies, heuristics, tricks are of great importance in **special** applications. In contrast to the intrinsic symmetry of pure logic the special nature of a particular application is reflected in some assymmetry of the form or role of the formulas representing the knowledge and statements within the topic in question. Since in most cases it is too complex to get hold of this assymmetry in precise mathematical terms (e.g. with a complete set of reductions as discussed in section 4), we must rely on strategical tools which take advantage of such special structures at least in an approximate way.

Even the way how humans represent knowledge is more specific than suggested by the general structure of logic. In this sense, dealing with **human** knowledge means already a special application from the pure logical point of view. This explains why natural deductive systems (see [B12] for an overview) sometimes are so successful although their deductive power in comparison with some resolution systems actually is relatively poor, since in contrast to the latter ones they do take advantage of the information provided by the special human form of representation.

For instance, we usually draw a conclusion C from certain assumptions $A_1, \ldots, A_n$, that is, we prove $A_1 \wedge \ldots \wedge A_n \rightarrow C$. Apparently, there is assymmetry in this structure, where a literal in C certainly plays a different role than one in A_i for $i \in \{1, \ldots, n\}$. The A_i themselves usually have this same structure $D_{i1} \wedge \ldots \wedge D_{im_i} \rightarrow E_i$. The success of PROLOG mentioned in section 2 relies to some extent upon the fact that it takes full use of the **procedural information** provided by humans when they represent knowledge in this form.

Hence it is mandatory also for a theorem proving system to take full advantage of such procedural information. As mentioned several times throughout this book, the connection method is particularly well suited to combining the deductive power of advanced resolution systems with such strategical information since it allows to retain the original structure of the formulas. In this connection it may well be expected that below the global structure of human statements as just described there is much more such strategic information to be found in the fine structure of these statements in their natural form.

Of course, this is only a very first step in specializing a proof system for a particular application. For instance, think of an application to a special field in mathematics like topology, say. Without any doubt the deductive strength of a human topologist heavily relies upon a very special, complex **structure** of all his previous topological **knowledge** . Clearly in this structure certain lemmas or theorems have a much higher priority than others, groups of theorems are clustered around particular notions, to mention only 2 among many possibilities. With an adequate way of storing information intrinsically structured in such a way and with special strategies encoding such priorities eventually one might be able to simulate the way of reasoning of an ingenious topologist.

This, of course, raises the question whether it might be possible to train a proof system which then would automatically learn the adequate structures and strategies by itself, as humans learn from their teachers. This is still science fiction; but we mention **learning** because the alternative of analyzing and encoding the particular structures and strategies for each of the many known special fields of applications by hand is certainly even less realistic simply because of the immense amount of work required for it.

Now assume we want to design such a proof system, be it with or without a strong strategical component, and with or without a richly structured **lemma base** , that is, a knowledge base containing lemmas and theorems, both these features built into the system by the designer or by training sessions via a learning component. In any case we have to consider a number of **design issues** . For instance, we have to make the important decision concerning the **external** and **internal representation** of all kinds of relevant knowledge, in particular of the formulas.

The decision w.r.t. the external representation has to compromise the 2 opposite demands from the user on the one side, who certainly will be happy if he can use his own familiar and natural way of representation, and from the system on the other side, which obviously is left with a lower load the more precise and less ambiguous the presentation will be.

For the internal representation the selection of data structures should be made in such a way that on the average proofs are found with less resources in time and storage (cf.

the discussion in section IV.3). Say, we have already decided upon the proof procedure to be based upon the connection method. Then the selection of data structures will influence the amount of time to perform a single step rather than the global behavior. With this selection thus we want to minimize the resources required to perform the actions within such a single step. For instance, if we think of the connection method in its simplest form this means that the data structure supports

(i)   the ability to access easily for a given set of literals (the active path) p_a and substition σ the set of literals in the remaining matrix which for some substitution of the form $\sigma\tau$ are complementary with some literal in p_a , further

(ii)   the ability to overlook the effect of selecting one out of several possible such connections in view of the spanning property.

If we have in mind the connection method in a more advanced form then the description of the required abilities will be much more involved, but nevertheless the features (i) and (ii) will be of a central importance even there. For other proof methods such as resolution or cg-resolution the required features will be somewhat different (e.g. see the features a) and b) in section 4.3 in [OLu]).

        Another issue of importance in the design of a proof system is the **organization of the information** kept in the memory during the proof process. Usually one distinguishes the **permanent** part from the **dynamic** one. In the connection method the given formula belongs to the permanent part since it never changes while for instance p_a and σ mentioned in (i) varies during the proof process. But of course this distinction is only a very first step towards an organization which supports a smooth and efficient run of the whole process.

        As a further issue we mention the **control architecture** of a proof system. With the capability of modern computers to carry out many processes in parallel it is certainly a natural idea to carry over some of the intrinsically indeterministic nature of theorem proving into parallel execution. In concrete terms, if there is, say, a possible choice among 2 connections for extension in the connection method with no clear priority for one of them according to the built-in strategies then the 2 possiblities might be pursued in parallel, possibly flowing together at some later point of the whole proof process. But even if we think of sequential execution we have to consider the fact that the various types of processes have to be invocated in some controlled way. For instance, during extension one unit might be activated to select a potential set of connections. Control might then be passed over to an evaluation unit which from this set further selects the subset for executing extension upon strategical considerations. For these connections the unification unit determines the necessary substitution unifying the respective terms. In fact these processes may even interfere with each other. Thus there is the need for a control unit supervising and directing the transfer of control among all available units.

Obviously, with these remarks we just scratch somewhat at the surface of the complex task of designing a powerful proof system. If someone intends the design and implementation of a system with the potential capability to compete in performance with well-known proof systems then he/she should plan for a number (possibly tens) of man-years. This brings us to the discussion of some of these systems in existence and in actual use.

The most successful proof system is **AURA** developed jointly at Argonne National Laboratory and Northern Illinois University under the leadership of L. Wos, with additional support from people at Northwestern University, all in Illinois, USA. This remarkable group has been working on the development of a powerful proof system for more than one and a half decades. This continuity, a rather permanent group with ingenious ideas, and adequate computing facilities are the distinctive features which to some extent explain the outstanding success of AURA (and its predecessor NIUTP).

This success is best illustrated by the fact that AURA was able to provide substantial assistance in proving open mathematical problems from various areas such as ternary boolean algebra, finite semigroups, electronic circuitry, and formal logic. Most of these problems have previously been considered by well-known mathematicians, that is, they are really interesting problems from a mathematical point of view, some with rather complicated proofs. An overview of these results may be found in [Wos]. Apart from these spectacular results it should be mentioned that the system has proved many known theorems from most of the major fields in mathematics.

The system is based on resolution. It is able, to control the resolution steps in a more global manner by using **hyper-resolution** , a variant due also to Robinson (see [Ro1]). It makes intensive use of subsumption. Equality is handled by paramodulation with extensive use of demodulation. In addition to its capability for finding proofs it has the ability to directly find models (i.e. examples) and counterexamples for given formulas (see the next section for this problem).

A key feature of the implementation (described in [OLu]) is the fact that there is only one copy of any clause, literal, or term in the permanent data structures. As we said further above, this feature anticipates one of the important aspects in the connection method. Incidentally, the global manner of controlling its steps is another strong virtue of the connection method (cf. the respective discussion preceding IV.1.7), which to some extent is realized in AURA via hyper-resolution as mentioned just before. It would be interesting to see the realization of a system which combines **all** the virtues of the connection method (e.g. non-normal form) with the theorem proving and programming expertise incorporated in AURA.

Another strong group developing powerful proof systems is centered at the University of Texas at Austin, headed by W. Bledsoe. They also have the experience of more than one and a half decades in the development of theorem provers.

Bledsoe was one of the first researchers working on resolution type systems who realized the importance of heuristics and user supplied knowledge, both of which are often domain dependent. In order to ease the incorporation of such features as well as to allow the human mathematician to interfere with the system during the proof process, this group implemented a system, called the **UT interactive prover** and described in [B1T], which is quite different from AURA, especially because it is not based on resolution but uses a natural style of reasoning with the flavor of the logical calculi of natural deduction which have been discussed in section (IV.7).

The central routine of this prover is called IMPLY. It takes formulas of the form H → C , and either is able to determine a most general unifier σ such that Hσ → Cσ is valid (usually a tautology in propositional logic) which substitution IMPLY returns as its value, or reduces the formula to simpler such formulas to which IMPLY recursively is applied again. Splitting, which has been discussed in section (IV.10), is one of the most important features in the reduction step.

This prover has been specialized for applications in various areas of mathematics such as (non-standard) analysis, set theory, Presburger arithmetic, algebra, etcetera (see [B12] for an overview and for references), and it has proved remarkable (known) theorems from these fields with many of the resultant proofs contained in the respective papers. The leitmotiv in all this work is the attempt to get hold of the heuristics that human experts in these fields would apply in their own approach.

This is even the case for a recent work on inequality reasoning [B1H] although the prover used for it is a new one based on resolution. This demonstrates that the human heuristic approach can well be combined with a less natural proof mechanism such as resolution. Naturalness is important at the surface of the prover, that is, at the human-machine interface; inside, however, efficiency is all that counts. Clearly this is exactly the position which has been taken throughout this book for the connection method.

The strong influence of Bledsoe's work may be seen in most major ATP projects, for instance, in the powerful **Boyer-Moore** proof system developed over a period of a decade by R.S. Boyer and J S. Moore at SRI International, Menlo Park, California. It is designed especially with the application to the construction of correct computer programs in mind, and therefore particular attention is payed to the mechanization of mathematical induction. With its strength in handling induction it is unique in comparison with the previous and other projects.

This strength has been demonstrated by the proof of hundreds of theorems, mostly by induction, which may be found in the comprehensive treatment [BoM] of this approach. Many of these theorems have arisen in correctness proofs for fairly complicated programs like for a simple optimizing compiler for expressions, for a tautology checker, and many others. The approach is built upon a formalism similar to pure LISP, and thus is of a functional nature. One would wish that its powerful proof techniques would be embedded into "natural" logic which certainly is feasible as we have indicated in section 5.

The **Stanford verifier** also is the product of a decade's work performed under the direction of D. Luckham at the Computer Systems Laboratory of Stanford University, California. It has been designed as a system for program verification in the Floyd-Hoare style, recently with the paradigm in mind that program development and verification go hand in hand. Its strength is due to the use of fast special purpose decision procedures (e.g. for arithmetic and data structures) used in a component where formulas are simplified. If a formula is valid, the result of the simplification will be **true** .

Specification and consistency analysis of hundreds of programs has been undertaken with this system. This includes the verification of a complete compiler for a Pascal-like language (about 150 pages of code) which is believed to be the largest verification task ever undertaken with the assistance of a mechanized verifier. A good overview of this work is given in [Pol].

The **AFFIRM theorem prover** [EMu], developed at the USC Information Sciences Institute at Marina del Rey, California, also is applied as a verification system for software. Again it has many of the flavors of the UT interactive prover, in particular it uses an interactive, natural deduction proof style, with an emphasis on simplification. This group preferred to use the language of abstract data types which naturally may be regarded as a well-defined sublanguage of logic.

The **Markgraf Karl refutation procedures** [ESS] is a proof system in development at the Informatik-Institut of the Universität Karlsruhe Germany. Like AFFIRM this is a relatively new project. The "logic engine" in this system essentially is a

classical theorem prover based on connection graph resolution
refined by a number of syntactic improvements or strategies.
However, the system is currently extended to contain several
other moduls for special handling of equality, for generalized
unification, for induction, and others.

Of course, with this overview of seven proof systems by
no means we claim to have covered all the valuable implementational work in ATP. One criterion for their selection was to
demonstrate the variety of different approaches which may be
taken in this field. They also demonstrate how many lucky
circumstances must come together and how much continuous
efforts must be invested until a system reaches the level of
performance which has been set by some of those above.

On the other side it must be emphasized that a lot of
progress was originated in small projects often with just one
or two individuals, their ideas later being absorbed in the big
ones, which is to say that it is still worth-wile to initiate
even small projects. Because of the close relationship with the
material presented in this book we therefore finally mention
two such small projects both concerned with the development of
a proof system essentially based on what we called the connection method. One is carried out in the Mathematics Department
of Carnegie-Mellon University at Pittsburgh, Pennsylvania,
under the direction of P. Andrews [An1], the other takes place
at the Informatik-Institut of the Technische Universität
München, Germany, under the direction of the author [Mül].

8.   OMISSIONS

In a wide field such as ATP it is hardly possible that a single
author covers all topics with competence. With this section we
just want to point out this fact by mentioning some of the
issues which for various reasons have not been raised in the
preceding sections.

Model or **(counter-)example generation** is one important issue which has not been treated. We have mentioned it in
connection with AURA in the previous section. It also plays a
role in the author's LOPS project with some results being given

in [Hö1] where further references may be found. This paper also
explains how to some extent a theorem prover, for instance one
based on the connection method, can directly be used for this
purpose. Nevertheless it is felt that a really satisfactory
approach so far does not exist, which is surprising since in
human theorem proving examples and counterexamples play an
essential role, and thus should be used in proof systems as
well.

They also play an important role in **learning** which is
another topic with strong ATP aspects omitted in this book (but
briefly mentioned in the previous section). A paper, which
particularly deals with aspects in learning of interest for
ATP, is [H-R]. Further a remarkable theory formation system
using a theorem prover is described in [Sha].

We also have left out the discussion of proof methods
for non-classical logics, for instance for **modal logic** (e.g.
[Br2]). Except for lacking competence this omission has its
reason also in an uncertainty about the importance of such
logics in the long run. "Modalities are important but modal
logic may not be the right way to deal with them" [McC]. For
several applications of modal logic, for instance as a logic of
programs or a logic of metatheory, it has been exemplified that
they can be treated with classical logic as well, perhaps even
in a more natural way (see [Wey], [Ko3], [BoK]).

Also we have by far not exhausted the tens or even
hundreds of syntactic strategies developed mainly for resolution provers because there are so many of them, in the first
place. But the author also admits a certain doubt about such
strategies independent of special applications which has been
specified to some extent in the previous section. Such general
doubts do not apply, however, to strategies for special
applications or even special proof methods. There are really
fascinating results like the proof techniques for inequality
resoning in [Sh2] and in [BlH], or for fragments of set theory
in [B13] and in [FOS], to mention just 2 out of a great variety
of results. It is simply their number which excludes them from
treatment.

As we already mentioned at the end of section 4, such
special methods may actually be regarded as proof processes

from which search has (partially) been eliminated by some control which takes advantage of the special proof situation under consideration. It seems to be very likely that there are common features or similarities in these various control mechanisms for various applications. Their detection might enable a common and more general treatment of this variety of special methods which today is so confusing because of its quantity.

9.   EXERCISES

(E1)   Referring to the fragment of a railway information system shown in figure 1, how could one formulate in logic and answer the following query: "When leaves a train to Salzburg, the departure time of which is as close as possible to 3 p.m."

(E2)   Show that for any formula F there exists a formula $\tilde{F}$ in normal form containing Horn clauses only such that F is valid iff $\tilde{F}$ is valid. (Hint: Use III.4.5)

(E3)   Represent each of the queries from section 1 both, as a logic program and as a matrix.

(E4)   Give a logic program for sorting lists, and represent it as a matrix. (Hint: Use the predicates $ORD(x)$ for expressing that x is ordered, $DELETE(x,y,z)$ for z resulting from deleting any one occurrence of x from y , $PERM(x,y)$ for y being a permutation of x , and $SORT(x,y)$ for y being a sorted version of x)

(E5)   Give a proof of the properties of commutativity and associativity of equality first by the connection calculus via the equality axioms, and then by the connection calculus with built-in equality.

(E6)   (3.6) is the result of incorporating equality into the version (III.6.4) of Herbrand's theorem. Give the analogue results for the versions (IV.8.5) and (IV.10.4).

(E7)   Elaborate the details of the connection calculus with equality as outlined in section (3) and the next exercise.

(E8)   The major partial problem in carrying out the previous exercise consists of a generalized form of unification as illustrated by the example in figure 3. Namely, one has to unify pairs of terms (such as g_2c and g_1e) by determining a sequence of substitutions $\sigma\tau_1...\tau_m$ where the τ_i , i=1,...,m , typically are not variable substitutions restricted to be taken from a predetermined set
(such as {a\b, b\a, ..., $g_2a\backslash g_1e$, $g_1e\backslash g_2a$}) , and σ is a variable substitution. Develop an algorithmic way for doing this in a "by-need" manner.

(E9)   Show how the rules $e^-{\cdot}x \rightarrow x$ and $x^{--}{\cdot}e \rightarrow x$ are obtained by superposition of rules (rg1) - (rg4). Continue this process, deleting any rule, the left side of which becomes reducible by a newly created rule. (Hint: The final set will be rg1 - rg10)

(E10)   For each of the rules (rg1) through (rg10) give the eq-connection proof which corresponds to it in the sense discussed in section 4.

(E11)   Specify the details of the algorithm mentioned in (5.4) and outlined before (5.4), and prove (5.4).

(E12)   Prove a number of arithmetic formulas both, by the limited approach discussed in the first part of section 5 and by the general approach discussed in the second one. Examples of provable formulas   are: (a+1)+b=(a+b)+1,   a+(b+c)=(a+b)+c, a+b=b+a, 0=0$\cdot$a, (a+1)$\cdot$b=(a$\cdot$b)+b, a$\cdot$(0+1)=a, (0+1)$\cdot$a=a, a$\cdot$b=b$\cdot$a, and so on.

(E13)   Define the **reverse** function on lists (which for instance reverses the list 5.8.4 to 4.8.5) and prove reverse(reverse(a))=a by both approaches as in (E12).

(E14)   Using the second-order definition of the equality pred-

icate EQ from section 6, show by a second-order connection
proof that the group axioms (g1), (g2), and (g3) imply the
equality of the left and right sides of each of the rules (rg4)
- (rg10) from section 4.

(E15)   Prove the theorems from (E12) with a second-order connection proof using the predicate NAT from section 6.

(E16)   For the predicate < defined in section 6 prove reflexivity, antisymmetry, and transitivity via a second-order connection proof.

10.   BIBLIOGRAPHICAL AND HISTORICAL REMARKS

Theorem proving methods were first applied in question answering by Green [Gre]. Sources for logic as framework for data
bases are [Ko3], [GaM] and [GMN]. For ways to organize knowledge bases see the references given in section (10.1.1) of
[Nil].
         The idea of logic as a programming language emerged in
the years 1973-74 at various places [Hay], [CKP], [Ko1], [Bi3]
with forerunners such as [Bur]. A comprehensive treatment is
given in [Ko3]. Program synthesis is first considered in [MaW].
[Bi8] is a more recent source for program synthesis, [BGK] more
generally for program construction, and [Man] for program verification.
         Paramodulation, which is the most widely used way of
building-in equality, has been introduced by Robinson and Wos
[RoW]. For forerunners and variants see the references provided
in [Lo4], p. 279. The need for a more global treatment of
equality has been realized in [Di2] and [WOH]. The connection
method with equality has not been published before.
         The paper by Knuth and Bendix [KnB] is considered as
the original work on rewrite rules although there are forerunners like Buchberger [Buc] anticipating the 2 essential ideas
of **critical pairs** and of **completion** (in a different but
closely related context where bases of vector spaces rather
than complete sets of reductions are considered). A survey of

the vast literature in this field can be found in [HOp].

Boyer and Moore [BoM] have done remarkable work on induction. Roughly, their approach is similar to the "lemma" approach described in section 5. Other work on induction may be found in [Bro], [Aub], and [Opp]. An algebraic approach is contained in [HuH].

The most important contributions to the mechanization of higher-order logic have been made by Andrews [AnC], Huet [Hu2], and Pietrzykowski [JeP]. The formal system GS^m has been adapted from chapter IV in [Sc4]. The theorem (6.4) in this form is an original result.

The first implementations of mathematical theorem provers were produced in the mid-fifties. For instance, Davis in 1954 implemented Presburger's decision procedure for the arithmetic of addition [Da1], while Newell, Shaw, and Simon in 1956 wrote a program called the **logic theorist** [NSS] for proving theorems in propositional logic in a way which simulates the human problem solver. A reference to other such early implementations may be found in [Wan] and [Coo]. The first implementation of a proof procedure for first-order logic was produced by D. Prawitz, H. Prawitz, and Voghera in the years 1957/1958 [PPV], but in the years 1958/1959 several others followed (see [Da3]).The first open mathematical problem solved with substantial support by a theorem prover is reported in [GOB].

References

[AHU]   Aho, A.V., Hopcroft, J.E., Ullmann, J.D.; The design and analysis of computer algorithms; Addison-Wesley, Reading, MA (1975)

[An1]   Andrews, P.B.; Refutations by matings; IEEE Transactions on Computers 25 , 801-807 (1976)

[An2]   Andrews, P.B.; Theorem proving via general matings; J.ACM 28 , 193-214 (1981)

[AnC]   Andrews, P.B., Cohen, E.L.; Theorem proving in type theory; Proc. IJCAI-5, Int. Joint Conferences on Artificial Intelligence, 566 (1977)

[Aub]   Aubin, R.; Mechanizing structural induction; Ph.D. thesis, U. of Edinburgh, Edinburgh, UK (1976)

[BaB]   Ballantyne, A.M., Bledsoe, W.W.; Automatic proofs and theorems in Analysis using non-standard techniques; J.ACM 24 , 353-374 (1977)

[Bax]   Baxter, L.D.; A practically linear unification algorithm; Report, Dept. Computer Science, U. of Waterloo, Waterloo, Canada (1976)

[B-A]   Ben-Ari, M.; A simplified proof that regular resolution is exponential; Information Processing Letters 10 , 96-98 (1980)

[Bet]   Beth, E.W.; The foundations of mathematics; North-Holland, Amsterdam (1965)

[Bi1]   Bibel, W.; Schnittelimination in einem Teilsystem der einfachen Typenlogik; Archiv f. Math. Logik 12 , 159-178 (1969)

[Bi2]   Bibel, W.; An approach to a systematic theorem-proving procedure in first-order logic; Computing 12 , 43-55 (1974)

[Bi3]   Bibel, W.; Programmieren in der Sprache der Prädikatenlogik; Habilitationsarbeit (abgelehnt), Techn. U., München (1975);
shortened version: Prädikatives Programmieren; Automata theory and formal languages, Lecture Notes in Computer Sci. 33 , Springer, Berlin, 274-283 (1975)

278

[Bi4]   Bibel, W.; Effizienzvergleiche von Beweisprozeduren; GI - 4. Jahrestagung, Lecture Notes in Computer Science **26** , Springer, Berlin, 153-160 (1975)

[Bi5]   Bibel, W.; Maschinelles Beweisen; Jahrbuch Überblicke Mathematik, Bibliographisches Institut, Mannheim, 115-142 (1976)

[Bi6]   Bibel, W.; A syntactic connection between proof procedures and refutation procedures; GI - 3. Fachtagung Theoretische Informatik, Lecture Notes in Computer Science **48** , Springer, Berlin, 215-225 (1977)

[Bi7]   Bibel, W.; Tautology testing with a generalized matrix reduction method; Theoretical Computer Science 8 , 31-44 (1979)

[Bi8]   Bibel, W.; Syntax-directed, semantics-supported program synthesis; Artificial Intelligence **14** , 243-261 (1980)

[Bi9]   Bibel, W.; A theoretical basis for the systematic proof procedure; Mathematical Foundations of Computer Science (Dembinski, ed.), Lecture Notes in Computer Science **88,** Springer, Berlin, 154-167 (1980)

[B10]   Bibel, W.; On matrices with connections; J.ACM **28** , 633-645 (1981)

[B11]   Bibel, W.; A comparative study of several proof procedures; Artificial Intelligence (to appear)

[B12]   Bibel, W.; A strong completeness result for connection graph resolution; Submitted to SICOMP (1979)

[B13]   Bibel, W.; The complete theoretical basis for the systematic proof method. Bericht ATP-6-XII-80, Projekt Beweisverfahren, Institut für Informatik, Technische U., München (1980); Submitted to J.ACM

[B14]   Bibel, W.; Matings in matrices; GWAI-81 (Siekmann, ed.), Informatik-Fachberichte **47** , Springer, Berlin, 171-187 (1981); Submitted to C.ACM

[B15]   Bibel, W.; Computationally improved versions of Herbrand's theorem; Proc. of the Herbrand Colloquium (Stern, ed.), North-Holland, Amsterdam (to appear)

[B16]   Bibel, W.; Logical program synthesis; Proc. Int. Conf. Fifth Generation Computer Systems (Moto-oka, ed.), North-Holland, Amsterdam (to appear)

[BiH]   Bibel, W., Hörnig, K.M.; LOPS - A system based on a strategical approach to program synthesis; In [BGK]

[BiK]   Bibel, W., Kowalski, R. (eds.); 5th Conference on Automated Deduction; Lecture Notes in Computer Sci. (Goos, Hartmanis, eds.) 87 , Springer, Berlin (1980)

[BiS]   Bibel, W., Schreiber, J.; Proof search in a Gentzen-
        like system of first-order logic; Proc. International
        Computing Symposium, North-Holland, Amsterdam, 205-212
        (1975)

[BGK]   Biermann, A., Guiho, G., Kodratoff, I. (eds.); Automa-
        tic program construction techniques; MacMillan (in
        print)

[BES]   Bläsius, K., Eisinger, N., Siekmann, J., Smolka, G.,
        Herold, A., Walther, C.; The Markgraf Karl refutation
        procedure (fall 1981); Proc. IJCAI-7, Int. Joint
        Conferences on Artificial Intelligence, 511-518 (1981)

[Bl1]   Bledsoe, W.W.; Splitting and reduction heuristics in
        automatic theorem proving; Artificial Intelligence 2 ,
        57-78 (1971)

[Bl2]   Bledsoe, W.W.; Non-resolution theorem proving; Artifi-
        cial Intelligence 9 , 1-35 (1977)

[Bl3]   Bledsoe, W.W.; Set variables; Proc. IJCAI-5, Int. Joint
        Conferences on Artificial Intelligence, 501-510 (1977)

[BlH]   Bledsoe, W.W., Hines, L.M.; Variable elimination and
        chaining in a resolution based prover for inequalities;
        In [BiK] 70-87

[BlT]   Bledsoe, W.W., Tyson, M.; The UT interactive prover;
        Report ATP 17, Dept. Mathem., U. of Texas, Austin
        (1975)

[BoK]   Bowen, K.A., Kowalski, R.A.; Amalgamating language and
        metalanguage in logic programming; Report 4/81,
        Computer and Information Sci., Syracuse U., Syracuse,
        N.Y. (1981)

[BM1]   Boyer, R.S., Moore, J S.; The sharing of structure in
        theorem proving programs; Machine Intelligence 7
        (Meltzer, Michie, eds.), Edinburgh University Press,
        101-116 (1972)

[BM2]   Boyer, R.S., Moore, J S.; A computational logic;
        Academic Press, New York (1979)

[Bro]   Brotz, D.K.; Proving theorems by mathematical induc-
        tion; PH.D. thesis, Stanford U., CA (1974)

[Br1]   Brown, F.; Notes on chains and connection graphs; Un-
        published (1976)

[Br2]   Brown, F.; A theorem prover for meta-theory; In [Joy]
        155-160

[BrP]   Bruynooghe, M., Pereira, L.M.; Revision of top-down
        logical reasoning through intelligent backtracking;
        Report CIUNL-8/81, Universid. Nova de Lisboa, Portugal
        (1981)

[Buc]   Buchberger, B.; Ein Algorithmus zum Auffinden der Basiselemente des Restklassenringes nach einem null-dimensionalen Polynomideal; Dissertation, Universität Innsbruck (1965)

[BuW]   Bundy, A., Welham, B.; Meta-level inference; In [BiK] 24-38

[Bur]   Burstall, R.M.; Formal description of program structure and semantics in first-order logic; Machine Intelligence 5 (Meltzer, Michie, eds.), American Elsevier, New York 79-98 (1970)

[ChK]   Chang, C.C., Keisler, H.J.; Model theory; North-Holland, Amsterdam (1973)

[ChL]   Chang, C.-L., Lee, R.C.-T.; Symbolic logic and mechanical theorem proving; Academic Press, New York (1973)

[CKP]   Colmerauer, A., Kanoui, H., Pasero, R., Roussel, P.; Un système de communication homme-machine en français; Rapport, Groupe Intelligence Artificielle, U. Aix-Marseille (1973)

[CKV]   Colmerauer, A., Kanoui, H., van Caneghem, M.; Last steps toward an ultimate PROLOG; Proc. IJCAI-7, Int. Joint Conferences on Artificial Intelligence, 947-948 (1981)

[Co1]   Cook, S.A.; The complexity of theorem proving procedures; Proc. 3rd ACM STOC, 151-158 (1971)

[CoR]   Cook, S.A., Reckhow, R.A.; On the lengths of proofs in the propositional calculus; Proc. 6th ACM STOC, 135-148 (1974)

[Coo]   Cooper, D.C.; Theorem proving in computers; Advances in programming and non-numerical computation (Fox, ed.), Pergamon Press, Oxford, 155-182 (1966)

[Da1]   Davis, M.; A computer program for Presburger's procedure; Summaries of talks presented at the Summer Institute for Symbolic Logic (1957); Second edition published by Institute for Defense Analysis, Princeton, N.J. (1960)

[Da2]   Davis, M.; Eliminating the irrelevant from mechanical proofs; Proc. Symp. Appl. Mathem. XV, Providence, R.I., 15-30 (1963)

[Da3]   Davis, M.; The prehistory of Automated Deduction; Invited lecture, 4th Workshop on Automated Deduction, Austin, Texas (1979); In [SiW]

[DaP]   Davis, M., Putmann, H.; A computing procedure for quantification theory; J.ACM 7 , 201-215 (1960)

[Di1]   Digricoli, V.J.; Resolution by unification and equality; In [Joy] 43-52

[Di2]   Digricoli, V.J.; Resolution by unification and equality; Report, Courant Inst. NYU, New York (1981)

[DrG]   Dreben, B.S., Goldfarb, W.D.; The decision problem:
solvable clases of the quantificational formulas;
Addision-Wesley, Reading, MA (1979)

[DuN]   Dunham, B., North, J.; Theorem testing by computer;
Proc. Sympos. Math. Theory of Automata, Polytechnic
Press, Brooklyn, N.Y., 173-177 (1963)

[DuW]   Dunham, B., Wang, H.; Towards feasible solutions of the
tautology problem; Annals of Mathem. Logic 10 , 117-154
(1976)

[ERa]   Elgot, C., Rabin, M.; Decidability and undecidability
of extensions of second (first) order theories of
(generalized) successor; J. of Symbolic Logic 31 ,
169-181 (1966)

[End]   Enderton, H.B.; A mathematical introduction to logic;
Academic Press, New York (1972)

[EMu]   Erickson, R.W., Musser, D.R.; The AFFIRM theorem
prover: proof forests and management of large proofs;
In [BiK] 220-231

[Ern]   Ernst, G.W.; The utility of independent subgoals in
theorem proving; Information and Control 18 , 237-252
(1971)

[FeF]   Feigenbaum, E., Feldmann, J. (eds.); Computers and
thought; McGraw-Hill, New York (1963)

[FOS]   Ferro, A., Omodeo, E.G., Schwartz, J.T.; Decision procedures for some fragments of set theory; In [BiK]
88-96

[Fis]   Fischer, P.; Entscheidbare Fälle in einem prädikaten-
logischen Beweisverfahren; Diplomarbeit, Fachbereich
Mathematik, Techn. U., München (1974)

[Fre]   Frege, G.; Begriffsschrift; Halle (1879);
Engl. transl. in [Hei]

[Gal]   Galil, Z.; On the complexity of regular resolution and
the Davis-Putnam procedure; Theoretical Computer
Sci. 4 , 23-46 (1977)

[GaM]   Gallaire, H., Minker, J. (eds.); Logic and data bases;
Plenum Press, New York (1978)

[GMN]   Gallaire, H., Minker, J., Nicolas, J.M. (eds.); Advances in data base theory, vol. 1 , Plenum Press, New
York (1981)

[Ge1]   Gentzen, G.; Untersuchungen über das logische Schlie-
ßen; Mathem. Ztschr. **39** , 176-210, 405-431 (1935);
Engl. transl. in [Sza]

[Ge2]   Gentzen, G.; Die Widerspruchsfreiheit der reinen Zahlentheorie; Math. Ann. **112** , 493-565 (1936);
Engl. transl. in [Sza]

[Gol]   Goldberg, A.; Average complexity of the satisfiability
problem; In [Joy] 1-6

[Go1]   Goldfarb, W.D. (ed.); Jacques Herbrand, Logical writ-
ings; Reidel, Dordrecht (1971)

[Go2]   Goldfarb, W.D.; The undecidability of the second-order
unification problem; Theoretical Computer Science **13** ,
225-230 (1981)

[Gre]   Green, C.; Theorem proving by resolution as a basis for
question-answering systems; Machine Intelligence **4**
(Meltzer, Michie, eds.), Edinburgh University Press
(1969)

[Gro]   Grosz, B.J.; Utterance and objective: issues in natural
language processing; Proc. IJCAI-6, Int. Joint Conferences on Artificial Intelligence, 1067-1076 (1979)

[GOB]   Guard, J., Oglesby, F., Bennett, J., Settle, L.; Semi-
automated mathematics; J.ACM **18** , 49-62 (1969)

[Hay]   Hayes, P.; Computation and deduction; Proc. 2nd MFCS
Symposium, Czechoslowak Academy of Sci., 105-118 (1973)

[H-R]   Hayes-Roth, F.; Theory-driven learning: proofs and
refutations as a basis for concept discovery; Papers of
the Workshop on Current developments in Machine Learning, Carnegie-Mellon U., Pittsburgh, PE (1980)

[Hei]   Heijenoort, J.v.; From Frege to Gödel; Harvard Univ.
Press, Cambridge (1967)

[Her]   Herbrand, J.J.; Recherches sur la thèorie de la dèmon-
stration; Travaux Soc. Sciences et Lettres Varsovie,
Cl. 3 (Math.,Phys.), 128 pp (1930);
English transl. in [Go1]

[He1]   Hermes, H.; Introduction to mathematical logic;
Springer, Berlin (1973)

[Hib]   Hibsch, G.; Ansatz für ein mechanisches Beweisverfahren
für die Prädikatenlogik zweiter Stufe mit Anwendungen
auf die Zahlentheorie; Diplomarbeit, Mathem. Instit.,
Techn. U., München (1973)

[HiA]   Hilbert, D., Ackermann, W.; Grundzüge der theoretischen
Logik; Springer (1928);
Engl. transl.: Mathematical logic; Chelsea (1950)

[Hö1]   Hörnig, K.M.; Generating small models of first-order axioms; GWAI-81 (Siekmann, ed.), Informatik-Fachberichte 47 , Springer, Berlin, 248-255 (1981)

[Hö2]   Hörnig, K.M.; Improvement and correctness proof of a tautology testing algorithm
(in preparation)

[HöB]   Hörnig, K.M.; Bibel, W.; Improvement and correctness proof of a tautology-testing algorithm; Bericht ATP-11-XI-81, Inst. f. Informatik, Technische U., München (1981)

[Hu1]   Huet, G.; Résolution d'équations dans des languages d'ordre 1,2,...,ω; Thèse de doctorat d'état, L'université Paris VII (1976)

[Hu2]   Huet, G.; Confluent reductions: abstract properties and applications to term rewriting systems; J.ACM 27 , 797-821 (1980)

[HuH]   Huet, G., Hullot, J.-M.; Proofs by induction in equational theories with constructors; 21st Annual IEEE Symposium on Foundations of Computer Sci., 96-107 (1980)

[HOP]   Huet, G., Oppen, D.; Equations and rewrite rules: a survey; Formal languages: perspectives and open problems (Book, ed.), Academic Press, 349-405 (1980)

[JeP]   Jensen, D.C., Pietrzykowski, T.; Mechanizing ω-order type theory through unification; Theoretical Computer Sci. 3 , 123-171 (1976)

[Joy]   Joyner, W.S. (ed.); Proc. 4th Workshop on Automated Deduction; Austin, Texas (1979)

[KnB]   Knuth, D.E., Bendix, P.B.; Simple word problems in universal algebras; Computational problems in abstract algebra (J. Leed, ed.), Pergamon Press, 263-297 (1970)

[Ko1]   Kowalski, R.; Predicate Logic as a programming language; Proc. IFIP-74, North-Holland, Amsterdam, 569-574 (1974)

[Ko2]   Kowalski, R.; A proof procedure using connection graphs; J.ACM 22 , 572-595 (1975)

[Ko3]   Kowalski, R.; Logic for problem solving; North-Holland, New York (1979)

[KoK]   Kowalski, R., Kuehner, D.; Linear resolution with selection function; Artificial Intelligence 2 , 227-260 (1971)

[Lew]   Lewis, H.R.; Unsolvable classes of quantificational formulas; Addison-Wesley, Reading (1979)

[Lo1]   Loveland, D.W.; A simplified format for the model elimination procedure; J.ACM **16** , 349-363 (1969)

[Lo2]   Loveland, D.W.; A linear format for resolution; Symp. on Automatic Demonstration (Laudet et al., eds.), Lecture Notes in Math. **125** ,Springer, Berlin, 147-162 (1970)

[Lo3]   Loveland, D.W.; A unifying view of some linear Herbrand procedures; J.ACM **19** , 366-384 (1972)

[Lo4]   Loveland, D.W.; Automated theorem proving; North-Holland, Amsterdam (1978)

[Luc]   Luckham, D.; Refinement theorems in resolution theory; Symp. Automatic Demonstration (Laudet et al., eds.), Lecture Notes in Math. **125** , Springer, Berlin, 163-190 (1970)

[Man]   Manna, Z.; Mathematical theory of computation; MacGraw Hill, New York (1974)

[MaW]   Manna, Z., Waldinger, R.; Towards automatic program synthesis; C.ACM **14** , 151-165 (1971)

[MaM]   Martelli, A., Montanari, U.; Unification in linear time and space: A structured presentation; Nota interna B76-16, Istituto di Elaborazione della Informazione, Pisa (1976)

[Mas]   Maslov, S.J.; The inverse method for establishing deducibility for logical calculi; Proc. Steklov Inst. Math. **98** (1968)

[McC]   McCarthy, J.; personal communication

[MOW]   McCharen, J., Overbeek, R., Wos, L.; Problems and experiments for and with automated theorem proving programs; IEEE Transactions on Computers, **C-25** , 773-782 (1976)

[Mel]   Meltzer, B.; Prolegomena to a theory of efficiency of proof procedures; Artificial Intelligence and Heuristic Programming (Findler, Meltzer, eds.), American Elsevier, New York, 15-33 (1971)

[Mül]   Müller, A.; Implementation of a theorem prover based on the connection method; Bericht ATP-12-XII-81, Projekt Beweisverfahren, Instit. f. Informatik, Techn. U. München, (1981)

[NSS]   Newell, A., Shaw, J., Simon, H.; Empirical explorations of the logic theory machine; Proc. West. Joint Computer Conf., vol. 15 , 218-239 (1957); Reprented in [Fef] , 109-133

[Nil]   Nilsson, N.J.; Principles of artificial intelligence; Tioga, Palo Alto (1980)

[Ove]   Overbeek, R.A.; An implementation of hyper-resolution;
          Comp. Math. with Appls. 1 , 201-214 (1975)

[OLu]   Overbeek, R.A., Lusk, E.L.; Data structures and control
          architecture for implementation of theorem-proving
          programs; In [BiK] 232-249

[PaW]   Paterson, M.S., Wegman, M.N.; Linear Unification; J. of
          Computer and Systems Sci. 16 , 158-167 (1978)

[Pol]   Polak, W.; Program verification at Stanford: past,
          present, future; GWAI-81 (Siekmann, ed.), Informatik-
          Fachberichte 47 , Springer, Berlin, 256-276 (1981)

[Pr1]   Prawitz, D.; An improved proof procedure; Theoria 26 ,
          102-139 (1960)

[Pr2]   Prawitz, D.; Advances and problems in mechanical proof
          procedures; Machine Intelligence 4 (Meltzer, Michie,
          eds.), Edinburgh University Press, 59-71 (1969)

[Pr3]   Prawitz, D.; A proof procedure with matrix reduction;
          Symposium on Automatic Demonstration (Laudet et al.,
          eds.), Lecture Notes in Math. 125 , Springer, Berlin,
          207-214 (1970)

[PPV]   Prawitz, D., Prawitz, H., Voghera, N.; A mechanical
          proof procedure and its realization in an electronic
          computer; J.ACM 7 , 102-128 (1960)

[Qui]   Quine, W.V.; A way to simplify truth functions; Amer.
          Math. Monthly 62 , 627-631 (1955)

[Rap]   Raphael, B.; Some results about proof by resolution;
          SIGART Newsletter 14 , 22-25 (1969)

[RoW]   Robinson, G., Wos, L.; Paramodulation and theorem prov-
          ing in first-order theories with equality; Machine
          Intelligence 4 (Meltzer, Michie, eds.), Edinburgh
          University Press, 103-133 (1969)

[Ro1]   Robinson, J.A.; A machine-oriented logic based on the
          resolution principle; J.ACM 12 , 23-41 (1965)

[Ro2]   Robinson, J.A.; Automatic deduction with hyper-resolu-
          tion; Int. J. Comput. Math. 1 , 227-234 (1965)

[Ro3]   Robinson, J.A.; Logic: Form and function; University
          Press, Edinburgh (1979)

[Rus]   Russel, B.; Mathematical logic as based on the theory
          of types; Americ. J. of Mathematics 30 , 222-262
          (1908);
          reprinted in [Hei]

[Sal]   Salomaa, A.; Formal languages; Academic Press, New York
          (1973)

286

[SaC]   Saya, H., Caferra, R.; A structure sharing technique
        for matrices and substitutions in Prawitz' theorem
        proving method; Rapport No. 101, U. of Grenoble (1977)

[Sc1]   Schlingloff, H.; Experimente zum systematischen Ver-
        gleich von Resolutions- und regulären Resolutionsab-
        leitungen; Fortgeschrittenenpraktikum, Inst. f.
        Informatik, Techn. U. München (1981)

[Sc2]   Schreiber, J.; Vergleichende qualitative und quantita-
        tive Untersuchungen von Beweisverfahren; Bericht 7411,
        Abteilung Mathematik, Techn. U. München (1974)

[SPe]   Schubert, L.K.; Pelletier, F.J.; From English to logic:
        context-free computation of "conventional" logical
        translations; submitted to J. Comput. Linguistics
        (1981)

[Sc3]   Schütte, K.; Beweistheoretische Erfassung der unend-
        lichen Induktion in der reinen Zahlentheorie; Math.
        Ann. **122** , 369-389 (1951)

[Sc4]   Schütte, K.; Proof theory; Springer, Berlin (1977)

[Sha]   Shapiro, E.Y.; An algorithm that infers theories from
        facts; Proc. IJCAI-7, Int. Joint Conferences on Artifi-
        cial Intelligence, 446-451 (1981)

[Sh1]   Shostak, R. E.; Refutation graphs; Artificial Intelli-
        gence 7 , 51-64 (1976)

[Sh2]   Shostak, R. E.; Deciding linear inequalities by comput-
        ing loop residues; In [Joy] 81-89

[Sic]   Sickel, S.; A search technique for clause interconnect-
        ivity graphs; IEEE Transactions on Computers 35 ,
        823-835 (1976)

[SiW]   Siekmann, J., Wrightson, G. (eds.); Collected papers on
        computational deduction, vol. I, II; Springer, Berlin
        (to appear)
        Contains an exhaustive bibliography on ATP upto 1970,
        while a list of more recent publications may be
        obtained from the editors (Inst. f. Informatik,
        Universität, Karlsruhe, Germany)

[Sko]   Skolem, T.; Logico-combinatorial investigations in the
        satisfiability or provability of mathematical proposi-
        tions; (1920); In [Hei] 252-263

[Smu]   Smullyan, R.M.; First-order logic; Springer, Berlin
        (1968)

[SSi]   Stephan, W., Siekmann, J.; Completeness and soundness
        of the connection graph proof procedure; Interner
        Bericht 7/76, Inst. f. Informatik, U. Karlsruhe (1976)

[Sza]   Szabo, M.E.; The collected papers of Gerhard Gentzen;
        North-Holland, Amsterdam (1969)

[TWi]   Trum, P., Winterstein, G.; Description, implementation,
        and practical comparison of unification algorithms;
        Interner Bericht 6/78, Fachbereich Informatik, U.
        Kaiserslautern (1978)

[Tse]   Tseitin, G.S.; On the complexity of derivations in the
        propositional calculus (transl. from Russian); Struct-
        ures in Constructive Mathematics and Mathematical Logic
        – part II (Slisenko, ed.); Consultants Bureau, New
        York, 115-125 (1968)

[TyB]   Tyson, M., Bledsoe, W.W.; Conflicting bindings and
        generalized substitutions; In [Joy] 14-18

[VFM]   VanderBrug, G.J., Fishman, D.H., Minker, J.; Outline,
        bibliography, and KWIC index on mechanical theorem
        proving and its applications; Report TR-159, Computer
        Sci. C., U. of Maryland (1971)

[Wan]   Wang, H.; Toward mechanical mathematics; IBM J. Res.
        Develop. 4 , 2-22 (1960)

[Wey]   Weyrauch, R.W.; Prolegomena to a theory of mechanized
        formal reasoning; Artificial Intelligence 13 , 133-170
        (1980)

[WiM]   Wilson, G.A., Minker, J.; Resolution, refinements and
        search strategies – a comparative study; IEEE Transac-
        tions on Computer, Vol. C-25 , 795-801 (1976)

[Win]   Winograd, T.; Language as a cognitive process; Addison
        Wesley, Reading, MA (1980)

[Wos]   Wos, L.; Solving open question with an automated
        theorem-proving program; Argonne Nat. Lab., IL (1981)

[WOH]   Wos, L., Oberbeek, R., Henschen, L.; Hyperparamodula-
        tion: A refinement of paramodulation; In [BiK] 208-219

[WRC]   Wos, L., Robinson, G., Carson, D., Shalla, L.; The
        concept of demodulation in theorem proving; J.ACM 14 ,
        698-709 (1967)

[YRH]   Yates, R.A., Raphael, B., Hart, T.P.; Resolution
        graphs; Artificial Intelligence 1 , 257-289 (1970)

List of symbols

(See also the tables on the pages X and XI)

P^O 12	$\vdash_C$ 39, 107	I 67
P, Q, R 12, 60	ι 40, 67	$\tau_I(F)$ 67
K, L, M 12	$\mathcal{F}$ 41	T^i 77
^0L, ^1L 12, 60	$\Sigma(F)$ 41	SP 77
R 12, 14, 60	$\mathcal{E}$ 41	$F^n(F)$ 81
D, E, F 12, 15, 63	$\vdash_{MULT}$ 46	H(F) 81
$\sigma(F)$ 12	$\vdash_{PURE}$ 46	ε 90
$\Omega(F)$ 12, 60	$\vdash_{TAUT}$ 47	DIFF(X,Y) 91, 202
$\delta(r)$ 12	$\vdash_{SUBS}$ 48	$UNIF_1$ 92
L^r 12	$\vdash_{UNIT}$ 48	μ 102
$\Omega(t)$ 14, 60	$\vdash_{RED}$ 49	F^μ 102
$A(t)$ 14	CP_1^O	CP_1^1 113
$t_{:r}$ 14	$\vdash_{DSTR}$ 54	$\vdash_r$ 122
$\lambda(t)$ 14	$\vdash_{CNCL}$ 54	CP_2^O 150
$\sigma(t)$ 14	V 59	CP_3^O 158
T, F 16, 18	x, y, z 59	NK 171
– 12, 16, 18, 60, 64	F 59	GS 174
$\to$ 16, 18	f, g, h 59	ND 177
$\leftarrow$ 16, 18, 50	P 60	<, <·, ◁ 181
$\leftrightarrow$ 16, 18	$\alpha(f)$, $\alpha(P)$ 60	~ 181
$\underset{\sim}{m}$ 19	F^n, P^n 60	$<_{F\mu}$ 183
$\underset{\sim}{ac}$ 19	a, b, c 60	$UNIF_{PW}$ 190
$\mathcal{M}$ 22	T 60	FINISH 190
$\tau_{\mathcal{M}}(i,F)$ 22	s, t 60	$UNIF_{MM}$ 192
$\models$ 22, 23, 24, 68	x^r 60	IGN_u 202
$\alpha(c)$ 37, 104	$f^r t_1 \ldots t_n$ 60	$PART_u$ 202
$\beta(L^r)$ 37, 104	$^m P t_1 \ldots t_n$ 60	CP^1 207
$\gamma(c)$ 37, 104	K, L, M 60	CP^0, CP_4^O 208
$\vdash$ 39, 40, 41, 42, 107, 174	$\forall$ 62	$\to$ 243
$\vdash^+$ 39, 40	$\exists$ 62	IND 248
$\vdash^*$ 40	cx 63	λ 255
	$x \backslash x\sigma$ 66	GS^m 257

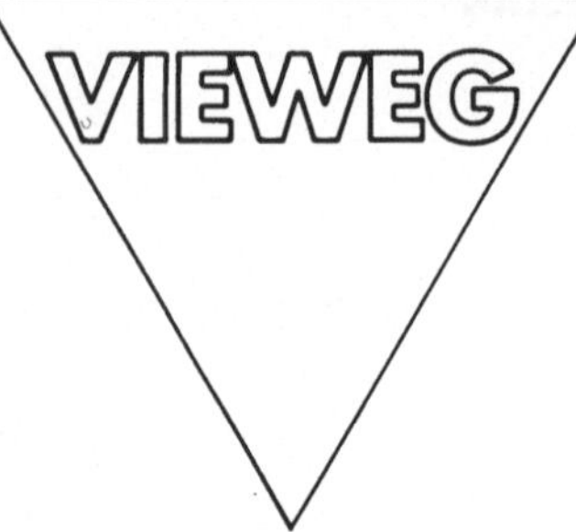

Michael M. Richter

Ideale Punkte, Monaden und Nichtstandard-Methoden

1982. VIII, 264 S. DIN C 5. Kartoniert

<u>Inhalt:</u> Historisches und Grundsätzliches über das Unendliche und den Gebrauch idealer Punkte — Der axiomatische Rahmen für die Nichtstandard-Analysis — Erstes Kapitel über die reelle und komplexe Nichtstandard-Analysis — Die Methode der Nichtstandarderweiterung im allgemeinen Fall — Fortgeschrittenes Kapitel zur Analysis — Topologische Räume — Algebra und Zahlentheorie — Vermischte Anwendungen — Mathematische Logik und Grundlagenfragen.

Für Mathematiker und Mathematikstudenten ab dem 4. Semester. Darstellung und Rechtfertigung der klassischen Infinitesimalienrechnung aus der Zeit von Leibniz und Euler im Rahmen der Nichtstandardanalysis auf axiomatischer Grundlage. Ausweitung der Nichtstandardmethoden zu einer allgemeinen axiomatischen Theorie der idealen Punkte. Anwendung und Beispiele: Differentialgleichungen, Distributionen, Topologie, Galoistheorie, algebraische Zahlentheorie, Programmiersprachen, Ökonomie. Das Schlußkapitel enthält die zur Begründung nötigen Elemente der mathematischen Logik, Modelltheorie und Mengenlehre.